THE EMERGING SEMANTIC WEB

Frontiers in Artificial Intelligence and Applications

Series Editors: J. Breuker, R. López de Mántaras, M. Mohammadian, S. Ohsuga and W. Swartout

Volume 75

Previously published in this series:

Vol. 74, M. Blay-Fornarino et al. (Eds.), Cooperative Systems Design
Vol. 73, In production
Vol. 72, A. Namatame et al. (Eds.), Agent-Based Approaches in Economic and Social Complex Systems
Vol. 71, J.M. Abe and J.I. da Silva Filho (Eds.), Logic, Artificial Intelligence and Robotics
Vol. 70, B. Verheij et al. (Eds.), Legal Knowledge and Information Systems
Vol. 69, N. Baba et al. (Eds.), Knowledge-Based Intelligent Information Engineering Systems & Allied
     Technologies
Vol. 68, J.D. Moore et al. (Eds.), Artificial Intelligence in Education
Vol. 67, H. Jaakkola et al. (Eds.), Information Modelling and Knowledge Bases XII
Vol. 66, H.H. Lund et al. (Eds.), Seventh Scandinavian Conference on Artificial Intelligence
Vol. 65, In production
Vol. 64, J. Breuker et al. (Eds.), Legal Knowledge and Information Systems
Vol. 63, I. Gent et al. (Eds.), SAT2000
Vol. 62, T. Hruška and M. Hashimoto (Eds.), Knowledge-Based Software Engineering
Vol. 61, E. Kawaguchi et al. (Eds.), Information Modelling and Knowledge Bases XI
Vol. 60, P. Hoffman and D. Lemke (Eds.), Teaching and Learning in a Network World
Vol. 59, M. Mohammadian (Ed.), Advances in Intelligent Systems: Theory and Applications
Vol. 58, R. Dieng et al. (Eds.), Designing Cooperative Systems
Vol. 57, M. Mohammadian (Ed.), New Frontiers in Computational Intelligence and its Applications
Vol. 56, M.I. Torres and A. Sanfeliu (Eds.), Pattern Recognition and Applications
Vol. 55, G. Cumming et al. (Eds.), Advanced Research in Computers and Communications in Education
Vol. 54, W. Horn (Ed.), ECAI 2000
Vol. 53, E. Motta, Reusable Components for Knowledge Modelling
Vol. 52, In production
Vol. 51, H. Jaakkola et al. (Eds.), Information Modelling and Knowledge Bases X
Vol. 50, S.P. Lajoie and M. Vivet (Eds.), Artificial Intelligence in Education
Vol. 49, P. McNamara and H. Prakken (Eds.), Norms, Logics and Information Systems
Vol. 48, P. Návrat and H. Ueno (Eds.), Knowledge-Based Software Engineering
Vol. 47, M.T. Escrig and F. Toledo, Qualitative Spatial Reasoning: Theory and Practice
Vol. 46, N. Guarino (Ed.), Formal Ontology in Information Systems
Vol. 45, P.-J. Charrel et al. (Eds.), Information Modelling and Knowledge Bases IX
Vol. 44, K. de Koning, Model-Based Reasoning about Learner Behaviour
Vol. 43, M. Gams et al. (Eds.), Mind Versus Computer
Vol. 41, F.C. Morabito (Ed.), Advances in Intelligent Systems
Vol. 40, G. Grahne (Ed.), Sixth Scandinavian Conference on Artificial Intelligence
Vol. 39, B. du Boulay and R. Mizoguchi (Eds.), Artificial Intelligence in Education
Vol. 38, H. Kangassalo et al. (Eds.), Information Modelling and Knowledge Bases VIII
Vol. 37, F.L. Silva et al. (Eds.), Spatiotemporal Models in Biological and Artificial Systems

ISSN: 0922-6389

The Emerging Semantic Web

Selected Papers from the first Semantic Web Working Symposium

Edited by

Isabel Cruz
University of Illinois at Chicago, USA

Stefan Decker
Stanford University, USA

Jérôme Euzenat
INRIA, France

and

Deborah McGuinness
Stanford University, USA

IOS Press

Ohmsha

Amsterdam • Berlin • Oxford • Tokyo • Washington, DC

ISBN 1 58603 255 0 (IOS Press)
ISBN 4 274 90513 6 C3055(Ohmsha)
Library of Congress Control Number: 2002105619

Publisher
IOS Press
Nieuwe Hemweg 6B
1013 BG Amsterdam
The Netherlands
fax: +31 20 620 3419
e-mail: order@iospress.nl

Distributor in the UK and Ireland
IOS Press/Lavis Marketing
73 Lime Walk
Headington
Oxford OX3 7AD
England
fax: +44 1865 75 0079

Distributor in the USA and Canada
IOS Press, Inc.
5795-G Burke Centre Parkway
Burke, VA 22015
USA
fax: +1 703 323 3668
e-mail: iosbooks@iospress.com

Distributor in Germany, Austria and Switzerland
IOS Press/LSL.de
Gerichtsweg 28
D-04103 Leipzig
Germany
fax: +49 341 995 4255

Distributor in Japan
Ohmsha, Ltd.
3-1 Kanda Nishiki-cho
Chiyoda-ku, Tokyo 101-8460
Japan
fax: +81 3 3233 2426

Foreword

The World Wide Web has been the main source of an important shift in the way people get information and order services. However, the current Web is aimed at people only. Information can be found in pages written in natural language. Similarly, many existing Web services provide their modus operandi through natural languages. In spite of remarkable success in information extraction and page indexing, today's search engines are of little use when one wants to find precise information in a web page or when one wants to find two complementary services for joint usage. *"Semantic Web"* is a term coined by Tim Berners-Lee for denoting a Web defined and linked in such a way that it can be used by machines as well as people, not just for display purposes, but for automation, integration and reuse of data across various applications.

The Semantic Web will be beneficial for companies that will interoperate with each other more closely, that will provide services in an integrated framework and thus find more customers. It will be beneficial for individuals who can automatically access a wide range of resources and services according to their preferences and constraints.

In order for computers to provide more help to people, the Semantic Web augments the current Web with formalized knowledge and data that can be processed by computers. So the Semantic Web can also be thought of as an infrastructure for supplying the Web with formalized knowledge in addition to its actual informal content. It thus needs a *language* for expressing knowledge. This knowledge is used to describe the content of information sources, through *ontologies*, and the terms and requirements of Web *service* operation. No consensus exists on how far the formalization should go: it ranges from metadata schemes (like the Dublin core metadata markers) to fully-fledged logical representation languages. Such a level of formalization exists only for particular applications. One of the challenges of the current Semantic Web development is the design of a framework in which these various approaches can be jointly used, because the full benefit of the Semantic Web can only be attained when computers relate resources from various sources, that is when they allow these resources to *interoperate*.

In order for the Semantic Web to be realized, supporting standards, technologies and policies must be designed to enable machines to "understand" the resources of the Web, with the result of making the Web more useful for humans. Facilities and technologies to put machine understandable data on the Web are rapidly becoming a high priority for many communities. While the emerging Semantic Web community is working on progress with markup languages, ontologies, environments, services, and interoperability, the commercial companies, which cannot wait, address their own interoperability problems in a way that meets their needs and also contributes to global progress on the topic. For the Semantic Web to scale, programs must be able to share and process data even when these programs have been designed totally independently. The Web can reach its full potential only if it becomes a place where data can be shared and processed by automated agents as well as by people, by research software as well as by commercial products.

The Semantic Web is yet to be transformed from a general vision to a practical infrastructure. This book aims to contribute to this goal by providing technical contributions that will facilitate realizing the Semantic Web. It contains revised versions of a selection of papers presented at the International Semantic Web Working Symposium (SWWS, http://www.semanticweb.org/SWWS/). The symposium took place in Stanford, California, from July 30 through August 1, 2001. Fifty-nine papers were submitted and there were two hundred and forty five registered participants from all over the world, encompassing a wide range of scientific backgrounds.

This book presents the state of the art in the development of the principles and technologies that will allow for the Semantic Web to become a reality. It is organized in three parts.

Languages for the Semantic Web. The first part of this book is dedicated to languages for the Semantic Web. It is crucial that knowledge be expressed in a language so that computers can take advantage of it. The lower layer of the Semantic Web is based on XML (eXtensible Markup Language). RDF (Resource Description Framework) is a language recommended by the W3C (World Wide Web Consortium) and is built on top of XML. RDF-Schema is a proposed schema language for RDF defined in RDF. Stephen Cranefield ("UML and the semantic web") shows how to use the UML (Unified Modeling Language) specification language for expressing ontologies and producing a schema RDF. The following chapters address some of the existing problems with RDF and RDF-Schema. Jeff Pan and Ian Horrocks ("Metamodeling architecture of web ontology languages") deal with the meta-model described in RDF-Schema and propose to reengineer it following the approach taken by UML. Other problems such as the interpretation of reification (the expression of an RDF statement as statements about that statement) and containers (the gathering of several RDF objects) are addressed by Wolfram Conen *et al.* ("RDF M&S revisited: From reification to nesting, from containers to lists, from dialect to pure XML"). Chris Goad ("Describing computation within RDF") presents an RDF extension for expressing scripts and programs within it. The programs can be manipulated just like ordinary RDF statements and provide access to RDF statements and resources. Chutiporn Anutariya *et al.* ("Semantic web modeling and programming with XDD") present an experimental language based on XML that also provides programming capabilities within a cleanly defined representation language.

Ontologies and services. Once knowledge representation languages for the Web are available, they may be used for expressing ontologies and knowledge used by applications and services. The second part of this book deals with the content of the Semantic Web as presented through ontologies, i.e., domain knowledge formalization, and services, i.e., operation knowledge representation. The management of ontologies, i.e., their creation, evolution and maintenance is the theme of the chapter by Aseem Das *et al.* ("Industrial strength ontology management"). It provides a set of requirements for ontology environments as motivated by commercial needs and presents a toolkit designed to meet those needs. Mark Tuttle *et al.* ("The semantic web as "perfection seeking": a view from drug terminology") consider the evolution of drug terminologies over several years and the solutions that can be developed for managing this evolution. Well-described services available for agents on the Web are one of the benefits that the Semantic Web can bring to its users, because it will enable service composition (such as joint hotel/plane/train booking). Anupriya Ankolenkar *et al.* ("DAML-S: Semantic markup for web services") propose a language for describing Web services based on RDF and DAML+OIL (an agent markup language built on top of RDF-Schema). Then, Mark Klein and Abraham Bernstein ("Searching for services on the semantic web using process ontologies") describe the use of process ontologies that describe Web services for retrieval. The last two chapters of this part of the book are more specifically related to annotating resources with knowledge. In "CREAM: Creating relational metadata with a component-based, ontology-driven annotation framework", Siegfried Handschuh *et al.* present an architecture for ontology-based document annotation. Emmanuel Desmontils and Christine Jacquin ("Indexing a web site with a terminology oriented ontology") consider the automatic indexing of Web sites with an ontology extracted from the site itself and processed by natural language analysis techniques.

Interoperability, integration, and composition. Relating resources is both the motivation of the Semantic Web and one of its challenges. An ontology can be the foundation of interoperability when it is shared by the different sources. However, when that sharing does not occur, ontology exchange or alignment must be addressed. The focus of the last part of the book is the main problem that the Semantic Web must solve: interoperability. Different approaches are considered here. The two first chapters introduce formal approaches inspired from databases and data integration. Diego Calvanese *et al.* ("A framework for ontology integration") propose a theoretical approach to the problem based on mapping and views expressed over a description logic language. Prasenjit Mitra *et al.* ("A scalable framework for interoperation of information sources") deal with the generation of articulation rules for expressing the correspondence between two ontologies. The two next chapters deal with mismatches across languages. Drew McDermott *et al.* ("Overcoming ontology mismatches in transactions with self-describing agents") consider the composition of services based on service description and apply techniques coming from the planning area for that purpose. It discusses the automatic generation of glue code for data mismatch. Jérôme Euzenat ("An infrastructure for formally ensuring interoperability in a heterogeneous semantic web") proposes an infrastructure based on transformations and proofs of their properties for supporting safe interoperability. The last chapters explore concrete cases of semantic interoperability problems. David Allsopp *et al.* ("Towards semantic interoperability in agent-based coalition command systems") discuss the problems and potential contributions of Semantic Web technologies to the interoperability between heterogeneous agents that must work together. Isabel Cruz and Paul Calnan consider the problem of integrating several geospatial sources of information based on associated metadata in "Object interoperability for geospatial applications".

The Semantic Web is only in its infancy. The various topics considered in this book are central to the Semantic Web and are still under consideration by researchers, engineers and users. They constitute valuable contributions to the Web to come, though they have to be evaluated for scaling to the great open Web.

The editors thank all those who made possible the success of the Semantic Web Working Symposium and who have a share in the birth of this book: track chair people (Jim Hendler, Vipul Kashyap, Sheila McIlraith, Charles Petrie, Mark Tuttle), program committee members (Dan Brickley, Tiziana Catarci, Vassilis Christophides, Dan Connolly, Steve Demurjian, Max J. Egenhofer, Peter Eklund, Dieter Fensel, Asunciòn Gomez-Perez, Benjamin Grosof, Natasha Fridman Noy, Nicola Guarino, Pat Hayes, Jim Hendler, Masahiro Hori, Ian Horrocks, Ora Lassila, Raphael Malyankar, Massimo Marchiori, Brian McBride, Sheila McIlraith, Robert Meersman, Eric Miller, Enrico Motta, Amedeo Napoli, Dimitris Plexousakis, Peter Patel-Schneider, Guus Schreiber, Amit Sheth, Steffen Staab, Heiner Stuckenschmidt and Frank van Harmelen) and tutorial presenters (Natasha Fridman Noy, Christoph Bussler, Fabio Casati and Ming-Chien Shan). We also thank those who provided local support including Marianne Siroker and Jennifer Espinoza. The event was sponsored by the Information and Data Management Program of the National Science Foundation, the European Union IST OntoWeb network, DARPA (DAML program), INRIA, and by the following corporate sponsors: VerticalNet, Nokia, SpiritSoft, Enigmatec.net, Empolis, Language and Computing, Network inference, Mondeca, LC4, Connotate technologies, and Ontoprise. Special thanks go to IOS Press publisher Einar Fredriksson and Series editor Joost Breuker who have been very supportive of the publication of this book from the beginning.

During the Semantic Web Working Symposium, a steering committee was established for monitoring future meetings and for setting directions for the Semantic Web. The steering committee has been named the Semantic Web Science Foundation (http://swsf.semanticweb.org/). The Semantic Web Science Foundation organizes a yearly event in continuation of the Semantic Web Working Symposium under the name of International Semantic Web Conference (http://iswc.semanticweb.org/). The next event will be held in Sardinia, Italy, in June 2002. The Semantic Web Science Foundation will also serve as a focal point for related Semantic Web efforts including the collection of educational materials, supporting research journals in the area, and helping to coordinate and support other workshops and related efforts.

We hope that this book and the future work of the Semantic Web Science Foundation will contribute to the quick progress of the Semantic Web.

Isabel Cruz, University of Illinois at Chicago,
Stefan Decker, Stanford University,
Jérôme Euzenat, INRIA Rhône-Alpes,
Deborah McGuinness, Stanford University,

March 15th, 2002.

Contents

Part 1:
Languages for
the Semantic Web

The Emerging Semantic Web
I.F. Cruz et al. (Eds.)
IOS Press, 2002

UML and the Semantic Web

Stephen Cranefield

Department of Information Science, University of Otago
PO Box 56, Dunedin, New Zealand
scranefield@infoscience.otago.ac.nz

Abstract. This paper discusses technology to support the use of UML for representing ontologies and domain knowledge in the Semantic Web. Two mappings have been defined and implemented using XSLT to produce Java classes and an RDF schema from an ontology represented as a UML class diagram and encoded using XMI. A Java application can encode domain knowledge as an object diagram realised as a network of instances of the generated classes. Support is provided for marshalling and unmarshalling this object-oriented knowledge to and from an RDF/XML serialisation. The paper also proposes an extension to RDF allowing the identification of property–resource pairs in a model for which 'closed world' reasoning cannot be used due to incomplete knowledge.

1   Introduction

The vision of the Semantic Web is to let computer software relieve us of much of the burden of locating resources on the Web that are relevant to our needs and extracting, integrating and indexing the information contained within. To enable this, resources on the Web need to be encoded in, or annotated with, structured machine-readable descriptions of their contents that are expressed using terms or structures that have been explicitly defined in a domain *ontology.*

Currently, there is a lot of research effort underway to develop ontology representation languages compatible with World Wide Web standards, particularly in the Ontology Inference Layer (OIL) [1] and DARPA Agent Markup Language (DAML) [2] projects. Derived from frame-based representation languages from the artificial intelligence knowledge representation community, OIL and DAML build on top of RDF Schema [3] by adding modelling constructs from description logic [4]. This style of language has a well understood semantic basis but lacks both a wide user community outside AI research laboratories and a standard graphical presentation—an important consideration for aiding the human comprehension of ontologies.

This paper discusses Semantic Web technology based on an alternative paradigm that also supports the modelling of concepts in a domain (an ontology) and the expression of information in terms of those concepts. This is the paradigm of object-oriented modelling from the software engineering community. In particular, there is an expressive and standardised modelling language, the Unified Modeling Language (UML) [5], which has graphical and XML-based formats, a huge user community, a high level of commercial tool support and an associated highly expressive constraint language. Although developed to support analysis and design in software engineering, UML is beginning to be used for other modelling problems, one notable example being its adoption by the Meta Data Coalition [6] for representing metadata schemas for enterprise data[1].

The proposed application of UML to the Semantic Web is based on the following three claims:

- UML class diagrams provide a static modelling capability that is well suited for representing ontologies [7].

- UML object diagrams can be interpreted as declarative representations of knowledge [8].

- If a Semantic Web application is being constructing using object-oriented technology, it may be advantageous to use the same paradigm for modelling ontologies and knowledge.

However, there is one significant current shortcoming of UML: it lacks a formal definition. The semantics of UML are defined by a metamodel, some additional constraints expressed in a semi-formal language (the Object Constraint Language, OCL), and descriptions of the various elements of the language in English. The development of formal semantics for UML is an active area of research as evidenced by a number of recent workshops [9, 10, 11] and the formation of an open-membership international research group to facilitate work in this area [12]. In particular, as UML is a very large language with some redundancy, research is underway to identify a core of UML modelling constructs from which the other language elements can be derived [13, 14]. A formal definition of this core will then indirectly provide semantics for the complete language.

This author believes that future developments in this area will provide at least a subset of UML with the formal underpinnings required for the unambiguous interpretation of ontologies. For the present, the use of the more basic features of class and object diagrams for representing ontologies and knowledge seems no more prone to misinterpretation than the use of the Resource Description Framework [15]—a language which underlies the Semantic Web but which also originally lacked formal semantics (although a model theory is now under development [16]). It is also worth noting that many of the difficulties in providing precise semantics for UML lie with its features for the dynamic modelling of systems, rather than the static models used in the work presented here.

Further discussion of the benefits and limitations of UML for ontology modelling is beyond the scope of this paper which focuses on technology to support the use of object-oriented modelling for the Semantic Web. An overview of this technology is given in Section 2. Section 3 presents an example ontology in UML and gives a brief description of the features of UML used in this example (for a good introduction to a much larger subset of the language see Muller [17]). Section 4 describes the techniques used to generate an RDF schema and a set of Java classes (complete with RDF-based object marshalling support) from a UML ontology. Section 5 proposes an extension to RDF that allows the inclusion in an RDF model of information on how complete that model is for particular property–resource pairs. Some preliminary thoughts on the possibility of performing reasoning with ontologies and knowledge expressed in UML are presented in Section 6. Finally, Section 7 gives an overview of related work and Section 8 concludes the paper.

---

[1]The MDC has since merged with the Object Management Group (OMG) to work jointly on the OMG's Common Warehouse Metamodel for data warehousing, business intelligence, knowledge management and portal technology metadata.

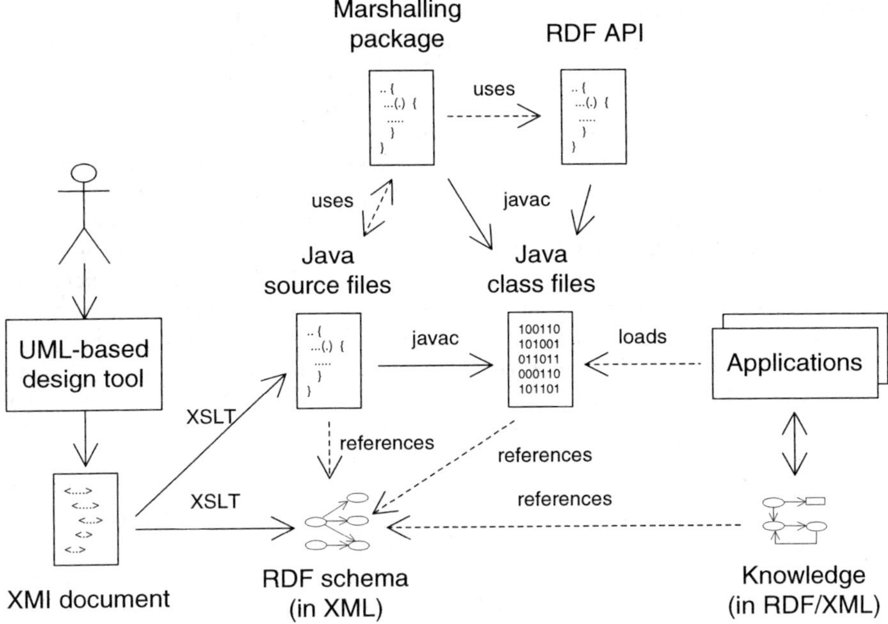

Figure 1: Overview of the implemented technology for object-oriented knowledge representation

2   Required Technology for UML and the Semantic Web

To enable the use of UML representations of ontologies and knowledge, standard formats are needed to allow both ontologies and knowledge about domain objects to be published on the Web and transmitted between agents. In addition, there is a need for code libraries to help application writers parse and internalise this serialised information.

This technology already exists for UML class diagrams. The XML Metadata Interchange (XMI) specification defines a standard way to serialise UML models as XML documents. There are also a number of Java class libraries existing or under development to provide a convenient interface for applications to access this information. However, there is currently no similar technology available to help Java applications construct, serialise and read object-oriented encodings of knowledge that are conceptualised as UML object diagrams. XMI documents can encode the structure of object diagrams, but this is necessarily done in a domain-independent way using separate but cross-referenced XML elements for each object, link, link end and attribute–value binding. What is required is a way to generate from an ontology a domain-specific encoding format for knowledge about objects in that domain, and an application programmer interface (API) to allow convenient creation, import and export of that knowledge.

Figure 1 shows an approach to object-oriented ontological and object-level knowledge representation that has been implemented and is described in this paper. First, a domain expert designs an ontology graphically using a CASE tool supporting the Unified Modeling Language, and then saves it using the XMI format. A pair of XSLT (Extensible Stylesheet

Language Transformations) stylesheets then take the XMI representation of the ontology as input and produce (i) a set of Java classes and interfaces corresponding to those in the ontology, and (ii) a representation of the ontology using the Resource Description Framework (RDF) [15] and the modelling concepts defined in RDF Schema [3]. The generated Java classes allow an application to represent knowledge about objects in the domain as in-memory data structures. The generated schema in RDF defines domain-specific concepts that an application can reference when serialising this knowledge using RDF (in its XML encoding). The marshalling and unmarshalling of object networks to and from RDF/XML documents is performed by a pair of Java classes: `MarshalHelper` and `UnmarshalHelper`. These delegate to the generated Java classes decisions about the names and types of fields to be serialised and unserialised, but are then called back to perform the translation to and from RDF, making use of an existing Java RDF application programmer's interface [18].

Note that the generated RDF schema does not contain all the information from the original UML model. If an application needs access to full ontological information, it can use the original XMI document with the help of one of the currently available Java APIs supporting the processing of UML models (e.g. NSUML [19]). The purpose of the RDF schema is to define RDF resources corresponding to all the classes, interfaces, attributes and associations in the ontology in order to support RDF serialisation of instance information. For the sake of human readers, the schema records additional information such as subclass relationships and the domains and ranges of properties corresponding to attributes and associations. However, this information is not required for processing RDF-encoded instance information because each generated Java class contains specialised methods `marshalFields` and `unmarshalFields` containing hard-coded knowledge about the names and types of the class's fields. This is a design decision intended to avoid potentially expensive analysis of the schema during marshalling and unmarshalling. This it should be possible to use this serialisation mechanism in situations where optimised serialisation is important, such as in agent messaging systems.

3   An Example Domain

This section presents an example ontology modelled as a UML class diagram and some knowledge encoded as an object diagram. The ontology defines a subset of the concepts included in the CIA World Factbook and is adapted from an OIL representation of a similar subset [20].

3.1   An Ontology in UML

Figure 2 presents the CIA World Factbook ontology represented as a UML class diagram. The version shown here is not a direct translation from the representation in OIL: there is an additional class `AdministrativeDivision`, UML association classes are used where appropriate, and instead of defining the classes `City` and `Country` as specialised types of `Region` (GeographicalLocation in the OIL original), the ontology represents these as optional roles that a region may have.

The boxes in the diagram represent classes, and contain their names and (where applicable) their attributes. The lines between classes depict association relationships between classes. A class A has an association with another class B if an object of class A needs to

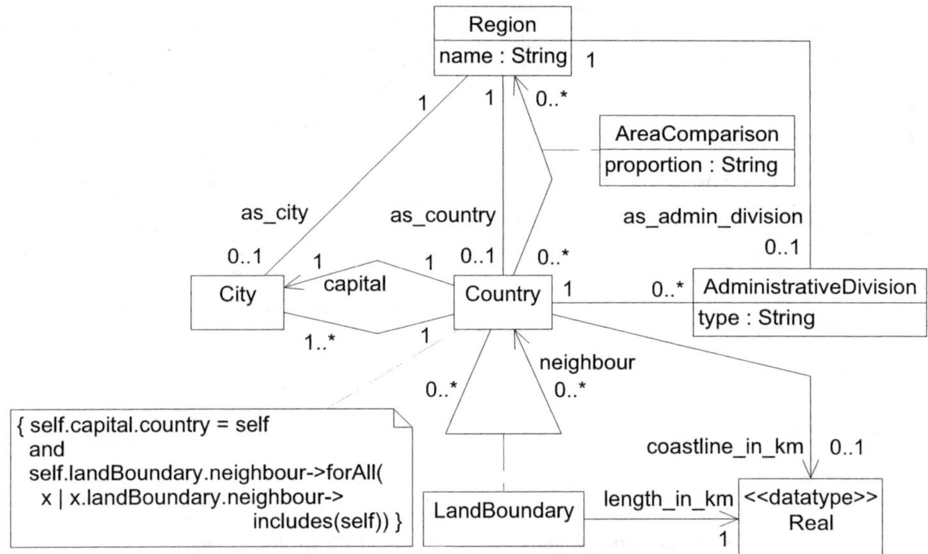

Figure 2: A UML ontology for a subset of the CIA World Factbook

maintain a reference to an object of class B. An association may be bidirectional, or (if a single arrowhead is present) unidirectional. A 'multiplicity' expression at the end of an association specifies how many objects of that class may take part in that relationship with a single object of the class at the other end of the association. This may be expressed as a range of values, with '*' indicating no upper limit. Association ends may be optionally named. In the absence of a name, the name of the adjacent class, with the initial letter in lower case, is used as a default name. Associations can be explicitly represented as classes by attaching a class box to an association (see LandBoundary and AreaComparison in Figure 2). This is necessary when additional attributes or further associations are required to clarify the relationship between two classes.

The dog-eared rectangle in the lower left corner of the figure contains a constraint in the Object Constraint Language (OCL). This language provides a way to constrain the possible instances of a model in ways that cannot be expressed using UML's structural modelling elements alone. The constraint shown here states that i) a country's capital is a city in that country, and ii) if a country c has another as a neighbour, then that neighbouring country has c as a neighbour. Finally, the keyword "datatype" appearing in guillemets (French quotation marks) above the class Real indicates that this is a pre-existing built-in datatype. OCL defines a minimal set of primitive datatypes and it is currently assumed that the ontology designer has used these primitive types.

Note that UML includes notation for class generalisation/specialisation relationships, although this is not required for the example presented in this paper.

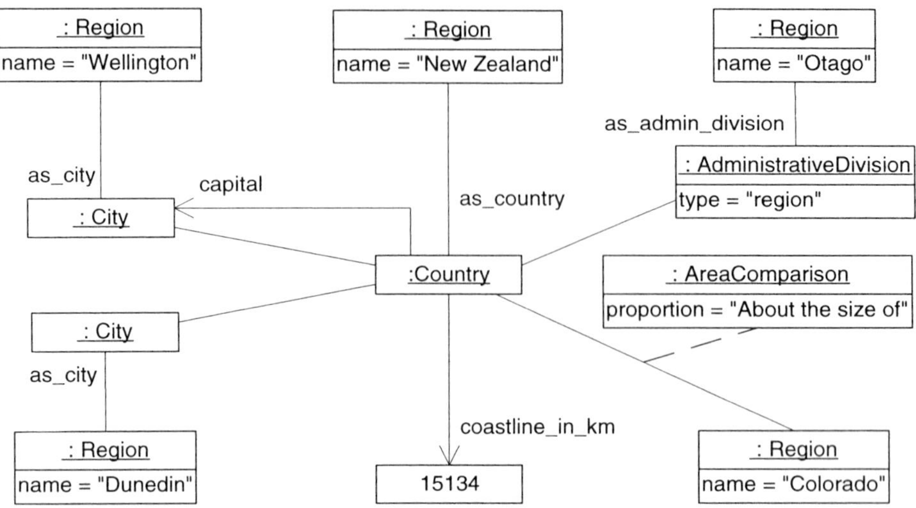

Figure 3: Information about New Zealand as a UML object diagram

3.2   Knowledge as an Object Diagram

Figure 3 presents some knowledge about New Zealand from the CIA World Factbook, expressed as an object diagram. For brevity, this diagram omits most of New Zealand's cities and administrative divisions, and provides no information about the region named Colorado, to which New Zealand is compared in terms of area.

In object diagrams, rectangles denote objects, specifying their class (after an optional name and a colon) and the object's attribute values. The lines between objects show 'links': instances of associations between classes.

4   From UML to RDF and Java

The previous section presented some knowledge expressed as a UML object diagram. This is an abstract representation of that knowledge. To enable this style of knowledge representation to be used for Semantic Web applications it is necessary to define an API to allow creation of the knowledge in this form and a serialisation format to allow Web publication and transmission of the knowledge. These can be generated automatically from an XML encoding of the Word Factbook using the XSLT stylesheets that have been developed. One stylesheet produces an RDF schema corresponding to the ontology and the other produces a corresponding set of Java classes and interfaces.

XSLT is a language for transforming XML documents into other documents. An XSLT stylesheet is comprised of a set of templates that match nodes in the input document (represented internally as a tree) and transform them (possibly via the application of other templates) to produce an output tree. The output tree can then be output as text or as an HTML or XML document.

The main issue common to both mappings is the problem of translating from UML classes, which may have different types of features such as attributes, associations and association classes, to a model where classes only have fields or (in RDF) properties. It was also necessary to generate default names for fields where association ends are not named in the UML model. The OCL conventions for writing navigation paths through object structures were used to resolve these issues. Also, attributes and association ends with a multiplicity upper limit greater than one are represented as set-valued fields (bags in RDF Schema) or, in the case of association ends with a UML "ordered" constraint, list-valued fields (sequences in RDF Schema). Further details about the mappings have been discussed elsewhere [21] and are beyond the scope of this paper.

4.1 The Generated RDF Schema

The Resource Description Framework (RDF) [15] is a simple resource–property–value model designed for expressing metadata about resources on the Web. RDF has a graphical syntax as well as an XML-based serialisation syntax. For readability, examples in this paper are presented in the graphical syntax, although in practice they are generated in the XML format.

RDF Schema [3] is a set of predefined resources (entities with uniform resource identifiers) and relationships between them that define a simple meta-model including concepts of classes, properties, subclass and subproperty relationships, a primitive type `Literal`, bag and sequence types, and domain and range constraints on properties. Domain schemas (i.e. ontologies) can then be expressed as sets of RDF triples using the (meta)classes and properties defined in RDF Schema. Schemas defined using RDF Schema are called RDF schemas (small 's').

The main issue in generating an RDF schema that corresponds to an object-oriented model is that RDF properties are first-class objects and are not defined within the context of a particular class. This can lead to conflicting range declarations if the same property (e.g. `head`) is used to represent a field in two different classes (e.g. `Brew` and `Department`). The solution chosen was to prefix each property name representing a field with the name of the class. This has the disadvantage that in the presence of inheritance a class's fields may be represented by properties with different prefixes: some specifying the class itself and some naming a parent class. This might be confusing for a human reader but is not a problem for the current purpose: to specify a machine-readable format for object-oriented knowledge interchange.

Figure 4 presents a subset of the generated RDF schema corresponding to the UML model presented in Figure 2. Only the classes `Country` and `Region` and the relationships between them are included in the figure.

In the standard RDF graphical notation used in the figure an ellipse represents a resource with its *qualified name* shown inside as a namespace prefix followed by a local name. A namespace prefix abbreviates a Uniform Resource Identifier (URI) associated with a particular namespace, and the URI for the resource can be constructed by appending the local name to the namespace URI. A property is represented by an arc, with the qualified name for the property written beside the arc (in this case the arcs are given labels with the corresponding URIs shown in the table).

Figure 4 includes one property that is not part of RDF Schema. There is no mechanism in RDF Schema to parameterise a collection type (such as `rdf:Bag`) by the class of elements it may contain. Therefore, the non-standard property `rdfsx:collectionElementType` was introduced to represent this information (this is abbreviated in the figure by the arc label `et`). The definition of this property is shown in Figure 5. The object serialisation mechanism

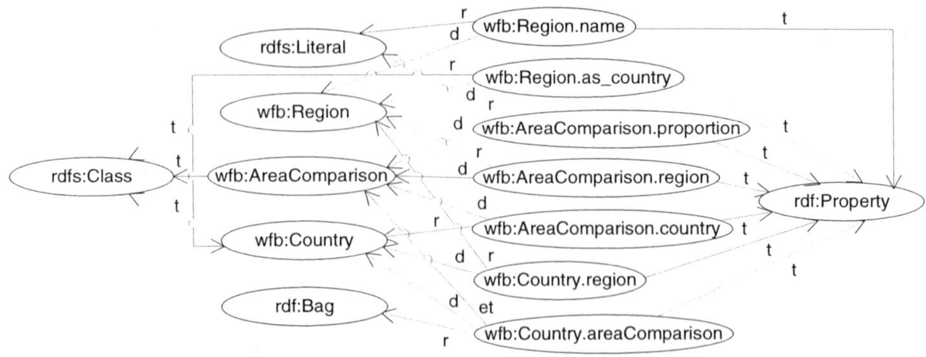

Property labels	Name space abbreviations
t = rdf:type	rdf = http://www.w3.org/1999/02/22-rdf-syntax-ns#
d = rdfs:domain	rdfs = http://www.w3.org/2000/01/rdf-schema#
r = rdfs:range	rdfsx = http://nzdis.otago.ac .nz/0_1/rdf-schema-x#
et = rdfsx:collectionElementType	wfb = *any new namespace chosen for this schema*

Figure 4: Part of the World Factbook schema in RDF

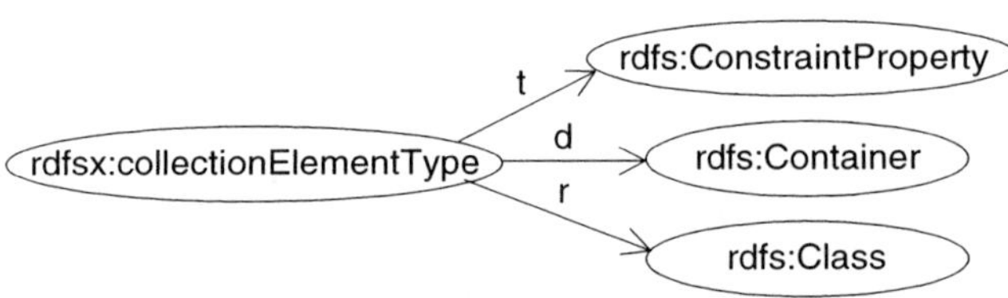

Property labels	Name space abbreviations
t = rdf:type	rdfs = http://www.w3.org/2000/01/rdf-schema#
d = rdfs:domain	rdfsx = http://nzdis.otago.ac.nz /0_1/rdf-schema-x#
r = rdfs:range	

Figure 5: An extension to RDF Schema

described in this paper does not require this information but it is useful to people reading the schema.

The schema in Figure 4 completely defines the encoding of instance data in RDF. Figure 6 shows how an object diagram is encoded in RDF with reference to the schema. This corresponds to the central `Region` and `Country` objects from Figure 3 together with the `AreaComparison` link to the Colorado `Region` object. The five resources outlined in bold are the ones being defined. There are two resources of type `wfb:Region`, one of type `wfb:Country`, one of type `rdf:Bag` (representing the set of the country's area comparisons) and one element in the bag: an instance of the area comparison association class (which is represented in RDF as the type `wfb:AreaComparison`). Depending on the needs of the application, defined objects might be assigned URIs or represented as anonymous resources. In this case, they are anonymous—the labels x and y are added to allow reference to these

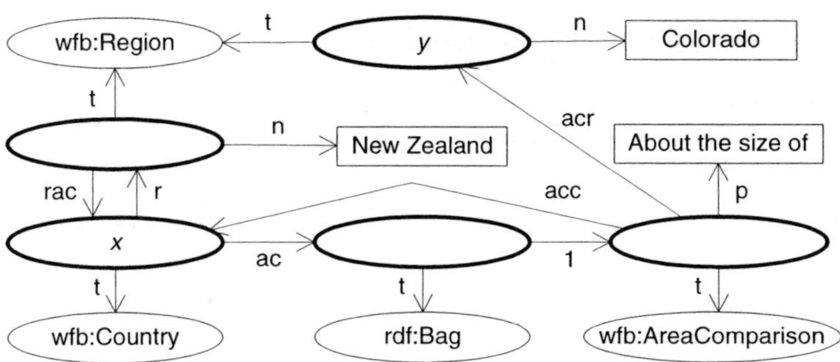

Property labels	Name space abbreviations
t = rdf:type 1 = rdf:_1 n = wfb:Region.name rac = wfb:Region.as_country r = wfb:Country.region ac = wfb:Country.areaComparison p = wfb:AreaComparison.proportion acr = wfb:AreaComparison.region acc = wfb:AreaComparison.country	rdf = http://www.w3.org/1999/02/22-rdf-syntax-ns# wfb = *namespace chosen for the World Factbook schema*

Figure 6: Information about New Zealand encoded in RDF

resources later in this paper. The rectangles represent RDF literals.

Note that while this graphical notation for RDF looks complicated, its encoding in XML only requires five XML elements to represent the information, as shown in the appendix.

4.2   The Generated Java Classes and Marshalling Framework

The generated RDF schema described in the previous section defines a domain-specific serialisation format for object-oriented representation of knowledge about the domain. To facilitate the processing of knowledge communicated in this form, a set of Java classes can also be generated from the ontology using XSLT. These allow Java applications to instantiate instances of the domain concepts. In addition, the generated classes, along with some additional utility classes, allow these in-memory structures to be marshalled and unmarshalled to and from the RDF serialisation format defined by the generated RDF schema. The aim of the marshalling code is to allow a Java application to maintain an internal representation of object-oriented knowledge and to easily read and write parts of this knowledge to and from a format suitable for transmission or publication on the Web.

Figure 7 presents a UML class diagram outlining the structure of the generated Java classes and the marshalling framework. The class `MarshalHelper` is part of a support package used by the generated classes. A static method `marshalObjects` provides the entry point for an application to marshal a network of objects. An `UnmarshalHelper` class is also provided, but is not discussed here. The class `DomainObject` is an abstract base class that all generated classes specialise (the specialisation relationship is represented

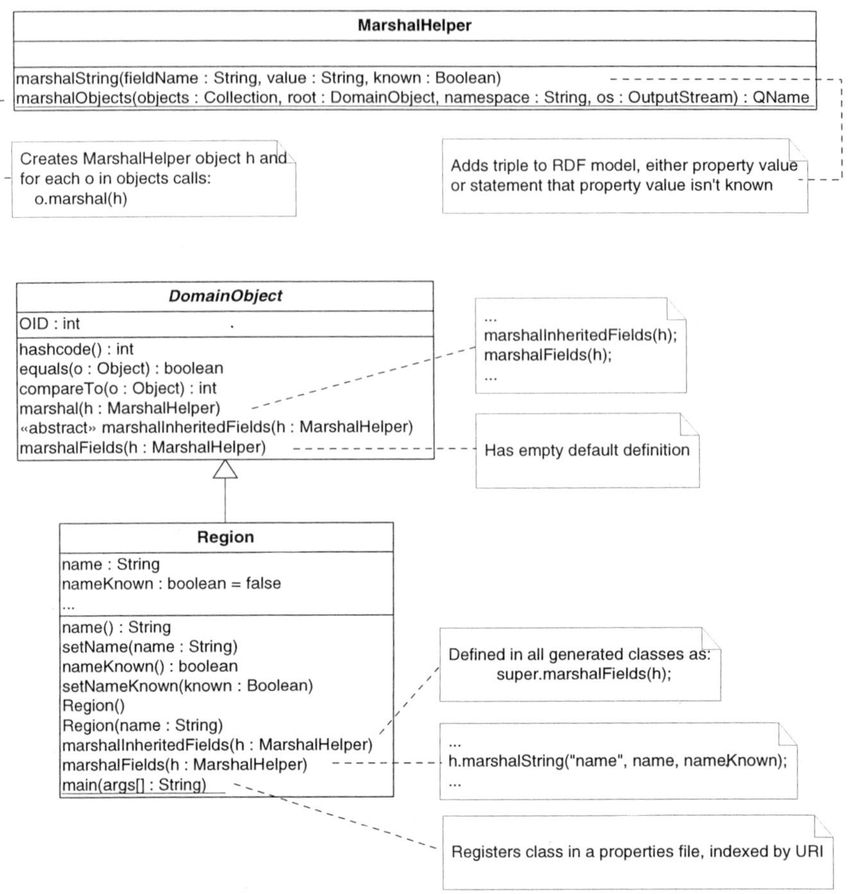

Figure 7: The structure of the generated classes and the marshalling methods

by a closed arrow pointing to the more general class). The class `Region` is shown as an example of a generated class.

The diagram does not show all the fields and methods. In particular, the class `Region` also contains fields and methods related to the association ends `as_city`, `as_country` and `as_admin_division` from the ontology shown in Figure 2. There are some fields and methods depicted that are related to whether or not a field value is "known". This is discussed in Section 5.

There is a significant difference between knowledge represented propositionally and knowledge represented in the form of an object diagram. Propositions are self-contained statements of knowledge whereas object diagrams are networks of objects. When serialising knowledge, an application may only wish to include some of the information it knows about a domain. For example, Figure 6 compares New Zealand's area to that of Colorado, but doesn't provide the information that Colorado is an administrative division of the United States. To allow

```
// Build object diagram
Region rNZ = new Region("New Zealand");
Country cNZ = new Country();
AreaComparison ac = new AreaComparison();
ac.setCountry(cNZ);
ac.setRegion(rNZ);
ac.setProportion("About the size of");
Set comparisons = new HashSet();
comparisons.add(ac);
Region rColorado = new Region("Colorado");
rNZ.setAs_country(cNZ);
cNZ.setRegion(rNZ);
cNZ.setAreaComparisonSet(comparisons);
// Now marshal it
Set toMarshal = new HashSet();
toMarshal.add(rNZ); toMarshal.add(cNZ);
toMarshal.add(ac); toMarshal.add(rColorado);
try {
  QName rootQName =
    MarshalHelper.marshalObjects(
      toMarshal, rNZ, "http://nzdis.otago.ac.nz/nzdata1#",
      new FileOutputStream("nz.xml"));
}
catch (MarshallingException e) { ... }
```

Figure 8: Sample Java code to create and marshal an object diagram

this selectivity, the `marshalObjects` method takes a collection of objects as an argument. Links to any objects outside this collection will not be serialised. To allow a particular entry point into the knowledge structure to be identified, a root object is specified and the method returns the qualified name of the RDF resource in the serialised model that represents that object. A namespace for the serialised information is also provided.

Figure 8 shows the Java code that would produce the RDF serialisation in Figure 6.

5 Modelling Incomplete Knowledge

Because object diagrams are inter-linked networks of objects rather than sets of discrete facts, and because classes may have attributes or associations that are optional (i.e. have a multiplicity lower bound of zero), it is important to be able to distinguish between a statement that there are no values for a given property and the omission or lack of knowledge about a given property. In other words, the recipient of object-oriented information needs a way of knowing for which objects and which properties a closed world assumption can safely be made. This is achieved by including extra boolean fields in the generated Java classes that record for each regular field whether or not its value is 'known' or, for set- or list-valued fields, 'closed'— meaning that the contents of the set or list provide complete knowledge of that field. Setting the value of a single-valued field sets its 'known' field to true and all fields also have a method allowing the programmer to explicitly specify the status of the field.

When unmarshalling an object diagram from the RDF encoding it is assumed that com-

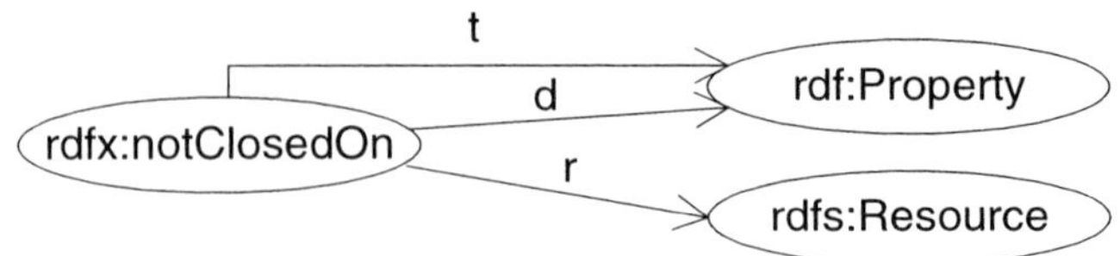

Property labels	Name space abbreviations
t = rdf:type	rdf = http://www.w3.org/1999/02/22-rdf-syntax-ns#
d = rdfs:domain	rdfs = http://www.w3.org/2000/01/rdf-schema#
r = rdfs:range	rdfx = http://nzdis.otago.ac.nz /0_1/rdf-x#

Figure 9: Schema for the notClosedOn property

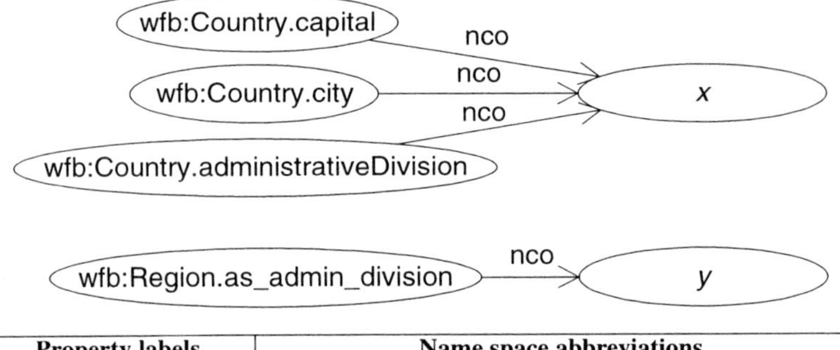

Property labels	Name space abbreviations
nco = rdfx:notClosedOn	rdfx = http://nzdis.otago.ac .nz/0_1/rdf-x#
	wfb = *namespace chosen for the World Factbook schema*

Figure 10: Meta-knowledge about incomplete information

plete information about all properties is included unless otherwise specified (although the opposite could equally well be implemented as the default assumption). Incomplete information is indicated using a non-standard RDF property notClosedOn that associates a property with a resource, meaning that complete information is not provided for that property applied to that resource. Figure 9 shows the declaration of the notClosedOn property.

Figure 10 presents an example of this property applied to the encoding of knowledge about New Zealand that was shown in Figure 6. When combined with the RDF-encoded information in Figure 6, this specifies that the RDF model does not contain complete (or possibly any) information about the capital, cities and administrative divisions of the country represented by the resource labelled x. Also, there is possibly information missing about the administrative division property of the region represented by the resource labelled y.

In order to have this meta-level information added to the RDF serialisation, the Java code shown in Figure 8 must have the following lines added before the call to marshalObjects:

```
cNZ.setCapitalKnown(false);
cNZ.setCitySetClosed(false);
cNZ.setAdministrativeDivisionSetKnown(false);
rNZ.setAs_admin_divisionKnown(false);
```

Similar mechanisms for handling incomplete knowledge have been used in the knowledge representation systems LOOM [22] (which includes :closed-world and :open-world relation properties) and CLASSIC [23] (which allows roles to be declared to be 'closed'). This notion has also been formalised in description logic by the use of epistemic operators that modify roles, and in AI planning by the use of "local closed world" formulae [24]. The notClosedOn property used in this work should also include a reference to the current RDF model, but this is not currently possible as RDF does not provide a way to declare that a set of statements collectively constitute a model with a given URI.

6   Reasoning with OCL

The Semantic Web, as envisioned by Tim Berners-Lee [25], includes a logical layer which allows "the deduction of one type of document from a document of another type; the checking of a document against a set of rules of self-consistency; and the resolution of a query by conversion from terms unknown into terms known". One of the biggest challenges for the Semantic Web community is to find interoperable ways of incorporating inference rules into ontologies. There is much research to be done in this area. For example, although the XML DTD for OIL 1.0 defines a rule-base element, its content is unconstrained text and no semantic connection is made between this rule base and the rest of the language. The RDF schemas defining later versions of OIL and DAML do not currently contain any way of representing rules, although it is a goal of the DAML project to produce an enhanced language, DAML-L, with support for rules.

It is therefore an important question to evaluate how well UML fares in this regard. In fact, UML includes a powerful mechanism for expressing inference rules: the Object Constraint Language. OCL has been claimed to be "essentially a variant of [first order predicate logic] tuned for writing constraints on object structures" [26]. This claim is true from a syntactic viewpoint: OCL is sufficiently expressive to represent any first-order inference rules that an ontology designer may wish to specify (although this expressiveness also means that reasoning about unconstrained OCL expressions is likely to be undecidable in general). From a semantic viewpoint, the above claim cannot be verified as OCL currently lacks a formal specification. However, this shortcoming has been recognised in the UML 2.0 OCL RFP [27] and at least one proposal for formal semantics for OCL has already been made [28].

The object-oriented syntax of OCL is also unlike any commonly used logical language, and attempting to write rules in OCL can be frustrating for the inexperienced. A constraint can often be expressed in several different ways and the resulting expression can look quite unlike its counterpart in first-order logic. Consider the constraint in Figure 2. The second conjunct specifies that the neighbourhood relationship between countries is reflexive. The form of this constraint might be immediately recognised as a standard pattern by an OCL expert but it is not obvious to the uninitiated.

To enable tractable reasoning about ontologies in UML, and to avoid the awkward syntax of OCL, it would be useful to define a macro language on top of OCL comprising predicates such as reflexive(*path-expression*) which are defined in terms of OCL. The set

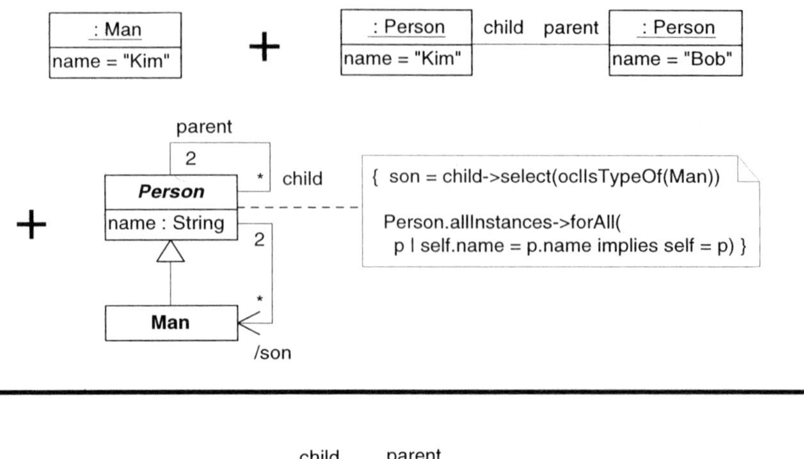

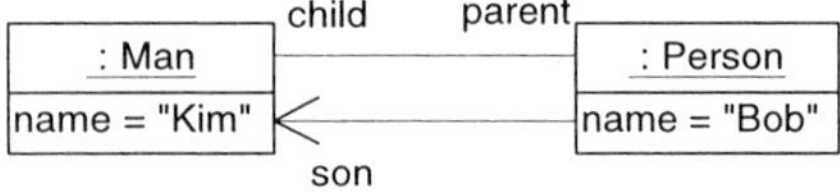

Figure 11: An example of inference over knowledge in UML

of macros could be chosen to ensure that reasoning over these expressions is tractable. This would also help to allow the translation of rules between UML-based and other representations of an ontology.

Recent research has also shown how inference rules in UML can be expressed as graph transformations on the UML metamodel [29, 14]. To give a taste of what inference with UML might look like, Figure 11 shows how new knowledge in the form of an object diagram can be generated by combining existing knowledge and information about the ontology. In this example, one agent has communicated to another that there is an object of class Man with "Kim" as the value of its name attribute. The other agent knows that there is a Person object with name Kim and that this object is the child of a Person object with name Bob. The ontology for this domain states that Man is a specialisation of Person, and includes two OCL constraints: one defining the derived (indicated by '/') role son (a son is a child that is a man), and the other stating (rather unrealistically) that the name attribute uniquely identifies objects of class Person. Over several steps of inference the agent can conclude that the two objects with name Kim are the same and therefore Kim is a male child, i.e. a son. Implementing this style of deduction in UML is a subject for future research.

7   Related Work

A number of other projects have investigated the serialisation of instances of ontological models.

Skogan [30] defined a mechanism for generating an XML document type definition (DTD) from a UML class diagram and implemented this as a script for the UML-based modelling tool Rational Rose. This is being used for the interchange of geographical information. The mapping is only defined on a subset of UML and many useful features of class diagrams, including generalisation relationships, are not supported.

Work has also been done on producing DTDs [31] and XML schemas [20] from models expressed in ontology modelling languages (Frame Logic and OIL respectively). The latter work reported that the XML Schema notion of type inheritance does not correspond well to inheritance in object-oriented models, which was a factor in the choice of RDF as a serialisation format in the research described here.

Since its initial proposal, OIL has been redesigned as an extension of RDFS [32]. This means that an ontology in OIL is also an RDF schema and therefore knowledge about resources in a domain modelled by an OIL ontology can easily be expressed using RDF.

The UML-based Ontology Toolset (UBOT) project at Lockheed Martin is working on tools to map between UML and DAML representations of ontologies [33]. This project has a different focus from the work described in this paper. Rather than using the existing features of UML to describe ontologies, the language is being extended with a set of UML 'stereotypes' (specialisations of UML modelling constructs) that correspond to classes and properties in the RDF schema for DAML. A proposal has also been made for an extension to the UML metamodel that would allow global properties in DAML ontologies to be modelled as aggregations of UML association ends (which are local to classes) [34].

The Web site http://www.interdataworking.com provides a number of 'gateways' that can be used to convert between different data formats. One particular 'gateway stack' can be used to produce an RDF schema from an XMI document, although no information is given about the mapping and how much of UML is supported. The resulting schema is defined using a mixture of properties and (meta)classes from RDF Schema (such as `rdfs:subClassOf`) and from Sergey Melnik's RDF representation of the UML metamodel [35]. The schema defines properties and classes that can be referenced when encoding object information in RDF, and could itself be used as an alternative to an XMI encoding for publishing and serialising an ontology modelled using UML. However, as XMI is an Object Management Group standard for model interchange, it is being supported by an increasing number of tools and APIs and there seem to be few advantages in using a different format for encoding UML models. If it is required to annotate an ontology with additional information that is not part of the XMI format (one of Melnik's desiderata) this could be achieved using external annotations and XLink [36].

Xpetal [37] is a tool that converts models in the 'petal' output format of the UML-based modelling tool Rational Rose to an RDF representation. No details are provided about the mapping from UML to RDFS and which UML features are supported.

8 Conclusion

This paper has described technology that facilitates the application of object-oriented modelling, and the Unified Modeling Language in particular, to the Semantic Web. From an ontology specified in UML, a corresponding RDF schema and a set of Java classes can be automatically generated to facilitate the use of object diagrams as internal knowledge representation structures and the import and export of these as RDF documents. A mechanism was also introduced for indicating when an object diagram has missing or incomplete knowledge.

Important areas for future work are the identification of tractable subsets of OCL for encoding inference rules and the definition of mappings between object-oriented representations of ontologies and knowledge and more traditional description logic-based formalisms. This would allow applications to choose the style of modelling most suitable for their needs while retaining interoperability with other subsets of the Semantic Web.

The software described in this paper is publicly available at http://nzdis.otago.ac.nz/ resources/allprojects.xml#uml-data-binding.

Acknowledgements

This work was done while visiting the Network Computing Group at the Institute for Information Technology, National Research Council of Canada, Ottawa, Canada. Thanks are due to Larry Korba and the NRC for hosting me and to the University of Otago for approving my research and study leave.

References

[1] D. Fensel, I. Horrocks, F. Van Harmelen, S. Decker, M. Erdmann, and M. Klein. OIL in a nutshell. In R. Dieng and O. Corby, editors, *Proceedings of the 12th International Conference on Knowledge Engineering and Knowledge Management (EKAW 2000)*, Lecture Notes in Artificial Intelligence 1937, pages 1–16. Springer, 2000.

[2] DAML project home page. http://www.daml.org, 2000.

[3] World Wide Web Consortium. Resource Description Framework (RDF) Schema Specification 1.0. http://www.w3.org/TR/rdf-schema, 2000.

[4] F. Donini, M. Lenzerini, D. Nardi, and A. Schaerf. Reasoning in description logics. In G. Brewka, editor, *Principles of Knowledge Representation and Reasoning*, Studies in Logic, Language and Information, pages 193–238. CLSI Publications, 1996.

[5] J. Rumbaugh, I. Jacobson, and G. Booch. *The Unified Modeling Language Reference Manual*. Addison-Wesley, 1999.

[6] Meta Data Coalition home page. http://www.mdcinfo.com/, 2000.

[7] S. Cranefield and M. Purvis. UML as an ontology modelling language. In *Proceedings of the Workshop on Intelligent Information Integration, 16th International Joint Conference on Artificial Intelligence (IJCAI-99)*, 1999. http://CEUR-WS.org/Vol-23/cranefield-ijcai99-iii.pdf.

[8] S. Cranefield and M. Purvis. Extending agent messaging to enable OO information exchange. In R. Trappl, editor, *Proceedings of the 2nd International Symposium "From Agent Theory to Agent Implementation" (AT2AI-2) at the 5th European Meeting on Cybernetics and Systems Research (EMCSR 2000)*, pages 573–578, Vienna, 2000. Austrian Society for Cybernetic Studies. Published under the title "Cybernetics and Systems 2000". An earlier version is available at http://www.otago.ac.nz/informationscience/publctns/complete/papers/dp2000-07.pdf.gz.

[9] Ana Moreira, L. F. Andrade, A. R. Deshpande, and S. Kent. Formalizing UML. Why? How? In *Addendum to the Proceedings of the Conference on Object Oriented Programming Systems Languages and Applications (OOPSLA'98)*. ACM/SIGPLAN, 1998.

[10] S. Kent, A. Evans, and B. Rumpe. UML semantics FAQ. In A. Moreira and S. Demeyer, editors, *Object-Oriented Technology: ECOOP'99 Workshop Reader*, Lecture Notes in Computer Science 1743. Springer, 1999. http://www4.informatik.tu-muenchen.de/papers/KER99.html.

[11] J.-M. Bruel, J. Lilius, A. Moreira, and R.B. France. Defining precise semantics for UML. In J. Malenfant, S. Moisan, and A. Moreira, editors, *Object-Oriented Technology: ECOOP 2000 Workshop Reader*, Lecture Notes in Computer Science 1964. Springer, 2000.

[12] Precise UML Group Web site. http://www.puml.org, 2001.

[13] A. S. Evans and S. Kent. Meta-modelling semantics of UML: the pUML approach. In B. Rumpe and R. B. France, editors, *Proceedings of the 2nd International Conference on the Unified Modeling Language*, Lecture Notes in Computer Science 1723. Springer, 1999. http://www.cs.york.ac.uk/puml/papers/pumluml99.pdf.

[14] M. Gogolla. Graph transformations on the UML metamodel. In *Proceedings of the ICALP Workshop on Graph Transformations and Visual Modeling Techniques (GVMT'2000)*, pages 359–371. Carleton Scientific, 2000. ftp://ftp.informatik.uni-bremen.de/%2Flocal/db/papers/Gogolla_2000GraGra.ps.

[15] Ora Lassila and Ralph R. Swick. Resource Description Framework (RDF) model and syntax specification. Recommendation, World Wide Web Consortium, 1999. http://www.w3.org/TR/REC-rdf-syntax.

[16] P. Hayes (ed.). RDF Model Theory. W3C Working Draft, http://www.w3.org/TR/rdf-mt/, 2002.

[17] P.-A. Muller. *Instant UML*. Wrox Press, 1997.

[18] S. Melnik. RDF API homepage. http://www-db-stanford.edu/~melnik/rdf/api.html, 2000.

[19] Novosoft metadata framework and UML library. http://nsuml.sourceforge.net, 2002.

[20] M. Klein, D. Fensel, F. van Harmelen, and I. Horrocks. The relation between ontologies and schemalanguages: translating OIL-specifications in XML-Schema. In *Proceedings of the Workshop on Applications of Ontologies and Problem solving Methods, 14th European Conference on Artificial Intelligence (ECAI 2000)*, 2000. http://delicias.dia.fi.upm.es/WORKSHOP/ECAI00/7.pdf.

[21] S. Cranefield. Networked knowledge representation and exchange using UML and RDF. *Journal of Digital Information*, 1(8), 2001. http://jodi.ecs.soton.ac.uk/.

[22] D. Brill. *LOOM Reference Manual version 1.4*. USC-ISI, 4353 Park Terrace Drive, Westlake Village, CA 91361, 1991.

[23] R. J. Brachman, D. L. McGuinness, P. F. Patel-Schneider, and A. Borgida. "Reducing" CLASSIC to practice: Knowledge representation theory meets reality. *Artificial Intelligence*, 114(1–2):203–237, 1999.

[24] O. Etzioni, K. Golden, and D. Weld. Tractable closed world reasoning with updates. In L. Doyle, E. Sandewall, and P. Torasso, editors, *KR'94: Principles of Knowledge Representation and Reasoning*, pages 178–189. Morgan Kaufmann, San Francisco, California, 1994.

[25] T. Berners-Lee. Semantic Web road map. http://www.w3.org/DesignIssues/Semantic.html, 1998.

[26] T. Clark, A. Evans, S. Kent, S. Brodsky, and S. Cook. A feasibility study in rearchitecting UML as a family of languages using a precise OO meta-modeling approach. http://www.cs.york.ac.uk/puml/mml/mmf.pdf, 2000.

[27] UML 2.0 OCL request for proposal. OMG Document ad/2000-09-03, Object Management Group, 2000. http://www.omg.org/techprocess/meetings/schedule/UML_2.0_OCL_RFP.html.

[28] M. V. Cengarle and A. Knapp. A formal semantics for OCL 1.4. In M. Gogolla and C. Kobryn, editors, *Proceedings of the Fourth International Conference on UML (UML 2001)*, Lecture Notes in Computer Science 2185, pages 118–133. Springer, 2001.

[29] A. S. Evans. Reasoning with UML class diagrams. In *Proceedings of the Workshop on Industrial Strength Formal Methods (WIFT'98)*. IEEE Press, 1998. http://www.cs.york.ac.uk/puml/papers/evanswift.pdf.

[30] D. Skogan. UML as a schema language for XML based data interchange. http://www.ifi.uio.no/~davids/papers/Uml2Xml.pdf, 1999.

[31] M. Erdmann and R. Studer. Ontologies as conceptual models for XML documents. In *Proceedings of the 12th Workshop on Knowledge Acquisition, Modeling and Management (KAW'99)*. Knowledge Science Institute, University of Calgary, 1999. http://sern.ucalgary.ca/KSI/KAW/KAW99/papers.html.

[32] J. Broekstra, M. Klein, S. Decker, D. Fensel, and I. Horrocks. Adding formal semantics to the Web: building on top of RDF schema. In *Proceedings of the Workshop on the Semantic Web: Models, Architectures and Management, Fourth European Conference on Research and Advanced Technology for Digital Libraries (ECDL'2000)*, 2000. http://www.ics.forth.gr/proj/isst/SemWeb/proceedings/session2-2/paper.pdf.

[33] UBOT project home page. http://ubot.lockheedmartin.com/, 2001.

[34] K. Baclawski, M. K. Kokar, P. A. Kogut, L. Hart, J. Smith, W. S. Holmes III, J. Letkowski, and M. L.
      Aronson. Extending UML to support ontology engineering for the Semantic Web. In M. Gogolla and
      C. Kobryn, editors, *Proceedings of the Fourth International Conference on UML (UML 2001)*, Lecture
      Notes in Computer Science 2185, pages 342–360. Springer, 2001.

[35] S. Melnik. UML in RDF. http://www-db.stanford.edu/~melnik/rdf/uml/, 2000.

[36] XLink project home page. http://www.w3.org/XML/Linking, 2001.

[37] Xpetal sourceforge Web page. http://sourceforge.net/projects/xmodel, 2001.

Appendix

The following is an XML serialisation of the RDF model representing information about New
Zealand that was shown in Figure 6.

```
<rdf:RDF
  xmlns:wfb="http://nzdis.otago.ac.nz/0_1/world-fact-book#"
  xmlns:rdf="http://www.w3.org/1999/02/22-rdf-syntax-ns#">

<wfb:Region rdf:ID="region1">
  <wfb:Region.name>New Zealand</wfb:Region.name>
  <wfb:Region.as_country rdf:resource="#country1"/>
</wfb:Region>

<wfb:Country rdf:ID="country1">
  <wfb:Country.region rdf:resource="#region1"/>
  <wfb:Country.areaComparison rdf:resource="#bag1"/>
</wfb:Country>

<rdf:Bag rdf:ID="bag1">
  <rdf:li rdf:resource="#comparison1"/>
</rdf:Bag>

<wfb:AreaComparison rdf:ID="comparison1">
  <wfb:AreaComparison.country rdf:resource="#country1"/>
  <wfb:AreaComparison.region rdf:resource="#region2"/>
  <wfb:AreaComparison.proportion>About the size of
  </wfb:AreaComparison.proportion>
</wfb:AreaComparison>

<wfb:Region rdf:ID="region2">
  <wfb:Region.name>Colorado</wfb:Region.name>
</wfb:Region>

</rdf:RDF>
```

Metamodeling Architecture of Web Ontology Languages

Jeff Z. Pan and Ian Horrocks

Information Management Group
Department of Computer Science
University of Manchester
Oxford Road Manchester M13 9PL, UK
{pan,horrocks}@cs.man.ac.uk

Abstract. Recent research has shown that RDF Schema, as a schema layer Semantic Web language, has a non-standard metamodeling architecture. As a result, it is difficult to understand and lacks clear semantics. This paperproposes RDFS(FA) (RDFS with Fixed metamodeling Architecture) and demonstrates how the problems of RDF Schema can be solved under RDFS(FA). Based on the fixed metamodeling architecture, a clear model-theoretic semantics of RDFS(FA) is given. Interestingly, RDFS(FA) also benefits DAML +OIL by offering a firm semantic basis and by solving the "layer mistake" problem.

1 Introduction

The Semantic Web, with its vision stated by Berners-lee [1], aims at developing *languages* for expressing information in a machine understandable form. The recent explosion of interest in the World Wide Web has also fuelled interest in ontologies. It has been predicted (Broekstra et al. [3]) that ontologies will play a pivotal role in the Semantic Web since ontologies can provide shared domain models, which are understandable to both human being and machines.

Ontology (Uschold and Gruninger [21]) is, in general, a representation of a shared conceptualisation of a specific domain. It provides a shared and common understanding of a *domain* that can be communicated between people and heterogeneous and distributed application systems. An ontology necessarily entails or embodies some sort of world view with respect to a given domain. The world view is usually conceived as a hierarchical description of important concepts (is-a hierarchy), a set of crucial properties, and their inter-relationships.

Berners-lee [1] outlined the architecture of Semantic Web. We would like to call it a *functional architecture* because the expressive primitives are incrementally introduced from languages in the lowest layer (i.e. metadata layer) to those in the higher layer (e.g. logical layer), so that the languages in each layer can satisfy the requirements of different kinds (or levels) of applications:

1. In the *metadata layer*, a simple and general model of semantic assertions of the Web is introduced. The simple model contains just the concepts of *resource* and *property*, which are used to express the meta information and will be needed by languages in the upper layers. The Resource Description Framework (RDF) (Lassila and R.Swick [14]) is believed to be the general model in metadata layer.

2. In the *schema layer*, simple Web *ontology* languages are introduced, which will define a hierarchical description of concepts (is-a hierarchy) and properties. These languages use the general model in metadata layer to define the basic metamodeling architecture of Web ontology languages. RDF Schema (RDFS) (Brickley and Guha [2]) is a candidate schema layer language.

3. In the *logical layer*, more powerful Web *ontology* languages are introduced. These languages are based on the basic metamodeling architecture defined in schema layer, and defines a much richer set of modelling primitives that can e.g. be mapped to very expressive Description Logics (Horrocks et al. [11], Horrocks [10]) to supply reasoning services for the Semantic Web. OIL (Horocks et al. [9]) and DAML+OIL (van Harmelen et al. [23]) are well known logical layer languages.

This paper will focus on the *metamodeling architecture* other than the functional architecture. We should point out that "metamodeling" and the "metadata layer" in the functional architecture are not the same. Metadata means data about data. *Metamodeling* concerns the definition of the modelling primitives (vocabulary) used in a modelling language. Many software engineering modelling languages, including UML, are based on metamodels. Among the Semantic Web languages, the schema layer languages are responsible to build the metamodeling architecture.

₁In this paper, we argue that RDFS, as a schema layer language, has a non-standard and non-fixed layer metamodeling architecture, which makes some elements in the model have dual roles in the RDFS specification (Nejdl et al. [17]). Therefore, it makes the RDFS specification itself quite difficult to understand by the modellers. The even worse thing is that since the logical layer languages (e.g. OIL, DAML+OIL) are all based on the metamodeling architecture defined by schema layer languages (RDFS), these languages therefore have the similar problems, e.g. the "layer mistake" discussed in Section 2.3.

We propose *RDFS(FA)* (RDFS with Fixed metamodeling Architecture), which has a metamodeling architecture similar to that of UML. We analyse the problems of the non-fixed metamodeling architecture of RDFS and demonstrate how these problems can be solved under RDFS(FA). Furthermore, We give a clear model theoretic semantics to RDFS(FA).

The rest of the paper is organized as follows. In Section 2 we explain the data model of RDF, RDFS and DAML+OIL, the languages belonging to the metadata level, schema level and logical level of the Semantic Web Architecture respectively. We will focus on the metamodeling architecture of RDFS and locate what the problems are and where they come from. In Section 3 we discuss the advantages and disadvantages of fixed and non-fixed layer metamodeling architecture and then briefly explain the metamodeling architecture of UML. In Section 4 we propose RDFS(FA), and give a clear semantics to RDFS(FA). We also demonstrate how the "layer mistake" problem with DAML+OIL is solved in RDFS(FA). Section 5 briefly discuss the advantages of RDFS(FA) and our attitudes on how to make use of UML in the Web ontology languages.

2   Current Data Models of Semantic Web Languages

2.1   RDF Data Model

As a Semantic Web language in the *metadata layer* of the functional architecture, RDF is a foundation for processing metadata. It provides interoperability between applications that exchange machine-understandable information on the Web. The foundation of RDF is a model for representing named properties and property values. The RDF data model provides an abstract, conceptual framework for defining and using metadata. The basic data model consists of three object types:

Resources: All things being described by RDF expressions are called *resources*. A resource may be an entire Web page, a part of a Web page, a whole collection of pages (Web site); or an object that is not directly accessible via the Web, e.g. a printed book. Resources are always named by URIs.

Properties: A *property* is a specific aspect, characteristic, attribute, or relation used to describe a resource.

Statements: A specific resource together with a named property plus the value of that property for that resource is an RDF *statement*.

In a nutshell, the RDF data model is an object-property-value mechanism. The metadata information is introduced by a set of statements in RDF. There are several ways to express RDF statements. First, we can use the binary predicate form Property(object,value), e.g. Title('http://img.cs.man.ac.uk/jpan/Zhilin', "Home Page of Jeff Z. Pan"). Secondly, we can diagram an RDF statement pictorially using directed labeled graphs: '[object]-Property->[value]' (see Figure 1). Thirdly, RDF uses

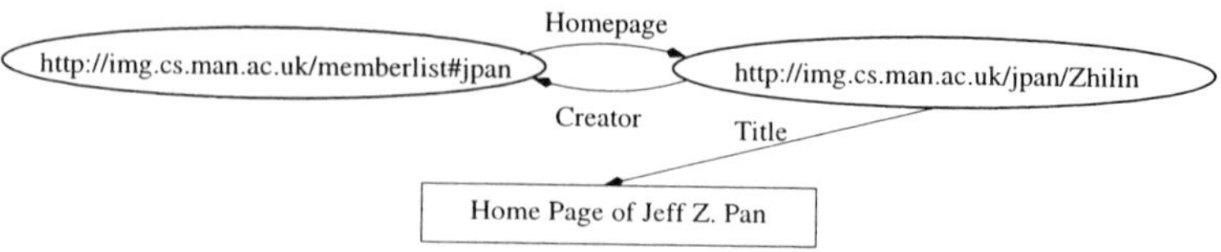

Figure 1: An Example of RDF in a Directed Labeled Graph

an Extensible Markup Language (XML) encoding as its interchange syntax:

```
<rdf:Description rdf:ID="http://img.cs.man.ac.uk/jpan/Zhilin">
  <Title>Home Page of Jeff Z. Pan</Title>
</rdf:Description>
```

The RDF data model is so called "property-centric". We can use the "about" attribute to add more properties to the existing resource. Generally speaking, with the object-property-value mechanism, RDF can be used to express:

- *attributes* of resources: in this case, the 'value' is a literal (e.g the "Title" property above);

- *relationships* between any two resources: in this case, the 'value' is a resource, and the involved properties represent different roles of the two resources with this relationship; in the following example, there exists a "creator-homepage" relationship between "http://img.cs.man.ac.uk/jpan/Zhilin" and "http://img.cs.man.ac.uk/memberlist#jpan" (see also Figure 1):

```
<rdf:Description rdf:ID="http://img.cs.man.ac.uk/memberlist#jpan">
  <Homepage rdf:resource="http://img.cs.man.ac.uk/jpan/Zhilin"/>
</rdf:Description>
<rdf:Description about="http://img.cs.man.ac.uk/jpan/Zhilin">
  <Creator rdf:resource="http://img.cs.man.ac.uk/memberlist#jpan"/>
</rdf:Description>
```

- *weak type* of resources: the 'type' is *weak* because RDF itself has no standard way to define a Class, so the type here is regarded only as a special attribute; for example,

```
<rdf:Description about="http://img.cs.man.ac.uk/memberlist#jpan">
  <rdf:type rdf:resource="#Person"/>
</rdf:Description>
```

- *statement about statement*: RDF can be used for making statements about other RDF statements, which are referred to as *higher-order statements*. This feature of RDF has yet to be clearly defined and is beyond the scope of this paper.

2.2　RDF Schema Data Model

As we have seen, on the one hand, RDF data model is enough for defining and using metadata. On the other hand, the modelling primitives offered by RDF are very basic. Although you can define "Class" and "subClassOf" as resources in RDF (no one can stop you doing that), RDF provides no standard mechanisms for declaring classes and (global) properties, nor does it provide any mechanisms for defining the relationships between properties or between classes. That is the role of RDFS–a Semantic Web language in the schema layer.

RDFS is expressed by using RDF data model. It extends RDF by giving an externally specified semantics to specific resources. In RDFS, rdfs:Class is used to define concepts, i.e. every class must be an instance of rdfs:Class. Resources that are described by RDF expressions are viewed to be instances of the class rdfs:Resource. The class rdf:Property is the class of all properties used to characterise instances rdfs:Resource. The rdfs:ConstraintResource defines the class of all constraints. The rdfs:ConstraintProperty is a subset of rdfs:ConstraintResource and rdf:Property, all of its instances are properties used to specify constraints, e.g. rdfs:domain and rdfs:range. For example, the following RDFS expressions

```
<rdfs:Class rdf:ID="Animal">
  <rdfs:comment>This class of animals is illustrative of a number of
  ontological idioms.</rdfs:comment>
</rdfs:Class>
<rdfs:Class rdf:ID="Person">
  <rdfs:subClassOf rdf:resource="#Animal"/>
</rdfs:Class>
<rdf:Description rdf:ID="John">
  <rdf:type rdf:resource="#Person"/>
  <rdfs:comment>John is a person.</rdfs:comment>
</rdf:Description>
<rdf:Description rdf:ID="Mary">
  <rdf:type rdf:resource="#Person"/>
  <rdfs:comment>Mary is a person.</rdfs:comment>
</rdf:Description>
```

define the classes "Animal" and "Person", with the latter being the subclass of the former, and two individuals "John" and "Mary", which are instances of the class "Person". Individual "John" can also be defined in this way,

```
<Person rdf:ID="John">
  <rdfs:comment>John is a person.</rdfs:comment>
</Person>
```

which is an implicit way to define rdf:type property. Note that here "Person" is a class.

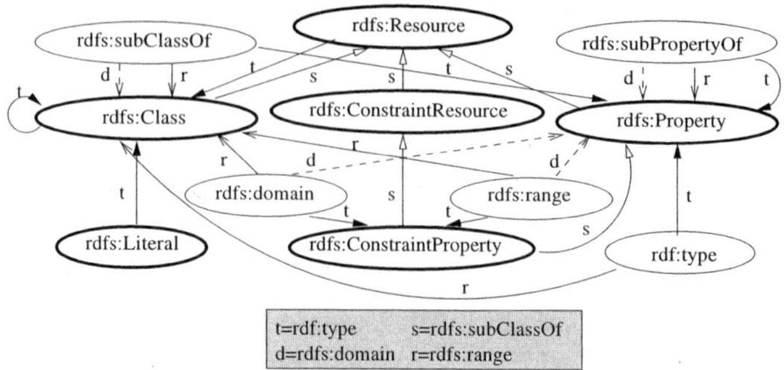

Figure 2: Directed Labeled Graph of RDF Schema

Figure 2 pictures the subclass-of and instance-of hierarchy of RDFS: rdfs:Resource, rdfs:Class, rdf:Property, rdfs:ConstraintResource and rdfs:ConstraintProperty are all instances of rdfs:Class, while rdfs:Class, rdf:Property and rdfs:ConstraintResource are subclass of rdfs:Resource. It is confusing that rdfs:Class is a sub-class of rdfs:Resource, while rdfs:Resource itself is an instance of rdfs:Class at the same time. It is also strange that rdfs:Class is an instance of itself.

In RDFS, all properties are instances of rdf:Property. The rdf:type property models instance-of relationships between resources and classes. The rdfs:subClassOf property models the subsumption hierarchy between classes, and is transitive. The rdfs:subPropertyOf property models the subsumption hierarchy between properties, and is also transitive. The rdfs:domain and rdfs:range properties are used to restrict domain and range properties. For example, the following RDFS expressions

```
<rdf:Property rdf:ID="hasFriend">
  <rdfs:domain rdf:resource="#Person"/>
  <rdfs:range rdf:resource="#Person"/>
</rdf:Property>
<rdf:Description about="#John">
  <hasFriend rdf:resource="#Mary"/>
</rdf:Description>
```

define a property "hasFriend" between two "Person"s and ⟨'John', 'Mary'⟩ is an instance of "hasFriend" (see Figure 3).

In RDFS, properties are regarded as sets of binary relationships between instances of classes, e.g. a property "hasFriend" is a set of binary tuples between two instances of the class "Person". One exception is the rdf:type, since it is just the *instance-of* relationship. In this sense, rdf:type is regarded as a special predefined property.

Figure 2 also shows the range and domain constraints in RDFS–rdfs:domain and rdfs:range can be used to specify the two classes that a certain property can asso-

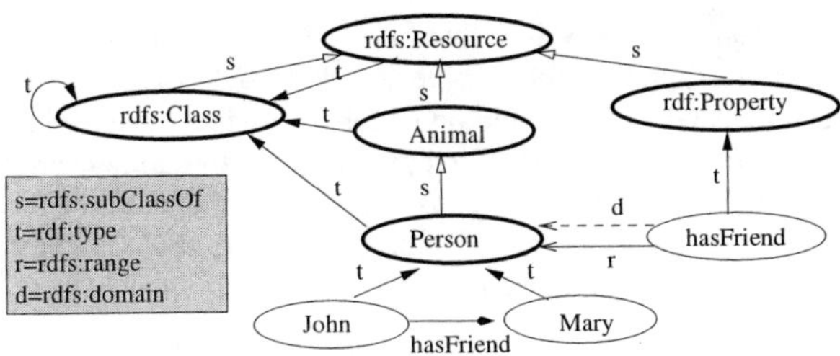

Figure 3: A "Person–hasFriend" Example of RDF Schema

ciate with. So the rdfs:domain of rdfs:domain and rdfs:range is the class rdf:Property, the rdfs:range of rdfs:domain and rdfs:range is the class rdfs:Class. The rdfs:domain and rdfs:range of rdfs:subClassOf is rdfs:Class. The rdfs:domain and rdfs:range of rdfs:subPropertyOf is rdf:Property. The rdfs:range of rdf:type is the class rdfs:Class. The rdf:type property is regarded as a set of binary links between *instances* and classes (as mentioned above), while the value of the rdfs:domain property should be a *class*, therefore rdf:type does not have the rdfs:domain property (cf. Brickley and Guha [2]).

As we have seen, RDFS use some primitive modelling primitives to define other modelling primitives (e.g. rdf:type, rdfs:domain, rdfs:range, rdf:type and rdfs:subClassOf). At the same time, these primitives can be used to define ontologies as well, which makes it rather unique when compared to conventional model and metamodeling approaches, and makes the RDFS specification very difficult to read and to formalise (Nejdl et al. [17], Broekstra et al. [3]). For example, in Figure 3, it is confusing that although rdfs:Class is the rdf:type of "Animal", both "Animal" and rdfs:Class are rdfs:subClassOf rdfs:Resource, where rdfs:Class is a modelling primitive and "Animal" is an user-defined ontology class.

2.3　DAML+OIL Data Model

DAML+OIL is an expressive Web ontology language in the logical layer. It builds on earlier W3C standards such as RDF and RDFS, and extends these languages with much richer modelling primitives. DAML+OIL inherits many aspects from OIL, and provides modelling primitives commonly found in frame-based languages. It has a clean and well defined semantics based on description logics.

A complete description of the data model of DAML+OIL is beyond the scope of this paper. However, we will illustrate how DAML+OIL extends RDFS by introducing some new subclasses of rdfs:Class and rdf:Property. One of the most important classes that DAML+OIL introduces is daml:Datatype. DAML+OIL divides the universe into two disjoint parts, the object domain and the datatype domain. The object domain consist of objects that are members of classes described in DAML+OIL. The datatype domain consists of the values that belong to XML Schema datatypes. Both daml:Class (object class) and daml:Datatype are rdfs:subClassOf rdfs:Class. Accordingly, properties in DAML+OIL should be either object properties, which relate objects to objects and are instances of daml:ObjectProperty; or datatype property, which relate objects to datatype values and are instances of daml:Datatype- Property. Both daml:ObjectProperty and daml:DatatypeProperty are rdfs:subClassOf rdf:Pro- perty. For example, we can define a datatype property called "birthday":

```
<daml:DatatypeProperty rdf:ID="birthday">
  <rdf:type rdf:resource="http://www.daml.org/2001/03/daml+oil#Uni-
  queProperty"/>
  <rdfs:domain rdf:resource="#Animal"/>
  <rdfs:range rdf:resource="http://www.w3.org/2000/10/XMLSchema#date"/>
</daml:DatatypeProperty>
```

Besides being an instance of daml:DatatypeProperty, the "birthday" property is also an instance of daml:UniqueProperty, which means that "birthday" can only have one (unique) value for each instance of the "Animal" class. In fact, daml:UniqueProperty is so useful that some people even want to use it to refine DAML+OIL predefined properties, e.g. daml:maxCardinality:

```
<rdf:Property rdf:about="#maxCardinality">
  <rdf:type rdf:resource="http://www.daml.org/2001/03/daml+oil#Uniq-
  ueProperty"/>
</rdf:Property>
```

This statement seems obviously right, however, it is wrong because the semantics of daml:UniqueProp- erty requires that only the ontology properties can be regarded as its instances (cf. van Harmelen et al. [22]). This is the so called "layer mistake". The reason that people can easily make the above "layer mistake" lies in the fact that the schema layer language RDFS doesn't *distinguish* the modelling information in the ontology level and that in the language level. Another example is what we had mentioned before in Figure 3, it is not appropriate that both rdfs:Class and "Animal" are rdfs:subClassOf rdfs:Resource.

It is the existence of the dual roles of some RDFS modelling elements, e.g. rdfs:sub-ClassOf, that makes RDFS have unclear semantics. This partially explains why Brickley and Guha [2] didn't define the semantics of RDFS. We should stress that DAML+ OIL is built on top of the *syntax* of RDFS, but not the *semantics* of RDFS. On the contrary, RDFS relies on DAML+OIL to give semantics to its modelling primitives. In other words, DAML+OIL not only defines the semantics of its newly introduced modelling primitives, e.g. daml:UniqueProperty, daml:maxCardinality etc., but also the modelling primitives of RDFS, e.g. rdfs:subClassOf, rdfs:subPropertyOf, rdfs:domain, rdfs:range etc (van Harmelen et al. [22]). This breaks the dependency between logical layer languages and schema layer languages and indicates that RDFS is not yet a fully qualified schema layer Semantic Web language.

3   Fixed or Non-fixed Metamodeling Architecture?

3.1   The Advantages and Disadvantages of Non-fixed Metamodeling Architecture

The dual roles of some RDFS modelling elements indicate that something might be wrong with the metamodeling architecture of RDFS. The RDFS has a non-fixed metamodeling architecture, which means that it can have possibly infinite layers of classes. The advantage is that it makes itself compact. However, it has at least the following three disadvantages or problems:

1. The class rdfs:Class is an instance of itself. Usually, a class is regarded as a set, and an instance of the class is a member of the set. A Class of classes can be interpreted as a set of sets, which means its members are sets. In RDFS, all classes (including rdfs:Class) are instances of rdfs:Class, which is suspicious by close to Russell paradox. The paradox arises when considering the set of all sets that are not members of themselves. Such a set appears to be a member of itself if and only if it is not a member of itself, hence the paradox.

2. The class rdfs:Resource is a superclass and instance of rdfs:Class at the same time, which means that the super set (rdfs:Resource) is a member of the subset (rdfs:Class).

3. The properties rdfs:subClassOf, rdf:type, rdfs:range and rdfs:domain are used to define both the other RDFS modelling primitives and the ontology, which makes their semantics unclear and makes it very difficult to formalise RDFS. E.g. it is not clear that the semantic of rdfs:subClassOf is a set of binary relationships between two sets of objects or a set of binary relationships between two sets of sets of objects, or else.

As a result, RDFS has no clear semantics, it even rely on DAML+OIL to give itself semantics, which makes RDFS a not so satisfactory schema layer semantic Web language.

3.2   The Advantages and Disadvantages of Fixed Metamodeling Architecture

We can demonstrate the advantages of fixed metamodeling architecture by showing how the problems of RDF Schema mentioned in Section 3.1 are solved under the fixed metamodeling architecture.

The reason that problem 1 exists is that RDFS uses a single primitive rdfs:Class to implicitly represent possibly infinite layers of classes. *But do we really need infinite layers of classes?* In practice, rdfs:Class usually acts as a modelling primitive in the ontology language and is used to define ontology classes (e.g. "Person"). One reasonable solution is to explicitly specify a certain number of layers of *class* primitives, with one being an instance of another, and the *class* primitives in the top layer having no type at all, which means that it is not an instance of anything. It isn't because it can't have a type, but because it doesn't have to have a type. From the pragmatic point of view, we are only interested in the several layers on the ground and it is very important that the modelling primitives in these layers have *clear semantics*. This is the main difference between the fixed and non-fixed metamodeling architecture.

So how many class primitives do we really need? Problem 2 indicates that we need at least *two* class primitives in different metamodeling layers — one as the type of rdfs:Resource, the other as a subclass of rdfs:Resource. In fact, in the four-layer metamodeling architecture of UML, there exist two class primitives in different metamodeling layers, which are *Class* in metamodel layer and *MetaClass* in meta-metamodel layer (see Section 3.3). In practice, it has not been found useful to have more than two class primitives in the metamodeling architecture (technology Inc. [20, pg. 298]). Therefore, it is reasonable to explicitly define two class primitives in different metamodeling layers of RDF Schema, one is MClass in Metalanguage Layer and the other is LClass in Ontology Language Layer[1] (see Section 4.1). This makes RDFS have a similar metamodeling architecture to that of the well known UML, so that it is easy for the modellers to understand.

Problem 3 is mainly about predefined properties. It can be solved by specifying which level of class we intend to refer to when we use these predefined properties. (see Section 4.1).

From the discussion above, we believe that although the schema layer language won't be as compact as it is, there will be several advantages if it has a fixed metamodeling architecture:

1. We don't have to worry about Russell's Paradox.

2. It has clear formalised semantics.

3. DAML+OIL and other logical layer Semantic Web languages can be built on top of both the syntax and semantics of the RDFS with fixed metamodeling architecture.

4. It is similar to the metamodeling architecture of UML, easy to understand and use.

---

[1]In this sense, there are three kinds of classes: meta classes in the Metalanguage Layer, language classes in the Language Layer and ontology classes, which are instance of LClass, in Ontology Layer.

3.3　UML Metamodeling Architecture

The Unified Modelling Language (OMG [18]) is a general-purpose visual modelling language that is designed to specify, visualise, construct and document the artifacts of a software system. It is a standard object-oriented design language that has gained virtually global acceptance. UML has a four-layer metamodeling architecture.

1) The *Meta-metamodel Layer* forms the foundation for the metamodeling architecture. The primary responsibility of this layer is to define the language for specifying a metamodel. A meta-metamodel can define multiple metamodels, and there can be multiple meta-metamodels associated with each metamodel. Examples of meta-objects in the metamodeling layer are: MetaClass, MetaAttribute.

2) A *Metamodel* is an instance of a Meta-metamodel. The primary responsibility of the Metamodel layer is to define a language for specifying models. Examples of meta-objects in the metamodeling layer are: Class, Attribute.

3) A *Model* is an instance of a Metamodel. The primary responsibility of the Model Layer is to define a language that describes an information domain. Examples in Model layer are class "Person" and property "hasFriend".

4) *User Objects* are an instance of a Model. The primary responsibility of the User Objects Layer is to describe a specific information domain. Examples in User Objects Layer are "John", "Mary" and $\langle$'John', 'Mary'$\rangle$.

The four-layer metamodel architecture is a proven methodology for defining the structure of complex models that need to be reliably stored, shared, manipulated and exchanged (Kobryn [13]). In the next section, we will use the metamodeling methods of UML to build a fixed layer metamodeling architecture for RDFS.

4　Web Ontology Language Data Model with Fixed Metamodeling Architecture

We will now illustrate what the data model of an RDF-based Web ontology language will look like under the fixed metamodeling architecture.

4.1　RDF Schema Data Model with Fixed Metamodeling Architecture

Firstly, we will map the original RDFS into RDFS with Fixed metamodeling Architecture (or RDFS(FA) for short). One principle during this mapping is that we try to minimise the changes we make to RDFS.

As we discussed in Section 3.2, we believe it is reasonable to define a four-layer metamodeling architecture for RDFS(FA). These four metamodeling layers are:

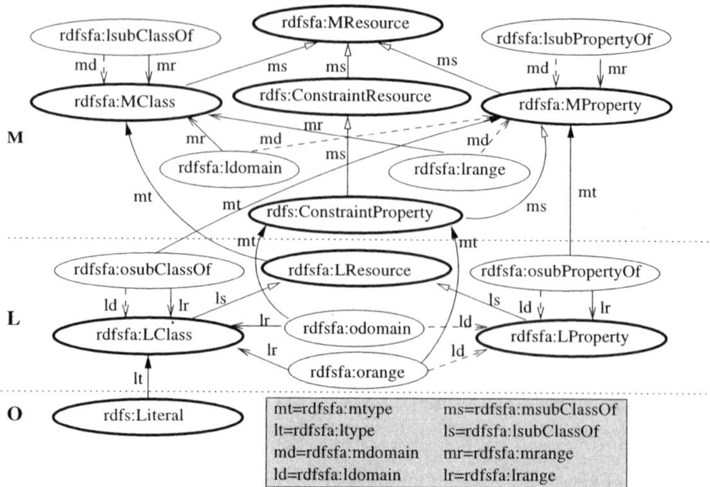

Figure 4: Directed Labeled Graph of RDFS(FA)

1. The *Metalanguage Layer* (M Layer, corresponding to the Meta-metamodel Layer in UML) forms the foundation for the metamodeling architecture. Its primary responsibility is to define the language layer. All the modelling primitives in this layer have no types (see Section 3.2). Examples of modelling primitives in this layer are rdfsfa:MClass and rdfsfa:MProperty.

2. The *Language Layer* (L Layer, corresponding to the Metamodel Layer in UML), or *Ontology Language Layer*, is an instance of the Metalanguage Layer. Its primary responsibility is to define a language for specifying ontologies. Examples of modelling primitives in this layer are rdfsfa:LClass, rdfsfa:LProperty. Both of them are instances of rdfsfa:MClass.

3. The *Ontology Layer* (O Layer, corresponding to the Model Layer in UML) is an instance of Language Layer. Its primary responsibility is to define a language that describes a specific domain, i.e. an ontology. Examples of modelling primitives in this layer are "Person" and "Car", which are instances of rdfsfa:LClass, and "hasFriend", which is an instance of rdfsfa:LProperty.

4. The *Instance Layer* (I Layer, corresponding to the User Objects Layer in UML) is an instance of Ontology Layer. Its primary responsibility is to describe a specific domain, in terms of the ontology defined in the Ontology Layer. Examples in this layer are "Mary", "John" and hasFriend⟨ 'John','Mary'⟩.

RDFS(FA) is illustrated in Figure 4. We map the modelling primitives of RDFS to the primitives in corresponding metamodeling layers of RDFS(FA), so that *no* modelling primitives will have dual roles in the metamodeling architecture of RDFS(FA).

First, we map rdfs:Class and its instance primitives in RDFS to the metamodeling architecture of RDFS(FA) as follows:

1. rdfs:Class is mapped to rdfsfa:MClass in Metalanguage Layer and rdfsfa:LClass in Language Layer, so that rdfsfa:LClass is an instance of rdfsfa:MClass.

```
<rdf:Description rdf:ID="MClass">
  <rdfs:comment>The concept of class in the Metalanguage Layer.
  </rdfs:comment>
  <rdfsfa:msubClassOf rdf:resource="#MResource"/>
</rdf:Description>
<rdfsfa:MClass rdf:ID="LClass">
  <rdfs:comment>The concept of class in the Language Layer.
  </rdfs:comment>
  <rdfsfa:lsubClassOf rdf:resource="#LResource"/>
</rdfsfa:MClass>
```

2. rdfs:Resource is mapped to rdfsfa:MResource in the Metalanguage Layer and rdfsfa:LResource in Language Layer, so that rdfsfa:MResource is the super class of all the modelling primitives in the Metalanguage Layer, while rdfsfa:LResource is an instance of rdfsfa:MClass and the superclass of rdfsfa:LClass.

```
<rdf:Description rdf:ID="MResource">
  <rdfs:comment>The most general resource in the Metalanguage
  Layer.</rdfs:comment>
</rdf:Description>
<rdfsfa:MClass rdf:ID="LResource">
  <rdfs:comment>The most general resource in the Language Layer.
  </rdfs:comment>
</rdfsfa:MClass>
```

3. The rdfs:Property is mapped to rdfsfa:MProperty in the Metalanguage Layer and rdfsfa:LProperty in the Language Layer.

```
<rdf:Description rdf:ID="MProperty">
  <rdfs:comment>The concept of property in the Metalanguage
  Layer.</rdfs:comment>
  <rdfsfa:msubClassOf rdf:resource="#MResource"/>
</rdf:Description>
<rdfsfa:MClass rdf:ID="LProperty">
  <rdfs:comment>The concept of property in the Language Layer.
  </rdfs:comment>
```

```
<rdfsfa:lsubClassOf rdf:resource="#LResource"/>
</rdfsfa:MClass>
```

4. The rdfs:ConstraintResource is in the Metalanguage Layer, where it is rdfsfa:msub-
ClassOf rdfsfa:MResource.

```
<rdf:Description rdf:ID="ConstraintResource">
  <rdfsfa:msubClassOf rdf:resource="#MResource"/>
</rdf:Description>
```

5. The rdfs:ConstraintProperty is in the Metalanguage Layer, where it is rdfsfa:msub-
ClassOf rdfsfa:MProperty and rdfs:ConstraintResource.

```
<rdf:Description rdf:ID="ConstraintProperty">
  <rdfsfa:msubClassOf rdf:resource="#MProperty"/>
  <rdfsfa:msubClassOf rdf:resource="#ConstraintResource"/>
</rdf:Description>
```

As shown in Figure 4, modelling primitives are divided into three groups in the
Metalanguage Layer, Language Layer and Ontology Layer. rdfsfa:LClass is not an
instance of itself, but an instance of rdfsfa:MClass. rdfsfa:LResource is an instance
of rdfsfa:MClass and a super class of rdfsfa:LClass. In general, there are three kinds
of "classes" in the metamodeling architecture of RDFS(FA)[2]: *meta classes* in the
Metalanguage Layer (e.g. rdfsfa:MClass, rdfsfa:MProperty), *language classes* in the
Language Layer (instances of rdfsfa:MClass, e.g. rdfsfa:LClass, rdfsfa:LProperty)
and *ontology class* in the Ontology Layer (instance of rdfsfa:LClass, e.g. "Person",
"Car").

In order to solve problem 3 mentioned in Section 3.1, we need to be able to specify
which kind of class (out of the three kinds of "classes" mentioned above) we want to
refer to. In RDFS(FA), we add the layer prefix (e.g. m- for Metalanguage Layer,
l- for Language Layer etc.) on the properties when we use the predefined property
primitives. Based on the above principle, we can map the property primitives in RDFS
to the metamodeling architecture of RDFS(FA) as follows:

1. rdfs:domain is a set of binary relationships between instances of rdf:Property and
rdfs:Class. As classes and properties occur in three different layers of RDFS(FA),
rdfs:domain is mapped to three different properties in RDFS(FA): rdfsfa:odomain,
rdfsfa:ldomain and rdfsfa:mdomain. As shown in Figure 4, the rdfsfa:ldomain
is defined in the Metalanguage Layer and used in the Language Layer, while
rdfsfa:odomain is defined in the Language Layer and used in the Ontology Layer
(see Figure 5).

---

[2]Accordingly, there are three kinds of "properties" as well.

```
<rdfs:ConstraintProperty rdf:ID="odomain">
  <rdfs:comment>This is how we specify that all instances of a
  particular ontology property describes instances of a partic-
  ular ontology class.</rdfs:comment>
</rdfs:ConstraintProperty>
<rdf:Description rdf:ID="ldomain">
  <rdfs:comment>This is how we specify that all instances of a
  particular language property describes instances of a partic-
  ular language class.</rdfs:comment>
</rdf:Description>
<rdf:Description rdf:ID="mdomain">
  <rdfs:comment>This is how we specify that all instances of a
  particular meta property describes instances of a particular
  meta class. </rdfs:comment>
</rdf:Description>
```

2. Similarly, rdfs:range is mapped to rdfsfa:orange, rdfsfa:lrange and rdfsfa:mrange.

```
<rdfs:ConstraintProperty rdf:ID="orange">
  <rdfs:comment>This is how we specify that all instances of a
  particular ontology property have values that are instances of
  a particular ontology class.</rdfs:comment>
</rdfs:ConstraintProperty>
<rdf:Description rdf:ID="lrange">
  <rdfs:comment>This is how we specify the values of an instance
  of a particular language property have values that are instanc-
  es of a particular language class. </rdfs:comment>
</rdf:Description>
<rdfsfa:MProperty rdf:ID="mrange">
  <rdfs:comment>This is how we specify the values of an instance
  of a particular meta property should be instances of a particu-
  lar meta class. </rdfs:comment>
</rdfsfa:MProperty>
```

3. rdf:type is a set of binary relationship between resource and rdfs:Class. As RDFS
   (FA) has meta classes, language classes and ontology classes, rdf:type is mapped
   to rdfsfa:otype, rdfsfa:ltype and rdfsfa:mtype. E.g. in Figure 4, rdfsfa:MClass is
   the rdfsfa:mtype of rdfsfa:LResource and rdfsfa:LClass.

```
<rdfsfa:MProperty rdf:ID="otype">
  <rdfs:comment>Indicates membership of an instance of rdfsfa:LC-
  lass.</rdfs:comment>
  <rdfsfa:lrange rdf:resource="#LClass"/>
```

```
</rdfsfa:MProperty>
<rdf:Description rdf:ID="ltype">
  <rdfs:comment>Indicates membership of rdfsfa:LClass or rdfsfa:
  LProperty.</rdfs:comment>
  <rdfsfa:mrange rdf:resource="#MClass"/>
</rdf:Description>
<rdf:Description rdf:ID="mtype">
  <rdfs:comment>Indicates membership of rdfsfa:MClass or rdfsfa:
  MProperty.</rdfs:comment>
</rdf:Description>
```

4. rdfs:subClassOf is a set of binary relationship between two instances of rdfs:Class, so rdfs:subClassOf is mapped to rdfsfa:osubClassOf and rdfsfa:lsubClassOf . E.g. in Figure 4, rdfsfa:LClass is an rdfsfa:lsubClassOf rdfsfa:LResource and rdfsfa:M-Class is an rdfsfa:msubClassOf rdfs:MResource.

```
<rdfsfa:MProperty rdf:ID="osubClassOf">
  <rdfs:comment>Binary relationship between two ontology classes.
  </rdfs:comment>
  <rdfsfa:ldomain rdf:resource="#LClass"/>
  <rdfsfa:lrange rdf:resource="#LClass"/>
</rdfsfa:MProperty>
<rdf:Description rdf:ID="lsubClassOf">
  <rdfs:comment>Binary relationship between two language classes.
  </rdfs:comment>
  <rdfsfa:mdomain rdf:resource="#MClass"/>
  <rdfsfa:mrange rdf:resource="#MClass"/>
</rdf:Description>
<rdf:Description rdf:ID="msubClassOf">
  <rdfs:comment>Binary relationship between two meta classes.
  </rdfs:comment>
</rdf:Description>
```

5. Similarly, rdfs:subPropertyOf is a set of binary relationships between instances of rdf:Property, so it is mapped to rdfsfa:osubPropertyOf, rdfsfa:lsubPropertyOf and rdfsfa:msubPropertyOf .

```
<rdfsfa:MProperty rdf:ID="osubPropertyOf">
  <rdfs:comment>Binary relationship between two ontology
  properties.</rdfs:comment>
  <rdfsfa:ldomain rdf:resource="#LProperty"/>
  <rdfsfa:lrange rdf:resource="#LProperty"/>
</rdfsfa:MProperty>
```

```
<rdf:Description rdf:ID="lsubPropertyOf">
  <rdfs:comment>Binary relationship between two language
  properties.</rdfs:comment>
  <rdfsfa:mdomain rdf:resource="#MProperty"/>
  <rdfsfa:mrange rdf:resource="#MProperty"/>
</rdf:Description>
<rdf:Description rdf:ID="msubPropertyOf">
  <rdfs:comment>Binary relationship between two meta properties.
  </rdfs:comment>
</rdf:Description>
```

6. The rdfs:comment, rdfs:label, rdfs:seeAlso and rdfs:isDefinedBy are treated as documentation in RDFS, and are not related to the semantics of RDFS(FA), so we are not going to discuss them in this paper.

Below is an RDFS(FA) version of the "Person–hasFriend" example. As with other Web ontology languages, these statements describe resources in the Ontology Layer and the Instance Layer.

```
<rdfsfa:LClass rdf:ID="Animal">
  <rdfs:comment>This class of animals is illustrative of a number of
  ontological idioms.</rdfs:comment>
</rdfsfa:LClass>
<rdfsfa:LClass rdf:ID="Person">
  <rdfs:osubClassOf rdf:resource="#Animal"/>
</rdfsfa:LClass>
<rdfsfa:LProperty rdf:ID="hasFriend">
  <rdfsfa:odomain rdf:resource="#Person"/>
  <rdfsfa:orange rdf:resource="#Person"/>
</rdfsfa:LProperty>
<rdf:Description rdf:ID="John">
  <rdfsfa:otype rdf:resource="#Person"/>
  <rdfs:comment>John is a person.</rdfs:comment>
</rdf:Description>
<rdf:Description rdf:ID="Mary">
  <rdfsfa:otype rdf:resource="#Person"/>
  <rdfs:comment>Mary is a person.</rdfs:comment>
</rdf:Description>
<rdf:Description about="#John">
  <hasFriend rdf:resource="#Mary"/>
</rdf:Description>
```

In the Ontology Layer, "Animal" and "Person" are ontology classes, so they are in-

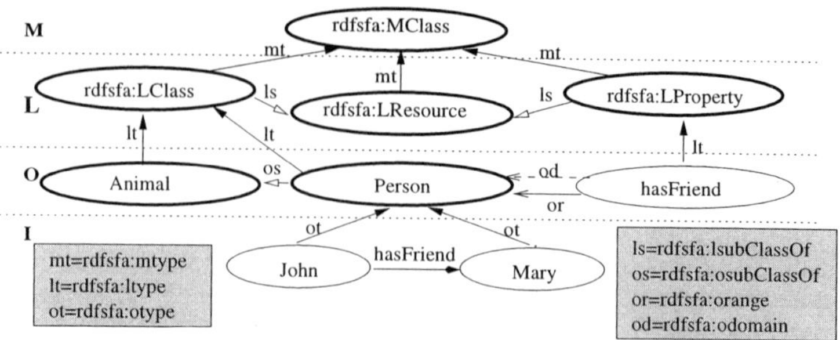

Figure 5: A "Person–hasFriend" example in RDFS(FA)

stances of rdfsfa:L- Class. The ontology class "Person" is the rdfsfa:odomain and
rdfsfa:orange of the property "hasFriend", so both the values of and resource described by instances of "hasFriend" are instances of "Person". In the Instance Layer,
the rdfsfa:otype of individuals such as "John" and "Mary" is the ontology class "Person". Figure 5 is a directed labeled graph of the above RDFS(FA) statements. Here
the rdfsfa:mtype of rdfsfa:LClass is the meta class rdfsfa:MClass, the rdfsfa:ltype of
"Person" is the language class rdfsfa:LClass and the rdfsfa:otype of "John" is the ontology class "Person". The language class rdf:Property is rdfsfa:lsubClassOf the language class rdfs:Resource while the ontology class "Person" is rdfsfa:osubClassOf
the ontology class "Animal". This example clearly shows that the modelling primitives in RDFS(FA) no longer have dual roles. Thus a clear semantics can be given to
them.

Note that, as in RDFS (see Section2.2), we can define rdfsfa:otype, rdfsfa:ltype
and rdfsfa:mtype properties within RDFS(FA) in an implicit way as well. E.g., individual "John" can also be defined as

```
<Person rdf:ID="John">
  <rdfs:comment>John is a person.</rdfs:comment>
</Person>
```

Here "Person" is an *ontology* class, so the above expressions use an implicit way to
define rdfsfa:otype property.

4.2   Data Model Semantics of RDFS(FA)

In this section, we use a Tarski style ([19]) model theoretic semantics to interpret the
data model of RDFS(FA). Classes and properties are taken to refer to sets of objects
in the domain of interests and sets of binary relationships (or tuples) between these
objects.

In RDFS(FA), the meaning of individuals, pairs of individuals, ontology classes and properties is given by an interpretation $\mathcal{I}$, which is a pair$(\Delta^{\mathcal{I}}, \cdot^{\mathcal{I}})$, where $\Delta^{\mathcal{I}}$ is the domain (a set) and $\cdot^{\mathcal{I}}$ is an interpretation function, which maps every individual name x to an object in the domain $\Delta^{\mathcal{I}}$:

$$x^{\mathcal{I}} \in \Delta^{\mathcal{I}}$$

every pair of individual names x, y to a pair of objects in $\Delta^{\mathcal{I}} \times \Delta^{\mathcal{I}}$:

$$\langle x^{\mathcal{I}}, y^{\mathcal{I}} \rangle \in \Delta^{\mathcal{I}} \times \Delta^{\mathcal{I}}$$

every ontology class name OC to a subset of $\Delta^{\mathcal{I}}$:

$$OC^{\mathcal{I}} \subseteq \Delta^{\mathcal{I}}$$

every ontology property name OP to a subset of $\Delta^{\mathcal{I}} \times \Delta^{\mathcal{I}}$:

$$OP^{\mathcal{I}} \subseteq \Delta^{\mathcal{I}} \times \Delta^{\mathcal{I}}.$$

In the Language Layer, the interpretation function $\cdot^{\mathcal{I}}$ maps rdfsfa:LClass (LC) to $2^{\Delta^{\mathcal{I}}}$:

$$LC^{\mathcal{I}} = 2^{\Delta^{\mathcal{I}}}$$

rdfsfa:LProperty (LP) to $2^{\Delta^{\mathcal{I}} \times \Delta^{\mathcal{I}}}$:

$$LP^{\mathcal{I}} = 2^{\Delta^{\mathcal{I}} \times \Delta^{\mathcal{I}}}$$

rdfsfa:LResource (LR) to $LC^{\mathcal{I}} \cup LP^{\mathcal{I}}$:

$$LR^{\mathcal{I}} = LC^{\mathcal{I}} \cup LP^{\mathcal{I}}$$

so that the interpretation of every possible ontology class ($OC^{\mathcal{I}}$) is an element of the interpretation of rdfsfa:LClass ($LC^{\mathcal{I}}$), the interpretation of every possible ontology property ($OP^{\mathcal{I}}$) is an element of the interpretation of rdf:Property ($LP^{\mathcal{I}}$). Note that $LR^{\mathcal{I}}$ is interpreted as the union of $LC^{\mathcal{I}}$ and $LP^{\mathcal{I}}$, and not as $2^{\Delta^{\mathcal{I}} \cup (\Delta^{\mathcal{I}} \times \Delta^{\mathcal{I}})}$, so instances of rdfsfa:LResource must be either ontology classes (sets of objects), or ontology properties (sets of tuples), and can't be interpreted as a "mixture" of sets of objects and tuples.

In the Metalanguage Layer, interpretation function $\cdot^{\mathcal{I}}$ maps rdfsfa:MClass (MC) to $2^{LR^{\mathcal{I}}}$:

$$MC^{\mathcal{I}} = 2^{LR^{\mathcal{I}}}$$

rdfsfa:MProperty (MP) to $2^{LC^{\mathcal{I}} \times LC^{\mathcal{I}}} \cup 2^{LC^{\mathcal{I}} \times LP^{\mathcal{I}}} \cup 2^{LP^{\mathcal{I}} \times LC^{\mathcal{I}}} \cup 2^{LP^{\mathcal{I}} \times LP^{\mathcal{I}}}$:

$$MP^{\mathcal{I}} = 2^{LC^{\mathcal{I}} \times LC^{\mathcal{I}}} \cup 2^{LC^{\mathcal{I}} \times LP^{\mathcal{I}}} \cup 2^{LP^{\mathcal{I}} \times LC^{\mathcal{I}}} \cup 2^{LP^{\mathcal{I}} \times LP^{\mathcal{I}}}$$

rdfsfa:MResource (MR) to $MC^{\mathcal{I}} \cup MP^{\mathcal{I}}$:

$$MR^{\mathcal{I}} = MC^{\mathcal{I}} \cup MP^{\mathcal{I}}$$

rdfs:ConstraintResource (CR) to subset of $MR^{\mathcal{I}}$:

$$CR^{\mathcal{I}} \subseteq MR^{\mathcal{I}}$$

rdfs:ConstraintProperty (CP) to subset of both $CR^{\mathcal{I}}$ and $MP^{\mathcal{I}}$:

$$CP^{\mathcal{I}} \subseteq CR^{\mathcal{I}} \cap MP^{\mathcal{I}}$$

so that the interpretations of rdfsa:LClass ($LC^{\mathcal{I}}$), rdfsa:LProperty ($LP^{\mathcal{I}}$) and rdfsa: LResource ($LR^{\mathcal{I}}$) are all elements of the interpretation of rdfsa:MClass ($MC^{\mathcal{I}}$), and all the possible pairs of subsets of $LC^{\mathcal{I}}$ and subsets of $LP^{\mathcal{I}}$ are elements of $MP^{\mathcal{I}}$.

Unlike rdfs:Class in RDFS, classes in RDFS(FA) have clear semantics. Clean semantics can also be given to the predefined properties of RDFS(FA) as shown in Figure 6, where

$$\Phi = 2^{MC^{\mathcal{I}} \times MC^{\mathcal{I}}} \cup 2^{MC^{\mathcal{I}} \times MP^{\mathcal{I}}} \cup 2^{MP^{\mathcal{I}} \times MC^{\mathcal{I}}} \cup 2^{MP^{\mathcal{I}} \times MP^{\mathcal{I}}}$$

As mentioned above, in order to specify which kind of class we want to refer to when we use the predefined properties, we add the layer prefixes to these properties. Subclass-of and subproperty-of are the subset relationship between the classes or properties within the same layer. Domain and range are foundation modelling primitives of RDFS(FA) properties, which can be used to specify two classes that a certain property can describe/use in descriptions in a certain layer. Type is a special cross-layer property, which is used to link instances to classes.

Predefined Property	Interpretation	Semantic Constraint
osubClassOf (OSC)	$OSC^{\mathcal{I}} \subseteq LC^{\mathcal{I}} \times LC^{\mathcal{I}}$	$\langle C_1^{\mathcal{I}}, C_2^{\mathcal{I}} \rangle \in OSC^{\mathcal{I}}$ iff. $C_1^{\mathcal{I}}, C_2^{\mathcal{I}} \in LC^{\mathcal{I}}$ and $C_1^{\mathcal{I}} \subseteq C_2^{\mathcal{I}}$
lsubClassOf (LSC)	$LSC^{\mathcal{I}} \subseteq MC^{\mathcal{I}} \times MC^{\mathcal{I}}$	$\langle C_1^{\mathcal{I}}, C_2^{\mathcal{I}} \rangle \in LSC^{\mathcal{I}}$ iff. $C_1^{\mathcal{I}}, C_2^{\mathcal{I}} \in MC^{\mathcal{I}}$ and $C_1^{\mathcal{I}} \subseteq C_2^{\mathcal{I}}$
msubClassOf (MSC)	$MSC^{\mathcal{I}} \subseteq 2^{MR^{\mathcal{I}}} \times 2^{MR^{\mathcal{I}}}$	$\langle C_1^{\mathcal{I}}, C_2^{\mathcal{I}} \rangle \in MSC^{\mathcal{I}}$ iff. $C_1^{\mathcal{I}}, C_2^{\mathcal{I}} \in 2^{MR^{\mathcal{I}}}$ and $C_1^{\mathcal{I}} \subseteq C_2^{\mathcal{I}}$
osubPropertyOf (OSP)	$OSP^{\mathcal{I}} \subseteq LP^{\mathcal{I}} \times LP^{\mathcal{I}}$	$\langle P_1^{\mathcal{I}}, P_2^{\mathcal{I}} \rangle \in OSP^{\mathcal{I}}$ iff. $P_1^{\mathcal{I}}, P_2^{\mathcal{I}} \in LP^{\mathcal{I}}$ and $P_1^{\mathcal{I}} \subseteq P_2^{\mathcal{I}}$
lsubPropertyOf (LSP)	$LSP^{\mathcal{I}} \subseteq MP^{\mathcal{I}} \times MP^{\mathcal{I}}$	$\langle P_1^{\mathcal{I}}, P_2^{\mathcal{I}} \rangle \in LSP^{\mathcal{I}}$ iff. $P_1^{\mathcal{I}}, P_2^{\mathcal{I}} \in MP^{\mathcal{I}}$ and $P_1^{\mathcal{I}} \subseteq P_2^{\mathcal{I}}$
msubPropertyOf (MSP)	$MSP^{\mathcal{I}} \subseteq \Phi \times \Phi$	$\langle P_1^{\mathcal{I}}, P_2^{\mathcal{I}} \rangle \in LSP^{\mathcal{I}}$ iff. $P_1^{\mathcal{I}}, P_2^{\mathcal{I}} \in \Phi$ and $P_1^{\mathcal{I}} \subseteq P_2^{\mathcal{I}}$
odomain (OD)	$OD^{\mathcal{I}} \subseteq LP^{\mathcal{I}} \times LC^{\mathcal{I}}$	$\langle P^{\mathcal{I}}, C^{\mathcal{I}} \rangle \in OD^{\mathcal{I}}$ iff. $P^{\mathcal{I}} \in LP^{\mathcal{I}}, C^{\mathcal{I}} \in LC^{\mathcal{I}}$ and $\forall x. \langle x^{\mathcal{I}}, y^{\mathcal{I}} \rangle \in P^{\mathcal{I}} \rightarrow x^{\mathcal{I}} \in C^{\mathcal{I}}$
ldomain (LD)	$LD^{\mathcal{I}} \subseteq MP^{\mathcal{I}} \times MC^{\mathcal{I}}$	$\langle P^{\mathcal{I}}, C^{\mathcal{I}} \rangle \in LD^{\mathcal{I}}$ iff. $P^{\mathcal{I}} \in MP^{\mathcal{I}}, C^{\mathcal{I}} \in MC^{\mathcal{I}}$ and $\forall x. \langle x^{\mathcal{I}}, y^{\mathcal{I}} \rangle \in P^{\mathcal{I}} \rightarrow x^{\mathcal{I}} \in C^{\mathcal{I}}$
mdomain (MD)	$MD^{\mathcal{I}} \subseteq \Phi \times 2^{MR^{\mathcal{I}}}$	$\langle P^{\mathcal{I}}, C^{\mathcal{I}} \rangle \in MD^{\mathcal{I}}$ iff. $P^{\mathcal{I}} \in \Phi, C^{\mathcal{I}} \in 2^{MR^{\mathcal{I}}}$ and $\forall x. \langle x^{\mathcal{I}}, y^{\mathcal{I}} \rangle \in P^{\mathcal{I}} \rightarrow x^{\mathcal{I}} \in C^{\mathcal{I}}$
orange (ORG)	$ORG^{\mathcal{I}} \subseteq LP^{\mathcal{I}} \times LC^{\mathcal{I}}$	$\langle P^{\mathcal{I}}, C^{\mathcal{I}} \rangle \in ORG^{\mathcal{I}}$ iff. $P^{\mathcal{I}} \in LP^{\mathcal{I}}, C^{\mathcal{I}} \in LC^{\mathcal{I}}$ and $\forall x. \langle x^{\mathcal{I}}, y^{\mathcal{I}} \rangle \in P^{\mathcal{I}} \rightarrow x^{\mathcal{I}} \in C^{\mathcal{I}}$
lrange (LRG)	$LRG^{\mathcal{I}} \subseteq MP^{\mathcal{I}} \times MC^{\mathcal{I}}$	$\langle P^{\mathcal{I}}, C^{\mathcal{I}} \rangle \in LRG^{\mathcal{I}}$ iff. $P^{\mathcal{I}} \in MP^{\mathcal{I}}, C^{\mathcal{I}} \in MC^{\mathcal{I}}$ and $\forall x. \langle x^{\mathcal{I}}, y^{\mathcal{I}} \rangle \in P^{\mathcal{I}} \rightarrow x^{\mathcal{I}} \in C^{\mathcal{I}}$
mrange (MRG)	$MRG^{\mathcal{I}} \subseteq \Phi \times 2^{MR^{\mathcal{I}}}$	$\langle P^{\mathcal{I}}, C^{\mathcal{I}} \rangle \in MRG^{\mathcal{I}}$ iff. $P^{\mathcal{I}} \in \Phi, C^{\mathcal{I}} \in 2^{MR^{\mathcal{I}}}$ and $\forall x. \langle x^{\mathcal{I}}, y^{\mathcal{I}} \rangle \in P^{\mathcal{I}} \rightarrow x^{\mathcal{I}} \in C^{\mathcal{I}}$
otype (OT)	$OT^{\mathcal{I}} \subseteq \Delta^{\mathcal{I}} \times LC^{\mathcal{I}}$	$\langle x^{\mathcal{I}}, C^{\mathcal{I}} \rangle \in OT^{\mathcal{I}}$ iff. $x^{\mathcal{I}} \in \Delta^{\mathcal{I}}, C^{\mathcal{I}} \in LC^{\mathcal{I}}$ and $x^{\mathcal{I}} \in C^{\mathcal{I}}$
ltype (LT)	$LT^{\mathcal{I}} \subseteq LR^{\mathcal{I}} \times MC^{\mathcal{I}}$	$\langle R^{\mathcal{I}}, C^{\mathcal{I}} \rangle \in LT^{\mathcal{I}}$ iff. $R^{\mathcal{I}} \in LR^{\mathcal{I}}, C^{\mathcal{I}} \in MC^{\mathcal{I}}$ and $x^{\mathcal{I}} \in C^{\mathcal{I}}$
mtype (MT)	$MT^{\mathcal{I}} \subseteq MR^{\mathcal{I}} \times 2^{MR^{\mathcal{I}}}$	$\langle R^{\mathcal{I}}, C^{\mathcal{I}} \rangle \in MT^{\mathcal{I}}$ iff. $R^{\mathcal{I}} \in MR^{\mathcal{I}}, C^{\mathcal{I}} \in 2^{MR^{\mathcal{I}}}$ and $x^{\mathcal{I}} \in C^{\mathcal{I}}$

Figure 6: Semantics of Predefined Properties in RDFS(FA)

4.3 DAML+OIL Data Model with Fixed Metamodeling Architecture

With a fixed metamodeling architecture, RDFS(FA) has its own semantics and makes itself a fully qualified schema layer Semantic Web language. Thus, DAML+OIL (or any other logical layer Semantic Web language) can be built on both its syntax and semantics.

From the point of view of metamodeling architecture, the modelling primitives that DAML+ OIL introduces are mainly located in the Language Layer (a complete description of the DAML+OIL data model with fixed metamodeling architecture will be given in a forthcoming paper). daml:Class is rdfsfa:lsubClassOf rdfsfa:LClass and daml:ObjectProperty is rdfsfa:lsubClassOf rdfsfa:LProperty; both daml:Datatype and daml:DatatypeProperty are rdfsfa:lsubClassOf rdfsfa:LResource. The above four are disjoint with each other. The "birthday" property lies in the Ontology Layer and can be defined in the following way:

```
<daml:DatatypeProperty rdf:ID="birthday">
  <rdfsfa:ltype rdf:resource="http://www.daml.org/2001/03/daml+oil#
  UniqueProperty"/>
  <damlfa:odatadomain rdf:resource="#Animal"/>
  <damlfa:odatarange rdf:resource="http://www.w3.org/2000/10/XMLSch-
  ema#date"/>
</daml:DatatypeProperty>
```

where damlfa:odatadomain is a set of binary relationships between instances of daml: DatatypeProperty and daml:Class, and damlfa:odatarange is a set of binary relationships between instances of daml:Data- typeProperty and daml:Datatype.

On the other hand, it is clear that Language Layer primitives can't be used to define/modify other Language Layer primitives, e.g. UniqueProperty can not be used to restrict the numbers of values of the maxCardinality as follows:

```
<rdfsfa:MProperty rdf:about="#maxCardinality">
  <rdfsfa:ltype rdf:resource="http://www.daml.org/2001/03/daml+oil#
  UniqueProperty"/>
</rdfsfa:MProperty>
```

In RDFS(FA), Language Layer properties can only be defined using Metalanguage Layer primitives, for which DAML+OIL doesn't provide any semantics. This is not clear in RDFS, where modellers might be tempted to think that they can modify DAML+OIL in the above manner, exploiting the semantics of DAML+OIL itself. To solve the above problem, one can define MUniqueProperty in the Metalanguage Layer and then set daml:maxCardinality as its instance.

In short, RDFS(FA) not only provides a firm semantic basis for DAML+OIL, it also eradicates the possibility of the "layer mistake" mentioned above.

5 Discussion

As we have seen, RDFS has at least the following problems:

1. Some elements of RDFS have dule roles, i.e. they have more than one semantics:

   (a) rdfs:Class is the type of both language classes, e.g. rdfs:Resource, and ontology classes, e.g. "Animal";

   (b) rdfs:Resource is the super-class of both language classes, e.g. rdfs:Class, and ontology classes, e.g. "Animal";

   (c) rdfs:subClassOf is used to express the sub-class/super-class relationship between both language classes, e.g. rdfs:Class is rdfs:subClassOf rdfs:Resource, and ontology classes. e.g. "Person" is rdfs:subClassOf "Animal".

2. Because of dule roles, RDFS doesn't have its semantics. DALM+OIL is only built on top of the syntax of RDFS. RDFS relies on DAML+OIL to give semantics to its modelling primitives. This indicates that RDFS is not yet a fully qualified schema layer Semantic Web language.

3. The even worse thing is that since the logical layer languages, e.g. DAML+OIL, are built on top of RDFS, affected by the dule roles problem of RDFS, people often make the "layer mistake" when using DAML+OIL.

A fixed layer metamodeling architecture for RDFS is proposed in this paper. We demonstrate how to map the original RDFS to RDFS(FA) (RDFS with Fixed metamodeling Architecture) and give a clear model-theoretic semantics to RDFS(FA). We believe that although RDFS(FA) won't be as compact as RDFS, there will be several advantages if RDFS has a fixed metamodeling architecture:

1. We don't have to worry about Russell's Paradox. (Other ways of thinking may include non well-founded sets.)

2. RDFS(FA) has a clear model theoretic *semantics* and there are no dule roles with its elements. RDFS(FA) eradicates the possibility of the "layer mistake".

3. DAML+OIL and other logical layer Semantic Web languages can be built on top of *both* the syntax and semantics of RDFS(FA).

4. The metamodeling architecture of RDFS(FA) is similar to that of UML, so it is *easy* for people to understand and use.

Some other papers have also talked about UML and the Web ontology language. Chang [4] summarised the relationship between RDF-Schema and UML. Melnik [15] tried to make UML "RDF-compatible", which allows mixing and extending UML models and the language elements of UML itself on the Web in an open manner.

Cranefield and Purvis [7] investigated the use of UML and OCL (Object Constraint Language) for the representation of information system ontologies. Cranefield [5] proposed UML as a Web ontology language. Cranefield [6] described technology that facilitates the application of object-oriented modelling, and UML in particular, to the Semantic Web. However, none of these works address the problem of the meta-modeling architecture of RDFS itself.

It is well known that UML has a well-defined metamodeling architecture (Kobryn [13]). It refines the semantic constructs at each layer, provides an infrastructure for defining metamodel extensions, and aligns the UML metamodel with other standards based on a four-layer metamodeling architecture, such as the Case Data Interchange Format (EIA [8]), Meta Object Facility (MOF-Parners [16]) and XMI Facility for model interchange (XMI-Parners [24]).

However, We believe Semantic Web languages and UML have different motivation and application domain. Besides the metamodeling architecture, Semantic Web languages also have a *functional architecture*. Within this functional architecture, RDF is a good candidate for the metadata layer language, while UML is obviously not designed as a metadata language. The schema layer languages must support global properties (anyone can say anything about anything) rather than the local ones, while the considerations of UML mainly focus on the local properties. The modelling primitives of logical layer languages, e.g. OIL and DAML+OIL, are carefully selected so that they can be mapped onto very expressive description logics (DLs), so as to facilitate the provision of reasoning support; on the UML side, reasoning over OCL is still under research.

Therefore, we prefer to enhance Web ontology languages by using the methodologies in UML, rather than making UML a component in Web ontology languages. Accordingly, we have used the metamodeling methods of UML to build a fixed layer metamodeling architecture for RDFS in this paper. And a similar approach can be found in Kampman and van Harmelen [12]. Further research will include a detailed study of the data model of DAML+OIL based on RDFS(FA) and the reasoning support provided by corresponding Description Logics.

References

[1] Tim Berners-lee. Semantic Web Road Map. W3C Design Issues. URL `http://www.w3.org/DesignIssues/Semantic.html`, Oct. 1998.

[2] Dan Brickley and R.V. Guha. Resource Description Framework (RDF) Schema Specification 1.0. W3C Recommentdation, URL `http://www.w3.org/TR/rdf-schema`, Mar. 2000.

[3] J. Broekstra, M. Klein, S. Decker, D. Fensel, F. can Harmelen, and I. Horrocks. Enabling knowledge representation on the Web by extending RDF Schema, Nov. 2000.

[4] Walter W. Chang. A Discussion of the Relationship Between RDF-Schema and UML. W3C Note, URL `http://www.w3.org/TR/NOTE-rdf-uml/`, Aug. 1998.

[5] Stephen Cranefield. Networked Knowledge Representation and Exchange using UML and RDF. In *Journal of Digital Information*, volume 1 issue 8. Journal of Digital Information, Feb. 2001.

[6] Stephen Cranefield. UML and the Semantic Web, Feb. 2001. ISSN 1172-6024. Discussion Paper.

[7] Stephen Cranefield and M. Purvis. UML as an ontology modelling language. In *IJCAI-99 Workshop on Intelligent Information Integration*, 1999.

[8] EIA. CDIF Framework for Modeling and Extensibility, EIA/IS-107. Nov. 1993.

[9] I. Horocks, D.Fensel, J.Broestra, S.Decker, M.Erdmann, C.Goble, F.van Harmelen, M.Klein, S.Staab, R.Studer, and E.Motta. The Ontology Inference Layer OIL. Aug. 2000.

[10] I. Horrocks. Benchmark Analysis with FaCT. In *TABLEAUX-2000*, number 1847 in LNAI, pages 62–66. Springer-Verlag, 2000.

[11] I. Horrocks, U. Sattler, and S. Tobies. Practical Reasoning for Expressive Description Logics. In H. Ganzinger, D. McAllester, and A. Voronkov, editors, *Proceedings of the 6th International Conference on Logic for Programming and Automated Reasoning (LPAR'99)*, number 1705 in Lecture Notes in Artificial Intelligence, pages 161–180. Springer-Verlag, 1999.

[12] Arjohn Kampman and Frank van Harmelen. Sesame's interpretation of RDF Schema. Aidministrator Nederland Note, URL `http://sesame.aidministrator.nl/doc/rdf-interpretation.html`, Apr. 2001.

[13] Cris Kobryn. UML 2001: A Standardization Odyssey. In *Communications of the ACM*, Vol.42, No. 10, Oct. 1999.

[14] Ora Lassila and Ralph R.Swick. Resource Description Framework (RDF) Model and Syntax Specification. Feb. 1999.

[15] S. Melnik. Representing UML in RDF. URL `http://www-db.stanford.edu/~melnik/rdf/uml/`, 2000.

[16] MOF-Parners. Meta Object Facility Revision 1.1b1. Jan. 1997.

[17] W. Nejdl, M. Wolpers, and C. Capelle. The RDF Schema Specification Revisited. In *Modelle und Modellierungssprachen in Informatik und Wirtschaftsinformatik, Modellierung 2000*, Apr. 2000.

[18] OMG. OMG Unified Modeling Language Specification vertion 1.3. Jun. 1999.

[19] A. Tarski. *Logic, Semantics, Mathemetics: Papers from 1923 to 1938.* Oxford University Press, 1956.

[20] PLATINUM technology Inc. Object Analysis and Design Facility, Response to OMG/OA&D RFP-1,Version 1.0, Jan. 1997.

[21] M. Uschold and M. Gruninger. Ontologies: Principles, Methods and Applications. *The Knowledge Engineering Review*, 1996.

[22] Frank van Harmelen, Peter F. Patel-Schneider, and Ian Horrocks. A Model-Theortis Semantics of DAML+OIL(March 2001). Mar. 2001.

[23] Frank van Harmelen, Peter F. Patel-Schneider, and Ian Horrocks. Reference Description of the DAML+OIL(March 2001) Ontology Markuk Language. DAML+OIL Document, URL `http://www.daml.org/2000/12/reference.html`, Mar. 2001.

[24] XMI-Parners. XML Metadata Interchange (XMI) v. 1.0. Oct. 1998.

The Emerging Semantic Web
I.F. Cruz et al. (Eds.)
IOS Press, 2002

RDF M&S revisited: From Reification to Nesting, from Containers to Lists, from Dialect to pure XML

Wolfram Conen[+], Reinhold Klapsing[++], and Eckhart Köppen[+++]

[+]XONAR GmbH,
Wodanstr. 7, 42555 Velbert, Germany,
Conen@xonar.biz

[++]Wirtschaftsinformatik und Softwaretechnik,
Universität Essen, 45117 Essen, Germany,
Reinhold.Klapsing@uni-essen.de

[+++]40Hz.org
343A Nature Drive, San Jose, CA 95123
eck@40hz.org

Abstract. The basic result presented is the following: with two assumptions about the intentions behind the RDF model, it can be shown that the RDF model and a model allowing for nested triples and lists of resources and triples, can be mapped to one another (in both directions). This allows to establish a close link between the RDF model and extended models previously suggested (SlimRDF [3], XRDF [4]). Further, the approach may help to clarify some problems related to interpreting the roles of reification and containers in the RDF model.

1 Introduction

As RDF is considered to be a key ingredient of the evolving semantic web, lack of clarity should be avoided. *Reification* and *Containers* gave rise to a number of discussions. In this paper, we propose an interpretation of these two constructs that may help to clarify this issue. It also demonstrates, how complex expressions can be constructed from RDF that allow a straightforward representation of the modeler's intentions. The basic idea is as follows: In RDF, if someone wants to express a relation between a statement and a resource or two statements, she has to utilize reification. If a relation between an entity (be it a resource or a triple or another group of entities) and a group of entities should be expressed, rdf:Bag, rdf:Seq or rdf:Alt have to be used. Essentially, both constructs are needed for expressing nested or grouped constructs with flat triples. Both constructs are not properly tied into the RDF model, for example, the meaning of attaching a predicate to a reificant[1] is not fixed in

---

[1]This terminology will be explained shortly.

the model (if r reifies $[s, p, o]$ and $[r, p_2, o_2]$ is given, is the intention to express $[s, p, o]$ *is p_2-related to o_2* or is the intention to take the triple literally, that is, *r is p_2-related to o_2?*).

We decided to fix the possible interpretation of the flat-triple constructs *reification* and *containers* by assuming that each reification is only a surrogate for the triple it represents and each container is only a surrogate for a list of entities (an entity may be a resource, a literal, a statement or a list of entities) that is, in a natural representation of the intentions, each reification and each container will be substituted by the represented triple or list and all only technically necessary triples of the flat model will be eliminated. We will argue that such a non-flat model captures the *essence* of the initial set of statements. Fig. 1 and Fig. 2 demonstrate this folding of a collection of flat-triple statements into one nested triple.

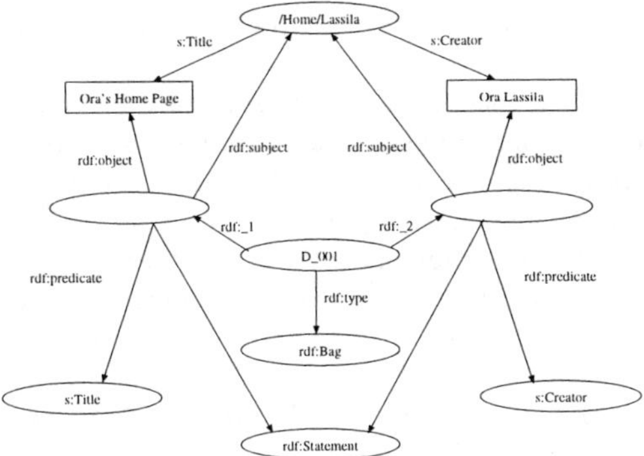

Figure 1: Demonstrating bags and reification (Figure 9 in [2])

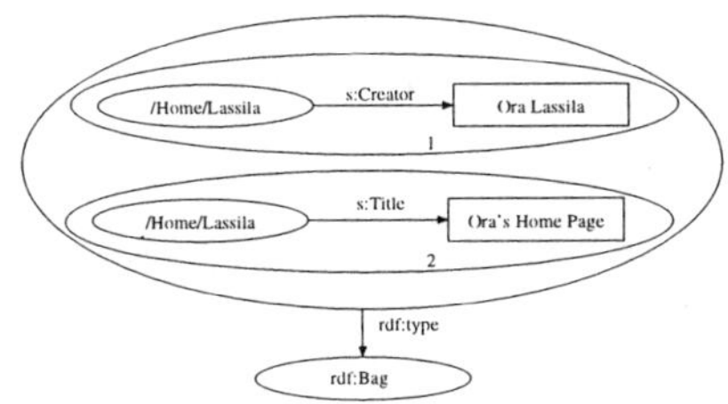

Figure 2: An intention-equivalent nested representation.

In the following, the two underlying assumptions will be presented more precisely. Let S be a set of flat-triple statements.

Assumption 1: Be r the *reificant*[2] of the triple $[s, p, o]$ as defined in [2], that is, the set S contains the triples $[r, \text{rdf:subject}, s]$, $[r, \text{rdf:predicate}, p]$, $[r, \text{rdf:object}, o]$ and $[r, \text{rdf:type}, \text{rdf:Statement}]$ (we will generally present triples in an infix[3] sequence, that is,

---

[2] In [2], this is called *reified statement* which might be a bit confusing–there is something that is reified, yes, but that is the "original" statement $[s, p, o]$. Instead of *reificant*, *reifying resource* could be used. Note that it would not be very useful to say *reifying statement* because r is **not** defined to be a member of the set **statement** (which is a concept of the RDF model defined in [2]), instead r has the **type** *rdf:Statement* which is, for the core RDF model, only a string representing a resource, and requires an interpretation in the context of RDF Schema and its constraints and concepts.

[3] infix with respect to the predicate.

as $[subject, predicate, object]$). The reification is used in another statement, say $[s_1, p_1, r]$. *Now, we assume that the intentions behind this subset of statements is to express that p_1 relates s_1 to $[s, p, o]$. This intention can easily be captured in a model allowing nested triples as $[s_1, p_1, [s, p, o]]$.*

Assumption 2: Be c a container, for example of type Seq, that is, $[c, \text{rdf:type}, \text{rdf:Seq}] \in S$. The n-ary sequence $R_C = (r_1, \ldots, r_n)$ of resources contains the elements of c, that is, $[c, \text{rdf:}\_i, r_i] \in S$ for all $i, 1 \leq i \leq n$. The container is used in another element of S, say $[s, p, c]$. *Now, we assume that the intentions behind this subset of statements is to express that p relates s to $(r_1, \ldots, r_n)$. This intention can easily be captured in a model allowing for lists of resources as $[s, p, (r_1, \ldots, r_n)]$.*[4]

Based on these two assumptions, the role of containers and reification can intuitively be described as allowing to express structure of arbitrary complexity with the limited instrument of a model based on flat triples.

In the next section, an extended model will be suggested that directly captures the underlying intentions of the constructs *reification* and *container* by introducing nesting and lists. In Section 3, we will prove that every RDF model can be expressed as an extended model *and* that every extended model can be expressed as an RDF model. This may suggest that the more comprehensive representation of the RDF model (read: the extended model) may be preferable when RDF is used for modeling. In Section 4 this aspect is briefly explored and two representations of the extended model, namely a nested graph notation and a straightforward XML DTD are suggested. In Section 5, two issues that explore the relation between structural and semantical aspects may give hints on possible directions for developing semantics for the extended models. Section 6 concludes the paper with a brief discussion.

2   An Extended Model

Let A be a reasonably selected alphabet. Let A^* be the set of strings defined over A. The following grammar defines expressions over A^* of the form R recursively as

$$R \quad ::= \quad r \quad | \quad '('\, R \,',' \, R \,')' \quad | \quad '['\, R \,',' \, R \,',' \, R \,']'$$

Here, r denote elements of A^*. (Sub-)Expressions of this form will be called *atomic*. A (sub-)expression of form R is called *resource*. A (sub-)expression of form R which matches the pattern $[R, R, R]$ is called *statement*. A (sub-)expression of form R which matches the pattern (R, R) is called *list*. Note that we will frequently use $(r_1, r_2, \ldots, r_n)$ instead of $(r_1, (r_2, (\ldots, (r_{n-1}, r_n) \ldots)$ where this can be done without the risk of misinterpretation. We will also leave out the comma regularly. Furthermore, we will only consider finite sets of finite expressions.

3   Relation between Extended model and RDF model

Let us begin with a remark: we will assume that the sets of statements of the RDF model that we will consider below are, in a certain sense, well-behaved, that is, we will assume that no reificant nor container is part of the (possibly complex) structure that it represents[5]. We will

---

[4]Note, that both assumptions together can be used to build list of statements etc.

[5]In the RDF model, as it is described in [2], it is, for example, possible to reify a statement that contains the representing reificant–which should, almost certainly, not be allowed. The same applies to containers containing themselves.

capture this more precisely in an algorithm that tries to order resources in strata so that each resource in a stratum represents structures that consist of resources of lower ranking strata only. The algorithm can also be used to detect whether its input (a set of statements of the RDF model), is not well-behaved.

Below, we will show that extended model and RDF model can be mapped to one another. First, some definitions are needed to set the stage. In the following, $s, p, o, s_1, o_1, r_1, \ldots, r_n$ will all be entities, that is, either an atom, a statement or a list if the extended model is considered or resources or literals (only possible in object position) if the RDF model is considered. Note that the definitions 1 and 3 can be applied to both models.

Definition 1 (Reification).
Given a resource r and the following set of statements, T^r:
$$T^r = \{ \quad [r, \text{rdf:subject}, s], [r, \text{rdf:predicate}, p],$$
$$[r, \text{rdf:object}, o], [r, \text{rdf:type}, \text{rdf:Statement}] \quad \}$$
Then, r is called a *reificant* of $[s, p, o]$ and T^r is called a *reification* of $[s, p, o]$.

Definition 2 (Reification: Derivation, Consequence).
Let u be a nested statement of the extended model of the form $[[s, p, o], p_1, o_1]$. Let r be a reificant of $[s, p, o]$ and T^r be the corresponding reification. The set $D = [r, p_1, o_1] \cup T^r$ is called a *derivation* of u. u, in turn, is called a *consequence* of D (analogously defined for $u = [s_1, [s, p, o], o_1]$ and $[s_1, p_1, [s, p, o]]$). With respect to a set C of statements, we say that u is *derivable* in C if $D \subseteq C$.

Definition 3 (Container).
Given a resource c and the following set of statements (with $X \in \{\text{rdf:Seq,rdf:Alt,rdf:Bag}\}$):
$T^c = \{ [c, \text{rdf:type}, X] \} \cup \{ [c, \text{rdf:}\_i, r_i] \mid i \in \mathbb{N}, 1 \leq i \leq n \}$. Then, c is called a *container*, T^c is called an n-ary *container definition* and the n-ary sequence $R_c = (r_1, \ldots, r_n)$ of entities is called the *elements* of c.

Definition 4 (Container: Derivation, Consequence).
Let u be a nested statement of the extended model of the form $[(r_1, \ldots, r_n), p, o]$. Let c be a container for the elements $(r_1, \ldots, r_n)$ of the Seq-type and let T^c be the corresponding container definition. The set $D = [c, p, o] \cup T^c$ is called a *derivation* of u. u, in turn, is called a *consequence* of D (analogously defined for $u = [s, (r_1, r_2, \ldots, r_n), o]$ and $[s, p, (r_1, r_2, \ldots, r_n)]$). With respect to a set C of statements, we say that u is *derivable* in C if $D \subseteq C$.

Note that a *consequence* can not be a statement from the flat RDF model. However, the *derivation* of a statement with only one level of nesting can completely consist of statements from the flat model. To be able to define some notion of equivalence between sets of statements from the extended and the flat model, we have to define how a deeply nested statement can be derived recursively from a set of flat statements.

Definition 5 (Rooted, Root, Hull). Be $\mathcal{O}$ a set of flat statements from the RDF model. Let $\mathcal{N}$ be a set of statements from the extended model. Let u be a statement from the extended model. We say that u is *rooted* in $\mathcal{O}$ if either

  (1) $u \in \mathcal{O}$ or

  (2) a derivation D of u can be given such that each statement $t \in D$ is *rooted* in $\mathcal{O}$.

We say that $\mathcal{N}$ is *rooted* in $\mathcal{O}$ if every statement n of $\mathcal{N}$ is *rooted* in $\mathcal{O}$. $\mathcal{O}$ is called *root* of u if u is rooted in $\mathcal{O}$; it is called *minimal root* of u if it is a root of u and for any statement

$t \in \mathcal{O}$, u is not rooted in $\mathcal{O} \setminus \{t\}$. $\mathcal{O}$ is called *root* of $\mathcal{N}$ if every statement $n \in \mathcal{N}$ is rooted in $\mathcal{O}$; it is called *minimal root* of $\mathcal{N}$ if it is a root of $\mathcal{N}$ and for any statement $t \in \mathcal{O}$ a statement $n \in \mathcal{N}$ can be found such that n is not rooted in $\mathcal{O} \setminus \{t\}$. We say that $\mathcal{N}$ is a *hull* of $\mathcal{O}$, if $\mathcal{O}$ is a minimal root of $\mathcal{N}$–we will alternatively say that $\mathcal{N}$ and $\mathcal{O}$ are *intention-consistent* (or simply *consistent*).

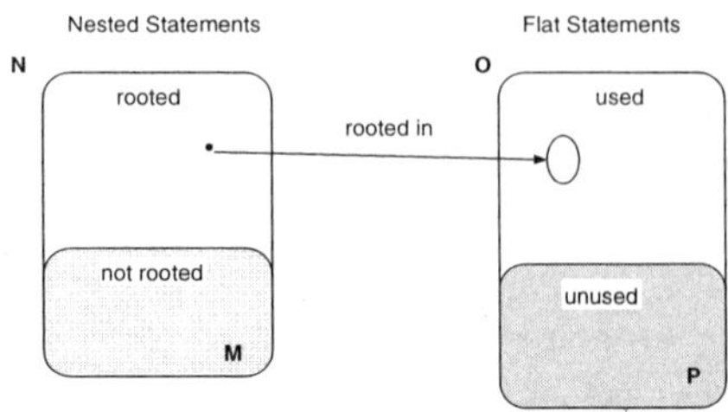

Figure 3: Relation between sets of extended and flat statements. If M is empty, $\mathcal{O}$ is a *root* of $\mathcal{N}$. If M and P are empty then $\mathcal{O}$ is a *minimal root* of $\mathcal{N}$.

Example 1. The following set $\mathcal{O}$ of flat statements is a *minimal root* (that is, no statement can be removed from $\mathcal{O}$) for the nested statement [GUSTAF SAYS [ECKI LIKES (REINHOLD WOLFRAM)]]: { [GUSTAF SAYS r_1], [r_1 RDF:TYPE RDF:STATEMENT], [r_1 RDF:SUBJECT ECKI], [r_1 RDF:PREDICATE LIKES], [r_1 RDF:OBJECT l_1], [l_1 RDF:TYPE RDF:SEQ], [l_1 RDF:_1 REINHOLD], [l_1 RDF:_2 WOLFRAM] }.

The sets { [GUSTAF SAYS [ECKI LIKES (REINHOLD WOLFRAM)]] } or { [GUSTAF SAYS [ECKI LIKES (REINHOLD WOLFRAM)]], [GUSTAF SAYS r_1], [r_1 RDF:PREDICATE LIKES] } are, among finitely many others[6], *hulls* of $\mathcal{O}$.

We look for hulls that contain only the minimally necessary number of statements to capture, with respect to the above assumptions, the intentions of the underlying set of flat statements.

Definition 6 (Essence). Be $\mathcal{O}$ a set of flat statements from the RDF model. Let $N^{\mathcal{O}} = \{\mathcal{N} | \mathcal{N}$ is a set of statements from the extended model $\wedge$ $\mathcal{N}$ is a hull of $\mathcal{O}\}$ be the *set of possible hulls* of $\mathcal{O}$. The subset $N^{\mathcal{O}}_{\min} = \{\mathcal{N} \in N^{\mathcal{O}} | \nexists \mathcal{M} \in N^{\mathcal{O}}$ with $|\mathcal{M}| < |\mathcal{N}|\}$ is the *set of minimal hulls*. An element of $N^{\mathcal{O}}_{\min}$ is called a *minimal hull* or *essence* of $\mathcal{O}$–we will alternatively say that $\mathcal{N}$ and $\mathcal{O}$ are *intention-equivalent* (or simply *equivalent*).

Note that due to the definitions of derivations, the minimal hull of a given set of statements from the RDF model is unique.

Example 2. The minimal hull for the set $\mathcal{O}$ of the above example is { [GUSTAF SAYS [ECKI LIKES (REINHOLD WOLFRAM)]] }.

Now the following two propositions can be proved. The first one essentially states that each set of extended statements can be expressed as an intention-consistent set of flat statements, while the second will show that each set of flat statements can be expressed as an intention-equivalent set of extended statements.

---

[6]In contrast, for a set of nested statements there is usually an infinite set of possible minimal roots due to the possible variations in naming the necessary containers and reificants.

Proposition 1. For each set $\mathcal{N}$ of statements from the extended model, a set $\mathcal{O}$ of statements from the RDF model can be found such that $\mathcal{O}$ is a minimal root of $\mathcal{N}$.

Proof: Intuitively, each nested statement can be expressed with a set of flat statements that allows to derive, possibly using intermediate nested statements, the initial statement (some care has to be taken not to confuse the *symbols* used in the model). Let us consider an example:

Initial Expression:	[GUSTAF SAYS [ECKI LIKES (REINHOLD WOLFRAM)]]
First Step:	[GUSTAF SAYS [ECKI LIKES l_1]]
(adds derivation of	[l_1 RDF:TYPE RDF:SEQ]
the list)	[l_1 RDF:_1 REINHOLD], [l_1 RDF:_2 WOLFRAM]
Second Step:	[GUSTAF SAYS r_1]
(adds derivation of	[r_1 RDF:TYPE RDF:STATEMENT], [r_1 RDF:SUBJECT ECKI]
the embedded	[r_1 RDF:PREDICATE LIKES], [r_1 RDF:OBJECT l_1]
statement)	[l_1 RDF:TYPE RDF:SEQ]
	[l_1 RDF:_1 REINHOLD], [l_1 RDF:_2 WOLFRAM]

This can be formalized as follows. Be C^E a set of statements[7] from the extended model. With the following construction, an intention-consistent set C^R of statements from the RDF model can be determined.

Algorithm *Flatten*(**In:** C^E)
    $C^R = \emptyset$. **Foreach** $t \in C^E$ **do**
        Expand(t,0,C^R)

Function *Expand* (**In:** Expression t, **In:** Int l, **InOut:** Set of Statements E) **returns** *Symbol*
    If $t \in A^*$ **then return** t
    If Match(t,$[s, p, o]$)[8] **then**　　/* Statement */
        s_r = Expand(s,l+1,E); s_p = Expand(p,l+1,E); s_o = Expand(o,l+1,E);
        r = Symbol[9](t);
        If $(l = 0)$[10] **then** $E = E \cup \{ [s_r, s_p, s_o] \}$; **return** *EmptySymbol*
            else $E = E \cup \{ [r, \text{rdf:type}, \text{rdf:Statement}], [r, \text{rdf:subject}, s_r],$
                    $[r, \text{rdf:predicate}, s_p], [r, \text{rdf:object}, s_o] \}$;
        return r
    If Match(t,$(r_1, \ldots, r_n)$) **then**　　/* List */
        r =Symbol(t); $E = E \cup \{ [r, \text{rdf:type}, \text{rdf:Seq}] \}$
        For $1 \leq i \leq n$ **do**
            s_i =Expand(r_i,l+1,E); $E = E \cup \{ [r, \text{rdf:}\_i, s_i] \}$
        return r

Let us sketch the proof of the correctness of the algorithm: (1) The algorithm terminates. To see this, consider the following: The function *Expand* recursively descents through the structure of its input expression. It will stop the descent in each branch of the structure as soon as

---

[7] Arbitrary sets of expressions resp. resources could also be allowed. This would require only a simple, but unnecessary (for this presentation) extension.

[8] The function *Match* makes the top level structure of t accessible by mapping it to the second argument if the structures match. In this case, *Match* returns true, otherwise false (similar to Perl's $=\sim$).

[9] The function *Symbol* returns a new symbol for each subexpression t that is not already represented in the flat model, otherwise, the already known symbol will be returned. This will be discussed below.

[10] The top-level expression is always a statement. There is no need to reify this statement because the reificant would be left unused (in this particular expansion).

an element of A^* is found (which will ultimately be the case, as the expressions have been assumed to be finite). Furthermore, each subexpression branch will be considered exactly once. (2) C^E and and the computed set C^R are intention-consistent. To see this, consider the following. First note that all statements added to C^R are flat. The algorithm constructs a derivation for each top-level statement by constructing derivations for each embedded expression while returning from the descent. Thus, each statements of C^E is rooted in the constructed C^R. C^R is a minimal root because no other statements but elements of derivations are added to C^R. $\boxminus$ A note regarding the function *Symbol*. In the algorithm, we have chosen to compute one *unique* name for literally identic subexpressions, that is, if, say, the statement [Ecki likes RDF] is encountered twice, it will be reified only once (although, to keep the algorithm above simple, it will be flattened twice but this will result in an identic set of flat statements and the redundancy will thus vanish due to considering sets). This makes it easy to identify literally equivalent expressions in the flat model (they have the same "name"), it, however, may make it more difficult to explore the differences in the meaning of multiple occurrences of literally identic expressions (this will have to consider the structural context of such expressions–sensibly dealing with this kind of context has to be made possible in the semantics build upon this models, so, for a full discussion of the implications, precise objectives for semantics are required. We will follow this line with some possible examples in Section 5. It is, nevertheless, easy to generate a new symbol for each occurrence of literally identic subexpressions, if this is found to be the better way to go).

Proposition 2. For each set $\mathcal{O}$ of statements from the RDF model, a set $\mathcal{N}$ of statements from the extended model can be found such that $\mathcal{N}$ is a minimal hull of $\mathcal{O}$.

Proof: The resources used in the RDF model can be arranged in strata if it is assumed that no circular definitions of reifications resp. containers exist (see below for details). The following algorithm will either determine a stratification or detect that circular references exist. Its input is a set of flat statements, C^R.

Algorithm Stratification(**In:** C^R)
Initially, all resources and literals are unmarked.
[Compute Stratum 0] Mark all literals as being in stratum 0. Mark all resources that are neither a reificant nor a container as being in stratum 0.
[Compute further Strata] **while** there is a resource r that is *unmarked* **and** all the resources or literals that are represented by r (this set of entities will be called E)[11] are marked **do**
    Determine the highest marking, say j, of a resource in E.
    Mark r to be in stratum $j + 1$.
[Check validity] **if** an unmarked resource exists
    then return "ERROR: there are mutually referencing structures"
    else return "OK - a stratification has been determined".

With the above assumption of a finite input set and finite expressions, the algorithm eventually terminates (in each round, an unmarked resource is marked). If the algorithm prints out the

---

[11]If r is a reificant and $[s, p, o]$ is a statement that r reifies then s,p and o are in E. If c is a container then the elements of R_c (as defined above) are in E. Note that with the definition of container above, a set of flat statements that defines a n-ary container also defines $(n - 1)$, $(n - 2)$ ... -ary containers. We assume that E contains all entities that are elements of the container with the largest arity. Besides the case in which r represents more than one structure, all other cases should most certainly be considered an error (for example, a resource that represents two statements or a statement and a container, or two non-inclusive containers).

"OK" message, the following condition will hold: each resource r that represents a structure belongs to a higher stratum then the resources/literals that are part of the represented structure. If the algorithm returns an ERROR message, at least one resource represents a structure that contains either the resource or a structure that, if recursively dereferenced, contains the resource.[12]

From finiteness follows that a highest ranking non-empty stratum, say k exists. Furthermore, it follows from the construction that the strata that are formed by marking resources and literals as their elements, are consecutively numbered.

Example 3. This is an example of a mapping from a stratified set of flat statements to an extended statement: The input set is { [GUSTAF SAYS r_1], [r_1 RDF:SUBJECT ECKI], [r_1 RDF:PREDICATE LIKES], [r_1 RDF:OBJECT l_1], [r_1 RDF:TYPE RDF:STATEMENT], [l_1 RDF:TYPE RDF:SEQ], [l_1 RDF:_1 REINHOLD], [l_1 RDF:_2 WOLFRAM] }

> *Stratum 0:* { GUSTAF REINHOLD ... RDF:SEQ RDF:_1 RDF:_2 }
> *Stratum 1:* {l_1}
> *Stratum 2:* {r_1}

Now a mapping along the stratification can be performed. First, { [l_1 RDF:TYPE RDF:SEQ], [l_1 RDF:_1 REINHOLD], [l_1 RDF:_2 WOLFRAM] } is mapped to (REINHOLD WOLFRAM), the statements are removed from the initial set, and each occurrence of l_1 is replaced by (REINHOLD WOLFRAM), leading to the next set of statements (now already extended): { [GUSTAF SAYS r_1], [r_1 RDF:SUBJECT ECKI], [r_1 RDF:PREDICATE LIKES], [r_1 RDF:OBJECT (REINHOLD WOLFRAM)], [r_1 RDF:TYPE RDF:STATEMENT], [(REINHOLD WOLFRAM) RDF:TYPE RDF:SEQ] }. Next, the set { [r_1 RDF:SUBJECT ECKI], [r_1 RDF:PREDICATE LIKES], [r_1 RDF:OBJECT (REINHOLD WOLFRAM)], [r_1 RDF:TYPE RDF:STATEMENT] } is mapped to [ECKI LIKES (REINHOLD WOLFRAM)] which replaces r_1, resulting in the minimal hull [GUSTAF SAYS [ECKI LIKES (REINHOLD WOLFRAM)]].

This procedure is captured in the following algorithm. It will determine an intention-equivalent extended model C^E from a set C^R of flat statements and a stratification $s[k]$.

*Algorithm Nest(***In:** C^R, **In:** stratum[], **In:** k)
For $s = 1$ to k **do**
   For all resources r in $stratum[s]$ **do**
     if r is a reificant **then**
       Remove from C^R the four statements defining the reification
        which has r as a reificant.
       Replace all occurrences of r in expressions in C^R by the statement that r reifies.
     if r is a container **then**
       Remove from C^R all statements of the form $[r, \_i, r_i]$ and
        build a list R_r from the resources r_i.
       Replace all occurrences of r in expressions in C^R by the list R_r.
Set $C^E = C^R$.
Again, the proposition follows from the construction.   ⊟

The relation between the RDF model and the extended model relies on the two assumptions. If these assumptions are not accepted as being a reasonable interpretation of the intentions behind the RDF model, then the propositions and proofs given above do not hold. However,

---

[12]Note that this can also be a chain of reifications and containers, that is, we consider it to be an error if a container contains a reificant that reifies a statement that contains the container etc.

the newly introduced model may still be considered as a reasonable, comprehensive alternative to the RDF model due to its ability to capture complex expressions naturally. We will try to illustrate this by suggesting two alternative representations in the next section, namely a graphical notation and a XML DTD, which both may be considered as advantageous[13] if compared to the alternatives offered in the RDF M&S specification.

4   Graphical and XML Representations of the Extended Model

The following graphical examples and the XML DTD largely follow the presentation in the XRDF discussion paper [4]. Both offer (bijectively mappable) alternatives to the statement/list notation of the extended model.

4.1   The Extended Model as a Graph

The graphical language for the extended model provides the constructs oval (representing resources) and directed labeled arcs (representing relations). Each oval representing a resource of the atom-type has inscribed a content taken from the alphabet A^*. Each embedded oval will be augmented with a number that is unique within the oval it is directly embedded in. Numbers will be left out where possible (ie., in statements, where the ordinal number follows from the direction of the arc, and in lists with one element only). A precise transformation to and from the nested-triple notation of the extended model is straightforward (compare [4]). Some examples of the graphical notation are given in the figures below.

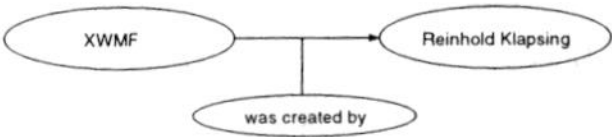

Figure 4: Representing "XWMF was created by Reinhold Klapsing"

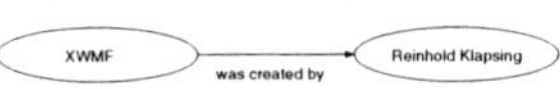

Figure 5: The same statement, now neglecting the fact that the predicate is also a resource (which is the usual way).

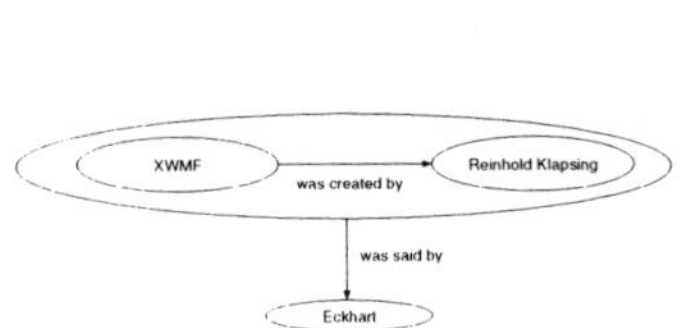

Figure 6: Representing "'XWMF was created by Reinhold Klapsing' was said by Eckhart", a statement about the previous statement.

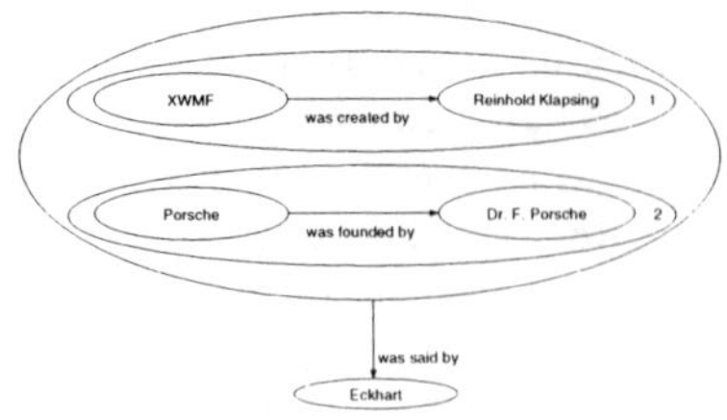

Figure 7: Eckhart made two statements.

It is left to the reader to flatten the graphically represented statements of the extended model to corresponding sets of flat RDF statements. This may suffice to demonstrate that already

---

[13]Beware: subjective judgment. We hope, however, that some readers may share our opinion.

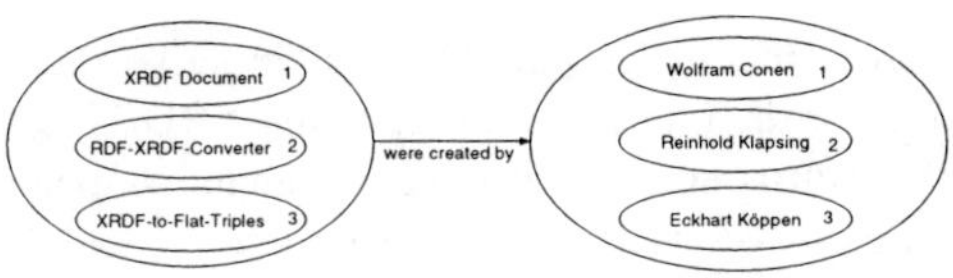

Figure 8: A group of people jointly created a collection of artifacts.

mildly complex examples of modeling tasks are much more straightforward to formulate (either graphical or in triple notation) with the extended model than with the flat model. Given the intention-equivalence of the two models (based on the two assumptions stated above), the extended model seems the more convenient way to express the intentions of sets of flat statements in which reification and containers are used.

4.2   A pure XML syntax for the Extended Model

It is straightforward to represent the (few) ingredients of the extended model as an XML-DTD (compare [4] with slightly different list and predicate definitions).

```
<!ELEMENT statement (subject, predicate, object)>
<!ELEMENT list      (statement | atom | list)+>
<!ELEMENT atom      (#PCDATA)>
<!ELEMENT subject   (atom|statement|list)>
<!ELEMENT predicate (atom|statement|list)>
<!ELEMENT object    (atom|statement|list)>
```

A conversion of an XML document that conforms to the above DTD into an extended model is immediate. The algorithm *Flatten* from above gives a conversion to an RDF model. From this, a XML/RDF representation (at least a direct, explicit representation where each statement results in one description) can be derived easily.

Example 4. The statement [([XWMF was_created_by Reinhold_Klapsing] [Porsche was_founded_by Dr._F._Porsche]) was_said_by Eckhart], compare Figure 7 above, can be "serialized" as follows:

```
<statement>
  <subject>
    <list>
      <statement>
        <subject><atom>XWMF</atom></subject>
        <predicate><atom>was created by</atom></predicate>
        <object><atom>Reinhold Klapsing</atom></object>
      </statement>
      <statement>
        <subject><atom>Porsche</atom></subject>
        <predicate><atom>was founded by</atom></predicate>
        <object><atom>Dr. F. Porsche</atom></object>
      </statement>
    </list>
  </subject>
  <predicate><atom>was said by</atom></predicate>
  <object><atom>Eckhart</atom></object>
</statement>
```

There is a number of reasons that make pure XML an attractive alternative to the RDF/XML serialization dialect, we refer the interested reader to the XRDF discussion paper for further details. We will now briefly turn our attention to basic semantic aspects that are closely related to the nested structure of expressions of the extended model.

5   Some brief considerations of Semantics

To facilitate the authoring and deployment of meta-data, syntactical and structural simplicity is needed. A layered approach has proven to be useful for the definition of models and techniques (this is especially obvious in the context of XML-based standards, where XML is the basis for other standards like name spaces which in turn are used in the definition of XSLT). With the extended model proposed above, we define the syntax of a lowest layer, making use of the structural primitives *statement* and *list*. On top of this basic structural model, semantic definitions and interpretations can be layered. Though this is not the main topic of the paper, we will briefly discuss two aspects that are related to semantical explorations of nested structures.

5.1   *Exploring/Propagating Meaning from Outside to Inside*

For the task of designing suitable semantics with the extended model we will have to consider a number of design options. We will propose one possible route and point out a few more things that might come in handy. Our route makes use of the following key observation: the semantics related to (sub-)expressions depend on their position within the surrounding structure–that is, the semantics will be explored starting from the outermost part of the structure and proceeding to the innermost part. Let's consider an example that demonstrates a simple kind of truth predicate.

[[sky color blue] hasTruthValue FALSE]]

or, in a flattened version

[r type statement][r subject sky][r predicate color][r object blue][r hasTruthValue FALSE]

The following transformation and constraints will give the flattened version some meaning in a FOL representation:

Transformation: Map each triple [s,p,o] into an instance of a predicate triple(s,p,o).

Constraints :
    (1) reifies(R,S,P,O) ←
         triple(R,type,statement) ∧ triple(R,subject,S) ∧
         triple(R,predicate,P) ∧ triple(R,object,O).
    (2) falsified_resource(R) ←
         statement_known_as_true(R,hasTruthValue,FALSE).
    (3) statement_known_as_false(S,P,O) ←
         triple(S,P,O) ∧ reifies(R,S,P,O) ∧ falsified_resource(R).
    (4) statement_known_as_true(S,P,O) ←
         triple(S,P,O) ∧ not(statement_known_as_false(S,P,O)).

The statement_ . . . -predicates could be used for further inferences. Note that further embedding works out fine also, ie. falsifying falsified statements is possible. The key point here is that the truth of the information contained in a triple will be propagated from the outer-most expression to the innermost. This principle can be used to define more sophisticated semantics as well, as would be necessary to give a proper meaning to expressions like

[Reinhold believes [Ecki assumes [[Wolfram is nice] hasTruthValue FALSE]]]

It is clear that the actual meaning of embedded expressions depends on the "semantical" scope that is propagated from the outer predicates to the inside.

```
Scope 3:  (believes  Reinhold
Scope 2:       (assumes  Ecki
Scope 1:           (hasTruthValue FALSE
Scope 0:                 (is Wolfram nice))))
```

What is actually *done* with this information will depend on the proper definition of semantics for predicates and their interaction. With respect to the above example the following ques-tion should be answered: what should be the meaning of an elementary statement of which someone believes that someone else assumes that its negation is true. Here, an "elementary" statement can be defined as a statement that has a predicate that does not modulate the truth value of the subject or object (like *is* in the above example). This may suffice to show how the meaning of statements generally depend on their *position*. From the intention-equivalence of extended and RDF model shown above, it follows that this is also true for RDF models–note, that the "position" of a statement in a complex structure is given by its occurrence in reifications/lists, for example, the following set of statements flattens the above expression:

[Reinhold believes r_3]
[r_3 subject Ecki] [r_3 predicate assumes] [r_3 object r_2] [r_3 type Statement]
[r_2 subject r_1] [r_2 predicate hasTruthValue] [r_2 object FALSE] [r_2 type Statement]
[r_1 subject Wolfram] [r_1 predicate is] [r_1 object nice] [r_1 type Statement]

Note that there is no need (or better: no use) to "materialize" the intermediate "propositions" like [Ecki assumes r_2], for, if this would be done, an intention-equivalent extended model would contain two statements:

[Reinhold believes [Ecki assumes [[Wolfram is nice] hasTruthValue FALSE]]]
[Ecki assumes [[Wolfram is nice] hasTruthValue FALSE]]

which is somewhat different from having only the first statement, because now, [Ecki ...] has become a factual statement. It should also be clear from this example that, within the scope of different statements, literally identic subexpressions can have different meaning. This also demonstrates that it is not necessary to give every occurrence of literally identic subexpressions an unique identity, because the actual meaning of each occurrence depends on its context, which is captured by the position of the occurrence as a subexpression within different expressions.

5.2 Abbreviating Expressions with Structural Transformations

It is possible to provide some kind of syntactic sugar with the help of structural transforma-tions that map a "sugarized" notation to the regular extended model. Some possible transfor-mations are discussed in [4]. This creates the possibility to specify for a predicate which type of transformation should be performed prior to interpreting the predicate. The transforma-tions can also be applied recursively and can make use of indirection (see example below).

This touches upon basic layers of semantics for which an extensive discussion is beyond the scope of this paper. We will therefore only give two brief examples.

The predicate *likes* is defined to be of the transformation type $n \times m$, that is, a statement of the form $[(n_1, \ldots, n_k)$ likes $(m_1, \ldots, m_l)]$ will be *expanded* to the list of statements $([n_1$ likes $m_1] \ldots [n_1$ likes $m_l] [n_2$ likes $m_1] \ldots [n_k$ likes $m_l])$. So,

[Wolli likes (Reinhold Eckhart)]

is transformed to

([Wolli likes Reinhold] [Wolli likes Eckhart])

Further assume that a specific predicate, *representedBy*, can be used to give *names* to lists (a similar predicate will exist for statements), like in

[(Reinhold, Eckhart) representedBy Friends]

Now, the transformation type of the predicate *likes* can be adapted to the possibilities of *indirection*, that is, if a *name* is encountered in subject or object position, the predicate will not be applied to the name (which is a resource itself) but to the resource or the list of resources that is represented by that name. We will denote the transformation type of *likes* accordingly as $n \times im$. Now, the following becomes possible:

[Wolli likes Friends]

which will result in the same list of statements as above. Note that this or similar kinds of indirection can be used to cleanly separate between relations to a resource and to the resources (lists/statements) that may be represented by a resource.

Whether this kind of transformations should be part of a basic layer of (pre-)semantics certainly remains to be discussed.

6   Discussion

We have presented an extended model for RDF that utilizes nested statements and lists to capture the intentions of reification and containers of the RDF model. The extended model can be represented comprehensibly as a nested graph, in nested triple notation or by utilizing a simple XML DTD. It provides a clean-cut basic structural layer. On top of this layer, semantics for predicates can be introduced without having to refer to syntactical elements of the structural layer.[14] We have formally demonstrated how the two models can be mapped into one another. Algorithms have been given to perform this transformations and to detect whether a set of flat statements is well-behaved (does not contain recursive (self-)inclusions of nested structures).

Let us briefly discuss one of the potential problems of upgrading from the RDF model to the extended model: the typing of containers. The issue is that two containers with definitions that refer to the same sequence of elements but with different types (e.g., one Bag, one Seq) become indistinguishable with the above mapping into the extended model. AHow two brief remarks: (1) one solution is to relegate this kind of typing of containers to a schema level. Together with, for example, the *representedBy* property described in 5.2, names for lists can be introduced and types for the lists represented by the names can be attached to the names

---

[14]No entities of the "rdf: ... "-kind are required on a higher layer, all those that are necessary in the RDF model to express structure will be "eaten up" in the transformation from flat to extended model. Remaining usages of rdf:type should be renamed (e.g. to a new property rdfs:type), to separate the layers cleanly.

etc. (2) Another solution is to drop the typing of containers and to simply regard them all as sequences – and to attach the information how a lists should be treated to the properties that make use of the list (each property can interpret a sequence as a Bag or an Alt construct if this suits the definition of the semantics of this property). More alternatives exist and a solution (an adaptation of the mapping) should be provided when defining a schema level for the extended model.

Certainly more details could be explored and more questions should be asked and answered.[15] However, this may suffice to demonstrate that the nesting of statements and the use of list of statements and resources provide a natural representation of useful structures that are cumbersome to model and difficult to use in RDF. Based on the interpretation of reification and containers given above, the RDF model (or, intention-equivalently, the extended model) can be seen as providing an abstract syntax to build rather complex expressions[16]. This may ease modeling with RDF (if the extended model is used) and may also provide a more clear-cut syntactic layer for the schema layer(s) to be put on top of this model.

References

[1] Dan Brickley and R.V. Guha. Resource Description Framework (RDF) Schema Specification 1.0. Candidate Recommendation, W3C, March 2000. http://www.w3.org/TR/2000/CR-rdf-schema-20000327.

[2] Ora Lassila and Ralph R. Swick. Resource Description Framework (RDF) Model and Syntax Specification. Recommendation, W3C, February 1999. http://www.w3.org/TR/1999/REC-rdf-syntax-19990222.

[3] Sergey Melnik. Slim RDF. Email to the RDF-IG, 12. February 2001.
     http://lists.w3.org/Archives/Public/www-rdf-interest/2001Feb/0090.html

[4] Wolfram Conen, Reinhold Klapsing and Eckhart Koeppen. XRDF - an eXtensible Resouce Description Framework Discussion Paper, November 2000. http://nestroy.wi-inf.uni-essen.de/rdf/xrdf/

[5] Drew McDemott, Jonathan Borden, Mark Burstein, Doug Smith and Richard Waldinger. A Proposal for Encoding Logic in RDF/DAML Discussion Paper, 8. August 2001.
     ftp://ftp.cs.yale.edu/pub/mcdermott/papers/noworry.ps.gz

---

[15]Don't hesitate to contact us if you found your questions unanswered, want to contribute ideas, or simply want to share your opinion on RDF/extended models with us. We thank Graham Klyne and an anonymous reviewer for comments on a previous version of the paper.

[16]A related approach to encode logic expressions in RDF can be found in [5].

The Emerging Semantic Web
I.F. Cruz et al. (Eds.)
IOS Press, 2002

Describing Computation within RDF

Chris Goad
Map Bureau
10 Sixth Street, Suite 108
Astoria, OR 97103
cg@mapbureau.com

Abstract. A programming language is described which is built within RDF. Its code, functions, and classes are formalized as RDF resources. Programs may be expressed directly using standard RDF syntax, or via a conventional JavaScript–based syntax. RDF constitutes not only the means of expression, but also the subject matter of programs: the native objects and classes of the language are RDF resources and DAML+OIL classes, respectively. The formalization of computation within RDF allows active content to be integrated seamlessly into RDF repositories, and provides a programming environment which simplifies the manipulation of RDF when compared to use of a conventional language via an API. The name of the language is "Fabl".

1. Introduction

Fabl[1] is a programming language which is built within RDF[1]. The constituents of the language - its code, functions, and classes - are formalized as RDF resources, as is the data over which computation takes place. This means that programs reside within the world of RDF content rather than being relegated to a separate realm connected to RDF via an API. The starting point for the formalization is DAML+OIL[2].

The language provides an efficient imperative programming framework for the RDF domain. Programs may be expressed as RDF objects using standard RDF syntax, or via a conventional syntax which might be described as JavaScript[2] enhanced with types and qualified property names. The language is designed to be easy to learn for programmers familiar with the conventional JavaScript/HTML/XML/DOM web–programming model. In fact, the conceptual cleanliness of RDF makes the language and its semantics far simpler than this conventional model. The initial implementation is similar in runtime efficiency to other scripting environments.

As a computational formalism for RDF, the neighboring points of comparison for Fabl are the RDF APIs (eg [3], [4]), in which computation is expressed in conventional ways, but the subject matter of the computation is expressed in RDF. Fabl has several advantages over APIs:

1. Simplicity of programming.
2. Functions and programs can be managed, inspected, manipulated, and annotated in the same manner as any other RDF resources; they are first–class citizens of the RDF world.

3. Fabl's type system exploits the RDF property–centric style. This yields a system of a kind different, and in some ways more expressive and flexible, than those found in the main thread of object–oriented type systems running from Simula through C++, Java, C#, and Curl.

4. Fabl programs are formalized within RDF in a manner that provides an open framework for extension of the language. The implementation of Fabl is, with the exception of a few low level utilities, written in Fabl itself. Further, the process by which programs are analyzed and converted into an efficiently executable form can be extended by addition of new RDF content. This means that extension of Fabl to include new language facilities, such as new control structures, new syntax, or new typing systems built on different principles can all be carried out in the RDF style: by extending the base of RDF files which describe the language.

Although Fabl defines a particular (albeit, extensible) textual format for programs on the one hand, and implements a particular byte–code and virtual machine for interpretation on the other, the core of the design is its formalism for describing imperative computation *as* RDF. This integrates computation into the RDF realm of distributed semantic description, decoupled from any particular source language and from any particular execution technique. Concretely, active entities, from simple spreadsheets to complex simulations, can be formalized in RDF, and made available to any agent that has a use for them, independent of the language (or graphical interface) from which they were created.

Whether or not the particular formalism introduced here is the right one, RDF can and should be used as a vehicle for standardizing computation as well as passive content. If nothing else, Fabl shows the practicality of this idea.

2. An Application

Our initial Fabl application illustrates one way in which the integration of computation with RDF facilitates the development of active RDF content. We have defined relatively simple ontologies for geography (themed maps, as in GIS), and for events located in a geographical context. This geographical and historical information is depicted by interactive web-delivered maps in the Macromedia Flash format (see our web site[5] for examples). The active aspect of our RDF repository consists primarily of handlers which generate interactive maps from the underlying geographical and historical information, and which maintain consistency between the data and its depiction as changes are made. The handlers are RDF resources and their relationship to other data is expressed by RDF statements. Regularities (eg all resources in *this* class have *that* handler) are asserted by DAML+OIL restrictions.

This application provides a template for a wide range of possible applications, wherein complex situations are represented in RDF, and where consistency constraints are automatically maintained by associated constraint propagation mechanisms which are at least partly algorithmic (rather than strictly deductive) in nature. The kind of complete integration proposed here is not the only possible approach to this kind of application, but we would argue that first-class status for computational entities in the RDF world removes a layer of indirectness and complexity that would otherwise be necessary.

3. An Example

Consider the simplest of data structures, a point on the plane with two coordinates, which can be expressed in Java by:

```
public class  Point {
    double xc;
    double yc;
}
```

Here is an extract from a Fabl RDF file at http://purl.oclc.org/net/fabl/examples/geom defining the same structure:

```
<rdf:RDF
  xmlns:rdf ="http://www.w3.org/1999/02/22-rdf-syntax-ns#"
  xmlns:rdfs="http://www.w3.org/2000/01/rdf-schema#"
  xmlns:xsd ="http://www.w3.org/2000/10/XMLSchema#"
  xmlns:daml="http://www.daml.org/2001/03/daml+oil#"
  xmlns:fabl="http://purl.oclc.org/net/nurl/fabl/"
  xmlns:nurl="http://purl.oclc.org/net/nurl/"
>

<daml:DatatypeProperty rdf:ID="xc"/>
<daml:DatatypeProperty rdf:ID="yc"/>

<daml:Class rdf:ID="Point">
  <rdfs:subClassOf>
    <daml:Restriction>
      <daml:onProperty rdf:resource="#xc"/>
      <daml:toClass
rdf:resource="http://www.w3.org/2000/10/XMLSchema#double"/>
      <daml:cardinality>1</daml:cardinality>
    </daml:Restriction>
  </rdfs:subClassOf>
  <rdfs:subClassOf>
    <daml:Restriction>
      <daml:onProperty rdf:resource="#yc"/>
      <daml:toClass
rdf:resource="http://www.w3.org/2000/10/XMLSchema#double"/>
      <daml:cardinality>1</daml:cardinality>
    </daml:Restriction>
  </rdfs:subClassOf>
</daml:Class>
```

The Fabl type system makes use of the March, 2001 version of DAML+OIL. The above RDF asserts that every member of **Point** has **xc** and **yc** properties, and that these properties each have exactly one value of type double. All of the examples in this paper use the name space declarations given just above, which will be abbreviated in what follows by *[standard–namespace–declarations]*. Here is vector addition for points:

```
<rdf:RDF
[standard-namespace-declarations]
  xmlns:geom="http://purl.oclc.org/net/fabl/examples/geom#"
>

<fabl:code>
geom:Point function plus(geom:Point x,y)
  {
  var geom:Point rs;
  rs = new(geom:Point);
  rs . geom:xc = x.geom:xc + y.geom:xc;
  rs . geom:yc = x.geom:yc + y.geom:yc;
  return rs;
  }
</fabl:code>
</rdf:RDF>
```

The above text is not, of course, legal RDF. Rather, it represents the contents of a file intended for analysis by the Fabl processor, which converts it into RDF triples. The pseudo–tag **<fabl:code>** encloses Fabl source code; everything not enclosed by the tag should be legal RDF.

Note that the syntax resembles that of JavaScript, except that variables and functions are typed. Fabl types are RDF classes, and are named using XML qualified[6] or unqualified names (details below).

Here are the contents of the file http://purl.oclc.org/net/fabl/examples/color:

```
<rdf:RDF
[standard-namespace-declarations]>

<daml:Class rdf:ID="Color"/>
<Color rdf:ID="yellow"/>
<Color rdf:ID="blue"/>
<rdf:Property rdf:ID="colorOf">
  <rdfs:range rdf:resource="#Color"/>
</rdf:Property>
```

The following fragment assigns a color to an existing **Point**: yellow if its **x** coordinate is positive, and blue otherwise:

```
<rdf:RDF
[standard-namespace-declarations]
   xmlns:geom="http://purl.oclc.org/net/fabl/examples/geom#"
   xmlns:color="http://purl.oclc.org/net/fabl/examples/color#"
>

<fabl:code>
fabl:void function setColor(geom:Point x)
   {
   if (x . geom:xc > 0) x.color:colorOf = color:yellow;
   else x.color:colorOf = color:blue;
   }
</fabl:code>
```

The expression **fabl:void** may only be used in a context where the return type of a function is indicated. It signifies that the function in question does not return a value. Note that **fabl:void** is not a class, and in particular is should not be identified with **daml:Nothing**. A function with return type **daml:Nothing** would indicate that the function returns a value belonging to **daml:Nothing** - an impossibility.

The setColor example illustrates the central difference between an RDF class and its counterparts in the object–oriented programming tradition. An RDF class is an assertion about properties possessed by a resource, which does not preclude the resource from having additional properties not mentioned in the class, nor from belonging to other classes, nor even from acquiring new properties and class memberships as time goes on. The progression of data types in programming languages exhibits growing freedom of type members: C or Pascal types exactly determine the structure of their members; C++ and Java classes determine the structure of members to a degree, but allow extension by subclasses; the RDF model leaves the structure of members free except as explicitly limited by the class definition.

Unless a property has been explicitly constrained to have only one value, Fabl interprets the value of a property selection:

```
x.P
```

as a bag. (Bags rather than sets are used here to avoid having the correctness of the collection stored for a property depend on the semantic distinctness of the collection's elements; determination of semantic identity is not always computationally feasible). In the following example, the first function returns the number of colors assigned to an object, and the latter returns its unique color if it has only one, and a nul value otherwise.

```
xsd:int function numColors(daml:Thing x)
{
    return cardinality(x.color:colorOf);
}

color:Color function theColorOf(daml:Thing x)
{
    var BagOf(color:Color) cls;
    cls = x.color:colorOf;
    if (cardinality(cls)==1) return cls[0];
    else return fabl:undefined;
}
```

fabl:undefined is a special identifier which denotes no RDF value, but rather indicates the absence of any RDF value in the contexts where it appears. **BagOf(T)** represents the class of bags whose elements lie in type **T** (see section 10).

4. RDF Computation in Fabl

RDF syntax and semantics can be viewed as having three layers: (1) a layer which assigns concrete syntax (usually XML) to RDF assertions, (2) the data model layer, in which RDF content is represented as a set of triples over URIs and literals, and (3) a semantic model, consisting of the objects and properties to which RDF assertions refer. DAML+OIL specifies semantics[7] constraining the relationship between the data model and the semantic model.

The proper level of description for computation over RDF is the data model; the state of an RDF computation is a set of triples **<subject,predicate,object>**. This triple set in turn can be construed as a directed labeled graph whose nodes are URIs and literals, and whose arcs are labeled by the URIs of properties.

Fabl is executed by a virtual machine. An invocation of the Fabl VM creates an initial RDF graph which is in effect Fabl's own self description: the graph contains nodes for the basic functions and constants making up the Fabl language. Subsequent activity modifies the RDF graph maintained by the VM, called the "active graph". The Fabl interpreter can accept input from a command shell, or can be configured as a server in a manner appropriate to the application.

The universe of RDF files on the web plays the role of the persistent store for Fabl. The command

```
loadRdf(U)
```

adds the triple set described in the RDF file at URL **U** to the active graph.

The active graph is partitioned into *pages*. The data defining a page includes: (1) the external URL (if any) from which the page was loaded, (2) the set of RDF triples which the page contains, (3) a dictionary which maps the ids appearing in the page (as values assigned to the rdf:ID attribute) to the resources which they identify, and (4) a set of namespace definitions (bindings of URIs to namespace prefixes). Many pages are the internal representations of external RDF pages, but new pages can be created which are not yet stored externally.

```
saveRdf(x,U)
```

saves the page upon which x lies at the file **U**. The current implementation interacts with the external world of RDF via simple loading and saving of pages, but there are interesting additional possibilities involving distributed computation, which are outlined in section 15.

A global variable or constant **X** with value **V** is represented by a **daml:UniqueProperty** named **X** whose value on the URI **fabl:global** is **V**. (It doesn't matter what values the property assumes when applied to other resources, nor does **fabl:global** play any other role.) For example, the following fragment defines the global **pi**:

```
<daml:DatatypeProperty rdf:ID="pi">
   <rdf:type
rdf:resource="http://www.daml.org/2001/03/daml+oil#UniqueProperty"/>
   <rdfs:range
rdf:resource="http://www.w3.org/2000/10/XMLSchema#double"/>
</daml:DatatypeProperty>

<daml:Class rdf:about="http://purl.oclc.org/net/nurl/fabl/global">
   <pi>3.14159265358979323846 </pi>
</daml:Class>
```

The values of global properties can be referred to directly by name in Fabl. For example, since http://purl.oclc.org/net/fabl/examples/geom includes the lines above defining **pi**, the following fragment illustrates reference to **pi** as a global:

```
<rdf:RDF
[standard-namespace-declarations]
   xmlns:geom="http://purl.oclc.org/net/fabl/examples/geom#"
>
<fabl:code>
xsd:double function timesPi(xsd:double x){return x * geom:pi}
</fabl:code>
```

As indicated in the initial example above, basic manipulation of the active graph is accomplished via conventional property access syntax: If **P** is the qualified name of a property, and **x** evaluates to an object, then

```
x.P
```

returns a bag of the known values of **P** on **x**, that is, the set of values **V** such that the triple <x,P,V> is present in the active graph. However, if **P** is asserted to be univalued - if it was introduced as a UniqueProperty, or has a cardinality restriction to one value - then

```
x.P
```

evaluates to the unique value instead. The assignment

```
x.P = E
```

for an expression **E** adds the triple <x,P,value(E)> to the active graph, unless **P** has been asserted to be a univalued, in which case the new triple replaces the previous triple (if any) which assigned a value to **P** on **x**. The command:

```
var Type name;
```

is equivalent to:

```
<daml:UniqueProperty rdf:ID="name">
  <rdfs:range rdf:resource="Type"/>
</daml:UniqueProperty>
```

The function:

```
new(Type)
```

creates a new node **N** in the active graph, and adds the triple **<N,rdf:type,Type>**. Initially, nodes created with the **new** operator lack an associated URI. However, Fabl allows URIs to be accessed and set as if they were properties, via the pseudo–property **uri**.

```
x.uri
```

is the current URI of **x** if it has one, and **fabl:undefined** if not.

```
x.uri = newURI;
```

assigns a new URI to **x**. If **newURI** is already assigned to another node **y** in the active graph, **x** is merged with **y**. The merged node will possess the union of the properties possessed by **x** and **y** prior to the merge.

5. RDF Computation Via an API: A Comparison

The Java code below uses the Jena API[4] to implement the function presented at the beginning of section 3: vector addition of points. This sample is included to give the reader a concrete sense of the difference between Fabl code, which expresses elementary RDF operations directly as basic operations of the language, and code using an API, in which the same elementary operations must be expressed as explicit manipulations of a representation of RDF content in the host language (here, Java). This is the only purpose of the sample. The details are not relevant to anything that appears later in this paper, and may be safely skipped by any reader who is willing to grant the point that an API adds complexity to the expression of RDF computation. This point applies equally to other RDF APIs.

Here is the definition of vector of addition using Jena:

```
import com.hp.hpl.mesa.rdf.jena.mem.ModelMem;
import com.hp.hpl.mesa.rdf.jena.model.*;
import com.hp.hpl.mesa.rdf.jena.vocabulary.*;
// The class GeomResources initializes variables
// xc, yc, and Point to RDF resources of the right kind.
public class GeomResources {
    protected static final String URI =
"http://purl.oclc.org/net/fabl/examples/geom#";
    public static String getURI(){return URI;}
    public static Property xc = null;
    public static Property yc = null;
    public static Resource Point = null;
    static {
        try {
            xc = new PropertyImpl(URI, "xc");
            yc = new PropertyImpl(URI, "yc");
            Point = new ResourceImpl(URI+"Point");
        } catch (Exception e) {
            System.out.println("exception: " + e);
        }
    }
}
```

```
public class GeomFunctions {
// PointPlus is vector addition
    public static Resource PointPlus(Resource x,Resource y) {
            Resource rs = x.getModel().createResource();
            rs.addProperty(RDF.type, GeomResources.Point);
            rs.addProperty(GeomResources.xc,
                x.getProperty(GeomResources.xc).getDouble() +
                y.getProperty(GeomResources.xc).getDouble());
            rs.addProperty(GeomResources.yc,
                x.getProperty(GeomResources.yc).getDouble() +
                y.getProperty(GeomResources.yc).getDouble());
            return rs;
            }
}
```

The Fabl implementation, we would argue, is easier to understand and easier to code. The difference is not due to any defect of the Jena API, but to the inherent indirectness of the API approach. Further, the direct expression of RDF primitives in Fabl is less than half the story with regards to ease of use. More significant is the fact that Fabl types *are* DAML+OIL classes, and type checking and polymorphism at the RDF level are implemented within the language. When using an API, type checking at the RDF level is the user's responsibility. For example, Java will not complain at compile time (nor run time) if the method *GeomFunctions.PointPlus* is applied to resources which are not members of **GeomResources.Point**.

6. Nurls

In normal RDF usage, locators (that is URLs) are often used as URIs whether or not the entities they denote exist on the web. However, nothing prevents the use of URIs which are completely unrelated to any web location, for example:

```
<rdf:Description rdf:about= "my_green_sedan">
```

Identifying an entity in a manner which does not make use of a WWW locator has two advantages. First, the question of where to find information about the entity is decoupled from naming the entity, which allows all of the different varieties of information about the entity to evolve without disturbing the manner in which the entity is named. Among other things, this simplifies the versioning of RDF data. Second, use of non–locating URIs frees up the content of the URI for expressing hierarchy information about the entities described.

In the Fabl implementation, the triple

```
<X,fabl:describedBy,U>
```

means that **U** denotes an RDF file which provides information about **X**. (**rdfs:isDefinedBy**[8] has a closely related, but not quite identical intent; descriptions need not always qualify as definitions). **U** is also taken as relevant to any subject **Y** whose URI (regarded as a pathname, with "." and "/" as delimiters) extends that of **X**. For example, if **my_green_sedan** is described by **U** , then so are **my_green_sedan.engine**, and **my_green_sedan/engine** but not **my_green_sedan_attenna**. The Fabl command:

```
getRdf(Y);
```

loads the files known to describe the resource **Y**; that is those files **F** for which the triple **<X,fabl:describedBy,F>** is present in the active graph, and **Y** is an extension of **X**. A typical Fabl initialization sequence involves first loading a configuration file containing

fabl:describedBy statements which indicate where to find information about basic resources. Then, as additional resources become relevant to computation, invocations of **getRdf** bring the needed data into the active graph. In future, lazy strategies may be implemented in which, for example, **getRdf(X)** is automatically invoked on the first access to a property of **X**. Also, nothing precludes future development of complex discovery technology for finding relevant RDF, rather than relying only on the simple **describedBy** mechanism.

It is desirable that non–locating URIs not conflict with URLs. For Fabl applications, we have reserved the URI http://purl.oclc.org/net/nurl/ as a root URI whose descendants will never serve as locators. This line appears in our standard namespace declaration:

```
xmlns:nurl="http://purl.olc.org/net/nurl"
```

Nurl stands for "Not a URL". The following fragment tells the Fabl VM where to find the description of the Fabl language, and illustrates the points just made:

```
<rdf:Description about= "http://purl.oclc.org/net/nurl/fabl">
    <fabl:describedBy
rdf:resource="http://purl.oclc.org/net/fabl/languageV0"/>
    </rdf:Description>
```

To access a future release of the language which resides at .../languageV1, only the configuration file need change; RDF which mentions language primitives via the namespace prefix "fabl:" may be left unchanged.

If **U** is the source URL of a page in the active graph, and the triple **<X,fabl:describedBy,U>** is present in the active graph, then **X** is said to be a *subject* of the page. That is, the page has as its subject matter the part of the hierarchical URI name space rooted at **X**. A page may have more than one subject. When a new triple **<A,P,B>** is created in the course of computation, and the URI of **A** is an extension of the subject of a page, the new triple is allocated to that page. (Slightly more complex rules - not covered here - govern the case where the subjects of pages overlap.)

7. Identifiers

Identifiers in Fabl represent XML qualified or unqualified names. However, since the "." character is reserved for property selection, "." is replaced by "\" when an XML name is transcribed into Fabl. For example:

```
fablex:automobiles\ford
```

is the Fabl identifier which would have been rendered as

```
fablex:automobiles.ford
```

in XML. The interpretation of unqualified names is governed by the *path* and the *home namespace*. The path is a sequence of namespaces. When an unqualified name **U** is encountered, the Fabl interpreter searches through the path for a namespace **N** such that **N:U** represents a node already present in the active graph. When a new unqualified name **U** is encountered, it is interpreted as **H:U**, where **H** is the home namespace. Normally, the "fabl:" and "xsd:" namespaces are included in the path, enabling unqualified reference to Fabl language primitives and XML Schema datatypes[9].

8. Types

Any RDF type is a legal Fabl type.

```
X.rdf:type = T;
```

asserts that **X** belongs to the type **T**; that is it adds the triple **<X,rdf:type,T>** to the active graph. (This statement is legal only if **T** is a daml:Class, not an XML Schema datatype). Of course, a value may have many types.

Fabl also includes its own primitives for constructing new types, that is, for introducing new resources whose type is **rdfs:Class**. The following lines of Fabl introduce the type **Point** which was discussed earlier.

```
class('Point');
var xsd:double geom:xc;
var xsd:double geom:yc;
endClass();
```

Any Fabl statement which introduces a type is equivalent to a set of DAML+OIL statements about the type. Thus, the Fabl class definition facility provides simplified syntax, not additional expressiveness. The Fabl class syntax covers only a part of DAML+OIL. More precisely, although any DAML+OIL class may appear as a legal Fabl type, Fabl syntax will only generate types in the following subset: A class within the subset can be introduced by subclassing a **daml:Restriction**. Within the **daml:Restriction**, properties may be restricted either (1) by **daml:hasValue**, or (2) by **daml:toClass** with an optional **daml:maxCardinality** or **daml:cardinality** restriction with value 1. The effect is that properties may be assigned values, or may be assigned types. If a property is assigned a type, it may optionally be restricted to have either exactly one, or at most one value of that type. A new class may also be introduced as a **daml:intersectionOf** existing classes. Fabl's type deduction mechanisms will not fully exploit available information in types outside this subset. Coverage of more of DAML+OIL can be implemented in future extensions of Fabl without disturbing the correctness of code written for the current subset.

Here are the details. A Fabl class definition starts with

```
class('classname');
```

and ends with

```
endClass();
```

Within the definition, statements of the form

```
var pathname = expression;
```

called an *assignment* and

```
var [qualifier] [type] pathname;
```

called an *assertion* may appear. The possible values of the optional qualifier are **exists**, **optional**, and **multivalued** (**exists** is the default). A pathname is a sequence of names of properties, separated by dots (".") and represents sequential selection of the values of properties along the path. The assertion:

```
var [qualifier] type pathname;
```

means that, for all elements **X** of the class being defined, if **v** is a value of **X.pathname**, then **v** belongs to **type**. The qualifier **exists** (resp. **optional**, **multivalued**) means that **X.pathname** must have exactly one value (resp. at most one value, any number of values).

```
var [qualifier] pathname;
```

makes no claim about the type of **X.pathname**, only about the cardinality of the set of values which it assumes (depending on the qualifier).

The assignment

```
var pathname = expression;
```

means that the value of the slot denoted by the pathname is initialized to the value of the expression at the time when the member **X** is created, or when the class is installed (see below). Here are examples:

```
class('Rectangle');
var Point geom:center;
var geom:width;   //already declared to be a xsd:double in geom:
var geom:height; //already declared to be a xsd:double in geom:
endClass();

class('RedObject');
var color:color = color:red;
endClass();

class('RedRectangleCenteredOnXaxis');
var Rectangle && RedObject this;
var geom:center.geom:xc = 0.0;
endClass();
```

In the last example, The && operator denotes conjunction, and the pathname **this** refers to members of the class being defined, so that

```
var A this;
```

means that the class within whose definition the statement appears is a subclass of **A**.

The translation of Fabl class definitions into DAML+OIL RDF is straightforward. Assertions translate into **toClass** restrictions, and their qualifiers to **cardinality** or **maxCardinality** restrictions. Assignments translate into **hasValue** restrictions. The only minor complication is that, when pathnames of length greater than one appear, helper classes are automatically generated which express the constraints on intermediate values in path traversal (details ommitted).

9. Dynamic Installation of Classes

Recall that

```
x.rdf:type = C;
```

asserts that **x** belongs to daml:Class **C**. Such statements can be executed at any time, thereby dynamically adding class memberships. The effect of the statement is not just to add the triple asserting class membership, but also to apply the constraints which **C** imposes on its members. Consider, for example:

```
var rect = new(Rectangle);
rect.rdf:type = RedRectangleCenteredOnXaxis;
```

Recall that **RedRectangleCenteredOnXaxis** asserts constant values for slots **geom:center.geom:xc** and **color:color**. Consequently, after the assertion that **x** belongs to this class, the following triples are added to the graph:

```
<x,rdf:type,RedRectangleCenteredOnXaxis>
<x,color:colorOf,color:red>,
<x,geom:center,center-uri>,
<center-uri,rdf:type,geom:Point>
<center-uri,geom:xc,0.0>
```

Here, **center–uri** represents an anonymous node which has been created to represent the value of the geom:center property of **x**.

10. Parametric Types

Fabl includes constructors **BagOf(T), ListOf(T), SeqOf(T),** and **Function(O,I_0,...,I_N)** which generate parametric types denoting the set of all bags (resp. lists,sequences) with members in type **T**, and of all functions from input types I_0,.... I_N to output type **O**, respectively.

Here is the definition of BagOf:

```
class('BagOf');
var daml:Class this;
var memberType;
endClass();

daml:Class function BagOf(rdfs:Class tp)
  {
    var BagOf rs;
    rs = new(BagOf);
    rs . memberType = tp;
    rs . uri = 'nurl:fablParametricTypes/' + 'BagOf(' + uriEncode(tp.uri)
+ ')';
    return rs;
  }
```

The above definition appears within the Fabl language definition, where **memberType** has already been declared to be a **UniqueProperty** of type **rdfs:Class**. The operator **uriEncode** encodes reserved characters (such as ":" and "/") as described in the URI standard[10]. Note that **BagOf** implements a one–to–one map from the URIs of types **T** to the URIs of **BagOf(T)**. So, this defines a way of building, for each type **T**, an RDF resource which represents the parametric type **BagOf(T)**. Note, however that it does nothing towards defining the semantics of the new type in terms of existing DAML+OIL primitives. This is normal practice for new ontologies: new notions are introduced, but explicit characterization of the semantics of these new notions in terms of preexisting primitives follows later, if ever.

The implementation of the other parametric types **ListOf, SeqOf,** and **Function** are analogous. Fabl programmers can introduce their own parametric types using the same strategy.

11. Types of Fabl Expressions

Fabl is not just a language in which types may be created and manipulated, but a *typed* language in the more usual sense that each Fabl expression **E** is assigned an **rdfs:Class**. Of course, any particular Fabl *value* (ie node in the active graph) may have arbitrarily many types, but a Fabl *expression* is assigned one of the types which the values of the expression is expected to assume. Types of function applications are deduced in the usual way. If a Fabl function **f** is defined by

```
O function f(I₀ a₀,... I_N a_N)
{
...
}
```

then the type of **f(i₀,...i_N)** is **O** if **i₀,...i_N** have types **I₀ ... I_N**. Range assertions are exploited in type deduction concerning property selections. If the triple

```
<P,rdfs:range,T>
```

is present in the active graph for property **P**, the expression

```
x.P
```

is given type **BagOf(T)**, unless **P** is asserted to be univalued, in which case the type of **x.P** is **T**. (If more than one range type is assigned to **P**, this is equivalent to assigning the conjunction of the range types.)

```
E ~ T
```

performs a type cast of the expression **E** to type **T**. Type casts are checked at runtime: if the value of **E** does not lie in **T** when **E~T** is executed, an error is thrown. Simple coercion rules are also implemented; for example ints coerce to doubles, and conjunctions coerce to their conjuncts.

12. Functions and Methods

A function definition:

```
O function fname (I₀ a₀,... I_N a_N))
{
...
}
```

adds a function to the active graph under the decorated name

```
'f'+hash(uri_encode(I₀.uri),...uri_encode(I_N.uri),fname)+'_'+fname;
```

The purpose of decoration is to support polymorphism by assigning different URIs to functions whose input types differ. If the function definition appears within the scope of a class definition, the function is added beneath the URI of the class, and is invoked in the usual manner of methods: **<object>.fname(...)**. The effect of a Java abstract method is obtained by including a property of functional type in a class definition. Overriding of methods takes place as a side effect of class installation when the class being installed assigns values to functional properties. This simple treatment of method overriding is more flexible than conventional treatments; for example, dynamic installation of classes may change the set of methods installed in an object at any time, not only at object-creation time as in Java or C++. These points are illustrated by examples just below. The Fabl expression:

```
f[I_0,...I_n]
```

denotes the variant of **f** with the given input types. For example, **twice[SeqOf(xsd:int)]** denotes the variant of **twice** which takes sequences of ints as input. The Fabl operator:

```
supplyArguments(functionalValue,a_0,...a_N)
```

returns the function which results from fixing the first **N** arguments to **functionalValue** at the values of $a_0,...a_N$. Now, consider the following code:

```
class('Displayable');
var Function(fabl:void) Displayable\display;
...
endClass();
```

Note that by giving **Displayable\display** as the name of the functional property, we have allocated a URI for that property in the hierarchy beneath the URI for **Displayable**. This technique can be used in any context where a property which pertains to only one class is wanted. Consider also a concrete variant which displays rectangles:

```
fabl:void function display(Rectangle r)
{
....
}
```

Then, with

```
class('DisplayableRectangle');
var Displayable && Rectangle this;
var Displayable\display = supplyArguments(display[Rectangle],this);
endClass();
```

a class is defined which is a subclass of both **Rectangle** and **Displayable**, and which assigns concrete functions to the corresponding functional properties in the latter class. This is similar to what happens when a C++ or Java class contains a virtual method which is implemented by a method defined in a subclass. As noted earlier, the wiring of virtual methods to their implementations can only take place at object creation time in Java or C++, and cannot be undone thereafter, whereas Fabl allows wiring of functional properties to their implementations to take place at any time during a computation, via, for example

```
someRectanglePreviouslyUndisplayable.rdf:type = DisplayableRectangle;
```

13. Code as RDF

The foregoing discussion has described how Fabl data and types are rendered as sets of RDF triples. The remaining variety of Fabl entity which needs expression in RDF is *code*.

Code is represented by elements of the class **fabl:Xob** (**Xob** = "eXecutable object"). **Xob** has subclasses for representing the atoms of code (global variables, local variables, and constants), and for the supported control structures (blocks, if–else, loops, etc). Here is the class **Xob**:

```
class('Xob');
//atomic Xob classes such as Xlocal do not require flattening
var optional Function(Xob,Xob) Xob\flatten;
var rdfs:Class Xob\valueType;
endClass();
```

Subclasses of **Xob** include:

```
class('Xconstant'); //Constant appearing in code
var Xob this;
var Xconstant\value;
endClass();

class('Xlocal'); //Local variable
var Xob this;
var xsd:string Xlocal\name;
endClass();

class('Xif');
var Xob this;
var Xob Xif\condition;
var Xob Xif\true;
var optional Xob Xif\false;
endClass();

class('Xapply'); //application of a function to arguments
var Xob this;
var AnyFunction Xapply\function;
var SeqOf(Xob) Xapply\arguments;
endClass();
```

(The type **AnyFunction** represents the union of all of the function types
Function(O,I$_0$...I$_N$)) The Fabl statement

```
if (test(x)) action(2);
```

translates to the Xob given by this RDF:

```
<fabl:Xif>
   <fabl:Xif.condition>
      <fabl:Xapply>
         <fabl:Xapply.function rdf:resource="#f001a0e6f_test"/>
         <fabl:Xapply.arguments>
            <rdf:seq>
               <rdf:li>
<fabl:Xlocal><fabl:Xlocal.name>x</fabl:Xlocal.name></fabl:Xlocal>
               </rdf:li>
            </rdf:seq>
         </fabl:Xapply.arguments>
      </fabl:Xapply>
   </fabl:Xif.condition>
   <fabl:Xif.true>
      <fabl:Xapply>
         <fabl:Xapply.function rdf:resource="#f001a0e6f_action"/>
         <fabl:Xapply.arguments>
            <rdf:seq>
               <rdf:li><fabl:Xconstant Xconstant.value=2/></rdf:li>
            </rdf:seq>
         </fabl:Xapply.arguments>
      </fabl:Xapply>
   </fabl:Xif.true>
 <fabl:Xif>
```

f001a0e6f_action is the decorated name of the variant of **action** which takes an **xsd:int** as input. Verbose as this is, it omits the **Xob** properties. Correcting this omission for the **Xlocal** would add the following lines in the scope of the **Xlocal** element:

```
<rdf:type rdf:resource = "http://purl.oclc.org/net/nurl/fabl/Xob"/>
<fabl:Xob.valueType rdf:resource =
"http://www.w3.org/2000/10/XMLSchema:int"/>
```

A full exposition of the set of all Xob classes is beyond the scope of this paper, but the above examples should indicate the simple and direct approach taken. The class

```
class('Xfunction');
var xsd:string Xfunction\name;
var rdfs:Class Xfunction\returnType;
var SeqOf(Xlocal) Xfunction\parameters;
var SeqOf(Xlocal) Xfunction\localVariables;
var Xob Xfunction\code;
var SeqOf(xsd:byte) Xfunction\byteCode;
endClass();
```

defines an implementation of a function. When a Fabl function is defined, the code is analyzed, producing an **Xfunction** as result. This **Xfunction** is assigned as the value of the decorated name of the function.

The following steps are involved in translating the source code of a Fabl function or command into an **Xfunction**:

```
Source code [Parser] ->
Parse tree    [Analyzer] ->
Type-analyzed form (Xob) [Flattener]->
Flattened form (Xob) [Assembler] ->
Byte Code (executed by the Fabl virtual machine)
```

All of these steps are implemented in Fabl. The parse tree is a hierarchical list structure in the Lisp tradition whose leaves are tokens; a token in turn is a literal annotated by its syntactic category. A *flat* Xob is one in which all control structures have been unwound, resulting in a flat block of code whose only control primitives are conditional and unconditional jumps. Separating out flattening as a separate step in analysis supports extensibility by new control structures, as will be seen in a moment.

The analysis step is table driven: it is implemented by an extensible collection of *constructors* for individual tokens. The constructor property of a token is a function of type **Function(Xob,daml:List)** which, when supplied with a parse tree whose operator is the token, returns the analysis of that tree. Here is the code for the constructor for **if**. The parse of an **if** statement is a list of the form (if **<condition> <action>**).

```
Xob function if_tf(daml:List x)
  {
  var Xob cnd,ift,Xif rs;
  cnd = analyze(x[1]); //the condition
  if (cnd.Xob\valueType!=xsd:boolean) error('Test in IF not boolean');
  ift = analyze(x[2]);
  rs = new(Xif);
  rs . Xif\condition = cnd;
  rs . Xif\true = ift; //no value need be assigned for Xif\false
  return rs;
  }
```

x[N] selects the Nth element of the list. Then, the statement

```
ifToken.constructor = if_tf[daml:List];
```

assigns this function as the constructor for the **if** token. More than one constructor may be assigned to a token; each is tried in turn until one succeeds.

The **Xif** class, like other non–primitive control structures, includes a method for flattening away occurences of the class into a pattern of jumps and gotos (details omitted). Constructors and flattening methods rely on a library of utilities for manipulating **Xobs**, such as the function **metaApply**, which constructs an application of a function to arguments, and **metaCast** which yields a **Xob** with a different type, but representing the same computation, as its argument.

This simple architecture implements the whole of the Fabl language. The crucial aspect of the architecture is that it is fully open to extension within RDF. New control structures, type constructors, parametrically polymophic operators, annotations for purposes such as aspect–oriented programming[11], and other varieties of language features can all be introduced by loading RDF files containing their descriptions. The core Fabl implementation itself comes into being when the default configuration file loads the relevant RDF; a different configuration file drawing on a different supply of RDF would yield another variant of the language. This is the sense in which the implementation provides an open framework for describing computation in RDF, rather than a fixed language.

Finally, note once again that **Xobs** provide a formalism for representing computation in RDF which does not depend for its definition on any particular source language nor on any particular method for execution. That is, it formalizes computation *within* RDF, as promised by the title of the paper, and can yield the benefits sketched in the introduction.

14. Implementation

The practicality of an RDF–based computational formalism is a central issue for this paper, so size and performance data for our initial implementation are relevant.

The implementation consists of a small kernel written in C. The size of the kernel as a WinTel executable is 150 kilobytes. The kernel includes the byte–code interpreter, a generation–scavenging garbage collector, and a loader for our binary format for RDF. The remainder of the implementation consists of Fabl's RDF self description, which consumes approximately one megabyte in our RDF binary format. A compressed self–installing version of the implementation, which includes the Fabl self description, consumes 450 kilobytes. Startup time (that is, load of the Fabl self description) is about one third of a second on a 400MHZ Pentium II. Primitive benchmarks show performance similar to scripting languages such as JavaScript (as implemented in Internet Explorer 5.0 by Jscript) and Python. However, further work on performance should yield much better results, since the language is strongly typed, and amenable to many of the same performance enhancing techniques as Java.

The full value of formalizing computation within RDF will be realized only by an open standard. We regard Fabl as a proof–of–concept for such a formalization.

15. Future Work

The current Fabl implementation treats the external RDF world as a store of RDF triple sets, which are activated explicitly via **loadRdf** or **getRdf**. However, an interesting direction for future work is the definition of a remote invocation mechanism for RDF–based computation. Here is an outline of one possibility.

Values of the **fabl:describedBy** property might include URLs which denote servers as well as RDF pages. In this case, **getRdf(U)** would not load any RDF. Instead, a connection would be made to the server (or servers) **S** designated by the value(s) of **fabl:describedBy** on **U**. In this scenario, the responsibility of **S** is to evaluate properties, globals, and functions in the URI hierarchy rooted at **U**. Whenever a property **E.P**, a global **G**, or a function application **F(x)** is evaluated in the client **C**, and the URI of **E**, **G**, or **F** is an extension of **U**, a request is forwarded to the server **S**, which performs the needed computation, and returns the result. The communication protocol would itself be RDF–based, along the lines proposed on the www–rdf–interest mailing list[12]. Such an approach would provide simple and transparent access to distributed computational resources to the programmer, while retaining full decoupling of description of computation in RDF from choices about source language and implementation.

16. Other XML Descriptions of Computation

Imperative computational constructs appear in several XML languages. Two prominent examples are SMIL[13] and XSLT[14], in which, for example, conditional execution of statements is represented by the **<switch>** and **<xsl:if>** tags, respectively. The aims of these formalizations are limited to specialized varieties of computation which the languages target. Scripting languages encoded in XML include XML Script[15] and XFA Script[16].

Footnotes

1. Fabl™ is a trademark of Map Bureau, and is pronounced "fable".
2. The standardization of JavaScript is ECMAscript[17]

References

[1] W3C RDF Model and Syntax Working Group. Resource Description Framework (RDF) Model and Syntax Specification, *http://www.w3.org/TR/1999/REC-rdf-syntax-19990222*, February 1999
[2] Ian Horrocks, Frank van Harmelen, Peter Patel–Schneider, eds. DAML+OIL (March 2001), *http://www.daml.org/2001/03/daml+oil-index.html*, March 2001
[3] Chris Waterson. RDF: back–end architecture, *http://www.mozilla.org/rdf/back–end–architecture.html*, August 1999
[4] Brian McBride. Jena - A Java API for RDF, *http://www.hpl.hp.com/semweb/jena-top.html*, January 2002 (last update)
[5] Map Bureau, *http://www.mapbureau.com*, March 2002 (last update)
[6] Tim Bray, Dave Hollander, Andrew Layman, eds. Namespaces in XML, *http://www.w3.org/TR/REC–xml–names/*, January, 1999
[7] Ian Horrocks, Frank van Harmelen, Peter Patel–Schneider, eds. A Model–Theoretic Semantics for DAML+OIL (March 2001), *http://www.daml.org/2001/03/model–theoretic–semantics.html*, March 2001
[8] Dan Brickley, R. V. Guha, eds. Resource Description Framework (RDF) Schema Specification 1.0, *http://www.w3.org/TR/2000/CR–rdf–schema–20000327*, March 2000
[9]Paul V. Biron, Ashok Malhotra, eds. XML Schema Part 2: Datatypes, *http://www.w3.org/TR/2001/REC–xmlschema–2–20010502*, May 2001
[10] T. Berners–Lee. Uniform Resource Identifiers (URI): Generic Syntax, *http://www.ietf.org/rfc/rfc2396.txt*, August 1998
[11] Gregor Kiczales, John Lamping, Anurag Mendhekar and Chris Maeda, Cristina Lopes, Jean–Marc Loingtier and John Irwin. Aspect–Oriented Programming , 11th European Conference on Object–Oriented Programming, LNCS, vol. 1241, Springer Verlag, 1997

[12] Ken MacLeod, and respondents. Toying with an idea: RDF Protocol,
http://lists.w3.org/Archives/Public/www–rdf–interest/2001Mar/0196.html, March 2001
[13] Jeff Ayars et al, eds. Synchronized Multimedia Integration Language (SMIL 2.0) Specification,
http://www.w3.org/TR/2001/WD–smil20–20010301/, March 2001
[14] James Clark, ed. XSL Transformations (XSLT), *http://www.w3.org/TR/xslt*, November 1999
[15] DecisionSoft Limited, XML Script, *http://www.xmlscript.org* May 2001
[16] XML For All, Inc. XFA Script, *http://www.xmlforall.com,* May 2001
[17] ECMA. Standard ECMA–262 – ECMAScript Language Specification,
http://www.ecma.ch/ecma1/stand/ecma–262.htm, December 1999

Semantic Web Modeling and Programming with XDD

Chutiporn Anutariya[1], Vilas Wuwongse[1], Kiyoshi Akama[2] and Vichit Wattanapailin[1]
[1] *Computer Science & Information Management Program,*
Asian Institute of Technology, Pathumtani 12120, Thailand
[2] *Center for Information and Multimedia Studies,*
Hokkaido Unversity, Sapporo 060, Japan

Abstract. *XML Declarative Description (XDD)* is a unified modeling language with well-defined declarative semantics. It employs XML as its bare syntax and enhances XML expressive power by provision of mechanisms for succinct and uniform expression of Semantic Web contents, rules, conditional relationships, integrity constraints and ontological axioms. Semantic Web applications, offering certain Web services and comprising the three basic modeling components: (i) application data, (ii) application rules and logic, (iii) users' queries and service requests, are represented in XDD language as *XDD descriptions*. By integration of XDD language, *Equivalent Transformation* computational paradigm and XML syntax, *XML Equivalent Transformation (XET)*—a declarative programming language for computation of XDD descriptions in Equivalent Transformation computational paradigm—is developed. By means of XDD and XET languages, a new declarative approach to the development and the execution of Semantic Web applications is constructed.

1 Introduction

The *Semantic Web* [6] is a vision of the next-generation Web which enables Web applications to automatically collect Web contents from diverse sources, integrate and process information, and interoperate with other applications in order to execute sophisticated tasks for humans. For the current Web to evolve from a global repository of information primarily designed for human consumption into the Semantic Web, tremendous effort has been devoted to definition and development of various supporting standards and technologies. Prominent markup languages with an aim to define a syntax convention for descriptions of the semantics of Web contents in a standardized interoperable manner include *XML, RDF, RDF Schema, OIL* [5, 7, 11] and *DAML+OIL* [12]. Moreover, for Web applications to effectively communicate and interoperate in the heterogeneous environment, a standard *Agent Communication Language (ACL)* [15] becomes a necessity. Two major current ACLs are *Knowledge Query and Manipulation Language (KQML)* [9] and *Foundation for Intelligent Physical Agents ACL (FIPA-ACL)* [9, 15].

With an emphasis on the modeling and the development of Semantic Web applications offering certain Web services, there arises a need for a tool which is capable of modeling their three major components: (i) *application data*, (ii) *application rules and logic*, (iii) *queries and requests*. *XML Declarative Description (XDD)* [4, 17]—a unified, XML-based Semantic

Web modeling language with well-defined semantics and a support for general inference mechanisms—aims to fulfill such a requirement. XDD does not only allow direct representation and manipulation of machine-comprehensible Web contents (such as documents, data, metadata and ontologies, encoded in XML, RDF, OIL or DAML+OIL syntax), but also provides simple, yet expressive means for modeling their conditional relationships, integrity constraints and ontological axioms as well as Semantic Web applications. XDD serves the three important roles: (i) *content language*, (ii) *application-rule language*, and (iii) *query or service-request language*, in modeling such three main components of Semantic Web applications.

Based on XDD language, a declarative programming language—*XML Equivalent Transformation (XET)*—is constructed. Given an application's model specification, represented in terms of an XDD description, an XET program capable of executing and handling the application's queries as well as service requests can be obtained directly. Thus, the developed technologies-XDD and XET languages-present a new paradigm for modeling and programming Semantic Web applications. By integration with existing Web and agent technologies, XDD and XET also allow both syntactic and semantic interoperability among Web applications, and hence enable the development of intelligent services as well as automated software agents.

Section 2 formalizes an extended XDD language with set-of-reference functions, Section 3 presents an XDD approach to modeling Semantic Web resources and applications, Section 4 describes XET programming language and outlines an approach to its employment in Web application development, Section 5 demonstrates a prototype system which adopts the developed technologies, Section 6 reviews current related works, and Section 7 draws conclusions.

2   XML Declarative Description

XDD [4, 17] is a language the *words* and *sentences* of which are *XML expressions* and *XML clauses*, respectively. XML expressions are used to express explicit and implicit as well as simple and complex facts, while XML clauses are employed to represent ontology, implicit and conditional relationships, constraints and axioms. First, the data structure of XML expressions and their sets, characterized by an *XML Specialization System*, will be given and then followed by the syntax and semantics of XML clauses.

2.1   XML Specialization System

XML expressions have a similar form to XML elements except that they can carry variables for representation of implicit information and for enhancement of their expressive power. Every component of an XML expression—the expression itself, its tag name, attribute names and values, pairs of attributes and values, contents, sub-expressions as well as some partial structures—can contain variables. XML expressions without variables are called *ground XML expressions* or simply *XML elements*, those with variables *non-ground XML expressions*. Table 1 defines all types of variables and their usages.

An *XML expression* takes formally one of the following forms:

1. *evar*,

Table 1: Variable types.

Variable Type	Variable Name Beginning with	Specialization into
N-variables: Name-variables	$N:	Names in N
S-variables: String-variables	$S:	Strings in C^*
P-variables: Attribute-value-pair-variables	$P:	Sequences of attribute-value pairs
E-variables: XML-expression-variables	$E:	Sequences of XML expressions
I-variables: Intermediate-expression-variables	$I:	Parts of XML expressions
Z-variables: Set-variables	$Z:	Sets of XML expressions

2. $<t \ \ a_1 = v_1 \ \ldots \ a_m = v_m \ \ pvar_1 \ \ldots \ pvar_k/>,$

3. $<t \ \ a_1 = v_1 \ \ldots \ a_m = v_m \ \ pvar_1 \ \ldots \ pvar_k> v_{m+1} </t>,$

4. $<t \ \ a_1 = v_1 \ \ldots \ a_m = v_m \ \ pvar_1 \ \ldots \ pvar_k> e_1 \ \ldots \ e_n </t>,$

5. $<ivar> e_1 \ \ldots \ e_n </ivar>,$

where
- $evar$ is an E-variable,
- $k, m, n \geq 0$,
- t, a_i are names or N-variables,
- $pvar_i$ is a P-variable,
- v_i is a string or an S-variable,
- $ivar$ is an I-variable,
- e_i is an XML expression.

The domain of XML expressions and their sets can be defined as follows:

- V_Z : the set of all Z-variables.

- $\mathcal{A}_X$: the set of all XML expressions,

- $\mathcal{G}_X$: the subset of $\mathcal{A}_X$ which comprises all ground XML expressions in $\mathcal{A}_X$,

- $\mathcal{A} = \mathcal{A}_X \cup 2^{(\mathcal{A}_X \cup V_Z)}$: the set of all XML expressions in $\mathcal{A}_X$ and sets of XML expressions and Z-variables in $2^{(\mathcal{A}_X \cup V_Z)}$, and

- $\mathcal{G} = \mathcal{G}_X \cup 2^{\mathcal{G}_X}$: the set of all ground XML expressions in $\mathcal{G}_X$, and sets of ground XML expressions in $2^{\mathcal{G}_X}$.

Note that elements of the sets $\mathcal{A}$ and $\mathcal{G}$ may be at times referred to as *objects* and *ground objects*, respectively, and when it is clear from the context, a singleton $\{X\}$, where $X \in V_Z$ is a Z-variable, will be written simply as X.

Instantiation of those various types of variables is defined by *basic specializations*, each of which has the form (v, w), where v specifies the name of the variable to be specialized and w the specializing value. For example, ($N:tag1, $N:tag2), ($N:tag2, Name) and ($E:e, ($E:e1, $E:e2)) are basic specializations which rename the N-variable $N:tag1 to $N:tag2, instantiate the N-variable $N:tag2 into the tagname Name, and expand the E-variable $E:e into the sequence of the E-variables $E:e1 and $E:e2, respectively. There are four types of basic specializations:

1. Rename variables.

2. Expand a P- or an E-variable into a sequence of variables of their respective types.

3. Remove P-, E- or I-variables.

4. Instantiate variables to XML expressions or components of XML expressions which correspond to the types of the variables, i.e., instantiate:

   - N-variables to element types or attribute names,

   - S-variables to strings,

   - E-variables to XML expressions in $\mathcal{A}_X$,

   - I-variables to XML expressions which contains their sub-elements at an arbitrary depth, or

   - Z-variables to sets of XML expressions and Z-variables.

The *data structure* of XML expressions and sets of XML expressions are characterized by a mathematical abstraction, called *XML Specialization System*, which will be defined in terms of *XML specialization generation system* $\Delta = \langle \mathcal{A}, \mathcal{G}, \mathcal{C}, \nu \rangle$, where

- $\mathcal{C}$ is the set of all basic specializations, and

- ν is a mapping from $\mathcal{C}$ to $partial\_map(\mathcal{A})$ (i.e., the set of all partial mappings on $\mathcal{A}$), called the *basic specialization operator*; it determines, for each basic specialization c in $\mathcal{C}$, the change of objects in $\mathcal{A}$ caused by c.

Figure 1 illustrates examples of a non-ground XML expression a in $\mathcal{A}_X$, basic specializations $c_1, \ldots, c_5$ in $\mathcal{C}$ and their successive applications to a by the operator ν in order to obtain a ground XML expression g in $\mathcal{G}_X$.

Denote a sequence of zero or more basic specializations in $\mathcal{C}$ by a *specialization*.

Based on the XML specialization generation system $\Delta = \langle \mathcal{A}, \mathcal{G}, \mathcal{C}, \nu \rangle$, the **XML Specialization System** is $\Gamma = \langle \mathcal{A}, \mathcal{G}, \mathcal{S}, \mu \rangle$, where

- $\mathcal{S} = \mathcal{C}^*$ is the set of all specializations, and

- $\mu : \mathcal{S} \to partial\_map(\mathcal{A})$ is the *specialization operator* which determines, for each specialization s in S, the change of each object a in A caused by s such that:

   - $\mu(\lambda)(a) = a$, where λ denotes the null sequence,

   - $\mu(c \cdot s)(a) = \mu(s)(\nu(c)(a))$, where $c \in \mathcal{C}$ and $s \in \mathcal{S}$.

Intuitively, the operator μ is defined in terms of the operator ν such that for each $a \in \mathcal{A}$ and $s = (c_1 \cdots c_n) \in \mathcal{S}$, $\mu(s)(a)$ is obtained by successive applications of $\nu(c_1), \ldots, \nu(c_n)$ to a. Note that, when μ is clear from the context, for $\theta \in \mathcal{S}$, $\mu(\theta)(a)$ will be written simply as $a\theta$.

With reference to Figure 1, let a specialization θ in $\mathcal{S}$ denote the sequence of the basic specializations c_1, c_2, c_3, c_4 and c_5; by the definition of μ, $g = \mu(\theta)(a) = a\theta$. Similarly, Figure 2 shows examples of a non-ground set of XML expressions A in $\mathcal{A}$, a specialization θ' in $\mathcal{S}$ and its application to A by the operator μ, in order to obtain a ground set of XML expressions G in $\mathcal{G}$, i.e., $G = \mu(\theta')(A) = A\theta'$.

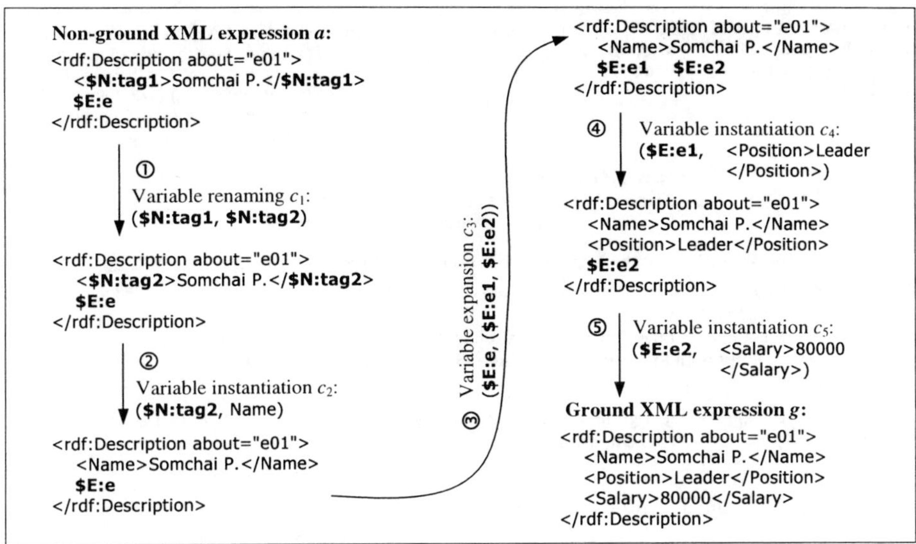

Figure 1: Successive applications of basic specializations $c_1, \ldots, c_5$ to a non-ground XML expression a in $\mathcal{A}_X$ by the operator ν, yielding a ground XML expression g in $\mathcal{G}_X$.

2.2   XDD: Syntax

The definitions of *XML declarative descriptions with references* and its related concepts are given next in terms of the XML specialization system Γ.

Let $\mathcal{K}$ be a set of *constraint predicates* and $\mathcal{F}$ the set of all mappings: $2^{\mathcal{G}} \to 2^{\mathcal{G}}$, the elements of which are called *reference functions*. An *XML declarative description* on Γ, simply called an *XDD description*, is a (possibly infinite) set of *XML clauses* on Γ. Table 2 defines concepts of *XML constraints*, *references* and *XML clauses* on Γ.

The notion of XML constraints introduced here is useful for defining restrictions on objects in $\mathcal{A}$, i.e., both on XML expressions in $\mathcal{A}_X$ and on sets of XML expressions in $2^{(\mathcal{A}_X \cup V_Z)}$. Given a ground constraint $q(g_1, \ldots, g_n), g_i \in \mathcal{G}$, its truth or falsity is assumed to be predetermined. Denote the set of all true ground constraints by $Tcon$. For instance:

- Define $\mathsf{GT}(a_1, a_2)$ as a constraint which will be true iff a_1 and a_2 are XML elements of the forms <Num>v_1</Num> and <Num>v_2</Num>, respectively, where v_1, v_2 are numbers and $v_1 > v_2$. Obviously, a constraint $\mathsf{GT}($<Num>10</Num>, <Num>5</Num>$)$ is a true ground constraint in $Tcon$.

- Define a constraint $\mathsf{Count}(G, g)$ which will be true, iff G is a set of XML elements and g the XML element <Result>v</Result>, where v denotes G's cardinality.

The concept of references defined here together with an appropriate definition of a *set-of-reference function* in $\mathcal{F}$ will be employed to describe complex queries/operations on sets of XML expressions such as set construction, set manipulation and aggregate functions, e.g., min, max and count in SQL. Given $e_c, e_p \in \mathcal{A}_X$, let $f_{e_c, e_p} \in \mathcal{F}$ denote a *set-of-reference*

A non-ground set of XML expressions $A \in \mathcal{A}$
{ <**$N:tag**>Somchai P.</**$N:tag**>,
 <**$N:tag**>Suwat K.</**$N:tag**>,
 $Z:set }

Specialized into
by $\mu\,(\theta')$

A ground set of XML expressions $G \in \mathcal{G}$
{ <Employee>Somchai P.</Employee>,
 <Employee>Suwat K.</Employee>,
 <Employee>Derek T.</Employee>,
 <Employee>Arunee I.</Employee> }

(**$N:tag**, Employee)
(**$Z:set**, { <Employee>Derek T.</Employee>,
 <Employee>Arunee I.</Employee> })

A specialization θ' which changes the non-ground set A to the ground set G by

- Instantiation of the N-variable **$N:tag** occurred in the elements of the set A into the tag name **Employee**,
- Instantiation of the Z-variable **$Z:set** into the set of two XML elements:
  { <**Employee**>**Derek T.**</**Employee**>, <**Employee**>**Arunee I.**</**Employee**> }.

Figure 2: Specialization of a non-ground set of XML expressions in $\mathcal{A}$ into a ground set of XML expressions $\mathcal{G}$ by the operator μ using a specialization θ' in $\mathcal{S}$.

function and be defined as follows: For each $G \subset \mathcal{G}_X$,

$$f_{e_c, e_p}(G) = \{\{e_c\theta \in \mathcal{G}_X | \theta \in \mathcal{S}, e_p\theta \in G\}\}. \tag{1}$$

In other words, for each subset G of $\mathcal{G}_X$, $f_{e_c, e_p}(G)$ is a singleton set, the element of which is a set of ground XML expressions of the form $e_c\theta$, where θ is a specialization in $\mathcal{S}$ that specializes e_p into a ground XML expression in G. Intuitively, objects e_p and e_c—*pattern* and *constructor* objects—are used to define the condition for constructing a set and to determine its elements, respectively. Given a specialization θ in $\mathcal{S}$, application of θ to $f_{e_c, e_p}(G)$ yields $f_{e_c, e_p}(G)\theta = f_{e_c\theta, e_p\theta}(G)$. For example, assuming that G is the set

> { <Employee division="IT"> Somchai </Employee>,
> <Employee division="HR"> Malee </Employee>,
> <Employee division="IT"> Suwat </Employee> }

then

> $f_{\langle \text{ITstaff name=\$S:n/}\rangle, \langle \text{Employee division="IT"}\rangle \$S:n\langle \text{/Employee}\rangle}(G)$
> = { { <ITstaff name="Somchai" />, <ITstaff name="Suwat" /> } }.

In other words, such a set-of function filters the XML elements of the set G with the pattern

> <Employee division="IT"> $S:n </Employee> — the pattern object,

and then constructs the resulting set of XML elements using

> <ITstaff name=$S:n/> — the constructor object.

Note that the effect of the binding of the variable $S:n in the pattern object will also cascade to the constructor object.

Based on the definition of the set-of function, a reference $r = \langle S, f_{e_c, e_p}, P \rangle$, for $e_c, e_p \in \mathcal{A}_X$ and $S \in 2^{(\mathcal{A}_X \cup V_Z)}$, is called *a set-of reference*.

Given an XML clause $C : (H \leftarrow B_1, \ldots, B_n)$, H is called the *head* and $\{B_1, \ldots, B_n\}$ the *body* of C, denoted by $head(C)$ and $body(C)$, respectively. The sets of all XML expressions,

Table 2: Definitions of the concepts *XML constraints, references* and *XML clauses* on Γ.

Concept	Having Ground Form Iff	Application of $\theta \in \mathcal{S}$ Yielding
XML constraint: $q(a_1, \ldots, a_n)$, where $n > 0, q \in \mathcal{K}$ and $a_i \in \mathcal{A}$	$a_i \in \mathcal{G}$ for $1 \leq i \leq n$	$q(a_1\theta, \ldots, a_n\theta)$
Reference: $r = \langle a, f, P \rangle$, where – $a \in \mathcal{A}$, – $f \in F$, and – P is an XDD description—called the *referred description* of r	$a \in \mathcal{G}$	$r\theta = \langle a, f, P \rangle\theta = \langle a\theta, f\theta, P \rangle$
XML Clause: $H \leftarrow B_1, \ldots, B_n$, where – $n \geq 0$ – H is an XML expression in $\mathcal{A}_X$, – B_i is an XML expression in $\mathcal{A}_X$, a constraint or a reference on Γ, and – the order of B_i is immaterial.	Comprising only ground objects, ground constraints, and ground references.	$H\theta \leftarrow B_1\theta, \ldots, B_n\theta$

constraints and references in the body of C are denoted by $object(C)$, $con(C)$ and $ref(C)$, respectively. Thus, $body(C) = object(C) \cup con(C) \cup ref(C)$. If $n = 0$, such a clause is called a *unit clause*, if $n > 0$, a *non-unit clause*. When it is clear from the context, a unit clause ($H \leftarrow$) is written simply as H, i.e., the left-arrow symbol is omitted. Therefore, every XML element can be considered as a ground XML unit clause, and moreover every XML document can be modeled as an XDD description comprising solely ground XML unit clauses.

The heights of an XML clause C and of an XDD description P, denoted by $hgt(C)$ and $hgt(P)$, are defined as follows:

- If $ref(C) = \emptyset$ (i.e., C contains no reference), then $hgt(C) = 0$; otherwise $hgt(C)$ is the maximum height of all the referred descriptions contained in its body plus one.

- $hgt(P)$ is the maximum height of all the clauses in P.

2.3 XDD: Declarative Semantics

Given an XDD description P on G, its declarative semantics, denoted by $\mathcal{M}(P)$, is defined inductively as follows:

1. Given the meaning $\mathcal{M}(Q)$ of an XDD description Q with the height m, a reference $r = \langle g, f, Q \rangle$ is a true reference, iff $g \in f(\mathcal{M}(Q))$. For any $m \geq 0$, define $Tref(m)$ as the set of all *true references*, the heights of the referred descriptions of which are smaller than or equal to m, i.e.:

$$Tref(m) = \{\langle g, f, Q \rangle | g \in \mathcal{G}, f \in \mathcal{F}, hgt(Q) \leq m, g \in f(\mathcal{M}(Q))\} \tag{2}$$

2. The meaning $\mathcal{M}(P)$ of the description P is the set of XML elements defined by:

$$\mathcal{M}(P) = \bigcup_{n=1}^{\infty} T_P^n(\emptyset) \tag{3}$$

where – $T_P^1(\emptyset) = T_P(\emptyset)$ and $T_P^n(\emptyset) = T_P(T_P^{n-1}(\emptyset))$ for each $n > 1$, and
     – the mapping $T_P : 2^{\mathcal{G}} \to 2^{\mathcal{G}}$ is:

For each $G \subset \mathcal{G}$, $g \in T_P(G)$ iff there exist a clause $C \in P$ and a specialization $\theta \in \mathcal{S}$ such that $C\theta$ is a ground clause, with head g and all objects, constraints and references in its body belong to G, $Tcon$ and $Tref(n)$, for some $n < hgt(P)$, respectively, i.e.:

$$T_P(G) = \{\ head(C\theta)\ \mid\ C \in P,\ \theta \in \mathcal{S}_X,\ C\theta \text{ is a ground clause,}$$
$$object(C\theta) \subset G,\ con(C\theta) \subset Tcon,$$
$$ref(C\theta) \subset Tref(n),\ n < hgt(P)\} \tag{4}$$

Intuitively, the meaning of a description P, i.e., $\mathcal{M}(P)$, is a set of all XML elements, which are directly described by and derivable from the unit and the non-unit clauses in P, respectively, i.e.:

- Given a unit clause $(H \leftarrow)$ in P, for $\theta \in \mathcal{S}$:

  $H\theta \in \mathcal{M}(P)$ if $H\theta$ is an XML element.

- Given a non-unit clause $(H \leftarrow B_1, \dots, B_i, B_{i+1}, \dots, B_j, B_{j+1}, \dots, B_n)$ in P, assuming without loss of generality that $B_1, \dots, B_i$ are XML expressions, $B_{i+1}, \dots, B_j$ are constraints, and $B_{j+1}, \dots, B_n$ are references, for $\theta \in \mathcal{S}$:

  $H\theta \in \mathcal{M}(P)$ if – $H\theta$ is an XML element,
              – $B_1\theta, \dots, B_i\theta \in \mathcal{M}(P)$,
              – $B_{i+1}\theta, \dots, B_j\theta$ are true constraints, and
              – $B_{j+1}\theta, \dots, B_n\theta$ are true references.

Based on the formalized concepts of XDD language, Figure 3 demonstrates two XDD descriptions denoted by Q and P, and then determines their semantics, which is sets of XML elements denoting certain objects and their relationships in a real-world domain.

3 Modeling Semantic Web Resources and Applications

XDD language allows collections of Semantic Web resources, such as documents, data, metadata and ontologies, encoded in XML, RDF, OIL or DAML+OIL syntax, to be represented in terms of XDD descriptions. In the descriptions, explicit information items are directly expressed as ground XML unit clauses, while rules, conditional relationships, integrity constraints and ontological axioms are formalized as XML non-unit clauses. The descriptions' semantics, which can be directly determined under the language itself, is defined as sets of XML elements—surrogates of objects and their relationships in a real-world domain.

Besides its employment to model various kinds of Semantic Web resources, XDD can also be applied to describe certain operations such as queries, document transformation and processing rules as well as program specifications. Figure 4 illustrates examples of Semantic Web resource modeling and a query formulation and shows that although information about senior employees and their bonuses is not explicit, it can be deductively inferred based on the clause R_3; this representation offers a more compact form and provides an easier way of information modification than explicit enumeration of such information. With this simple,

---

$\{\ C_1:$ <Employee division="IT">Somchai</Employee> $\leftarrow$
$C_2:$ <Employee division="HR">Malinee</Employee> $\leftarrow$
$C_3:$ <Employee division="IT">Suwat</Employee> $\leftarrow\ \}$

(a) XDD description Q.

- $hgt(C_1) = hgt(C_2) = hgt(C_3) = hgt(Q) = 0.$
- $\mathcal{M}(Q) = \{$ <Employee division="IT">Somchai</Employee>
  <Employee division="HR">Malinee</Employee>
  <Employee division="IT">Suwat</Employee> $\}.$

(b) The height and the meaning of Q.

$\{\ C_4:$ <ITStaffNumber>$S:num</ITStaffNumber>
$\leftarrow\ (\$Z{:}set,\ f_{\text{<ITstaff name=\$S:n/>,<Employee division="IT">\$S:n</Employee>}},\ Q),$
Count($Z:set, <Result>$S:num</Result>) $\}$

(c) XDD description P.

- $hgt(C_4) = hgt(Q) + 1 = 1$, and $hgt(P) = 1.$
- $f_{\text{<ITstaff name=\$S:n/>,<Employee division="IT">\$S:n</Employee>}}(\mathcal{M}(Q)) =$
  $\{\ \{$ <ITstaff name="Somchai"/>, <ITstaff name="Suwat"/> $\}\ \}$
- $(\$Z{:}set,\ f_{\text{<ITstaff name=\$S:n/>,<Employee division="IT">\$S:n</Employee>}},\ Q)$
  is a true reference, iff $Z:set is specialized into the set
  $\{\ \{$ <ITstaff name="Somchai"/>, <ITstaff name="Suwat"/> $\}\ \}.$
- Count is a true XML constraint, iff $S:num is specialized into the number 2.
- $\mathcal{M}(P) = \{$<ITStaffNumber>2</ITStaffNumber>$\}.$

(d) The height and the meaning of P.

Figure 3: XDD descriptions P, Q and their declarative semantics.

yet expressive modeling mechanism, XDD can readily be applied to model Semantic Web applications.

A Semantic Web application, offering certain Semantic Web services, comprises three main components: (i) *application data*, (ii) *application rules or logic*, and (iii) *users' queries or requests for services*. For instance: In a Semantic Web search engine, offering an information-gathering service,

- its application data: a catalog or descriptions of Semantic Web contents,
- its application rules: domain-model ontologies and axioms,
- its requests: user queries describing their informational needs.

In a business-2-business (B2B) commerce application, its three components are
- a catalog of available products and services,
- business rules and policies such as price discounting and refund rules,
- queries and business transactions such as a request for a quotation and an order placement.

XDD language provides means for modeling Semantic Web applications in that it enables direct representation of:

- application data (facts), encoded in XML, RDF, OIL or DAML+OIL syntax, in terms of ground XML unit clauses,

E_1:
```
<rdf:Description about="e01">
      <rdf:type resource="Employee"/>
      <e:Name>Somchai P.</e:Name>
      <e:Salary>80000</e:Salary>
</rdf:Description>
```

E_2:
```
<rdf:Description about="e02">
      <rdf:type resource="Employee"/>
      <e:Boss resource="e01"/>
      <e:Name>Sawat K.</e:Name>
      <e:Salary>50000</e:Salary>
</rdf:Description>
```

E_3:
```
<rdf:Description about="e03">
      <rdf:type resource="Employee"/>
      <e:Boss resource="e02"/>
      <e:Name>Derek T.</e:Name>
      <e:Salary>40000</e:Salary>
</rdf:Description>
```

E_4:
```
<rdf:Description about="e04">
      <rdf:type resource="Employee"/>
      <e:Boss resource="e02"/>
      <e:Name>Arunee I.</e:Name>
      <e:Salary>30000</e:Salary>
</rdf:Description>
```

(a) Modeling of application data – descriptions of employee objects, based on RDF infrastructure.

R_1:
```
<EmpRelation boss=$S:X subordinate=$S:Y level=1/>
   ←     <rdf:Description about=$S:Y>
             <rdf:type resource="Employee"/>
             <e:Boss resource=$S:X/>
             $E:emp
          </rdf:Description>.
```
% If Y is described as a resource of the type Employee and its Boss property is another resource X, then one can derive that X is the first-leveled boss of Y.

R_2:
```
<EmpRelation boss=$S:X subordinate=$S:Z level=$S:n1/>
   ←     <EmpRelation boss=$S:X subordinate=$S:Y level=$S:n/>,
          <rdf:Description about=$S:Z>
             <rdf:type resource="Employee"/>
             <e:Boss resource=$S:Y/> $E:emp
          </rdf:Description>,
          Add( <Num>$S:n</Num>, <Addendum>1</Addendum>,
               <Result>$S:n1</Result>).
```
% If X is the nth-leveled boss of Y and Y is referred to as a direct boss of an Employee Z, then one can imply that X is the $(n+1)$th-leveled boss of Z.

R_3:
```
<rdf:Description about=$S:X>
      <rdf:type resource="SeniorEmployee"/>
      <e:Bonus>$S:bonus</e:Bonus>
      <e:Subordinate>
          <rdf:Bag>$Z:set</rdf:Bag>
      </e:Subordinate>
      <e:Salary>$S:sal</e:Salary>  $E:emp
</rdf:Description>
   ←  <rdf:Description about=$S:X>
          <rdf:type resource="Employee"/>
          <e:Salary>$S:sal</e:Salary>  $E:emp
       </rdf:Description>,
       ⟨$Z:set, ƒ<rdf:Li resource=$S:Y/>,<EmpRelation boss=$S:X subordinate=$S:Y level=$S:any/>,
       {$E_1,…, E_4, R_1, R_2$}⟩,
       Count($Z:set, <Result>$S:num</Result>),
       GT(<Num>$S:num</Num>, <Num>3</Num>),
       Mul(<Num>$S:sal</Num>, <Multiplier>2</Multiplier>,
           <Result>$S:bonus</Result>).
```
% For an employee X who has more than 3 subordinates (of any level), then X is considered to be a SeniorEmployee and will receive a double-salary bonus. A list of all subordinates of X is also included in X's description.

(b) Modeling of application rules and logic – descriptions of relationships among employee objects.

Q:
```
<Answer>$S:name</Answer>
   ←     <rdf:Description about=$S:X>
             <rdf:type resource="Employee"/>
             <e:Name>Somchai P.</e:Name>  $E:emp1
          </rdf:Description>,
          <EmpRelation boss=$S:X subordinate=$S:Y level=2/>,
          <rdf:Description about=$S:Y>
             <rdf:type resource="Employee"/>
             <e:Name>$S:name</e:Name>  $E:emp2
          </rdf:Description>.
```
% A query Q finds names of all Somchai P.'s second-leveled subordinates.

(c) Modeling of a query.

Figure 4: Modeling of an application.

- application rules or logic in terms of XML non-unit clauses—the heads and bodies of the clauses describe the consequences and antecedents of the rules, respectively,
- users' queries or service requests in terms of XML non-unit clauses—the heads of the clauses describe the structure of the query results or the service responses and the bodies specify the queries' selection conditions or the service requests and their constraints.

Thus, XDD language has the three vital roles:

- *content language,*
- *application-rule language,*
- *query or service-request language.*

See Figure 4 for an example of each role. Basically, each query/request will be executed on a specified collection of application data and rules, and will return as its answer a set of XML elements, derivable from such a collection and satisfying all of its conditions. More precisely, given a set of application data and rules, modeled as an XDD description P, and a query/request, formulated as an XML clause $Q : (H \leftarrow B_1, \ldots, B_n)$, the response to Q is the set $\{H\theta \mid H\theta \in \mathcal{M}(P \cup \{Q\}), \theta \in \mathcal{S}\}$.

By employment of *Equivalent Transformation (ET)* computational paradigm [2, 14], which is based on semantics-preserving transformations (*equivalent transformations*) of declarative descriptions, the *computation* of an answer/response to such a query/request Q is carried out by successive transformations of the XDD description $P \cup \{Q\}$ into a simpler but equivalent description, from which the answer can be obtained readily and directly. In brief, $P \cup \{Q\}$ will be successively transformed until it becomes the description $P \cup \{Q_1, \ldots, Q_n\}$, where $n \geq 0$ and the Q_i are ground XML unit clauses.

Note that in order to guarantee correctness of a computation, only equivalent transformations are applied at every step. The unfolding transformation, a widely-used program transformation in conventional logic programming, is a kind of equivalent transformation. Other kinds of equivalent transformations can also be devised, especially for improvement of computation efficiency. Thus, ET provides a more flexible, efficient computational framework.

XET, a declarative programming language for computation of XDD descriptions in ET paradigm, will be presented next.

4   XET Programming Language

XET (XML Equivalent Transformation) [18] is a declarative programming language which can directly and succinctly manipulates XML data. By integration of XDD language, ET computational paradigm and XML syntax, XET possesses XDD's expressiveness and ET's computational power as well as XML's flexibility, extensibility and interchangeability. Therefore, XET naturally unifies "Documents", "Programs" and "Data", and with its computational and reasoning services, it also unifies "Document Processing (Transformation)", "Program Execution" and "Query Processing". Available XML editing and validating tools can also be employed to edit and validate XET programs. The syntax of XET language, described by XML Schema, is available in [18]. XET provides useful sets of built-in operations including:

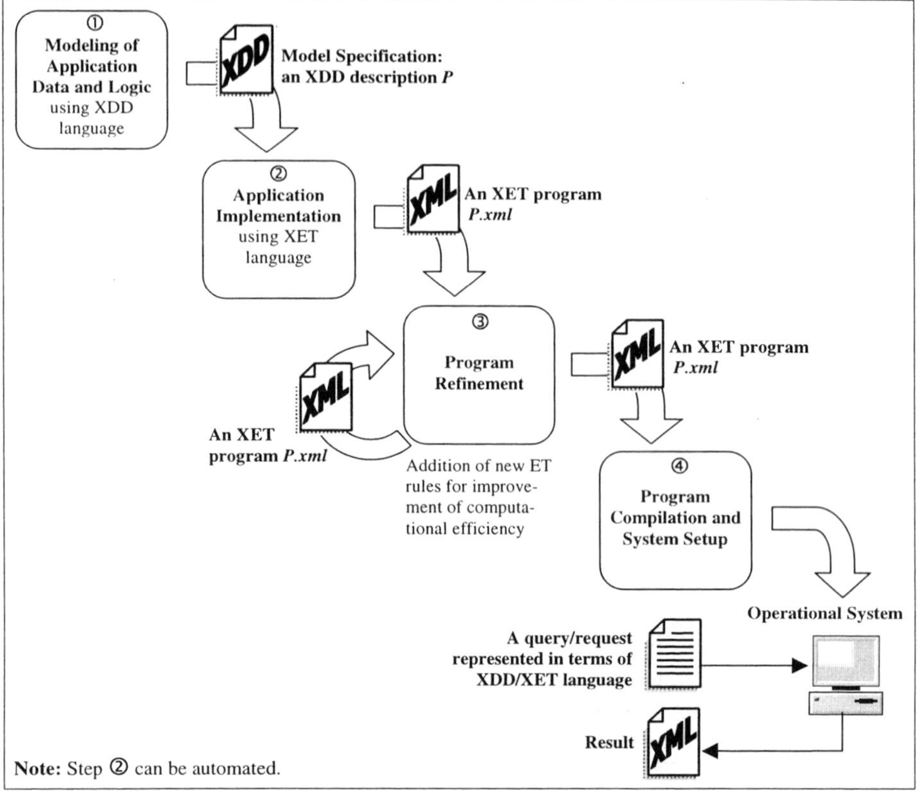

Figure 5: A declarative approach to Semantic Web application development.

- Data type checking,
- Document well-formedness and validity checking,
- Arithmetic operations and relations,
- String manipulation operations,
- XML expression unification and matching,
- XML expression operations,
- Input/Output operations,
- File manipulation operations,
- Communication services.

Once an XDD description which models a Semantic Web application's data and logic has been formulated, an XET program corresponding to such a description can be obtained directly. The obtained XET program can be iteratively refined, if new ET rules have been devised for improvement of computational efficiency. Finally, using *XET compiler* [18], the program is compiled and an operational system obtained. In response to a query/request submitted in terms of XDD or XET language, the system executes it and returns its result. Based on such processes, Figure 5 outlines a new declarative approach to Semantic Web application development. With reference to the XDD description and the query Q of Figure 4, an XET program corresponding to such a description is given by Figure 6 and the answer to the query Q by Figure 7.

```
<xet:Program   xmlns:xet="XET" xmlns:rdf="http://www.w3.org/1999/02/22-rdf-syntax-ns#"
               xmlns:e="http://emp.org/" xsi:schemaLocation="XET Grammar.xsd">
    <xet:RuleClassOrder>1 2 3 4</xet:RuleClassOrder>
    <xet:Fact>
        <rdf:Description about="e01">                              ⎤   A list of facts
            <rdf:type resource="Employee"/>                        |   corresponding to the
            <e:Name>Somchai P.</e:Name>             - - - - - - - -    XML unit clauses
            <e:Salary>80000</e:Salary>                             |   E₁, ..., E₄.
        </rdf:Description>                                         ⎦
            ⋮
    </xet:Fact>
    <xet:Rule name="EmpRelation" priority="4">                     ⎤
        <xet:Head>                                                |   An XET rule
            <EmpRelation boss="Svar-X" subordinate="Svar-Z" level="Svar-n1"/>   - - - - - -  corresponding to
        </xet:Head>                                               |   the XML non-unit
        <xet:Body>                                                |   clauses R₁ and R₂.
            <rdf:Description about="Svar-Z">
                <rdf:type resource="Employee"/>
                <e:Boss resource="Svar-X"/>   Evar-emp
            </rdf:Description>
            <xet:Unify>
                <Num>Svar-n1</Num>   <Num>1</Num>
            </xet:Unify>
        </xet:Body>
        <xet:Body>
            <EmpRelation boss="Svar-X" subordinate="Svar-Y" level="Svar-n"/>
            <rdf:Description about="Svar-Z">
                <rdf:type resource="Employee"/>
                <e:Boss resource="Svar-Y"/>   Evar-emp
            </rdf:Description>
            <xet:Add number="Svar-n" addendum="1" result="Svar-n1"/>
        </xet:Body>
    </xet:Rule>
    <xet:Rule name="SeniorEmp" priority="4">                       ⎤
        <xet:Head>                                                |   An XET rule
            <rdf:Description about="Svar-X">                       - - - - - - - corresponding to
                <rdf:type resource="SeniorEmployee"/>             |   the XML non-unit
                <e:Subordinate>        <rdf:Bag>Zvar-set</rdf:Bag> |   clause R₃.
                </e:Subordinate>
                <e:Bonus>Svar-bonus</e:Bonus>
                <e:Salary>Svar-sal</e:Salary>   Evar-emp
            </rdf:Description>
        </xet:Head>
        <xet:Body>
            <rdf:Description about="Svar-X">
                <rdf:type resource="Employee"/>
                <e:Salary>Svar-sal</e:Salary>   Evar-emp
            </rdf:Description>
            <xet:SetOf>
                <xet:Set>Zvar-set</xet:Set>
                <xet:Constructor>       <rdf:Li resource="Svar-Y"/>
                </xet:Constructor>
                <xet:Pattern>
                    <EmpRelation boss="Svar-X" subordinate="Svar-Y"/>
                </xet:Pattern>
            </xet:SetOf>
            <xet:Count>
                <xet:Set>Zvar-set</xet:Set>
                <xet:Result>Svar-num</xet:Result>
            </xet:Count>
            <xet:GE number1="Svar-num" number2="4"/>
            <xet:Mul number="Svar-sal" multiplier="3" result="Svar-bonus"/>
        </xet:Body>
    </xet:Rule>
</xet:Program>
```

Figure 6: An XET program P.xml.

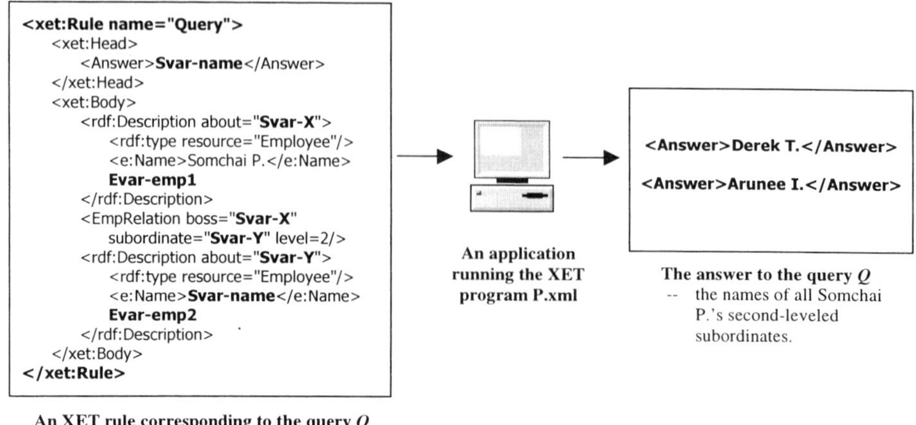

Figure 7: The answer to the query Q.

Note that the declarative semantics of an XET program can be determined based on that of its respective XDD description.

Figure 8 depicts an example scenario of Semantic Web service execution, which starts when a user or an application A issues a query describing a service need together with constraints and preferences to a Semantic-Web-Service Search Engine B, which will then searches, from its database of Web services, for Semantic Web applications offering the demanded service with the requested properties and restrictions. Based on the returned list of applications, A selects an appropriate one, say Semantic Web application C, and sends it a query or a service-request as well as user constraints and preferences. C then executes such a query or request with respect to its data and application rules and logic. During its execution, C may forward corresponding sub-queries and/or sub-requests to other related applications based on its defined rules and logic and wait for their replies and responses. Once the execution has been finished, a reply to A's query/request is returned. Note that Steps 1 and 2 can be skipped, if the user/application A knows at a priori which application provides the desired service. Similarly, at Steps 5.1 and 5.3 if the application C does not know which application it should interoperate, it may ask B for a list of applications offering the required services. In addition, during the execution, it is often a case that communicating parties may involve in a negotiation for modification of service conditions.

From the example scenario, one may observe that XDD and XET can serve as a tool for modeling and implementing a wide diversity of Semantic Web applications offering various kinds of services. Consider, for instance, the Semantic-Web-Service Search Engine B, which maintains a database of Web services described by means of Web-service metadata and provides a search facility for finding of particular services satisfying some specified criteria. Such a search engine is simply modeled as an XDD description comprising XML unit clauses, describing a collection of registered services and their properties/capabilities (in terms of Web-service metadata), and XML non-unit clauses, modeling Web-service ontologies as well as implicit relations among services in the collection. From such a description, an XET program which is capable of searching for services with desired properties and constraints can be ob-

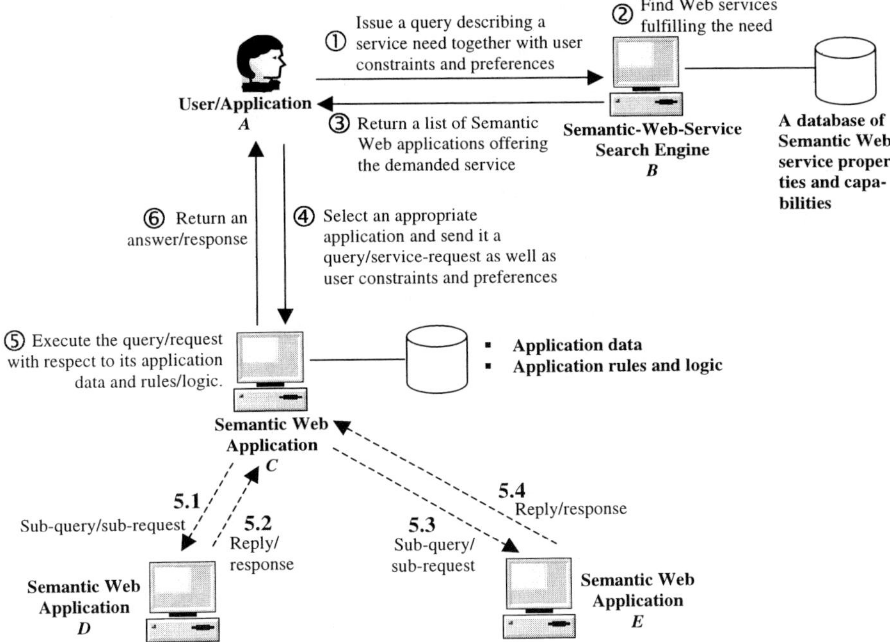

Figure 8: A scenario for Semantic Web service execution.

tained directly. Other applications C, D and E serving certain specific services can also be modeled and implemented in a similar manner.

5　Prototype Application

Founded on the proposed framework, a prototype Semantic Web application, which provides product-information-gathering as well as e-shopping services, has been implemented by means of XDD modeling language and XET programming language. The employed XDD and XET languages have been enhanced with the ability to handle rule conflicting problems using rule prioritization information [10]. Such an additional feature enables, for example, a formalization of a discounting policy stating that if a customer is a member of the store, a 10 percent discount is offered, and if a customer has a late-payment history, no discount is offered and that the latter has higher priority than the former [10]. Due to space limitation, declarative semantics of *prioritized XDD descriptions and XET programs* is omitted; its formal definition is available in [18].

To buy some products (Figure 9), a customer may fill out an order form and submit it on-line to the application Web site or directly send an HTTP request with appropriate parameters encoded in XML to the application URL. The application first checks its stock, and if the products are available, it will calculate the order's price, send a request to a credit card company (another Semantic Web application) for a debit of the customer's account, send a request to a shipping company and then wait for their responses. After the order process has

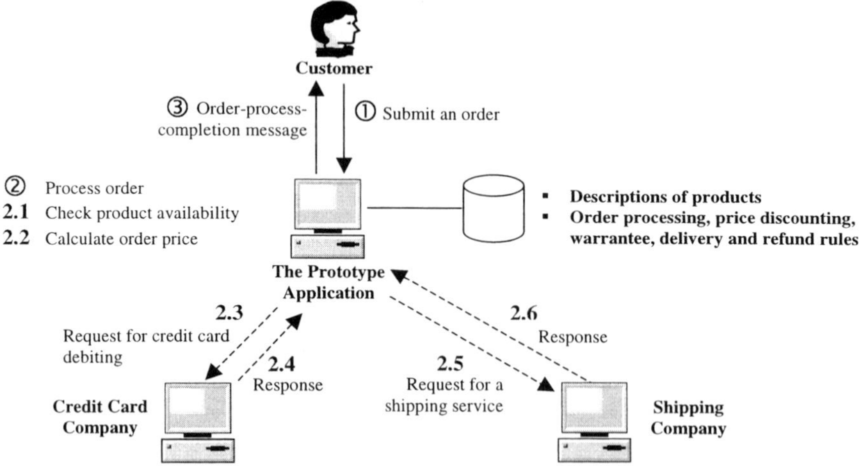

Figure 9: Prototype Semantic Web application.

been finished, the application notifies the customer of the completed process.

6 Related Work

Business Rule Markup Language (BRML) [10] is an XML-based language for encoding of *Courteous Logic Programs (CLP)*—an extension of conventional logic programs by inclusion of the ability to express prioritized conflict handling. BRML is a language in the RuleML Initiative, which has been specifically designed to represent business rules and policies. However, since BRML provides merely an XML embodiment of CLPs, its expressive power is relatively limited in that its sole permitted representation is atomic formulae with simple-structure terms. Complex XML data with nesting structures cannot be directly represented in BRML. Instead they require appropriate translations into corresponding sets of atomic formulae. Figure 10, for example, shows the CLP's and BRML's representations of the XML element E_1 and the XML clause R_1 of Figure 4. Comparing XDD with BRML, one can readily observe that XDD provides a more direct and succinct modeling mechanism; while possessing sufficient expressive power to represent simple as well as complex statements and relations, its representation is still readable.

OIL [5, 7, 11] and *DAML+OIL* [12] are the two most recent, improved ontology-based semantic markup languages for Web resources which extends RDF Schema by richer sets of modeling primitives. However, their current versions still lack expressive power in that arbitrary rules and axioms cannot be described [5]. Since these languages' schemas and instances, which are encoded in RDF/XML serialization, can be directly represented in XDD as XML unit clauses, XDD can be employed to serve as their foundation, in order to help enhance their expressiveness [17]. Therefore, resources and applications modeled by these languages become immediately instances of XDD language and hence directly programmable by XET language. Note that with the awareness of the DAML+OIL's limitation in representing rules and axioms, the language is being extended with the ability to express Horn clauses and will

```
rdf:type(e01, Employee)                      <clp>
e:Name(e01, Somchai P.)                        <erule>
e:Salary(e01, 80000)                             <head>
e:Position(e01, Project Leader)                    <cliteral predicate="rdf:type">
                                                     <function name="e01"/>
                                                     <function name="Employee"/>
                                                   </cliteral>
                                                 </head>
                                               </erule>
                                               ...
                                             </clp>
```

(a) The CLP's representation of the XML element E_1.　　**(b) The BRML's representation of the XML element E_1.**

```
R1:    EmpRelation(?X, ?Y, 1)                <clp>
         ←   rdf:type(?Y, Employee) ∧          <erule rulelabel="R1">
             e:Boss(?Y, ?X).                      <head>
                                                    <cliteral predicate="EmpRelation">
                                                      <variable name="X"/>
                                                      <variable name="Y"/>
                                                      <function name="1"/>
                                                    </cliteral>
                                                  </head>
                                                  <body>
                                                    <and>
                                                      <fcliteral predicate="rdf:type">
                                                        <variable name="Y"/>
                                                        <variable name="Employee"/>
                                                      </fcliteral>
                                                      <fcliteral predicate="e:Boss">
                                                        <variable name="Y"/>
                                                        <variable name="X"/>
                                                      </fcliteral>
                                                    </and>
                                                  </body>
                                                </erule>
                                              </clp>
```

(c) The CLP's representation of the XML clause R_1.　　**(d) The BRML's representation of the XML clause R_1.**

Figure 10: The CLP's and BRML's representations of the element E_1 and the clause R_1 of Figure 4.

be called *DAML-L* [16].

With reference to the overall process of Semantic Web service implementation defined in [10, 16], XDD can be uniformly employed to materialize each step of the process:

- *Service Advertisement and Discovery*: A collection of service properties and capabilities described by means of metadata or *Semantic Web Service Markup Language* [16] can be directly represented as XML unit clauses, and their additional constraints and relations modeled in terms of XML non-unit clauses. Based on such declarative advertisements of Web services, discovery of a particular service having specific properties and capabilities is expressed as an XML non-unit clause, which will be evaluated on the Web service database and return as its reply a list of applications or service providers offering the requested service.

- *Negotiation*: Given particular negotiation rules and procedures for selection of Web services (e.g., response time, data accuracy and cost conditions), corresponding XML non-unit clauses can be declaratively defined. Besides definition of such rules, an appropriate employment of *Agent Communication Language (ACL)* [15] which allows the negotiating parties to effectively communicate and interoperate must also be considered. By a careful formulation and implementation of the two major current ACLs (i.e., *KQML* [8] and *FIPA-ACL* [9, 15]) in XDD [13], XDD readily provides an effective communication in the negotiation stage, allowing every negotiating party to communicate with one another via XDD uniform interface, and hence enabling a higher level of interoperability.

- *Service Execution*: Execution of a service according to a given procedure can be represented in XDD by appropriate XML clauses. Based on such a declarative specification, an application can automatically execute the service.

- *Service Composition and Integration*: It is often a case that a service is designed as a composition or an integration of other existing services. The execution of such a composite service often requires interaction with those related services in terms of request-for-service calls and returned responses. Using XDD, one can represent service composition and integration by an XML clause, the head of which specifies the composite service and the body of which describes the composition rule as well as the service calls and the data to be exchanged with other services. Such service calls and exchanged data could be embodied in an ACL.

- *Service Customization*: In order to increase the level of share-ability, reusability and user's satisfactory of provided services, a service may be defined by a particular generic procedure which can then be customized for execution of a specific service request. Such a generic procedure is described by a set of XML clauses, and its customization is realized by either parameter instantiation or by addition of XML clauses into it—this latter case is equivalent to program refinement. Note that different customizations normally lead to different sequences and results of service execution.

In summary, with these supports, XDD readily provides sufficient Semantic Web modeling facilities for development of intelligent, automated Web applications requiring interoperation with other independently-developed applications.

7 Conclusions

The proposed XDD language is an expressive modeling language which allows collections of Semantic Web resources (modeled in terms of XML, RDF, OIL or DAM+OIL) to be directly represented with their semantics precisely and formally determined. In addition to such a resource modeling facility, XDD also provides a means for descriptions of Web resource manipulations, service provisions and business rules and processes. Moreover, its extension [18] by the ability to handle rule conflicting problems has enhanced its expressive power to be sufficient to capture and describe complex and conflicting rules and logic in Semantic Web applications.

Founded on XDD's expressive power and ET's computational efficiency, XET programming language and its compiler have also been developed. By means of XDD and XET languages, the paper has proposed a declarative framework for Semantic Web application development and has demonstrated that a variety of Semantic Web applications and services is simply expressible by XDD and hence programmable by XET. Moreover, the development of the prototype system based on the proposed framework has helped prove the framework's viability and potential in real applications. Integration of the proposed framework with appropriate Web and agent technologies allows intelligent as well as automated Web services, which demand syntactic and semantic interoperability, to be easily and rapidly developed. Note also that an XET program which performs particular tasks can be exchanged, shared and reused by multiple applications.

References

[1] K. Akama, Declarative Semantics of Logic Programs on Parameterized Representation Systems. Advances in Software Science and Technology **5** (1993) 45–63.

[2] K. Akama, T. Shimitsu and E. Miyamoto, Solving Problems by Equivalent Transformation of Declarative Programs. J. Japanese Society of Artificial Intelligence (JSAI) **13(6)** (1998) 944–952 (in Japanese).

[3] K. Akama, C. Anutariya, V. Wuwongse and E. Nantajeewarawat, A Foundation for XML Databases: Query Formulation and Evaluation. Technical Report, Computer Science and Information Management Program, Asian Institute of Technology, Thailand (1999).

[4] C. Anutariya, V. Wuwongse, E. Nantajeewarawat and K. Akama. Towards a Foundation for XML Document Databases. Proc. 1st Int. Conference on Electronic Commerce and Web Technologies (EC-Web 2000), London, UK. Lecture Notes in Computer Science, Springer Verlag **1875** (2000) 324–333.

[5] S. Bechhofer et al., An Informational Description of Standard OIL and Instance OIL. White Paper (Nov. 2000). Available at http://www.ontoknowledge.org/oil/downl/oil-whitepaper.pdf

[6] T. Berners-Lee, Weaving the Web. Harpur, San Francisco (1999).

[7] S. Decker et al., The Semantic Web: The Roles of XML and RDF, IEEE Internet Computing, (Sep./Oct. 2000) 63-74.

[8] T. Finin, Y. Labrou and J. Mayfield, KQML as an Agent Communication Language. Software Agents, AAAI/MIT Press (1997).

[9] FIPA: FIPA Specification, Version 2.0, Part 2: Agent Communication Language (1997) Available at http://www.fipa.org/spec/f8a22.zip

[10] B.N. Grosof, Y. Labrou, and H.Y. Chan, A Declarative Approach to Business Rules in Contracts: Courteous Logic Programs in XML. Proc. 1st ACM Conf. on Electronic Commerce (EC99), ACM Press (1999).

[11] F.V. Harmelen, and I. Harrocks, FAQs on OIL: The Ontology Inference Layer. IEEE Intelligent Systems **15(2)** (Nov./Dec. 2000) 69–72.

[12] J. Hendler and D. McGuinness, The DARPA Agent Markup Language. IEEE Intelligent Systems **15(2)** (Nov./Dec. 2000) 72–73.

[13] S. Jindadamrongwech, An Agent Communication Language using XML Declarative Description. Master's Thesis, Computer Science and Information Management Program, Asian Institute of Technology, Thailand (2000).

[14] H. Koike, K. Akama, H. Mabuchi, K. Okada, Correct Computation for Negation in Equivalent Transformation Paradigm. Proc. Int'l Conf. Information Systems, Analysis and Synthesis (ISAS 2001).

[15] Y. Labrou, T. Finin, and Y. Peng, Agent Communication Languages: The Current Landscape. IEEE Intelligent Systems, **14(2)** (Apr./May 1999) 45–52.

[16] S.A. McIlraith, T.C. Son, and H. Zeng, Semantic Web Services. IEEE Intelligent Systems, **16(2)** (Mar./Apr. 2001) 46–53.

[17] V. Wuwongse, C. Anutariya, K. Akama and E. Nantajeewarawat: XML Declarative Description (XDD): A Language for the Semantic Web. IEEE Intelligent Systems, **16(3)** (May/Jun. 2001) 54–65.

[18] V. Wattanapailin, A Declarative Programming Language with XML. Master's Thesis, Computer Science and Information Management Program, Asian Institute of Technology, Thailand (2000).

Part 2:
Ontologies and
Services

The Emerging Semantic Web
I.F. Cruz et al. (Eds.)
IOS Press, 2002

Industrial Strength Ontology Management

Aseem Das, *DemaVu Technologies, aseem@demavu.com*
Wei Wu, *Verticalnet Inc., wwu@verticalnet.com*
Deborah L. McGuinness, *Stanford University, dlm@ksl.stanford.edu*

Abstract. Ontologies are becoming increasingly prevalent and important in a wide range of e-business applications. E-business applications are using ontologies to support parametric searches, enhanced navigation and browsing, interoperable heterogeneous information systems, configuration management, e-marketplaces and visibility, and comprehension and response across extended enterprises. Applications such as information and service discovery and autonomous agents that are built on top of the emerging Semantic Web for the WWW also require extensive use of ontologies. Ontology-enhanced e-business applications, such as these and others require ontology management that is scalable (supporting thousands of simultaneous distributed users), available (running 365x24x7), fast, and reliable. This level of ontology management is necessary not only for the initial development and maintenance of ontologies, but is essential during deployment, when scalability, availability, reliability and performance are absolutely critical. Verticalnet's Ontology Builder and Ontology Server products are specifically designed to provide the ontology management infrastructure needed for e-business applications. These tools bring the best ontology and knowledge representation practices together with the best enterprise solutions architecture to provide a robust and scalable ontology management solution.

1 Introduction

Ontology Builder and Ontology Server were developed in response to the business needs for ontologies in Verticalnet's e-business and extended enterprise applications. Verticalnet is an enterprise software provider that helps businesses share information across business units, conduct commerce with trading partners and utilize, comprehend and respond to business-critical supply chain data across the extended enterprise. The use of ontologies was seen as the best solution for providing a common knowledge infrastructure for solving these particular and other future e-business problems [17, 18, 25]. Ontology Builder/Server are used internally to support critical Verticalnet e-business applications and provide a scalable and distributed ontology environment – a component critical to the success of these e-business applications. More broadly, however, this component is also critical to the success of any architecture, which leverages background information, such as the Semantic Web. The next generation web – commonly referred to as the Semantic Web – obtains its power and "intelligence" from utilizing markup information on content sources along with background information on terms and content. The success of such an endeavor relies on environments that support creation and maintenance of background information, while working in a broadly distributed environment like the web. Ontology Builder/Server provide such an environment in an industrial strength implementation.

2　Requirements

An extensive requirement gathering process was undertaken to compile requirements for Verticalnet's ontology management solutions. We identified the following key requirements for ontology management for Verticalnet:

1　Scalability, Availability, Reliability and Performance – These were considered essential for any ontology management solution in the commercial industrial space, both during the development and maintenance phase and the ontology deployment phase. The ontology management solution needed to allow distributed development of large-scale ontologies concurrently and collaboratively by multiple users with a high level of reliability and performance. For the deployment phase, this requirement was considered to be even more important. Applications accessing ontological data need to be up 365x24x7, support thousands of concurrent users, and be both reliable and fast.

2　Ease of Use – The ontology development and maintenance process had to be simple, and the tools usable by ontologists as well as domain experts and business analysts.

3　Extensible and Flexible Knowledge Representation – The knowledge model needed to incorporate the best knowledge representation practices available in the industry and be flexible and extensible enough to easily incorporate new representational features and incorporate and interoperate with different knowledge models such as RDF(S) [2, 16], OIL[9], DAML [12], (DAML-ONT[20], DAML+OIL [4]).

4　Distributed Multi-User Collaboration – Collaboration was seen as a key to knowledge sharing and building. Ontologists, domain experts, and business analysts need a tool that allows them to work collaboratively to create and maintain ontologies even if they work in different geographic locations.

5　Security Management – The system needed to be secure to protect the integrity of the data, prevent unauthorized access, and support multiple access levels. Supporting different levels of access for different types of users would protect the integrity of data while providing an effective means of partitioning tasks and controlling changes.

6　Difference and Merging – Merging facilitates knowledge reuse and sharing by enabling existing knowledge to be easily incorporated into an ontology. The ability to merge ontologies is also needed during the ontology development process to integrate versions created by different individuals into a single, consistent ontology.

7　XML interfaces – Because XML is becoming widely-used for supporting interoperability and sharing information between applications, the ontology solution needed to provide XML interfaces to enable interaction and interoperability with other applications.

8　Internationalization – The World Wide Web enables a global marketplace and e-business applications using ontological data have to serve users around the world. The ontology management solution needed to allow users to create ontologies in different languages and support the display or retrieval of ontologies using different locales based on the user's geographical location. (For example, the transportation ontology would be displayed in Japanese, French, German, or English depending on the geographical locale of the user.)

9　Versioning – Since ontologies continue to change and evolve, a versioning system for ontologies is critical. As an ontology changes over time, applications need to know what version of the ontology they are accessing and how it has changed from one version to another so that they can perform accordingly. (For example, if a supplier's database is mapped to a particular version of an ontology and the ontology changes, the database needs to be remapped to the updated ontology, either manually or using an automated tool.)

The requirements of scalability, reliability, availability, security, internationalization and versioning were considered to be the most important for an industrial strength ontology management solution.

3 Existing Ontology Environments

Given the above requirements, several existing ontology management environments were evaluated[1]:

- Ontolingua/Chimaera [7, 19]
- Protégé/PROMPT [11, 22]
- WebOnto/Tadzebao [5]
- OntoSaurus, a web browser for Loom [13] (http://www.isi.edu/isd/ontosaurus.html)

Some of these environments have already been compared based on different criteria than those formulated at Verticalnet [6]. Figure 1, shows a feature set matrix and our evaluation[2] of the tools based on Verticalnet's requirements. To keep the evaluation simple, a three level (+, 0, -) scale was used, where (+) indicates a requirement was surpassed, (0) indicates the requirement was met and (-) indicates that the tool failed to meet the requirement. Although, none of the existing ontology development environments provide all of the required features, they are nevertheless strong in particular features and have different but very expressive underlying knowledge representation models.

Figure 1: Comparison of Some Ontology Environments

	Scalable Available Reliable	Ease of Use	Knowledge Representation	Multi User Collaboration	Security Management	Diff & Merge	International ization	Versioning
Ontolingua/ Chimaera	-	-	+	0	-	+	-	-
Protégé/ PROMPT	-	0	+	-	-	+	-	-
WebOnto/ Tadzebao	-	0	+	+	-	-	-	-
OntoSaurus /Loom	-	-	+	0	-	-	-	-

Ontolingua provides a very powerful and expressive representation with its frame language and its support for KIF [10] – a first order logic representation. In combination with its theorem prover (ATP/JTP), Ontolingua provides extensive reasoning capabilities and with Chimaera [19,20], it supports ontology merging, diagnostics, and ontology evolution. Ontolingua also provides expressive and operational power not found in other environments such as support for generating and modifying disjoint covering partitions of classes.

WebOnto/Tadzebao provides very rich collaborative support for browsing, creating and editing ontologies, together with the ability to collaboratively annotate and hold synchronous and asynchronous ontology related discussions using the Tadzebao tool.

---

[1] The evaluation was done in Fall'99 and hence does not include ontology management environments such as OntoEdit (http://www.ontoprise.de), WebODE (http://delicias.dia.fi.upm.es/webODE/), and OILEd (http://img.cs.man.ac.uk/oil/), which were available for use after Fall'99.

[2] This was not a formal evaluation with published, unambiguous evaluation criteria. It was however a good faith effort to evaluate VerticalNet requirements as understood in the various tools.

OntoSaurus provides a graphical hyperlinked interface to Loom knowledge bases. Loom provides expressive knowledge representation, automatic consistency checking and deductive support via its deductive engine – the classifier.

Protégé is the easiest to use and supports the construction of knowledge-acquisition interfaces based on ontological data. It also has a component framework for easily integrating other components via plugins. Protégé already provides several plugins including PAL, a first order logical language for expressing constraints, and SMART/PROMPT [22,23], a tool for merging and alignment of ontologies

However, despite their strengths, all of the ontology solutions fell short on the scalability, reliability, and performance requirements, perhaps because industrial strength, commercial scalability was not seen as a important aspect of ontology management since most of the ontology usage until recently has been restricted to research and academia. Also, none of the tools provided security, internationalization, or versioning support – requirements considered critical for e-business applications.

After evaluating these solutions against our requirements, we decided to build our own ontology management solution with the goal of bringing the best ontology and knowledge representation practices together with the best enterprise solutions architecture to satisfy the requirements of ontology-driven e-business applications.

4 Ontology Builder

Ontology Builder is a multi-user collaborative ontology generation and maintenance tool designed to incorporate the best features of existing ontology toolkits in order to provide a simple, powerful and yet broadly usable tool. Ontology Builder uses a frame-based representation based on the OKBC Knowledge Model [3]. OKBC was developed recognizing the wide general acceptance of frame-based systems [14] and provides an API (Applications Programming Interface) for frame-like systems. Written entirely in Java, Ontology Builder can run on multiple platforms. It is based on the J2EE (Java 2 Enterprise Edition) platform (http://java.sun.com/j2ee), which is a standard for implementing and deploying enterprise applications. Ontology Builder also provides:

- Import and export based on XOL (XML-based Ontology Exchange Language) [15][3]
- A verification engine designed to maintain consistency of terms stated in the language
- A role-based security model for data security and ontology access
- An ontological difference and merging engine

---

[3] At the time of design and development, a DAML option did not exist. Today there are plans to support DAML+OIL and RDF as well.

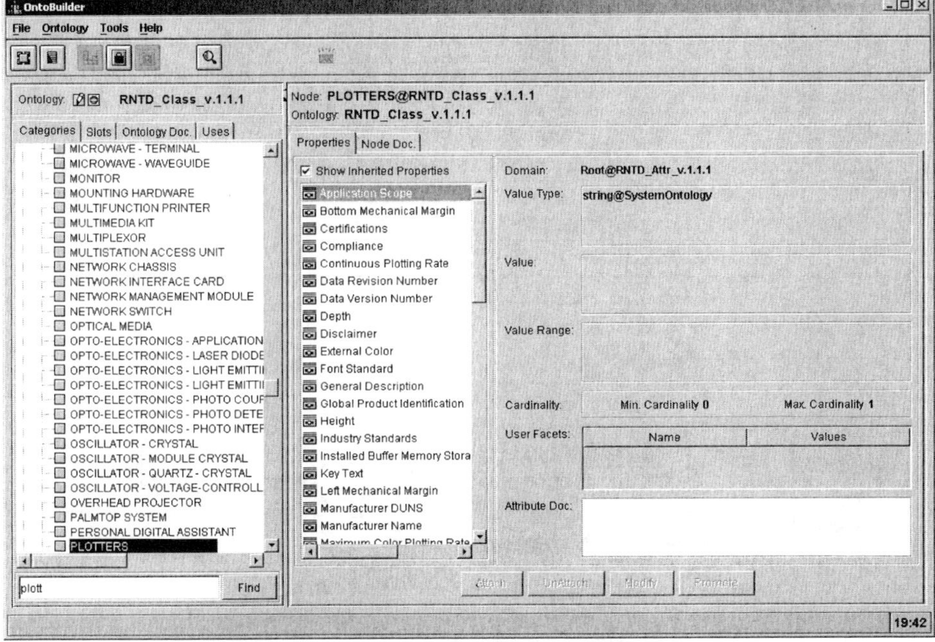

Figure 2: Ontology Builder Main Screen

4.1 Architecture

Ontology Builder is based on the J2EE (Java 2 Enterprise Edition) platform, a standard for implementing and deploying "enterprise" applications. The term "enterprise" implies highly-scalable, highly-available, highly-reliable, highly-secure, transactional, distributed applications. The J2EE technology is designed to support the rigorous demands of large-scale, distributed, mission-critical application systems and provides support for multi-tier application architecture. Multi-tier applications are typically configured to include:

- A client tier to provide the user interface
- One or more middle-tier modules that provide client services and business logic for an application
- A backend enterprise information system data tier that provides data management

The client tier is a very "thin" tier, that contains only presentation logic. The business and data logic are usually partitioned into separate components and deployed on one or more application servers. This partitioning of the application into multiple server components allows components to be easily replicated and distributed across the system, ensuring scalability, availability, reliability and performance.

Central to the J2EE platform architecture are application servers, which encapsulate the business and data logic and provide runtime support for responding to client requests, automated support for transactions, security, persistence, resource allocation, life-cycle management, and as well as lookup and other services.

Ontology Builder uses a 4-tier architecture comprised of a presentation tier, web tier, service tier, and data tier. This architecture, shown in Figure 3, can be deployed using a single application server. The application server encapsulates the service tier, which consists of the business and data logic. A single server can support many simultaneous connections and multiple servers can be easily clustered as needed for scalability, load balancing, and fault tolerance. Within the presentation tier, a client can be either a Java applet or application. The clients have easy-to-use interfaces written using the Java Swing APIs. Both applet and application-based clients communicate with the web tier via the HTTP protocol. The web-tier communicates with the service tier using RMI (Java Remote Method Invocation) (http://java.sun.com/products/rmi-iiop/index.html). The service tier communicates with the data tier through the JDBC (Java Data Base Connectivity) protocol (http://java.sun.com/products/jdbc). Collaboration is implemented using a JSDT (Java Shared Data Toolkit) server (http://java.sun.com/products/java-media/jsdt), which forwards all communication and change events to the respective clients.

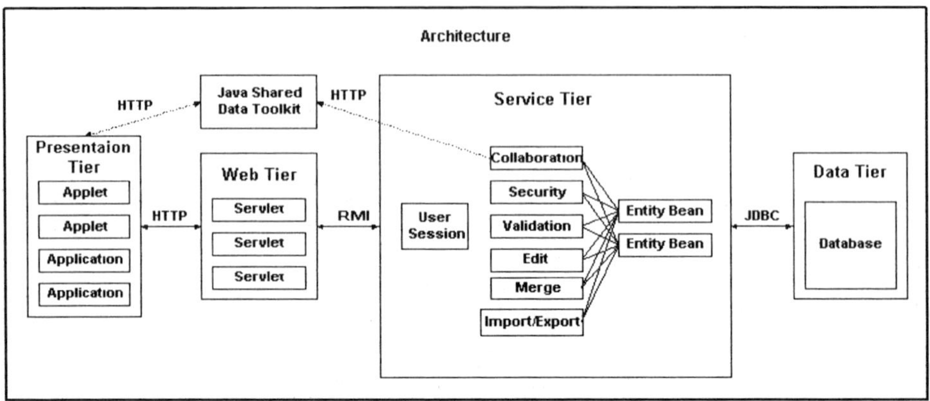

Figure 3: The Architecture of Ontology Builder

4.2   Knowledge Representation

Ontology Builder uses an object-oriented knowledge representation model based on and compatible with the OKBC knowledge model and is designed to use the best practices from other frame-based systems. Ontology Builder implementation supports the OKBC operations on classes, slots, facets, and individuals. Currently, however, no external interfaces are exposed to enable other knowledge systems to use Ontology Builder as an OKBC compliant server. Interoperability, knowledge sharing, and reuse are important goals and our future plans call for making Ontology Builder work as a fully compliant OKBC server.

Ontology Builder supports a metaclass architecture to allow the introduction of flexible and customizable behaviors into an ontology. This could potentially be used for incorporating other knowledge models or extending the existing knowledge model within Ontology Builder. Ontology Builder predefines certain system constants, classes, and primitives in a default upper ontology, which can be extended or refined to change the knowledge model and behaviors within the system. The main predefined concepts are:

- CLASS - the default metaclass for all classes, CLASS is an instance of itself
- SLOT – the default metaclass for all slots and an instance of CLASS
- T – the root in the default upper ontology (sometimes referred to as THING in other ontologies)

- INDIVIDUAL – the class of ground objects. Operationally, every entity that is not a class is an instance of INDIVIDUAL.[4]
- Predefined slots – slot-minimum-cardinality, slot-maximum-cardinality, slot-value-type, slot-value-range and domain. These are template slots on the class SLOT.
- Predefined facets– minimum-cardinality, maximum-cardinality, value-type, value-range and documentation-in-frame. These define the specific values for the slot as associated with either a class or a slot frame.
- Predefined primitive data types – boolean, string, integer, float, date, etc.

An ontology is composed of **classes**, **slots**, **individuals** and **facets**, which are all implemented as frames. **Ontology** itself is also defined as a frame and contains information such as author, date created and documentation. Both classes and slots support multiple-inheritance in an Ontology Builder ontology.

Classes are all instances of the metaclass CLASS by default, which is changeable by the user. Classes can be instances of multiple metaclasses and they may be subclasses of multiple superclasses.

Slots are defined independently of any class and are instances of the metaclass SLOT by default, which is also changeable by the user. They can also be instances of multiple metaclasses and parent classes. Like classes, slots also support a multiple-inheritance hierarchy. Slot hierarchies can be used to model naturally hierarchical relationships between terms. For example, you might need to model the notion of price along with the subrelations of wholesale-price, retail-price, and discount-price.

Slots can be attached to a class frame or a slot frame, as slots are themselves first-class objects and when attached describe the properties of the frame. A slot can be attached either as a **template** slot or as an **own** slot. Own slots cannot be directly attached to a frame, but are acquired by the frame (class, slot or individual) being an instance of another class. Template slots can be directly attached to either a class or a slot frame. The domain own slot (acquired by a slot frame from being an instance of class SLOT) is useful for limiting the applicability of the slot only to the specified domain class and its subclasses. If a slot does not define a domain, it can be applied to all classes in an ontology. This flexibility is often useful during the early stage of ontology development when the slots used in an ontology are still being refined. Later however, it is often useful to define a domain for slots so that they are only used in specific contexts.

Facets specify the specific values for a slot-class or a slot-slot association. A facet is considered associated with a frame-slot pair, if the facet has a value for that association. The predefined facets (value-type, value-range, minimum-cardinality, maximum-cardinality etc.) hold the values given to a slot's own slots (slot-value-type, slot-value-range, etc.) when the slot is associated with a frame. The facet values can only be a specialization of the slot frame's own slot values. For example, if slot *color* is defined to have a slot-value-type of "color", when it's attached to a frame, the value can only be changed to a specialization of "color", "rgbcolor" or "hsvcolor". If the value is changed, then the "value-type" facet will hold the changed value. In addition to predefined facets, Ontology Builder supports the creation and use of **user-defined facets**. A user-defined facet can be created and attached to a slot when the slot is attached to a frame. For example, a user-defined facet might be used to specify whether or not a slot is "displayable".

---

[4] Note: Slots and facets are instances of CLASSES. Currently, all entities are either CLASSES or INDIVIDUALS but for extensibility, we are not stating that INDIVIDUALS and CLASSES form a covering partition for all things.

4.3   Ontology Inclusion (Uses Relationship)

Ontology construction is time consuming and expensive. To lower development and maintenance cost, it is beneficial to build reusable and modular ontologies so that new ontologies can be created and assembled quickly by mixing and matching existing validated ontologies. Both Ontolingua and Protégé have the capability to include ontologies for the purpose of reuse [7, 24]. Protégé allows projects to be included, but the included projects cannot be easily removed and no duplicated names can exist across projects used (included projects plus the current working project) due to the requirement that names must be unique. This unique name requirement in Protégé is limiting because duplicate names occur in practice. Ontolingua provides facilities that allow flexible combination of axioms and definitions of multiple ontologies. Ontolingua eliminates symbol conflicts among ontologies in its internal representation by providing a local name space for symbols defined in each ontology.

Ontology Builder supports concepts reuse and ontology inclusion through the "uses" relationship. The "uses" relationship allows all classes, instances, slots, and facets from the included ontology to be visible and used by an ontology. For example, if ontology A "uses" ontology B, all of the concepts defined in ontology B (classes, instances, slots and facets) can be referenced from ontology A. A class in ontology A can be a subclass of a class in ontology B, and any class in A can use any slots defined in ontology B. The "uses" relationship can be added or removed easily from an ontology. When a "uses" relationship is removed, inconsistencies might exist in the current working ontology because concepts defined in the removed "uses" ontology still are being referenced, even though the ontology is not being used. Changes made to an ontology are propagated in real-time to all ontologies that use that ontology. Although this ensures that the latest concepts are available for use, it might also cause inconsistencies. Verification can be performed to diagnose and identify frames that have inconsistencies

The "uses" relationship is transitive. If ontology A "uses" ontology B, and ontology B "uses" ontology C, then ontology A "uses" ontology C automatically. Ontology Builder also allows cyclical "uses" relationship, that is ontologies A and B can both use each other. Concepts are unambiguously identified by using a globally unique identifier that is generated automatically when a concept is first created; or by using a fully qualified name. A fully qualified name is the concept name concatenated together with the "@" and the ontology name. For example, <u>car@transportation</u>. The fully qualified name is guaranteed to be unique as a concept name is enforced to be to be unique within a specific ontology and ontology names are unique across all ontologies in the knowledge base. The fully qualified names are used automatically when working with concepts in ontologies other than the ontology where they are initially defined.

4.4   Data Storage and Knowledge-Relational Mapping

Knowledge-base systems traditionally used the computer's main memory for storing the knowledge needed at run-time. The amount of information that can be stored is limited by the available memory and there might be an initial delay in loading all of the entities into memory from a flat file. Moreover, the storing of the knowledge model in flat files is not secure, is error-prone, and quickly becomes unmanageable as the size of the knowledge base increases. Object-Oriented Database Systems (OODS) can also be used to store the knowledge model and provide superior modeling for representing the relations and hierarchies within an ontology. However, when compared to relational DBMS (RDBMS), OODS lack in performance, enterprise usage and acceptance, internationalization support, and other features. RDBMS are still the storage mechanism of choice in enterprise computing when it comes to storing large amounts of performance-critical data. RDBMS can store gigabytes of data, search several million rows of data extremely quickly, and also support data replication and redundancy.

Ontology Builder uses an enterprise-class RDBMS so that very large-scale ontologies and large numbers of ontologies can be stored and retrieved quickly and efficiently. Several other knowledge based systems SOPHIA [1] and an environment for large ontologies motivated by PARKA [26] have also used RDBMS for these and other similar reasons. Ontology Builder currently supports the Oracle 8 and Microsoft SQL Server RDBMSs for data storage.

Ontology Builder employs a sophisticated database schema to represent the OKBC based knowledge model and can support all OKBC-defined operations that could be performed on classes, instances, slots and facets, as well as the operations specified by the OKBC ask/tell interface. The multiple-table database schema also supports internationalization, which permits ontologies to be developed in any language. Multiple translations of the same ontology can coexist in the same database and can be used to view the same ontology in different locales. The schema is normalized; each piece of information is stored in only one location so that modifications to a concept are automatically propagated to all entities that use that concept.

Knowledge-relational mapping is accomplished via a high-performance persistence layer that converts relational data to and from in-memory Java objects that represent the different entities and relationships of the knowledge model. Information retrieval is optimized to retrieve information about multiple concepts via one JDBC database call, which dramatically improves performance. Moreover, a lazy-loading algorithm is used to retrieve information on an as-need basis. For example, when an ontology is first loaded, only the classes and the class hierarchy are loaded; attached slots, slot values, and facet values are only loaded when a user decides to browse or edit a particular class.

4.5   Multi User Collaboration & Locking

Ontology construction is often a collaborative endeavor where the participants in the ontology building process share their knowledge to come to a common understanding and representation of the ontology. These participants might be geographically separated and for collaboration require the ability to hold discussions and view the changes made to the ontology by other collaborators. Ontology Builder provides this type of multi-user collaborative environment. Collaborators can hold discussions individually or in a group and see changes made to the ontology by other collaborators in real time.

Collaboration is implemented via the Java Data Shared Toolkit (JSDT), which provides the communication, messaging, and session management infrastructure for collaboration within Ontology Builder. As they log into the system, each user is registered with the JSDT server in a default "global" discussion room. Messages sent by any user in this discussion room are received by all other current users of the system. Each ontology also defines its own discussion room, which is created the first time any user opens the ontology for browsing or editing. Users who open the same ontology are added to that ontology's discussion room automatically and can see the messages from and collaborate with other users within that ontology's discussion room. A user can also open a private chat session with any other user who is logged on to the system.

Edits to any ontology in the system are broadcasted to all users, regardless of their interest. The change record indicates the type of edit operation, the affected concept and ontology, and the user who performed the action. Figure 4 is a snapshot of the collaboration window that shows the system log and a discussion between collaborators. Any changes to the ontology are committed to the database immediately, so that the changes are available to all other users in real time. An icon is displayed automatically next to the concepts within an open ontology that have been modified by other users, indicating to the user that the information currently displayed in the Ontology Builder client is no longer accurate. The user might already know what has changed based on the discussion with other collaborators or can look in the system messages to see exactly what was changed in the affected concept. An ontology can be refreshed at any point to retrieve the latest state.

Since multiple collaborators can make changes to the same ontology, some kind of locking scheme is necessary to prevent users from overwriting each other's changes. Ontology Builder uses a pessimistic locking strategy that requires an explicit lock to be acquired by a collaborator before any edits are allowed to a concept. Explicitly locking a concept implicitly locks all of the parents and children of the locked concept, preventing other users from editing either the children or the parents of the locked node. Explicitly locking a concept still allows other users to edit the siblings of the locked concept. Locked concepts are shown with a locked icon in all of the clients, indicating which concepts are currently being edited. This locking strategy enables multi-user collaboration and reduces inconsistencies generated from multiple collaborators working on the same ontology.

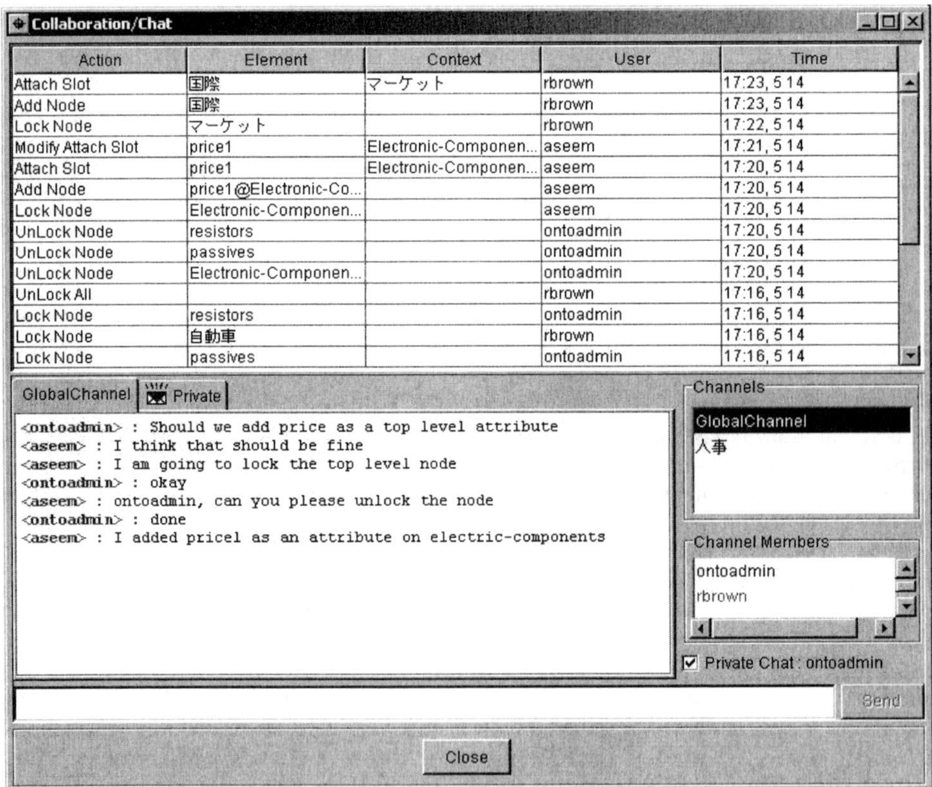

Figure 4: Collaboration Window in Ontology Builder

4.6 Verification

Ontology Builder provides a verification engine to resolve any inconsistencies that might have been introduced during the ontology development and maintenance process. Maintaining consistency is not only critical during the development process where a particular ontology might "use" other ontologies, it is even more critical during the deployment phase where the ontologies have to be valid and consistent so that they can be used by applications without any errors. Real-time verification is a fairly complex task and requires a truth maintenance system (TMS) of some sort in order to have acceptable performance. If a TMS is not used, thorough checks of all of the elements of the ontology need to be done, which is not acceptable from a performance perspective. Ontology Builder does some real-time verification during the edit/creation process itself (for example, it checks for value-type and cardinality violations), but for a full consistency check, the verification engine needs to be explicitly invoked by the user. The verification engine checks for:

- Cycles
- Domain of slots is valid for the classes to which they are attached
- Minimum cardinality <= maximum cardinality
- Minimum cardinality <= num of values <= maximum cardinality
- Values are of specified value-types
- Undefined symbols – symbols that are being used but not defined in the current ontology or any of the ontologies it uses
- Attached slots are consistent with the slot definition (Specialization of value-types, value-ranges and cardinalities is checked for consistency)

4.7 Difference & Merging

Merging ontologies becomes necessary when there is a need to consolidate concepts defined in multiple ontologies, often developed by different teams or gathered from various sources, into a consistent and unified ontology that can be deployed with e-business applications. Because the general task of merging ontologies can become arbitrarily difficult, extensive human intervention and negotiation are required. Chimaera [19] and PROMPT [23] provide semi-automated tools to facilitate the merging process. The merging tools in Chimaera and PROMPT suggest a list of merging candidates and present available operations on the candidate frames. Once a user finishes a particular merge operation, more suggestions could be generated and the tool guides the users to finish the merging process. Chimaera also provides diagnostics on the results of merging and other ontology modifications.

Ontology Builder follows a different path in that the initial list of merging candidate frames is not generated. Instead, Ontology Builder relies on the user to decide where to start the merging process. Essentially the user determines when two concepts mean the same thing semantically. The rationale behind the decision is that in practice a user often knows the structures and contents of the ontologies to be merged, and thus has the knowledge to determine where to start the merging process. The goal of the difference and merge service in Ontology Builder is to speed up the merge process once the initial merging candidate frames have been chosen, rather than being a general-purpose merging tool like those provided by Chimaera and PROMPT.

In Ontology Builder, the merge operation does not generate a third ontology that contains the merged results from two input ontologies. Instead, Ontology Builder defines a base ontology and merge ontology where the differences between the two ontologies can be initially identified and then, if desired, the differences can be merged into the base ontology.

Ontology Builder currently has a simplistic algorithm for reporting the differences between two ontologies. Differences are reported for the two concepts selected for comparison as well as for their children that have matching names. If there are no matching names, the differencing stops. Ontology Builder reports the following differences:

- Missing children/parents
- Missing slots
- Value, value-type, value-range, domain, documentation, and cardinality differences for matched concepts

If desired, the differences can be merged. The merge operation

- Copies missing children recursively to the base ontology
- Copies missing slots to the base ontology
- Merges documentation, slot values, value-types, value-ranges and cardinalities for the matched concepts

The difference and merge feature of Ontology Builder is simple compared to the merging features available in other tools like PROMPT or Chimaera, but future plans call for enhancing this functionality based on further requirements and proposed usage.

4.8   Role Based Security

Ontology Builder provides a flexible security model designed to allow client access to the back-end services. Every user has an account on the system and is only allowed to access the back-end services if properly authenticated. Each user is assigned a role, which denotes the level of access for ontology management. Users assigned a particular role can only perform the operations allowed by that role, however, users can be assigned different roles for different ontologies. The security model also enables a much finer-grained permissions system where individual edit operations in an ontology (such as modify-documentation) can be enabled for particular users.

By protecting ontology data and controlling access to back-end services, Ontology Builder's security model meets one of the critical requirements for enterprise class applications.

4.9   Internationalization

Ontology Builder is fully internationalized and can support the browsing and editing of ontologies in multiple locales. A single representation of the ontology is maintained for all locales. Names from each of the locales are linked to this one representation so that changes in ontology structure in one locale are propagated and available in all the other locales. Concepts, which have not been translated in a particular locale, are shown in the locale in which they were initially created. For example, if the ontology was initially created in English and then partially translated into Japanese, browsing it in Japanese will show the names in English for the concepts that have not yet been translated. Ontology Builder also provides support for translating from one locale into another locale. Hooks are provided to use a translation tool or service if desired to semi-automate the translation process. The snapshot in Figure 5 shows a Japanese ontology with some untranslated words in English and French.

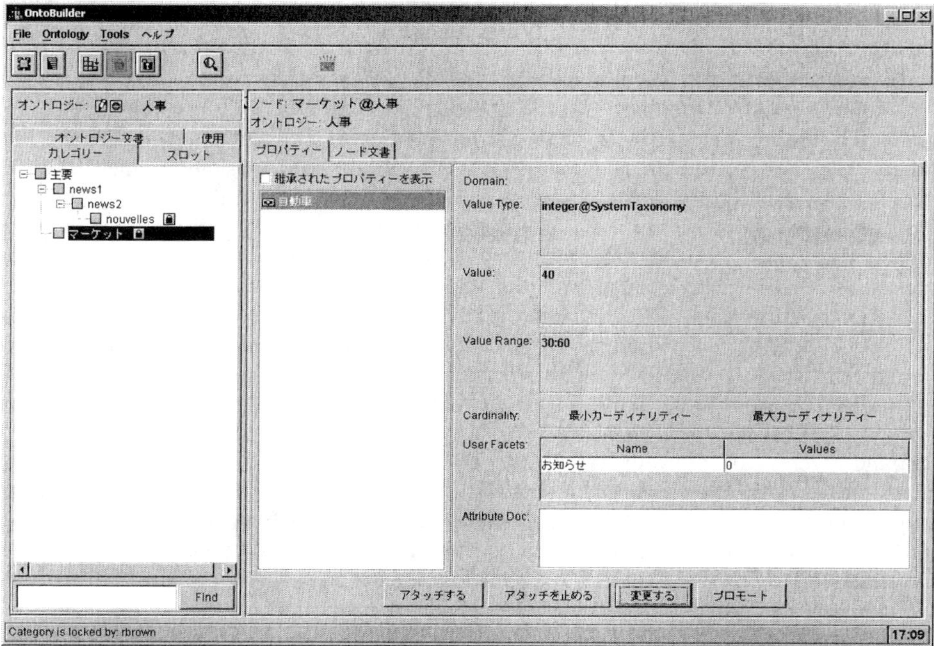

Figure 5: Ontology creation in Japanese

4.10 Import & Export

Ontology Builder provides import and export functionality based on XOL (XML based Ontology Exchange Language) [15]. XOL is based on OKBC-Lite, a simplified form of the OKBC knowledge model, and is "designed to provide a mechanism for encoding ontologies within a flat file that may be easily published on the WWW for exchange among a set of application developers." In Fall' 99, when the decision to use XOL was made, XOL was considered to be an emerging standard for exchange and publication of ontologies. Since, then other ontology representation and exchange standards such as RDF(S) and DAML+OIL have emerged or gained support and the W3C has started a web ontology working group within its semantic web activity to provide an ontology web language (OWL). -Future plans include supporting emerging standards such as these. The XOL DTD used by Ontology Builder has been modified to support internationalization, metaclass, uses, and facet definitions, which are not part of the original DTD.

5 Ontology Server

Ontology Server is a scalable, high-performance server and is a critical component for e-business applications that require ontologies to drive their services. It provides a very scalable, available, reliable, and high-performance solution. Ontology Server uses exactly the same architecture and representation as Ontology Builder and provides XML and Java RMI interfaces for access to the ontological data. It is optimized for read-only access, which facilitates the use of data-caching mechanisms to enhance performance, which is critical for e-business applications. Ontology Server defines its own interfaces, which are simpler and more suitable for e-business applications than the general OKBC interface.

6 Usage & Performance

Ontology Builder was released internally for use by Verticalnet ontologists and domain experts in April 2000, following a beta release in February 2000. The server - a Sun Ultra 1/60, 1 Gigabyte of RAM, with Oracle 8.0.4 - is hosted out of Palo Alto and accessed mainly from Horsham, Pennsylvania but it is also accessed from several other locations. Over the past year 84 different users have created 974 ontologies on the server. Concurrent usage peaked at about 20 users using the system at one time. The current database has over 5 million records, consisting of 650,000 classes, 480,000 slots, 680,000 frame-slot relations, 220,000 frame-slot-facet relations, 650,000 parent-child relations and 1,100,000 meta-class relations. Specific ontologies have been imported into various Ontology Servers to support e-business applications like spend analysis, services based event management, unified distributed catalogs, RFQ/RFP, auctions and structured negotiation.

Ontology Builder and Ontology Server both use the same architecture and back-end services. However, Ontology Server is optimized for read-only access to the ontological data and gives better performance than Ontology Builder for read operations. Figure 6, shows the performance graph for read operations for Ontology Server. 25 to 1000 clients were simulated accessing 100 different frames, each frame being accessed by each client 100 times. The performance tests were done on a Windows 2000 Pentium III (800 mHz) machine with 512 megabytes of RAM, using SQLServer 2000 default configuration without any tuning. Multiple clients were simulated using multiple threads on a Windows 2000 Pentium III (800 mHz) machine. The performance data is given for **average response time** - the time experienced by a client to retrieve a frame, including server processing time, networking delay, lookup and Java serialization/deserialization and for **overall requests per second** – the number of frame accesses per second or the server throughput.

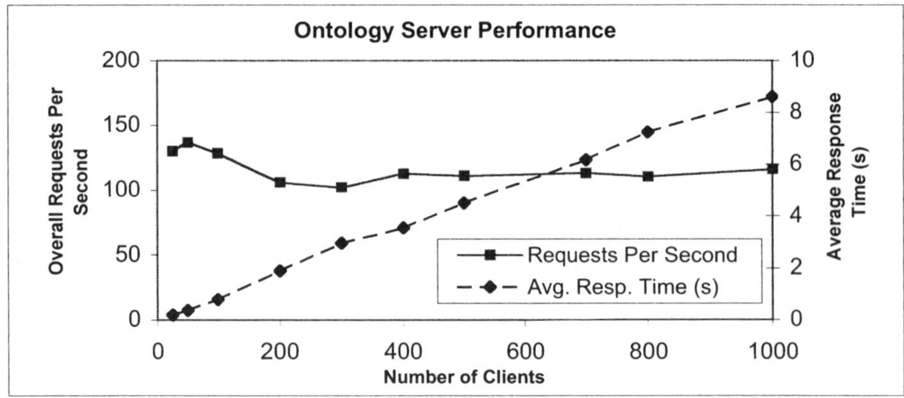

Figure 6: Performance graph for Ontology Server

The graph shows that as the number of clients increases, the throughput remains almost the same but the average response time increases, as now clients have to wait for previous requests from other clients to complete. The average response time for 200 users is about 2 seconds, but as the number of users increases the response time gets much longer, which may not be acceptable. To allow a more scalable solution multiple servers can be clustered together to handle thousands of users concurrently with a reasonable response time. The choice of application server can also significantly impact the response time and the server throughput as some application servers provide better performance and scalability than others. The choice of database and fine-tuning of the database can also increase performance and scalability.

Excluding the networking, serialization and lookup time, Ontology Server's **actual processing time** is only 1-3 milliseconds and does not vary significantly with the number of clients, once the frame has been initially loaded from the database. The initial loading time is about 20–250 milliseconds for each frame, depending on the number of slots, facets, class, parents, children and metaclass relations to be retrieved. Once retrieved, the application server caches the frame and subsequent requests to retrieve that frame take only 1-3 milliseconds regardless of the client requesting the frame. The number of frames to be cached can be specified as a parameter. Frames not being accessed for a while are cached out and replaced with the newly requested frames as the caching limit is reached. Since, all of our tables use primary keys, the size of the database and tables does not significantly increase the initial loading time of the frame. Figure 7, shows the access time in milliseconds for retrieving a bare frame (with no relational information) from the frame table with different sizes.

Figure 7: Access time for retrieving from database table with different sizes

Num. Of Rows	Min. Time	Max. Time	Avg. Time	Iterations
1000	3.12	14.45	7.2	200
10,000	3.84	17.12	7.75	200
100,000	3.23	15.78	9.35	200
1,000,000	4.52	19.35	11.85	200

Ontology Builder does not use caching for retrieving ontological data, but uses lazy loading to retrieve information as needed. Each piece of information is retrieved from the database every time it is requested. For the same machine configuration as described above, the **average response time** to retrieve a simple frame with parents, children, metaclasses and slots (without slot values and frame-slot-facets) is about 50 milliseconds, which translates into 20 read transactions per second. The average time to create a simple frame in Ontology Builder is about 35 milliseconds, which translates into 30 write transactions per second. In practice this level of performance for Ontology Builder has proved to be acceptable, as the ontology development and maintenance is not a performance intensive process. Clustering multiple servers, choice of application server and tuning the database can further improve Ontology Builder's performance.

7 Discussion

Ontologies are becoming much more common as a core component of e-business applications. Industrial strength solutions are needed and, in fact, critical for the success and longevity of these applications. We have presented two Vertical Net products: Ontology Builder and Ontology Server. We believe these products bring together the best knowledge management and ontology practices and the best enterprise architectures to provide industrial-strength solutions for ontology creation, maintenance, and deployment.

When evaluated against our initial product requirements, Ontology Builder and Ontology Server meet or surpass most of the requirements. Figure 8, shows this evaluation and compares Ontology Builder with the ontology environments compared in Figure 1. Even though we have provided reasonable solutions to most requirements, designated by a 0, we believe there is still considerable room for improvement and plan to continue to enhance functionality in these particular areas.

Figure 8: Comparison of Ontology Builder with other Ontology Environments

	Scalable Available Reliable	Ease of Use	Knowledge Representation	Multi User Collaboration	Security	Diff & Merge	Internationali zation	Versioning
Ontolingua/ Chimaera	-	-	+	0	-	+	-	-
Protégé/ PROMPT	-	0	+	-	-	+	-	-
WebOnto Tadzebao	-	0	+	+	-	-	-	-
OntoSaurus /Loom	-	-	+	0	-	-	-	-
Ontology Builder	+	0	0	0	0	0	+	-

We believe we have delivered a robust solution for our most critical requirements –scalability, availability, reliability and performance. By using an enterprise architecture (J2EE) and an enterprise RDBMS as the back end storage, we have provided an enterprise-class scalable, reliable, available, and high-performance ontology management solution.

The Ontology Builder client provides an easy-to-use interface for ontologists, domain experts, and business analysts. Though, we have not done formal usability studies, many domain experts and analysts have been able to use the tool productively, with a minimum of training and we plan to continue to enhance the user-interface based on user studies and analysis.

Our knowledge model is based on the OKBC knowledge model and provides flexibility and extensibility for incorporating new features and existing knowledge models. OntologyBuilder is only compliant with a subset of OKBC. Full compatibility along with support for emerging standards such as RDF and DAML+OIL are future plans.

We have provided a multi-user collaborative environment to facilitate the ontology building, sharing, and maintenance process. Collaborators can hold discussions and see changes committed by other users. The collaborative environment could be further improved by providing optimistic locking (where a frame is not allowed to be edited, only when it is being updated) instead of pessimistic locking. We are also investigating a more complete conferencing and whiteboarding solution, perhaps by integrating a third party tool like Microsoft NetMeeting (http://www.microsoft.com/windows/netmeeting/default.asp).

Our role-based security model provides data security, data integrity, user authentication and multiple levels of user access. A fine-grained model in which a set of permissions could be assigned to a user of a particular ontology has also been designed.

The difference and merging engine currently uses a simple algorithm. Future plans call for a more sophisticated difference and merging algorithm

Ontology Builder is fully internationalized and can be used in multiple languages and ontologies can be created and displayed in multiple locales.

Ontology Builder currently does not provide any versioning support. Versioning of ontologies is needed so that changes from one version to another can be tracked and managed and so that applications can determine what specific version of an ontology is being accessed. We hope to provide fine-grain versioning control functionality in the future.

Ontology Builder/Server have been used within Verticalnet to produce and maintain ontologies used in critical e-business applications such as spend analysis where ontologies are used to drive normalization, classification, and data cleansing processes for managing distributed heterogeneous business data and services based event management where ontologies are used to extend a web-service style architecture for service and process specifications. We view the tool suite as one of Verticalnet's differentiators in being able to offer cutting-edge intelligent e-business solutions.

8 Acknowledgements

We like to thank the many people who have contributed to these products - Mark Yang for design, Howard Liu, Don McKay, Keith Thurston, Lisa Colvin, Patrick Cassidy, Mike Malloy, Leo Orbst, Eric Elias, Craig Schlenoff, Eric Peterson for their use of the products and feedback, Joel Nava, Faisal Aslam, Hammad Sophie, Doug Cheseney, Nigel McKay for implementation, and Hugo Daley and Adam Cheyer for their support.

9 References

[1]　Neil F. Abernethy, Russ B. Altman, "SOPHIA: Providing basic knowledge services with a common DBMS", *Proceedings of the 5ᵗʰ KRDB Workshop*, Seattle, WA, 1998.

[2]　Dan Brickley & R.V.Guha, "Resource Description Framework (RDF) Schema Specification 1.0", World Wide Web Consortium, Cambridge, MA, 1999

[3]　Vinay Chaudhri, Adam Farquhar, Richard Fikes, Peter Karp, James Rice, "Open Knowledge Base Connectivity 2.0", Knowledge Systems Laboratory, 1998.

[4]　Dan Connolly, Frank van Harmelen, Ian Horrocks, Deborah L. McGuinness, Peter F. Patel-Schneider, and Lynn Andrea Stein. "DAML+OIL (March 2001) Reference Description". World Wide Web Committee (W3C) Note 18 December 2001. Also available from http://www.daml.org/2001/03/daml+oil-index.

[5]　J. Domingue, "Tadzebao and WebOnto: Discussing, Browsing, and Editing Ontologies on theWeb", *Proceedings of the Eleventh Workshop on Knowledge Acquisition, Modeling and Management*, Banff, Canada, 1998.

[6]　J. Duineveld, R. Stoter, M. R. Weiden, B. Kenepa & V. R. Benjamins, "WonderTools? A comparative study of ontological engineering tools", *Proceedings of the Twelfth Workshop on Knowledge Acquisition, Modeling and Management*, Banff, Canada, 1999.

[7]　Adam Farquhar, Richard Fikes, James Rice, "The Ontolingua Server: a Tool for Collaboartive Ontology Construction", *International Journal of Human-Computer Studies*, 46, 707-727, 1997.

[8]　Adam Farquhar, Richard Fikes, James Rice, "Tools for assembling modular ontologies in Ontolingua", Knowledge Systems Laboratory, Stanford University, April, 1997.

[9]　Dieter Fensel, Ian Horrocks, Frank van Harmelen, Deborah L. McGuinness, and Peter F. Patel-Schneider. ``OIL: An Ontology Infrastructure for the Semantic Web ''. In IEEE Intelligent Systems, Vol. 16, No. 2, March/April 2001.

[10]　Michael Genesereth and Richard Fikes, "Knowledge Interchange Format, Version 3.0 Reference Manual", Knowledge System Laboratory, Stanford University, 1992.

[11]　W. E. Grosso, H. Eriksson, R. W. Fergerson, J. H. Gennari, S. W. Tu, & M. A. Musen, "Knowledge Modeling at the Millennium (The Design and Evolution of Protege-2000)". *Twelfth Banff Workshop on Knowledge Acquisition, Modeling, and Management*. Banff, Alberta, 1999.

[12]　James Hendler and Deborah L. McGuinness, ``The DARPA Agent Markup Language''. *IEEE Intelligent Systems*, Vol. 15, No. 6, November/December 2000, pages 67-73.

[13]　ISX Corporation (1991). "LOOM Users Guide, Version 1.4".

[14]   Peter D. Karp, "The design space of frame knowledge representation systems", Technical Report 520, SRI International AI Center, 1992.

[15]   Peter D. Karp, Vinay K. Chaudhri, and Jerome F. Thomere, "XOL: An XML-Based Ontology Exchange Language," Technical Note 559, AI Center, SRI International, 1999.

[16]   Ora Lassila & Ralph Swick, "Resource Description Framework (RDF) Model and Syntax Specification", W3C Recommendation 22 February 1999, World Wide Web Consortium, Cambridge (MA); available on-line as http://www.w3.org/TR/REC-rdf-syntax/.

[17]   Deborah L. McGuinness ``Ontologies and Online Commerce". In IEEE Intelligent Systems, Vol. 16, No. 1, January/February 2001, pages 8-14.

[18]   Deborah L. McGuinness. "Ontologies Come of Age". To appear in D. Fensel, J. Hendler, H. Lieberman, and W. Wahlster (editors). Semantic Web Technology, MIT Press, Boston, Mass., 2002.

[19]   Deborah L. McGuinness, Richard Fikes, James Rice, and Steve Wilder, "An Environment for Merging and Testing Large Ontologies. *Proceedings of the Seventh International Conference on Principles of Knowledge Representation and Reasoning,* Breckenridge, Colorado, April 2000.

[20]   Deborah L. McGuinness, Richard Fikes, James Rice, and Steve Wilder, "The Chimaera Ontology Environment", *Proceedings of the The Seventeenth National Conference on Artificial Intelligence,* Austin, Texas, July 2000.

[21]   Deborah L. McGuinness, Richard Fikes, Lynn Andrea Stein, and James Hendler. ``DAML-ONT: An Ontology Language for the Semantic Web ". To appear in Dieter Fensel, Jim Hendler, Henry Lieberman, and Wolfgang Wahlster, editors. The Semantic Web: Why, What, and How, MIT Press, 2002.

[22]   Natalya F. Noy & Mark A. Musen, "SMART: Automated Support for Ontology Merging and Alignment", *Proceedings of the Twelfth Workshop on Knowledge Acquisition, Modeling and Management*, Banff, Canada, July 1999.

[23]   Natalya F. Noy & Mark A. Musen, "PROMPT: Algorithm and Tool for Automated Ontology Merging and Alignment", *Seventeenth National Conference on Artificial Intelligence*, Austin, Texas, 2000.

[24]   Protégé Users Guide, http://www.smi.stanford.edu/projects/protege/doc/users_guide/index.html

[25]   Navi Radjou, Bill Doyle, Stuart Woodring, Marli Porth "The X Internet Invigorates B2B apps", The Forrester Report. Cambridge, Mass., October 2001.

[26]   Kilian Stoffel, Merwyn Taylor, James Hendler, "Efficient Management of Very Large Ontologies", *Proceedings of American Association for Artificial Intelligence Conference*, (AAAI-97), AAAI/MIT Press 1997.

The Emerging Semantic Web
I.F. Cruz et al. (Eds.)
IOS Press, 2002

The Semantic Web As "Perfection Seeking": A View from Drug Terminology

Mark S. Tuttle, *Apelon, Inc.*, <u>mtuttle@apelon.com</u>
Steven H. Brown, MD, *Vanderbilt University / Veterans Administration*
Keith E. Campbell, MD, PhD, *Inoveon, Inc.*
John S. Carter, *University of Utah / Apelon, Inc.*
Kevin D. Keck, *Keck Labs*
Michael Lincoln, MD, *University of Utah / Veterans Administration*
Stuart J. Nelson, MD, *National Library of Medicine*
Michael Stonebraker, PhD, *Massachusetts Institute of Technology*

Abstract. To date, the Semantic Web has viewed formal terminology, or ontology, as either immutable, or something that can change but that has no past and no future – only a present. Change, or process – such as "perfection seeking," is outside the scope of the proposed "semantics," except in so far as it is represented in attributes. In contrast, current U.S. Government efforts to formalize drug (medication) terminology are being driven by the need to manage changes in this terminology asynchronously and longitudinally. For example, each year the FDA (Federal Drug Administration) approves about 150 new drugs and thousands of changes to the "label" of existing drugs, the VHA (Veterans Health Administration) must manage new drugs, label changes, and tens of thousands of drug "packaging" changes, and the NLM (National Library of Medicine) must maintain a current index of references to proposed or approved medications in the world's biomedical literature. We propose that an emerging multi-federal-agency reference terminology model for medications, mRT, be used to drive development of the necessary repertoire of "semantic" change management mechanisms for the Semantic Web, and that these "process" mechanisms be organized into an ontology of change.

1. Overview – Using mRT to drive the development of Semantic Web change management

Creating standards, especially standards that create information industry infrastructure, is difficult, time-consuming and at constant risk for irrelevance and failure. One way to mitigate this risk, and secure the participation of the diverse interest groups required to make such standards a success is to focus on process – as in the process that produces and maintains a good standard. This is in contrast to an approach that says some existing artifact selected from a list will be THE standard, and all the others will NOT be the standard. An observation that we attribute to Betsy Humphreys from the National Library of Medicine in the context of biomedical terminology standards is that it doesn't matter where you start, i.e., it doesn't much matter which terminology or terminologies one selects as a starting point; instead what does matter is the process by which the proposed standard evolves to achieve and sustain the desired degree of quality, comprehensiveness, and functionality. The process is what determines where the standard ends up.

Seen in this light, change, even a large amount of change, will be a feature of successful formal terminologies, or ontologies. We hope to demonstrate the feasibility and utility of this approach. The challenge in the context of the Semantic Web is to choose a representation for change that makes it explicit. Viewed this way the Semantic Web would be "perfection seeking,"[1] and the ongoing changes would be part of the semantics. The challenge with this approach is the formulation of the units of change and the creation of an ontology of these change units. This follows a Semantic Web notion expressed by Tim Berners-Lee in a discussion of Metadata Architecture [1] "… metadata itself may have attributes such as ownership and an expiry date, and so there is meta-metadata but we don't distinguish many levels, we just say that metadata is data and that from that it follows that it can have other data about itself. This gives the Web a certain consistency." Making change part of the Semantic Web would preserve that consistency.

One way to focus the development of the desired units, inter-relationships, and uses is to solve real problems and gain experience from deployments of these solutions; we propose to do this by formulating, deploying and evaluating what we now call "The New Drug Transaction." This transaction needs to supply diverse, operating healthcare and biomedical information systems with the requisite formal definition of a new drug, given a reference model, and do so at Web scale. The main challenge is how to do this in a way that first avoids breaking working applications that use the drug terminology and second preserves the longitudinal value of existing and future patient descriptions of medication use.

More generally, healthcare and biomedicine undergo constant change – some of it perfection seeking and some of it clerical – and the relevant terminology needs to change in parallel. Again, the challenge is to the extent possible to accommodate change without breaking what already works, and without losing the value of historical data.

A simple, large-scale model of longitudinal change management is that used by MEDLINE, the National Library of Medicine's citation database (http://www.ncbi.nlm.nih.gov/entrez/query.fcgi). The formal "semantics" of MEDLINE are supported by MeSH (Medical Subject Headings), a concept-based biomedical terminology that is updated annually (http://www.nlm.nih.gov/mesh/meshhome.html). Each year, rules are written that transform citations indexed using the previous year's MeSH into citations indexed using the new version of MeSH. In this way, by "re-writing history," old citations can be retrieved as appropriate using current terminology. As can be appreciated, formulating the rules requires manual intervention and testing, but more than 11 million citations, each tagged with about a dozen index terms selected from some 18,000 concepts, are maintained longitudinally in this way. While MEDLINE has always been a pre-eminent and exemplar information retrieval system, the notion of "history re-writing" implies a loss of information; the declining cost of secondary storage may eliminate one of the reasons for such information loss, a theme that will be re-examined below.

2. Background - The Semantic Web is a generalization of formalization efforts already underway in healthcare and biomedicine

In his recent Scientific American article Berners-Lee argues that the Semantic Web is infrastructure, and not an application [2]. We couldn't agree more. To us, this view is a top-down and horizontal approach to Semantic Web objectives, and it is this kind of disciplined thinking that made the Web the success that it is today.

In parallel with this effort, progress toward related goals is occurring in healthcare and biomedicine and we think of this progress as bottom-up and vertical. Thus, at present,

---

[1] Peri Schuyler, then head of the MeSH (Medical Subject Headings) at the NLM, used this term in the context of the UMLS (Unified Medical Language System) Project in 1988.

healthcare and biomedicine have a repertoire of standard terminologies and standard messages and, in some instances, their use is or will be mandated by law.[2] While current deployments of these artifacts lack the formality required for the Semantic Web they nevertheless represent a rehearsal of many of the processes that the Semantic Web will require. Further, as will be described in a later section, the shortfalls of current healthcare terminology and message standards are driving a new generation of healthcare terminologies and messages that do have some of the desired formal properties. All this is part of a gradual evolution in healthcare information technology that is changing its focus from "systems" to "data," [3] [4] a trend predicted in [5]. The authors believe that the major forcing function for this evolution is the need to "scale" healthcare information technology to ever larger enterprises and collections of individuals and enterprises; while this trend began before the Web, the presence of the Web has accelerated the change.

What is missing in healthcare and biomedicine is a way to link its relevant progress and experience with that occurring in the Semantic Web community. The Web influences healthcare information technology, but the Web is little influenced by lessons learned in healthcare IT. We believe that medications represent a domain in which these two activities can be joined productively. The potential significance of such a joining cannot be over-estimated. Healthcare now costs the U.S. more than $1 trillion/year, and medications are the largest single category of cost and the fastest growing category of cost.[3] They are also involved in a significant number of life-threatening medical errors. [6]

At a deeper level, we believe that the Semantic Web is an opportunity to shrink the "formalization gap" described by Marsden S. Blois, PhD, MD (1918-88). Blois argued that overcoming this gap was the fundamental challenge of medical informatics: 'This discontinuity in formalization between a manual (human) medical information process and the machine code necessary to accomplish comparable ends begins at a very high descriptive level and it is not itself a concern of computer science. If this concern is to be given a name at all, it must be regarded as concerning medical applications, and it is increasingly being referred to as "medical information science" in the United States, and as "medical informatics" in Europe. It will be the task of this new discipline to better understand and define the medical information processes we have considered here, in order that appropriate activities will be chosen for computerization, and to improve the man-machine system.' [7] One rationale for a "perfection seeking" approach to the Semantic Web is the difficulty of getting the formalizations right, and of maintaining them, and the patient descriptions based on them, in the face of change.

---

[2] HIPAA (Health Insurance Portability and Accountability Act).
[3] Last year, VHA (Veterans Health Association) spent about $2.5 billion on medications, and MHS (Military Health System – covering active duty personnel and their dependents) spent about $1.5 billion. Personal conversation, Donald Lees, RPh, 6/01.

                    M.S. Tuttle et al. / The Semantic Web as "Perfection Seeking"

3. A model - semantic definitions for medication active ingredients

If change management were not such a critical issue, already complete approximations of the medication reference model shown in *Figure 1* could be used by Semantic Web developers to test proposed representations. Carter, et al. [8] describe how about 1,000 active ingredients

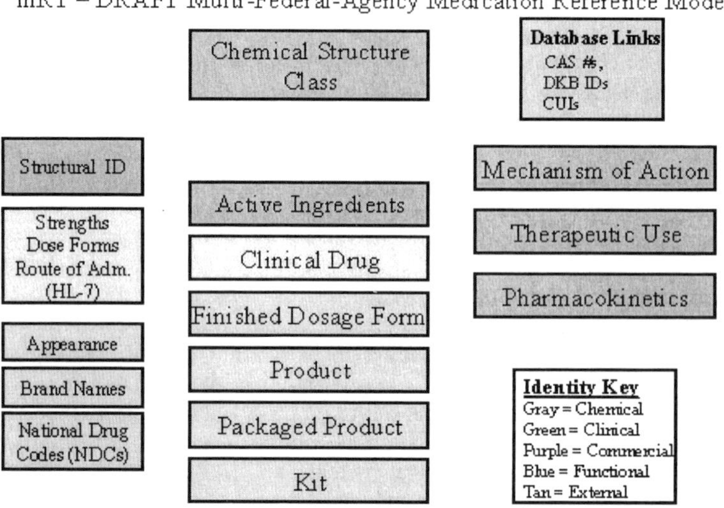

were given "Aristotelian" definitions represented in Description Logic and "published" in XML. One result of this effort was a focus on the emerging importance of "The New Drug Transaction" as a necessary conjunct to expansion of the model to cover all important active ingredients, and to trial deployments.

Figure 1 – DRAFT formal model of medications for potential use by three Federal Agencies: Active ingredients have "Aristotelian" definitions represented using Description Logic; these definitions will place each Active Ingredient in an IS_A hierarchy of Chemical Structure Classes, and describe each Active Ingredient using named relationships into reference taxonomies for, respectively, Mechanism of Action, Therapeutic Use, and Pharmacokinetics. Each Active Ingredient (molecule) will also have a machine-processible three-dimensional structural description (identifier). Not shown are inactive ingredients and other necessary details.

This model, developed over the last few years, has proven remarkably robust in the face of multi-disciplinary and multi-institutional inspection, and sample instantiations. Its next test will be to represent portions of various order-entry formularies used by the public and private sectors. A typical formulary covers about 10,000 – 100,000 "orderables" and the goal will be to produce "useful" definitions of the active ingredients contained in these orderables using early versions of the reference taxonomies for Chemical Structure, Mechanism of Action, Therapeutic Use, and Pharmacokinetics. This test will also allow us to gain experience assembling and formalizing medication information obtained from multiple authorities and disciplines that is used for related but still different purposes. For example, there will be at least three different kinds of "Therapeutic Use," also called "indications" – "FDA approved", "VA approved"(generally a superset of FDA approved), and "Described in the Literature".[4] The whole notion of "orderables" will also force clarification of the boundary between the so-called "terminology model" (categories and hierarchies) and the "instance" or "database" model (the orderables themselves, along with all their attributes). Everyone agrees that that the former is a good way to organize the latter, and that there should be a boundary between the two models – that is, the two models are similar and related but not the same, but few agree on where the implementation boundary should be, especially in light of emerging interoperation requirements based on re-usable objects. This dilemma should resonate with those working on the Semantic Web.

4. A process – embracing change and making it explicit

The model presented in Figure 1 is little more than an academic exercise without accompanying productive change management. Currently, excepting MeSH and MEDLINE (described above), change management in authoritative, deployed biomedical terminologies is at best primitive. [9] [10] As a result, there are few "warehouses" of patient descriptions that can be searched over time, that is across changes in the terminologies used to formalize the descriptions. Of the few patient description repositories that support such "time travel" no two do so in the same way, and none use existing or proposed standards. An explicit goal of the mRT project is to begin to overcome this shortfall at least in the context of medications.

The view of change management presented here is a synthesis of current and emerging practices in healthcare terminology, e.g., the use of Description Logic, earlier and current work on the handling of time-oriented data in database system models, e.g., POSTGRES [11] and T-SQL [12] [13], and our current understanding of the Semantic Web. This synthesis can be summed up by the conclusion that "Process is more important than representation."

4.1 A "new drug" transaction

The first step in making formal terminology changes into a terminology/ontology "thing," or unit, is to create a unit of change that has the same general properties as any other "thing-ness" unit. For example, given the appropriate reference taxonomies, used to (in the Description Logic sense) "classify" medications, one can create the desired reference terminology – mRT – by "adding" the (Aristotelian) definitions of each drug, one drug at a time. But, of course, this ignores, among many other things, the fact that the reference taxonomies need to be changed, too. Frequently, new drugs come with new mechanisms of action and new indications (therapeutic objectives), and thus the corresponding "new drug transaction" may need to update the reference taxonomies before adding the definition of the new drug. These latter cases will be covered in "Other transactions" below.

To make the simple case more tangible, here is one potential near term future of the kind of "New Drug Transaction" that does not require updating the reference taxonomies:

---

[4] An important side-effect of this effort will be an authoritative collection of so-called "off-label" uses of medications; such uses represent legal, but not FDA-approved, medication indications.

1) The FDA will approve a new drug and "publish," as XML, a newly "structured" version of the traditional package insert, or "label," designed to "explain" that drug to both humans and computers. (One can think of this document as a "contract" between the FDA and the drug manufacturer.) The data that will appear in the new drug transaction is the result of processes now in place at the FDA; regulations are pending that will increase the degree of machine-processibility and formality of this data. [14]

2) The NLM will further process and enhance the parts of the label that can be processed usefully by computers, and then "publish" it, once again in XML. The "enhancements" may include connections to the biomedical literature, related terminology and foreign language names.

3) Applications or servers electing to process the new drug transaction will see that the XML indicates that it is an "add," the simplest kind of transaction to process. That is, the transaction will add a new concept – the new drug, the appropriate relationships to other concepts in the various reference taxonomies, and attributes of the new drug. (In every formulary or medication reference terminology known to the authors this is done manually, at present.)

It is not hard to imagine that most applications, e.g., drug order-entry systems, would be tolerant of such an insertion and subsequently "do the right thing." However, the problem with this simple form of the new drug transaction is that, as described by domain experts, most new drugs represent "changes in understanding," and it is not at all clear how existing applications can deal with such changes in understanding automatically, or know when they need help from humans. An extreme instance of such new understanding would be a drug that triggered a reorganization of the Aristotelian classification of existing drugs. (Changes in understanding due to pharmacogenetics may cause these kinds of "re-organizing" updates.)

4.2 Other transactions

In this context, "changes in understanding" are represented by changes in the reference taxonomies, e.g., for chemical structure, mechanism of action, pharmacokinetics, and therapeutic use. That is, a typical "new drug transaction" will need to include one or more changes to the reference taxonomies along with the (simple) "add" described above, and these changes will represent "changes in understanding." It can be assumed that changes to the reference taxonomies will "break" existing applications, e.g., the decision support that operates in conjunction with order entry. The authors claim that to the degree that we can overcome this problem in the context of medication terminology maintenance that we are solving a problem that will be faced by the Semantic Web.

As presently planned our solution will be built on two foundations: First, mRT will not "overwrite" information; that is, per POSTGRES [15] any "garbage collection" or "archiving" will be handled asynchronously with new drug transactions, the practical effect being that an explicit, time-oriented, history of mRT is available to applications at all times. Second, appropriate use of Description Logic permits consistency-preserving updates; for example, if prior to execution of the new drug transaction an off-line, an updated copy of mRT is "reclassified" successfully (in the DL sense), then, in principle, mechanisms exist that can correctly update a run-time database (terminology server) "incrementally" (and thus quickly). Thus, such updates represent one useful repertoire of units of change.

Per earlier work of Stonebraker, et al. and more recent work of Snodgrass, et al., one can view a "database" as a time-oriented accumulation of changes. Thus the current "state" of the database is acquired through a computation, or "view," on the transactions accumulated over time. (See [13], for an enumeration of the many subtleties implicit here.) Part of the desired functionality is implemented, currently, in the MEME (Metathesaurus Enhancement and Maintenance Environment) deployed at the NLM. [16] The Metathesaurus (http://www.nlm.nih.gov/pubs/factsheets/umlsmeta.html) is a gigabyte+ synthesis of most authoritative biomedical terminologies, now released multiple times per year. Increasingly, a "release" is becoming a report on a time-oriented database.[5] Gradually, the whole notion of a "release" will become less important, and, instead, the Metathesaurus will be seen as a time-oriented record – a no-information-loss history – of authoritative terminologies. Of interest to those trying to deploy solutions on the Semantic Web, in run-time systems, use of incremental "write-once / read-many" databases make locking and error recovery significantly simpler.

We expect that the simple new drug transaction will be the easiest formal unit of change to specify. Quantitatively, the most important unit of change will be a transaction that introduces a change to the definition of an existing medication. For practical reasons the latter transactions are both the most important to accommodate in existing medication order entry systems and the most difficult. Frequently, they affect how drugs are to be used, e.g., the change may be a new contraindication.

Complicating this approach are the presence of larger changes-in-understanding – so-called "lumps" and "splits" - that, seemingly, violate the "axioms" implicit or explicit in DL tools. "Splits" occur when a concept is "split" into two or more concepts, typically because of the emergence of new knowledge. The latter may be new concepts or existing concepts. And the original concept that is split may be retired, or it may be retained as a subsumer of the "split" concepts. Splits are most often prompted by new information system needs, related to the emergence of new knowledge. Similarly, "lumps" – the merging of two previously distinct concepts – is usually prompted by the detection of clerical errors, or by the discovery that two things we thought were different proved not to be. As will be appreciated by those who favor the use of Description Logic (DL) in these contexts, a feature of DL, namely its support for formal definitions, helps to decrease the number of inadvertent "missed synonyms". Alternatively, some less mature domains, e.g., Bioinformatics, avoid the problem by using terminologies in which terms are freely lumped or split as needs dictate.

4.3 An ontology of change

If we view a formal terminology or ontology as a corpus of "facts," or assertions, collected over time, then one can contemplate an ontology of such facts, or changes. This much is straightforward. The difficulty is defining and implementing the semantics to be attached to each type of "change unit." One step toward such semantics is the simple expedient of tagging each terminologic unit – concept, term, relationship, and attribute - with a "Start Date" and (any) "End Date"; then, in principle, an application can know the state of the terminology at any point in time. More disciplined and complete forms of such semantics are what are needed to preserve the longitudinal functionality of systems that use the ontology, and what will be needed to transfer knowledge gained from a successful test of the new drug transaction to the Semantic Web.

In the MEDLINE - "rewriting history" - example described above, semi-automated methods accommodate the effects of new concepts, retired concepts, split concepts and lumped concepts in MeSH, as best as can be done each year. Thus, one "blunt instrument" approach to

---

[5] Brian Carlsen, personal conversation.

the analogous problem in the Semantic Web is for every repository of historical information to have a companion "warehouse" that is consistent with the current relevant ontologies. The semantics of change are then implemented in the potentially frequent re-computation of this warehouse, as appropriate. The companion argument here is that so-called Clinical Data Repositories (CDRs) and some biomedical research databases are being implemented as "write-only" databases because they represent the authoritative archive of record. Any so-called "data-healing" is done outside the CDR in adjacent data warehouses that are built from queries that run against the authoritative archive. Such pragmatics may evolve into functional requirements for the Semantic Web.

Regardless, the challenge posed by "ontologizing" these units of change is to represent what, for example, should be inherited or shared by other units. Thus, the new drug transaction is a specialized version of the change transaction and thus should inherit any properties of the former. At present, it is not clear how "split" and "lump" should be handled, formally.

4.4 "Perfection Seeking"

While the notion of "perfection seeking" has been very helpful in that it helps those in an inter-disciplinary project "satisfice" in particular domains so as to make progress toward the over-all goal, it has not yet been formalized, e.g., in the form of a metric. At present, terminology and terminology process are bereft of quality metrics. One exception is some work by Campbell, et al., that measured the degree to which lexically implied subsumption (one term appearing within, or sharing sub-strings with, another term) had been represented logically, i.e., in DL, in a large healthcare terminology. [17] While the metric was aimed at measuring the yield of "lexically suggested logical closure" it also revealed the degree to which the lexical suggestions were not converted to logical relationships, e.g., because of linguistic ambiguity.

A related hypothesis was that expressed by Blois, namely that conceptualization and naming was more stable and predictable at "lower" biological levels, e.g., for molecules. [18] Thus, we would expect fewer synonyms and fewer changes to the Chemical Structure portion of the formal definitions of ingredients.

The fact remains, however, that we've yet to "formalize" (or even measure) perfection-seeking to any useful degree. It is still an entirely human process. However, there is some evidence that tools can aid formalization and while doing so improve conceptualization. [19] [20] Specifically, when a user, in this case a physician, is given the task of entering a formal term for a patient "problem," an interface that displays potentially related formal terms in response to the input of a casual term can help the user better conceptualize the concept being entered. Thus, even when the user interface returns an exact equivalent for the casual term, users may choose a "better" formal term from the displayed semantic neighborhood. The simple explanation for this phenomenon is that humans are better at recognition than recall. Those developing ontologies will be familiar with the phenomenon; once domain experts can "see" a domain model they can almost always make it better.

4.5 Architecture, tools and the local enhancement problem

Implicit in much that has been written here is the architectural notion of vocabulary servers, or in this context, formal terminology or ontology servers. That is, such servers "normalize" terminology functions for enterprises, some at Web scale. [See for example the National Cancer Institute's EVS (Enterprise Vocabulary Server) http://ncievs.nci.nih.gov/NCI-

Metaphrase.html] We believe that such servers will be essential to the support of the Semantic Web, and as usual on the Web, the challenge will be how to maintain them in loose synchrony as appropriate.

A clear result of experience to date shows that terminology development, especially formal terminology development cannot be undertaken for long without non-trivial supporting tools and software. Foremost among the required tools is a scalable terminology editing workstation, one evolutionary sequence of which was begun by Mays, et al. [21] The fact that formal terminologies will almost always be constructed and maintained by geographically separated domain experts implies additional requirements for "configuration management," conflict resolution, and the like. One approach to these problems is described in [22]. Further, experience in both the U.S. and United Kingdom has shown that the rate-limiting factor for large-scale terminology development is workflow management, rather than the editing work itself.

One short-term reality is the need for what we call "local enhancement." In the healthcare domain, enterprises will have some locally produced, i.e. "locally mixed and prepared," medications for the foreseeable future, and academic medical centers will always have new terms and concepts in substantive use locally. For these and other reasons, an authoritative reference terminology will need to be enhanced locally. The so-called "update paradox" is that those who add the greatest quantity of local enhancements incur the greatest maintenance burden as the external terminology authority evolves. This tradeoff is made more complex by external reimbursement and reporting requirements.

5. Additional exemplars - reference terminologies and semantic messages in healthcare and biomedicine

In response to the shortfalls of current authoritative biomedical terminologies a number of efforts are underway focused on the development of so-called "principled" reference terminologies. For the purposes of this paper the "principles" in question are those that are computer-empowering, indeed the whole point of a reference terminology is to empower computers, particularly, as with the Semantic Web, to empower computer-to-computer interoperation. Several examples are represented in Figure 2.

Emerging Reference Models

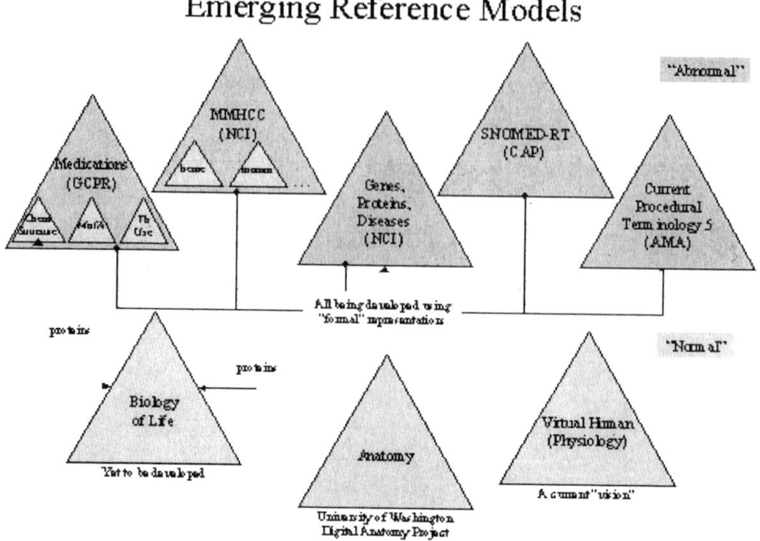

Figure 2 – Emerging Reference Terminologies in Biomedicine: The GCPRMedications reference terminology defined some 1,000 medication active ingredients in terms of Chemical Structure Class, Mechanism of Action, and Therapeutic Use. The NCI MMHCC (Mouse Models of Human Cancer Consortium) is developing detailed diagnostic terminologies for eight organ sites in mice, as a prelude to "certification" of the models as representative of human cancer behavior. NCI is also "modeling" about 250 genes known to be associated with cancer; in particular the association between these genes, the proteins they produce (or do not produce), and diseases is being made explicit. SNOMED-RT is a large (100K+ concept) effort by CAP (College of American Pathologists) and Kaiser Permanente Healthcare to "formalize" SNOMED International (SNOMED = Systematic Nomenclature of Medicine). The AMA (American Medical Association) is formalizing CPT-4 (Current Procedural Terminology). Each of these efforts employs a Description-Logic-based representation. The modular approach implied by this repertoire of reference terminologies in turn creates a need for a reference terminology for Biology that would represent the considerable commonality in, for instance, mice and humans. Similarly, a formal model of human anatomy being developed by Rosse, et al., at the University of Washington may evolve into a reference terminology for vertebrate anatomy as a way to, again, capture inter-species commonality for reuse in other models. A terminology model of Physiology, now being contemplated by some groups, may represent another piece of the "normal" reference model. Not shown is a laboratory testing method terminology being developed by the CDC (Centers for Disease Control and Prevention) .[23]

As recently as a few years ago such a (relative) "explosion" of formal terminology efforts would have been inconceivable. Now such efforts are taking on, in specific domains, the challenge implied by the Semantic Web, namely the development of ontologies for specified domains. Early versions of some of these terminologies are being deployed this year.

HL7, version 3 (http://www.hl7.org/page.cfm?p=524), is a proposed standard for semantic messages in healthcare. It builds on the widely deployed HL7, version 2, standard syntax by using "value sets" taken from external, authoritative, formal terminologies.

6. Summary – healthcare and biomedicine are a rehearsal for the Semantic Web

We are building on our experience with the use of formalization processes for update management in critical working systems. We believe that the challenges we face are specialized equivalents of challenges to be faced by Semantic Web developers as more and more sophisticated systems are deployed and become critical. Among other things these experiences reveal the critical role of process, and that this process needs to be made explicit and intrinsic. We are attempting to fulfill this requirement through the development of an ontology of change, and a recognition that process is more important than representation. If successful, the Semantic Web community may be able to generalize this ontology sufficiently to allow it to be migrated into the "horizontal" Semantic Web infrastructure, and support a "perfection-seeking" Semantic Web.

Acknowledgements

This work was partially supported by Contracts with NLM (National Library of Medicine), NCI (National Cancer Institute), and GCPR (Government Computer-based Patient Record). The GCPR (Government Computer-based Patient Record) medication Reference Terminology Model project team also included Ha Nguyen and Joanne Wong, University of California Berkeley, Munn Maung, University of California Davis, Maung Than, Tun Tun Naing, Apelon, Richard Dixon, MD, FACP and Joe Awad, MD, Vanderbilt. Also contributing were Betsy Humphreys, MLS, William T. Hole, MD, Suresh Srinivasan, PhD, Alexa McCray, PhD, Frank Hartel, PhD, Sherri De Coronado, Robert Cardiff, MD, PhD, Scott Kogan, MD, Mark Erlbaum, MD, David Sperzel, MD, David Sherertz, Brian Carlsen, Cornelius Rosse, MD, DrSc, and Randy Levin, MD, and several others at the FDA (Food and Drug Administration), though as customary they should not be held responsible. Eric Mays, PhD and Bob Dionne from Apelon clarified some of the utility of Description Logic. Important feedback regarding the utility of the model presented in Figure 1 was received from the HL7 Vocabulary Committee and from NCVHS (National Committee on Vital and Health Statistics), including assistance from Jeff Blair, Stan Huff, MD, Christopher Chute, MD, DrPH, James Cimino, MD, Jeff Blair, Ed Hammond, PhD, Michael Fitzmaurice, PhD, Joan Kapusnick-Uner, PharmD, and William Braithwaite, MD. Related material was presented at Pharmacology Grand Rounds Vanderbilt University, Informatics Seminars at the University of Utah, the University of California San Francisco, and the University of California Davis, and also at the Department of Defense, the FDA (Federal Drug Administration), the HL7 (Health Level 7) Vocabulary Standards Committee, and TEPR (Toward Electronic Patient Record) 2001.

References

[1]   Berners-Lee, T., "Metadata Architecture," W3C, January 6, 1997.
[2]   Berners-Lee, T., Hendler, James, Lassila, Dra, "The Semantic Web," Scientific American, May, 2001.
[3]   Tuttle, MS, Information technology outside health care: what does it matter to us? J Am Med Inform Assoc. 1999 Sep-Oct;6(5):354-60.
[4]   Kuhn, KA, Guise, DA, "Review: From Hospital Information Systems to Health Information Systems – Problems, Challenges, Perspectives," Haux, R, Kulikowski, C., Editors, *Yearbook of Medical Informatics 2001*, Schattuer, pp 63-76.
[5]   Brodie, Michael L., M. Stonebraker, *Migrating Legacy Systems: Gateways, Interfaces and the Incremental Approach*, Freeman, 1995.
[6]   Kohn, L., J. Corrigan, and M. Donaldson, *To Err is Human: Building a Safer Health System*. 2000, Institute of Medicine Report, Washington, DC: National Academy Press, 2000.
[7]   Blois, M.S., ***Information and Medicine: The Nature of Medical Descriptions*** (University of California Press, 1984), p. 284.

[8]   Carter, J., et al., "The Creation and Use of a Reference Terminology for Inter-Agency Computer-based Patient Records: The GCPR RTM Demonstration Project," Fall AMIA Symposium, 2001 (to be presented).

[9]   Cimino, JJ, An approach to coping with the annual changes in ICD9-CM., Methods Inf Med. 1996 Sep;35(3):220.

[10]   Tuttle, MS, Nelson, SJ, A poor precedent. Methods Inf Med. 1996 Sep;35(3):211-7. (A companion article to [9] above.)

[11]   Michael Stonebraker. ``The POSTGRES Next-Generation Database Management System", *CACM*, 34(10)78-93, October 1991. (Available on-line at http://www.acm.org/pubs/articles/journals/cacm/1991-34-10/p78-stonebraker/p78-stonebraker.pdf.)

[12]   Snodgrass, RT, ed., *The TSQL2 Temporal Query Language*, Kluwer, Boston, 1995. http://www.wkap.nl/kapis/CGI-BIN/WORLD/book.htm?0-7923-9614-6

[13]   Snodgrass, RT, *Developing Time-Oriented Database Applications in SQL*, Morgan Kaufman, 1999.

[14]   Randy Levin, MD, personal conversation.

[15]   Michael Stonebraker, "The Design of the POSTGRES Storage System," Proceedings of the 13th VLDB Conference, Brighton 1987, pp. 289-300. (Available on-line at http://www.informatik.uni-trier.de/~ley/db/conf/vldb/Stonebraker87.html.)

[16]   Suarez-Munist, O, et al., "MEME-II supports the cooperative management of terminology. Proc AMIA Annu Fall Symp. 1996;:84-8.

[17]   Campbell, KE, Tuttle, MS, Spackman, KA, A "lexically-suggested logical closure" metric for medical terminology maturity. Proc AMIA Symp 1998;:785-9.

[18]   Blois, MS, Medicine and the nature of vertical reasoning. N Engl J Med. 1988 Mar 31;318(13):847-51.

[19]   Tuttle, MS, et al., "Metaphrase: an aid to the clinical conceptualization and formalization of patient problems in healthcare enterprises" Methods Inf Med. 1998 Nov;37(4-5):373-83.

[20]   Cimino, JJ, Patel, VL, Kushniruk, AW, Studying the human-computer-terminology interface. J Am Med Inform Assoc. 2001 Mar-Apr;8(2):163-73.

[21]   Mays, E, et al., Scalable and expressive medical terminologies. Proc AMIA Annu Fall Symp. 1996;:259-63.

[22]   Campbell, KE, *Distributed Development of a Logic-Based Controlled Medical Terminology* (CS-TR-97-1596). Dissertation available from elib.Stanford.ledu, Stanford: Stanford University.

[23]   Steindel, Steven, Granade, SE, "Monitoring Quality Requires Knowing Similarity: The NICLTS Experience," Fall AMIA Symposium, 2001 (to be presented).

DAML-S: Semantic Markup For Web Services

The DAML Services Coalition[1]:
Anupriya Ankolekar[2], Mark Burstein[3], Jerry R. Hobbs[4], Ora Lassila[5],
David L. Martin[4], Sheila A. McIlraith[6], Srini Narayanan[4], Massimo Paolucci[2],
Terry Payne[2], Katia Sycara[2], Honglei Zeng[6]

Abstract.

The Semantic Web should enable greater access not only to content but also to services on the Web. Users and software agents should be able to discover, invoke, compose, and monitor Web resources offering particular services and having particular properties. As part of the DARPA Agent Markup Language program, we have begun to develop DAML-S, a DAML+OIL ontology for describing the properties and capabilities of web services, and that supports the automatic discovery, invocation, composition and monitoring of these services. In this paper we describe the overall structure of the ontology, the service profile for advertising services, and the process model for the detailed description of the operation of services. We also compare DAML-S with several industry efforts to define standards for characterizing services on the Web.

1   Introduction: Services on the Semantic Web

Efforts toward the creation of the Semantic Web are gaining momentum [2] through the development of Semantic Web markup languages such as DAML+OIL [10]. Such markup languages enable the creation of arbitrary domain ontologies that support unambiguous description of web content. Web services are resources that do not merely provide static information but allow one to effect some action or change in the world, such as the sale of a product or the control of a physical device. Software agents should be able to locate, select, employ, compose, and monitor Web-based services automatically. To achieve this, an agent needs a computer-interpretable description of the service and how it can be invoked.

Web-based services are garnering a great deal of interest from industry, and standards are being developed for low-level descriptions of these services. Languages such as WSDL (Web Services Description Language) provide a communication level description of messages and simple protocols used by services. An important goal for DAML is to complement this effort by establishing a higher-level framework within which semantic descriptions of services can be made and shared. Web sites should be able to employ a set of basic classes and properties for declaring and describing services, and the ontology structuring mechanisms of DAML provide the appropriate framework within which to do this.

---

[1] Authors' names are in alphabetical order.
[2] The Robotics Institute, Carnegie Mellon University, Pittsburgh, PA
[3] BBN Technologies, Cambridge, Massachusetts
[4] Artificial Intelligence Center, SRI International, Menlo Park, California
[5] Nokia Research Center, Burlington, Massachusetts
[6] Knowledge Systems Laboratory, Stanford University, Stanford, California

This paper describes a collaborative effort by BBN Technologies, Carnegie Mellon University, Nokia, Stanford University, and SRI International to define just such an ontology. We call this language DAML-S. We first motivate our effort with some sample tasks. In the central part of the paper we describe the upper ontology for services that we have developed, including the ontologies for profiles, processes, and time, and thoughts toward a future ontology of process control. We then compare DAML-S with a number of recent industrial efforts to standardize a markup language for services.

2　Some Motivating Tasks

Services can be simple or primitive in the sense that they invoke only a single Web-accessible computer program, sensor, or device that does not rely upon another Web service, and there is no ongoing interaction between the user and the service, beyond a simple response. For example, a service that returns a postal code or the longitude and latitude when given an address would be in this category. Alternately, services can be complex, composed of multiple primitive services, often requiring an interaction or conversation between the user and the services, so that the user can make choices and provide information conditionally. For example, one's interaction with a book retail service such as *Amazon.com* might proceed as follows: the user searches for books by various criteria, perhaps reads reviews, may or may not decide to buy, and gives credit card and mailing information. DAML-S is meant to support both categories of services, but complex services have provided the primary motivations for the features of the language. The following four sample tasks will illustrate the kinds of tasks we expect DAML-S to enable [13, 14].

1. **Automatic Web Service Discovery.** This involves the automatic location of Web services that provide a particular service and that adhere to requested constraints. For example, the user may want to find a service that sells airline tickets between two given cities and accepts a particular credit card. Currently, this task must be performed by a human who might use a search engine to find a service, read the Web page, and execute the service manually, to determine if it satisfies the constraints. With DAML-S markup of services, the information necessary for Web service discovery could be specified as computer-interpretable semantic markup at the service Web sites, and a service registry or ontology-enhanced search engine could be used to locate the services automatically. Alternatively, a server could proactively advertise itself in DAML-S with a service registry, also called a *Middle Agent* [5, 12, 24], so that requesters can find this service by querying the registry. Thus, DAML-S must provide declarative advertisements of service properties and capabilities that can be used for automatic service discovery.

2. **Automatic Web Service Invocation.** This involves the automatic execution of an identified Web service by a computer program or agent. For example, the user could request the purchase of an airline ticket from a particular site on a particular flight. Currently, a user must go to the Web site offering that service, fill out a form, and click on a button to execute the service. Alternately the user might send an HTTP request directly to the service with the appropriate parameters in HTML. In either case, a human in the loop is necessary. Execution of a Web service can be thought of as a collection of function calls. DAML-S markup of Web services provides a declarative, computer-interpretable API for executing these function calls. A software agent should be able to interpret the markup to

understand what input is necessary to the service call, what information will be returned, and how to execute the service automatically. Thus, DAML-S should provide declarative APIs for Web services that are necessary for automated Web service execution.

3. **Automatic Web Service Composition and Interoperation.** This task involves the automatic selection, composition and interoperation of Web services to perform some task, given a high-level description of an objective. For example, the user may want to make all the travel arrangements for a trip to a conference. Currently, the user must select the Web services, specify the composition manually, and make sure that any software needed for the interoperation is custom-created. With DAML-S markup of Web services, the information necessary to select and compose services will be encoded at the service Web sites. Software can be written to manipulate these representations, together with a specification of the objectives of the task, to achieve the task automatically. Thus, DAML-S must provide declarative specifications of the prerequisites and consequences of individual service use that are necessary for automatic service composition and interoperation.

4. **Automatic Web Service Execution Monitoring.** Individual services and, even more, compositions of services, will often require some time to execute completely. Users may want to know during this period what the status of their request is, or their plans may have changed requiring alterations in the actions the software agent takes. For example, users may want to make sure their hotel reservation has already been made. For these purposes, it would be good to have the ability to find out where in the process the request is and whether any unanticipated glitches have appeared. Thus, DAML-S should provide descriptors for the execution of services. This part of DAML-S is a goal of ours, but it has not yet been defined.

Any Web-accessible program/sensor/device that is *declared* as a service will be regarded as a service. DAML-S does not preclude declaring simple, static Web pages to be services. But our primary motivation in defining DAML-S has been to support more complex tasks like those described above.

3 An Upper Ontology for Services

The class *Service* stands at the top of a taxonomy of services, and its properties are the properties normally associated with all kinds of services. The upper ontology for services is silent as to what the particular subclasses of *Service* should be, or even the conceptual basis for structuring this taxonomy, but it is expected that the taxonomy will be structured according to functional and domain differences and market needs. For example, one might imagine a broad subclass, *B2C-transaction*, which would encompass services for purchasing items from retail Web sites, tracking purchase status, establishing and maintaining accounts with the sites, and so on.

Our structuring of the ontology of services is motivated by the need to provide three essential types of knowledge about a service (shown in Figure 1), each characterized by the question it answers:

- *What does the service require of the user(s) or other agents, and provide for them?* This is answered by the "profile"[7]. Thus, the class *Service* presents a *ServiceProfile*.

---

[7] A service profile has also been called service capability advertisement [20].

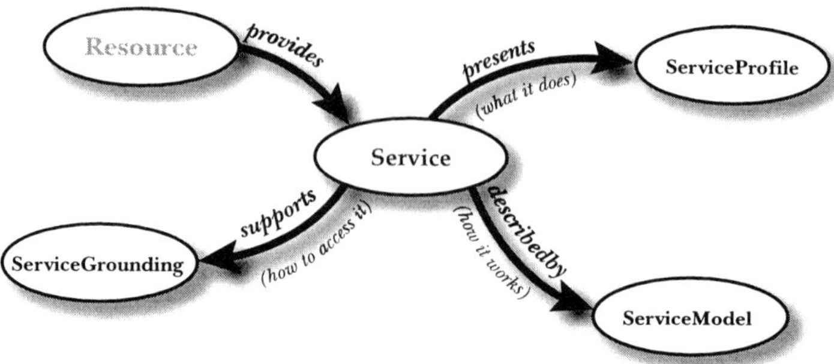

Figure 1: Top level of the service ontology

- *How does it work?* The answer to this question is given in the "model." Thus, the class *Service* is `describedBy` a *ServiceModel*.

- *How is it used?* The answer to this question is given in the "grounding." Thus, the class *Service* `supports` a *ServiceGrounding*.

The properties `presents`, `describedBy`, and `supports` are properties of *Service*. The classes *ServiceProfile*, *ServiceModel*, and *ServiceGrounding* are the respective ranges of those properties. We expect that each descendant class of *Service*, such as *B2C-transaction*, will `present` a descendant class of *ServiceProfile*, be `describedBy` a descendant class of *ServiceModel*, and `support` a descendant class of *ServiceGrounding*. The details of profiles, models, and groundings may vary widely from one type of service to another—that is, from one descendant class of *Service* to another. But each of these three classes provides an essential type of information about the service, as characterized in the rest of the paper.

The service profile tells "what the service does"; that is, it gives the type of information needed by a service-seeking agent to determine whether the service meets its needs (typically such things as input and output types, preconditions and postconditions, and binding patterns). In future versions, we will use logical rules or their equivalent in such a specification for expressing interactions among parameters. For instance, a rule might say that if a particular input argument is bound in a certain way, certain other input arguments may not be needed, or may be provided by the service itself. As DAML+OIL and DAML-S and their applications evolve, logical rules and inferential approaches enabled by them are likely to play an increasingly important role in models and groundings, as well as in profiles. See [6] for additional examples.

The service model tells "how the service works"; that is, it describes what happens when the service is carried out. For non-trivial services (those composed of several steps over time), this description may be used by a service-seeking agent in at least four different ways: (1) to perform a more in-depth analysis of whether the service meets its needs; (2) to compose service descriptions from multiple services to perform a specific task; (3) during the course of the service enactment, to coordinate the activities of the different participants; (4) to monitor the execution of the service. For non-trivial services, the first two tasks require a model of action and process, the last two involve, in addition, an execution model.

A service grounding ("grounding" for short) specifies the details of how an agent can access a service. Typically a grounding will specify a communications protocol (e.g., RPC, HTTP-FORM, CORBA IDL, SOAP, Java RMI, OAA ACL [12]), and service-specific details such as port numbers used in contacting the service. In addition, the grounding must specify, for each abstract type specified in the *ServiceModel*, an unambiguous way of exchanging data elements of that type with the service (i.e., the marshaling/serialization techniques employed).

Generally speaking, the *ServiceProfile* provides the information needed for an agent to discover a service. Taken together, the *ServiceModel* and *ServiceGrounding* objects associated with a service provide enough information for an agent to make use of a service. The upper ontology for services deliberately does not specify any cardinalities for the properties `presents`, `describedBy`, and `supports`. Although, in principle, a service needs all three properties to be fully characterized, it is possible to imagine situations in which a partial characterization could be useful. Hence, there is no specification of a minimum cardinality. Furthermore, it should be possible for a service to offer multiple profiles, models, and/or groundings. Hence, no maximum cardinality is specified. In addition, there need not exist a one-to-one correspondence between profiles, models, and/or groundings. The only constraint among these three characterizations that might appropriately be expressed at the upper level ontology is that for each model, there must be at least one supporting grounding.

The service profile and the service model are described in detail in the following two sections. A discussion of the grounding and it's synergy with WSDL can be found in [4].

4   Service Profiles

A service profile provides a high-level description of a service and its provider [21, 20]; it is used to request or advertise services with discovery services and capability registries. Service profiles consist of three types of information: a human readable *description* of the service; a specification of the *functionalities* that are provided by the service; and *functional attributes* which provide additional information that may assist when reasoning about services with similar capabilities. Service functionalities are represented as a transformation from the inputs required by the service to the outputs produced. For example, a news reporting service would advertise itself as a service that, given a date, will return the news reported on that date. Functional attributes specify additional information about the service, such as what guarantees of response time or accuracy it provides, or the cost of the service.

While service providers define advertisements for their services using the profile ontology, service requesters utilize the profile to specify what services they need and what they expect from such a service. For instance, a requester may look for a service that reports current market and stock quotes. Middle Agents and other discovery services then match the request against the advertised profiles, and identify which services provide the best match.

Implicitly, the service profiles specify the intended purpose of the service, because they specify only those functionalities that are publicly provided. A book-selling service may involve two different functionalities: it allows other services to browse its site to find books of interest, and it allows them to buy the books they found. The book-seller has the choice of advertising just the book-buying service or both the browsing functionality and the buying functionality. In the latter case the service makes public that it can provide browsing services, and it allows everybody to browse its registry without buying a book. In contrast, by advertising only the book-selling functionality, but not the browsing, the agent discourages browsing by requesters that do not intend to buy. The decision as to which functionalities to advertise determines how the service will be used: a requester that intends to browse but not to buy would select a service that advertises both buying and browsing capabilities, but not one that advertises buying only.

The service profile contains only the information that allows registries to decide which advertisements are matched by a request. To this extent, the information in the profile is a summary of the information in the process model and service grounding. Where, as in the above example, the service does not advertise some of its functionalities, they will not be part of the service profile. But they *are* part of the service model to the extent that they are needed for *achieving* the advertised services. For example, looking for a book is an essential prerequisite for buying it, so it would be specified in the process model, but not necessarily in the profile. Similarly, information about shipping may appear within the process model but not the profile.

The following subsections break down the type of information represented by the profile into the three categories: *description, functionalities* and *functional attributes*.

4.1　Description

The profile includes high-level information about the service and it's provenance. This information has two roles: to describe the service and the service provider (or requester) in a human readable format; and to provide semi-structured semantics that may support service matchmaking. Typically, this information would be presented to users when browsing a service registry. The *description* properties are listed in Table 1.

Table 1: Description Properties - defining the provenance of the service.

Property	Description
serviceName	The name of the service.
intendedPurpose	A high-level description on what constitutes successful accomplishment of a service execution.
textDescription	A brief, human readable description of the service, summarizing what the service offers or what capabilities are being requested.
role	An abstract link to *Actors* that may be involved in the service execution.
requestedBy	A sub-property of role that links the service to the *Actor* that requests a service.
providedBy	A sub-property of role that links the service to the *Actor* that advertised the service.

The class *Actor* is also defined to describe entities (e.g. humans or organizations) that provide or request web services. Two specific classes are derived from the *Actor* class; the *ServiceRequester* class and *ServiceProvider* class, to represent the requester and provider of the service respectively. Properties of *Actor* include physicalAddress, webURL, name, phone, email, and fax.

4.2　Functionality Description

An essential component of the profile is the specification of what the service provides and the specification of the conditions that have to be satisfied for a successful result. In addition, the profile specifies what conditions result from the service including the expected and unexpected results of the service activity.

The service is represented by `input` and `output` properties of the profile. The input property specifies the information that the service requires to proceed with the computation. For example, a book-selling service could require the credit-card number and bibliographical information of the book to sell. The outputs specify the result of the operation of the service. For the book-selling agent the output could be a receipt that acknowledges the sale.

```
<rdf:Property rdf:ID="input">
  <rdfs:comment>
    Property describing the inputs of a service in the Service Profile
  </rdfs:comment>
  <rdfs:domain rdf:resource="#ServiceProfile"/>
  <rdfs:subPropertyOf rdf:resource="#parameter"/>
</rdf:Property>
```

While inputs and outputs represent the service, they are not the only things affected by the operations of the service. For example, to complete the sale the book-selling service requires that the credit card is valid and not overdrawn or expired. In addition, the result of the sale is not only that the buyer owns the book (as specified by the outputs), but that the book is physically transferred from the the warehouse of the seller to the house of the buyer. These conditions are specified by `precondition` and `effect` properties of the profile. Preconditions present one or more logical conditions that should be satisfied prior to the service being requested. These conditions should have associated explicit effects that may occur as a result of the service being performed. Effects are events that are caused by the successful execution of a service.

Finally, the profile allows the specification of what `domainResources` are affected by the use of the service. These domain resources may include computational resources such as bandwidth or disk space as well as more material resources consumed when the service controls some machinery. This type of resource may include fuel, or materials modified by the machine.

4.3 Functional Attributes

In the previous section we introduced the functional description of services. Yet there are other aspects of services that the users should be aware of. While a service may be accessed from anywhere on the Internet, it may only be applicable to a specific audience. For instance, although it is possible to order food for delivery from a Pittsburgh-based restaurant Web site in general, one cannot reasonably expect to do this from California. The functional attributes described in Table 2 address the problem that there are properties that can be used to describe a service other than as a functional process.

5 Modeling Services as Processes

A more detailed perspective on services is that a service can be viewed as a *process*. We have defined a particular subclass of *ServiceModel*, the *ProcessModel* (as shown in Figure 2), which draws upon well-established work in a variety of fields, such as AI planning and

Table 2: Functional Attributes

Property	Description
geographicRadius	The geographic scope of the service, either at the global scale (e.g. for e-commerce) or at a regional scale (e.g. pizza delivery).
degreeOfQuality	Quality qualifications, such as providing the cheapest or fastest possible service.
serviceParameter	An expandable list of properties that characterize the execution of a service, such as averageResponseTime or invocationCost.
communicationThru	High-level summary of how a service may communicate, e.g. what agent communication language (ACL) is used (e.g., FIPA, KQML, SOAP). This summarizes, but does not replace, the descriptions provided by the service grounding.
serviceType	Broad classification of the service that might be described by an ontology of service types, such as B2B, B2C etc.
serviceCategory	Categories defined within some service category ontology. Such categories may include *Products, Problem-Solving, Commercial Services* etc.
qualityGuarantees	Guarantees that the service promises to deliver, e.g. guaranteeing to provide the lowest possible interest rate, or a response within 3 minutes, etc.
qualityRating	Industry-based ratings, such as the "Dun and Bradstreet Rating" for businesses, or the "Star Rating" for Hotels.

workflow automation, and which we believe will support the representational needs of a very broad array of services on the Web.

The two chief components of a process model are the *process model*, which describes a service in terms of its component actions or processes, and enables planning, composition and agent/service interoperation; and the *process control model*, which allows agents to monitor the execution of a service request. We will refer to the first part as the Process Ontology and the second as the Process Control Ontology. Only the former has been defined in the current version of DAML-S, but below we briefly describe our intentions with regard to the latter. We have defined a simple ontology of time, described below; in subsequent versions this will be elaborated. We also expect in a future version to provide an ontology of resources.

5.1   The Process Ontology

We expect our process ontology to serve as the basis for specifying a wide array of services. In developing the ontology, we drew from a variety of sources, including work in AI on standardizations of planning languages [9], work in programming languages and distributed systems [16, 15], emerging standards in process modeling and workflow technology such as the NIST's Process Specification Language (PSL) [19] and the Workflow Management Coalition effort (http://www.aiim.org/wfmc), work on modeling verb semantics and event structure [17], previous work on action-inspired Web service markup [14], work in AI on modeling complex actions [11], and work in agent communication languages [12, 8].

The primary kind of entity in the Process Ontology is, unsurprisingly, a "process". A process can have any number of inputs, representing the information that is, under some conditions, required for the execution of the process. It can have any number of outputs, the information that the process provides, conditionally, after its execution. Besides inputs and outputs, another important type of parameter specifies the participants in a process. A variety of other parameters may also be declared, including, for physical devices, such things as rates, forces, and knob-settings. There can be any number of preconditions, which must

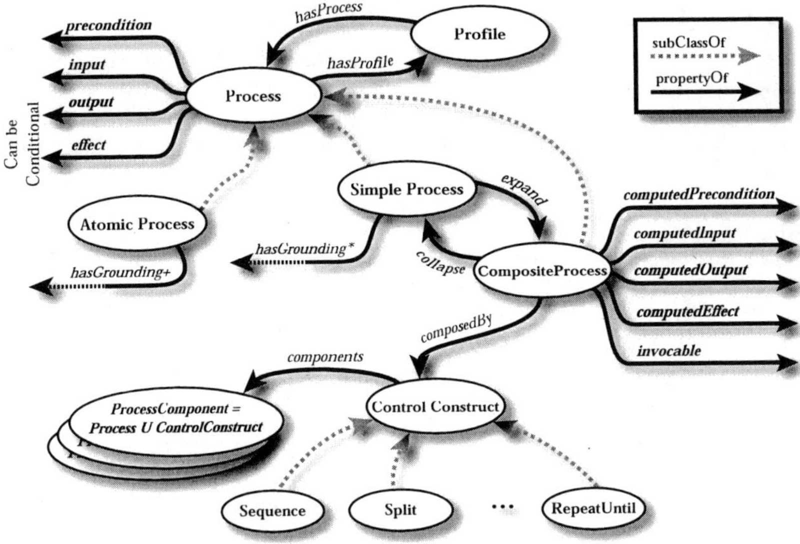

Figure 2: Top level of process modeling ontology

all hold in order for the process to be invoked. Finally, the process can have any number of effects. Outputs and effects can have conditions associated with them.

More precisely, in DAML-S, we have:

- **Process**

  Class *Process* has related properties `parameter`, `input`, (conditional) `output`, `participant`, `precondition`, and (conditional) `effect`. Input, `output`, and `participant` are categorized as subproperties of `parameter`. The range of each of these properties, at the upper ontology level, is *Thing*; that is, left totally unrestricted. Subclasses of *Process* for specific domains can use DAML language elements to indicate more specific range restrictions, as well as cardinality restrictions for each of these properties.

```
<rdfs:Class rdf:ID="Process">
  <rdfs:comment>
    Top-level class for describing how a service works
  </rdfs:comment>
</rdfs:Class>
```

In addition to its action-related properties, a *Process* has a number of bookkeeping properties such as `name`, `address`, `documentsRead`, `documentsUpdated`, and so on.

In DAML-S, as shown in Figure 2, we distinguish between three types of processes: *atomic*, *simple*, and *composite*.

- **AtomicProcess**

  The *atomic* processes are directly invocable (by passing them the appropriate messages), have no subprocesses, and execute in a single step, from the perspective of the service requester. That is, they take input message(s) all at once, execute, and then return their output message(s) all at once. Atomic processes must provide a grounding that enables a service requester to construct these messages.

  ```
  <daml:Class rdf:ID="AtomicProcess">
    <daml:intersectionOf rdf:parseType="daml:collection">
      <daml:Class rdf:about="#Process"/>
      <daml:Restriction daml:minCardinality="1">
        <daml:onProperty rdf:resource="#hasGrounding"/>
      </daml:Restriction>
    </daml:intersectionOf>
  </daml:Class>
  ```

- **SimpleProcess**

  Simple processes, on the other hand, are not normally invocable and not normally associated with a grounding, but, like atomic processes, they *are* conceived of as having single-step executions. Simple processes are used as elements of abstraction; a simple process may be used either to provide a view of (a specialized way of using) some atomic process, or a simplified representation of some composite process (for purposes of planning and reasoning). In the former case, the simple process is `realizedBy` the atomic process; in the latter case, the simple process `expands` to the composite process.

  ```
  <daml:Class rdf:ID="SimpleProcess">
    <daml:subClassOf rdf:resource="#Process"/>
  </daml:Class>

  <rdf:Property rdf:ID="realizedBy">
    <rdfs:domain rdf:resource="#SimpleProcess"/>
    <rdfs:range rdf:resource="#AtomicProcess"/>
    <daml:inverseOf rdf:resource="#realizes"/>
  </rdf:Property>

  <rdf:Property rdf:ID="expand">
    <rdfs:domain rdf:resource="#SimpleProcess"/>
    <rdfs:range rdf:resource="#CompositeProcess"/>
    <daml:inverseOf rdf:resource="#collapse"/>
  </rdf:Property>
  ```

- **CompositeProcess**

  Composite processes are decomposable into other (non-composite or composite) processes; their decomposition can be specified by using control constructs such as *Sequence* and *If-Then-Else*, which are discussed below. Such a decomposition normally shows, among other things, how the various inputs of the process are accepted by particular subprocesses, and how its various outputs are returned by particular subprocesses.

```
<daml:Class rdf:ID="CompositeProcess">
  <daml:intersectionOf rdf:parseType="daml:collection">
    <daml:Class rdf:about="#Process"/>
    <daml:Restriction daml:minCardinality="1">
      <daml:onProperty rdf:resource="#composedOf"/>
    </daml:Restriction>
  </daml:intersectionOf>
</daml:Class>
```

A process can often be viewed at different levels of granularity, either as a primitive, un-decomposable process or as a composite process. These are sometimes referred to as "black box" and "glass box" views, respectively. Either perspective may be the more useful in some given context. When a composite process is viewed as a black box, a simple process can be used to represent this. In this case, the relationship between the simple and composite is represented using the expand property, and its inverse, the collapse property. The declaration of expand is shown above, with *SimpleProcess*.

A *CompositeProcess* must have a composedOf property by which is indicated the control structure of the composite, using a *ControlConstruct*.

```
<rdf:Property rdf:ID="composedOf">
  <rdfs:domain rdf:resource="#CompositeProcess"/>
  <rdfs:range rdf:resource="#ControlConstruct"/>
</rdf:Property>

<daml:Class rdf:ID="ControlConstruct"/>
```

Each control construct, in turn, is associated with an additional property called components to indicate the ordering and conditional execution of the subprocesses (or control constructs) from which it is composed. For instance, the control construct, *Sequence*, has a components property that ranges over a *ProcessComponentList* (a list whose items are restricted to be *ProcessComponent*s, which are either processes or control constructs).

```
<rdf:Property rdf:ID="components">
  <rdfs:comment>
    Holds the specific arrangement of subprocesses.
  </rdfs:comment>
  <rdfs:domain rdf:resource="#ControlConstruct"/>
</rdf:Property>

<daml:Class rdf:ID="ProcessComponent">
  <rdfs:comment>
    A ProcessComponent is either a Process or a ControlConstruct.
  </rdfs:comment>
  <daml:unionOf rdf:parseType="daml:collection">
    <daml:Class rdf:about="#Process"/>
    <daml:Class rdf:about="#ControlConstruct"/>
  </daml:unionOf>
</daml:Class>
```

In the process upper ontology, we have included a minimal set of control constructs that can be specialized to describe a variety of Web services. This minimal set consists of *Sequence, Split, Split + Join, Choice, Unordered, Condition, If-Then-Else, Iterate, Repeat-While*, and *Repeat-Until*. In the following, due to space constraints, we give (partial) code samples only for *Sequence* and *If-Then-Else*.

Sequence : A list of Processes to be done in order. We use a DAML restriction to restrict the components of a Sequence to be a List of process components — which may be either processes (atomic, simple and/or composite) or control constructs.

```
<rdfs:Class rdf:ID="Sequence">
  <daml:intersectionOf rdf:parseType="daml:collection">
    <rdfs:Class> rdf:about="#ControlConstruct" </rdfs:Class>
    <daml:Restriction>
      <daml:onProperty rdf:resource="#components"/>
      <daml:toClass rdf:resource="#ProcessComponentList"/>
    </daml:Restriction>
  <daml:intersectionOf>
</rdfs:Class>
```

Split : The components of a *Split* process are a bag of process components to be executed concurrently. No further specification about waiting or synchronization is made at this level. The components are restricted similarly to those of *Sequence*, except to a bag rather than a list.

Split is similar to other ontologies' use of Fork, Concurrent, or Parallel. We use the DAML `sameClassAs` feature to accommodate the different standards for specifying this.

Unordered : Here a bag of process components can be executed in any order. No further constraints are specified. All process components must be executed.

Split+Join : Here the process consists of concurrent execution of a bunch of process components with barrier synchronization. With *Split* and *Split+Join*, we can define processes that have partial synchronization (e.g., split all and join some sub-bag).

Choice : *Choice* is a control construct with additional properties `chosen` and `chooseFrom`. These properties can be used both for process and execution control (e.g., choose from `chooseFrom` and do `chosen` in sequence, or choose from `chooseFrom` and do `chosen` in parallel) as well for constructing new subclasses like "choose at least n from m", "choose exactly n from m", "choose at most n from m" [8], and so on.

If-Then-Else : The *If-Then-Else* class is a control construct that has properties `ifCondition`, `then` and `else` holding different aspects of the *If-Then-Else*. Its semantics is intended as "Test `ifCondition`; if True do `then`, if False do `else`." (Note that the class *Condition*, which is a place-holder for further work, will be defined as a class of logical expressions.) We show here just the property definitions.

```
<rdf:Property rdf:ID="ifCondition">
  <rdfs:domain rdf:resource="#If-Then-Else"/>
  <rdfs:range> rdf:resource ="#Condition" </rdfs:range>
</rdf:Property>

<rdf:Property rdf:ID="then">
```

---

[8]This can be obtained by restricting the size of the Process Bag that corresponds to the `components` of the chosen and chooseFrom subprocesses using cardinality, min-cardinality, max-cardinality to get choose(n, m)$(0 \leq n \leq |components(chooseFrom)|, 0 < m \leq |components(chosen)|)$.

```
  <rdfs:domain rdf:resource="#If-Then-Else"/>
  <rdfs:range rdf:resource="#ProcessComponent"/>
</rdf:Property>

<rdf:Property rdf:ID="else">
  <rdfs:domain rdf:resource="#If-Then-Else"/>
  <rdfs:range rdf:resource="#ProcessComponent"/>
</rdf:Property>
```

Iterate : *Iterate* is a control construct whose `nextProcessComponent` property has the same value as the current process component. *Repeat* is defined as a synonym of the *Iterate* class. The repeat/iterate process makes no assumption about how many iterations are made or when to initiate, terminate or resume. The initiation, termination or maintenance condition could be specified with a `whileCondition` or an `untilCondition` as below.[9]

Repeat-Until : The *Repeat-Until* class is similar to the *Repeat-While* class in that it specializes the *If-Then-Else* class where the `ifCondition` is the same as the `untilCondition` and different from the *Repeat-While* class in that the `else` (compared to `then`) property is the repeated process. Thus the process repeats till the `untilCondition` becomes true.

5.2   Process Control Ontology

A process instantiation represents a complex process that is executing in the world. To monitor and control the execution of a process, an agent needs a model to interpret process instantiations with three characteristics:

1. It should provide the mapping rules for the various input state properties (inputs, preconditions) to the corresponding output state properties.

2. It should provide a model of the temporal or state dependencies described by the sequence, split, split+join, etc constructs.

3. It should provide representations for messages about the execution state of atomic and composite processes sufficient to do execution monitoring. This allows an agent to keep track of the status of executions, including successful, failed and interrupted processes, and to respond to each appropriately.

We have not defined a process control ontology in the current version of DAML-S, but we plan to in a future version.

5.3   Time

For the initial version of DAML-S we have defined a very simple upper ontology for time. There are two classes of entities: *Instants* and *intervals*. Each is a subclass of *TemporalEntity*.

There are three relations that may obtain between an instant and an interval, defined as DAML-S properties:

---

[9] Another possible extension is to ability to define counters and use their values as termination conditions. This could be part of an extended process control and execution monitoring ontology.

1. The `startOf` property whose domain is the *Interval* class and whose range is an *Instant*.

2. The `endOf` property whose domain is the *Interval* class and whose range is an *Instant*.

3. The `inside` property whose domain is the *Interval* class and whose range is an *Instant*.

No assumption is made that intervals *consist of Instants*.

There are two possible relations that may obtain between a process and one of the temporal objects. A process may be in an *at-time* relation to an instant or in a *during* relation to an interval. Whether a particular process is viewed as instantaneous or as occurring over an interval is a granularity decision that may vary according to the context of use. These relations are defined in DAML-S as properties of processes.

1. The `atTime` property: its domain is the Process class and its range is an *Instant*.

2. The `during` property: its domain is the Process class and its range is an *Interval*.

Viewed as intervals, processes could have properties such as `startTime` and `endTime` which are synonymous (daml:samePropertyAs) with the `startOf` and `endOf` relation that obtains between intervals and instants.

One further relation can hold between two temporal entities: the *before* relation. The intended semantics is that for an instant or interval to be before another instant or interval, there can be no overlap or abutment between the former and the latter. In DAML-S the `before` property whose domain is the *TemporalEntity* class and whose range is a *TemporalEntity*.

Different communities have different ways of representing the times and durations of states and events (processes). For example, states and events can both have durations, and at least events can be instantaneous; or events can only be instantaneous and only states can have durations. Events that one might consider as having duration (e.g., heating water) are modeled as a state of the system that is initiated and terminated by instantaneous events. That is, there is the instantaneous event of the start of the heating at the start of an interval, that transitions the system into a state in which the water is heating. The state continues until another instantaneous event occurs—the stopping of the event at the end of the interval. These two perspectives on events are straightforwardly interdefinable in terms of the ontology we have provided. Thus, DAML-S supports both.

The various relations between intervals defined in Allen's temporal interval calculus [1] can be defined in a straightforward fashion in terms of *before* and identity on the start and end points. For example, two intervals meet when the end of one is identical to the start of the other. Thus, in the near future, when DAML is augmented with the capability of defining logical rules, it will be easy to incorporate the interval calculus into DAML-S. In addition, in future versions of DAML-S we will define primitives for measuring durations and for specifying clock and calendar time.

6 Example Walk-Through

To illustrate the concepts described in this paper, we have developed an example of a fictitious book-buying service offered by the Web service provider, Congo Inc. Congo has a suite of programs that they are making accessible on the Web. Congo wishes to compose these individual programs into Web services that it offers to its users. We focus here on the Web service of buying a book, CongoBuy. In the DAML-S release, we present a walk-through that steps through the process of creating DAML-S markup for Congo[10].

We take the perspective of the typical Web service provider and consider three automation tasks that a Web service provider might wish to enable with DAML-S: 1) automatic Web service discovery, 2) automatic Web service invocation, and 3) automatic Web service composition and interoperation. For the purposes of this paper, we limit our discussion to the second and third tasks.

6.1　Web Service Invocation

To automate Web Service Invocation, DAML-S markup must tell a program how to automatically construct an (http) call to execute or invoke a Web service, and what output(s) may be returned from the service. To enable such functionality, the process ontology in DAML-S provides markup to describe individual and composite Web-accessible programs as either simple or composite processes.

6.1.1　Define the Service as a Process

Congo Inc. provides the CongoBuy Web service to its customers. We view the CongoBuy Web service as a simple process, i.e., it is a subclass of the class *SimpleProcess* in the process ontology.

```
<rdfs:Class rdf:ID="CongoBuy">
  <rdfs:subClassOf rdf:resource=
    "http://www.daml.org/services/.../Process.daml#SimpleProcess"/>
</rdfs:Class>
```

Although the CongoBuy service is actually a predetermined composition of several of Congo's Web-accessible programs, it is useful to initially view it as a black-box process. The black-box process, CongoBuy has a variety of invocation-relevant properties, including input, (conditional) output and parameter. For example, input to the CongoBuy book-buying service includes the name of the book (bookName), the customer's credit card number, and their account number and password. If the service being described is simple in that it is not the composition of other services or programs, then the service inputs are simply the set of inputs that must be provided in the service invocation. The outputs are the outputs returned from the service invocation. Note that these outputs may be conditional. For example the output of a book-buying service will vary depending upon whether the book is in or out of stock.

In contrast, if the service is composed of other services, as is the case with CongoBuy, then the rationale for specification of the inputs, outputs and parameters is more difficult, and the utility of these properties is limited. In the simplest case, the inputs and outputs of the black-box process can be defined to be the composition of all the possible inputs and all the possible (conditional) outputs of the simple services that the black-box process may invoke, taking every possible path through the composition of simple services. Note however that this is not a very exacting specification. In particular, the collection of outputs may be contradictory (e.g., one path of CongoBuy may lead to confirmation of a purchase, while another may lead to confirmation of no purchase). The conditions under which inputs and

---

[10]This Congo example can be found at http://www.daml.org/services/daml-s/2001/06/Congo.daml

outputs arise are encoded exactly in the expand of this black-box process, and can be retrieved from the expanded process. The inputs, outputs and parameters for the black-box process are designed to be a useful shorthand. Thus, it could be argued that the inputs and outputs should describe the most likely inputs and outputs through the system. However, in some cases, even this is difficult to define. For now, DAML-S leaves this decision up to the Web service provider.

The following is an example of one input to CongoBuy. Note that it is a subproperty of the property `input` of *Process*.

```
<rdf:Property rdf:ID="bookName">
  <rdfs:subPropertyOf rdf:resource=
    "http://www.daml.org/services/daml-s/2001/06/Process.daml#input"/>
  <rdfs:domain rdf:resource="#CongoBuy"/>
  <rdfs:range rdf:resource="http://www.w3.org/2000/10/XMLSchema#string"/>
</rdf:Property>
```

An output can similarly be defined as a subproperty of the property `output` of *Process*. In a real book-buying service, this output would likely be conditioned on the book being in stock, or the customer's credit card being valid, but to simplify our example, we assume Congo has an infinite supply of books, and infinite generosity.

```
<rdf:Property rdf:ID="eReceiptOutput">
  <rdfs:subPropertyOf rdf:resource=
    "http://www.daml.org/services/daml-s/2001/06/Process.daml#output"/>
  <rdfs:range rdf:resource="#EReceipt"/>
</rdf:Property>
```

In addition to input and output properties, each service has parameter properties. A parameter is something that affects the outcome of the process, but which is not an input provided by the invoker of the process. It may be known by the service, or retrieved by the service from elsewhere. For example, the fact that the customer's credit card is valid, is a parameter in our CongoBuy process, and is relevant when considering the use of the CongoBuy, but it is not an input or output of CongoBuy.

```
<rdf:Property rdf:ID="creditCardValidity">
  <rdfs:subPropertyOf rdf:resource=
    "http://www.daml.org/services/.../Process.daml#parameter"/>
  <rdfs:range rdf:resource="#ValidityType"/>
</rdf:Property>
```

6.1.2 *Define the Process as a Composition of Processes*

Given the variability in the specification of inputs, outputs and parameters, it is generally insufficient to simply specify a service as a black-box process, if the objective is to automate service invocation. We must expand the black-box service to describe its composite processes. This is achieved by first defining the individual processes and then defining their composition as a composite process.

Define the Individual Processes

We define each of the simple services in CongoBuy, i.e., LocateBook, PutInCart, etc.[11]

```
<rdfs:Class rdf:ID="LocateBook">
  <rdfs:subClassOf rdf:resource=
    "http://www.daml.org/services/.../Process.daml#SimpleProcess"/>
</rdfs:Class>

<rdfs:Class rdf:ID="PutInCart">
  <rdfs:subClassOf rdf:resource=
    "http://www.daml.org/services/.../Process.daml#SimpleProcess"/>
</rdfs:Class>

<rdf:Property rdf:ID="bookSelected">
  <rdfs:subPropertyOf rdf:resource=
    "http://www.daml.org/services/.../Process.daml#input"/>
  <rdfs:domain rdf:resource="#PutInCart"/>
  <rdfs:range rdf:resource="http://www.w3.org/2000/10/XMLSchema#string"/>
</rdf:Property>
```

Define the Composition of the Individual Processes

The composition our simple services can be defined by using the composition constructs created in the process ontology, i.e., *Sequence, Split, Split + Join, Unordered, Condition, If-Then-Else, Repeat-While, Repeat-Until.* Using these constructs, we specify a *CompositeProcess*, ExpandedCongoBuy, which is composed from simple services such as those shown above. For lack of space, the definition of ExpandedCongoBuy is omitted here, but may be seen at the URL mentioned in the last footnote.

Having defined ExpandedCongoBuy, its relationship to CongoBuy can be indicated using the `expand` (and `collapse`) properties.

6.1.3 *Automated Service Composition and Interoperation*

The DAML-S markup required to automate service composition and interoperation builds directly on the markup for service invocation. In order to automate service composition and interoperation, we must also encode the effects a service has upon the world, and the preconditions for performing that service. For example, when a human being goes to www.congo.com and successfully executes the CongoBuy service, the human knows that they have purchased a book, that their credit card will be debited, and that they will receive a book at the address they provided. Such consequences of Web service execution are not part of the input/output markup we created for automating service invocation.

The process ontology provides precondition and effect properties of a process to encode this information. As with our markup for automated service invocation, we define preconditions and effects both for the black-box process CongoBuy and for each of the simple processes that define its composition, and as with defining inputs and outputs, it is easiest to define the preconditions and effects for each of the simple processes first, and then to aggregate them into preconditions and effects for CongoBuy. The markup is analogous to the markup for input and (conditional) output, but is with respect to the properties precondition and (conditional) effect, instead.

---

[11] Additional DAML code is needed here to specify the relationship between the bookName property of CongoBuy and the bookSelected property of PutInCart. As of this writing, discussions are underway to determine the best way to indicate this relationship in DAML+OIL.

7   Related Efforts

Industry efforts to develop standards for electronic commerce, and in particular for the description of Web-based services currently revolve around UDDI, WSDL, and ebXML [23]. There have also been company-specific initiatives to define architectures for e-commerce, most notably E-speak from Hewlett-Packard.

Nevertheless, we believe that DAML-S provides functionality that the other efforts do not. In comparison to the DAML-S characterization of services, the industry standards mostly focus on presenting a *ServiceProfile* and a *ServiceGrounding* of services (to use DAML-S terminology). *ServiceGroundings* are supported by all the standards. However, they are limited with respect to DAML-S profiles in that they cannot express logical statements, e.g. preconditions and postconditions, or rules to describe dependencies between the profile elements. Input and output types are supported to varying extents. Furthermore, DAML-S supports the description of certain functional attributes of services, which are not covered in the other standards, such as qualityGuarantees and serviceType.

With respect to the four tasks of automatic Web service discovery, automatic Web service invocation, automatic Web service interoperation and composition, and automatic Web service execution monitoring that DAML-S is meant to support, the standards primarily enable the first and the second tasks to a certain extent. These standards are still evolving and it is unclear at present to what extent composition will be addressed. At the moment, the standards do not consider the *ServiceModel* of a service and thus, they also do not support execution monitoring, as defined in this paper.

In the following sections, we look in greater detail at each of these technologies in turn and compare them to DAML-S.

7.1   UDDI

UDDI (Universal Description, Discovery and Integration) is an initiative proposed by Microsoft, IBM and Ariba to develop a standard for an online registry, and to enable the publishing and dynamic discovery of Web services offered by businesses [22]. UDDI allows programmers and other representatives of a business to locate potential business partners and form business relationships on the basis of the services they provide. It thus facilitates the creation of new business relationships.

The primary target of UDDI seems to be integration and at least semi-automation of business transactions in B2B e-commerce applications. It provides a registry for registering businesses and the services they offer. These are described according to an XML schema defined by the UDDI specification. A Web service provider registers its advertisements along with keywords for categorization. A Web services user retrieves advertisements out of the registry based on keyword search. The UDDI search mechanism relies on pre-defined categorization through keywords and does not refer to the semantic content of the advertisements. The registry is supposed to function in a fashion similar to white pages or yellow pages, where businesses can be looked up by name or by a standard service taxonomy as is already used within the industry. UDDI attempts to cover all kinds of services offered by businesses, including those that are offered by phone or e-mail and similar means; in principle, DAML-S could do this, but it has not been our focus.

Technically speaking, each business description in UDDI consists of a businessEntity element, akin to a White Pages element describing the contact information for a business. A businessEntity describes a business by name, a key value, categorization, services offered (businessService elements) and contact information for the business. A businessService element describes a service using a name, key value, categorization and multiple "bindingTemplate" elements. This can be considered to be analogous to a Yellow Pages element that categorises a business. A bindingTemplate element in turn describes the kind of access the service requires (phone, mailto, http, ftp, fax etc.), key values and tModelInstances. tModelInstances are used to describe the protocols, interchange formats that the service comprehends, that is, the technical information required to access the service. It is also used to describe the "namespaces" for the classifications used in categorization. Many of the elements are optional, including most of the ones that would be required for matchmaking or service composition purposes.

UDDI aims to facilitate the discovery of potential business partners and the discovery of services and their groundings that are offered by known business partners. This may or may not be done automatically. When this discovery occurs, programmers affiliated with the business partners program their own systems to interact with the services discovered. This is also the model generally followed by ebXML. DAML-S enables more flexible discovery by allowing searches to take place on almost any attribute of the ServiceProfile. UDDI, in contrast, allows technical searches only on tModelKeys, references to tModelInstances, which represent full specifications of a kind of service.

UDDI does not support semantic descriptions of services. Thus, depending on the functionality offered by the content language, although agents can search the UDDI registry and retrieve service descriptions, a human needs to be involved in the loop to make sense of the descriptions, and to program the access interface.

Currently, UDDI does not provide or specify content languages for advertisement. Although WSDL is most closely associated with UDDI as a content language, the specification refers to ebXML and XML/edi also as potential candidates. Content languages could be a possible bridge between UDDI and DAML-S. DAML-S is also a suitable candidate for a content language and in this sense, DAML-S and UDDI are complementary. A higher-level service or standard defined on top of UDDI could take advantage of the additional richness of content DAML-S has to offer within the UDDI registries.

7.2 WSDL

WSDL (Web Services Description Language) is an XML format, closely associated with UDDI as the language for describing interfaces to business services registered with a UDDI database. Thus, it is closer to DAML-S in terms of functionality than UDDI. Like DAML-S, it attempts to separate services, defined in abstract terms, from the concrete data formats and protocols used for implementation, and defines bindings between the abstract description and its specific realization [3]. However, the abstraction of services is at a lower level than in DAML-S.

Services are defined as sets of ports, i.e. network addresses associated with certain protocols and data format specifications. The abstract nature of a service arises from the abstract nature of the messages and operations mapped to a port and define its port type. Port types are reusable and can be bound to multiple ports [18]. There are four basic types of operations in WSDL: a one-way, a (two-way) request-response, a (two-way) solicit-response and a (one-way) notification message. A message itself is defined abstractly as a request, a response or even a parameter of a request or response and its type, as defined in a type system like XSD.

They can be broken into parts to define the logical break-down of a message.

Messages and operations are defined abstractly and are thus reusable and extensible and correspond roughly to the DAML-S ServiceProfile. The service element itself incorporates both a ServiceProfile and ServiceGrounding information. WSDL service descriptions are not as expressive as DAML-S profiles. Preconditions, postconditions and effects of service access cannot be expressed within WSDL.

Like UDDI, WSDL does not support semantic description of services. WSDL focuses on the grounding of services and although it has a concept of input and output types as defined by XSD, it does not support the definition of logical constraints between its input and output parameters. Thus its support for discovery and invocation of services is less versatile than that of DAML-S.

7.3   E-speak

Hewlett-Packard is collaborating with the UDDI consortium to bring E-speak technology to the UDDI standard. E-speak and UDDI have similar goals in that they both facilitate the advertisement and discovery of services. E-speak is also comparable to WSDL in that it supports the description of service and data types [7]. It has a matching service that compares service requests with service descriptions, primarily on the basis of input-output and service type matching.

E-speak describes services (known as "Resources") as a set of attributes within several "Vocabularies". Vocabularies are sets of attributes common to a logical group of services. E-speak matches lookup requests against service descriptions with respect to these attributes. Attributes take common value types such as String, Int, Boolean and Double. There is a base vocabulary which defines basic attributes such as Name, Type (of value String only), Description, Keywords and Version. Currently, there is no semantic meaning attached to any of the attributes. Any matching which takes place is done over the service description attributes which does not distinguish between any further subtypes. DAML-S had a much richer set of attributes; in DAML-S terminology, the input/output parameters, effects and additional functional attributes. In addition, dependencies between attributes and logical constraints on them are not expressible within E-speak.

Unlike UDDI, which was intended to be an open standard from the beginning, e-speak scores relatively low on interoperability. It requires that an e-speak engine be run on all participating client machines. Furthermore, although e-speak is designed to be a full platform for Web services and could potentially expose a execution monitoring interface, service processes remain a black-box for the e-speak platform and consequently no execution monitoring can be done.

7.4   ebXML

ebXML, being developed primarily by OASIS and the United Nations, approaches the problem from a workflow perspective. ebXML uses two views to describe business interactions, a Business Operational View (BOV) and a Functional Service View (FSV) [23]. The BOV deals with the semantics of business data transactions, which include operational conventions, agreements, mutual obligations and the like between businesses. The FSV deals with the supporting services: their capabilities, interfaces and protocols. Although ebXML does not concentrate on only Web services, the focus of this view is essentially the same as that of the current DAML-S effort.

It has the concept of a Collaboration Protocol Profile (CPP) "which allows a Trading Partner to express their supported Business Processes and Business Service Interface requirements [such that they are understood] by other ebXML compliant Trading Partners", in effect a specification of the services offered by the Trading Partner. A Business Process is a set of business document exchanges between the Trading Partners. CPPs contain industry classification, contact information, supported Business Processes, interface requirements etc. They are registered within an ebXML registry, in which there is discovery of other Trading Partners and the Business Processes they support. In this respect, UDDI has some similarities with ebXML. However, ebXML's scope does not extend to the manner in which the business documents are specified. This is left to the Trading Partners to agree upon a priori by the creation of a Collaboration Protocol Agreement.

In conclusion, the kind of functionality, interoperability and dynamic matchmaking capabilities provided by DAML-S is only partially supported, as the standards are currently positioned, by WSDL and UDDI. UDDI may become more sophisticated as it incorporates e-speak-like functionalities, but it will not allow automatic service interoperability until it incorporates the information provided by DAML-S.

8 Summary and Current Status

DAML-S is an attempt to provide an ontology, within the framework of the DARPA Agent Markup Language, for describing Web services. It will enable users and software agents to automatically discover, invoke, compose, and monitor Web resources offering services, under specified constraints. We have released an initial version of DAML-S. It can be found at the URL: http://www.daml.org/services

We expect to enhance it in the future in ways that we have indicated in the paper, and in response to users' experience with it. We believe it will help make the Semantic Web a place where people can not only find out information but also get things done.

Acknowledgments

The authors have profited from discussions about this work with Ron Fadel, Richard Fikes, Jessica Jenkins, James Hendler, Mark Neighbors, Tran Cao Son, and Richard Waldinger. The research was funded by the Defense Advanced Research Projects Agency as part of the DARPA Agent Markup Language (DAML) program under Air Force Research Laboratory contract F30602-00-C-0168 to SRI International, F30602-00-2-0579-P00001 to Stanford University, and F30601-00-2-0592 to Carnegie Mellon University. Additional funding was provided by Nokia Research Center.

References

[1] J. F. Allen and H. A. Kautz. A model of naive temporal reasoning. In J. R. Hobbs and R. C. Moore, editors, *Formal Theories of the Commonsense World*, pages 251–268. Ablex Publishing Corp., 1985.

[2] T. Berners-Lee, J. Hendler, and O. Lassila. The Semantic Web. *Scientific American*, 284(5):34–43, 2001.

[3] E. Christensen, F. Curbera, G. Meredith, and S. Weerawarana. Web Services Description Language (WSDL) 1.1. http://www.w3.org/TR/2001/NOTE-wsdl-20010315, 2001.

[4] DAML-S Coalition:, A. Ankolekar, M. Burstein, J. Hobbs, O. Lassila, D. McDermott, D. Martin, S. McIlraith, S. Narayanan, M. Paolucci, T. Payne, and K. Sycara. DAML-S: Web Service Description for the Semantic Web. Submitted to the First International Semantic Web Conference (ISWC01), 2002.

[5] K. Decker, K. Sycara, and M. Williamson. Middle-Agents for the Internet. In *IJCAI97*, 1997.

[6] G. Denker, J. Hobbs, D. Martin, S. Narayanan, and R. Waldinger. Accessing Information and Services on the DAML-Enabled Web. In *Proc. Second Int'l Workshop Semantic Web (SemWeb'2001)*, 2001.

[7] E-Speak and the HP Web Services Platform. http://www.e-speak.net/, 2001.

[8] T. Finin, Y. Labrou, and J. Mayfield. KQML as an agent communication language. In J. Bradshaw, editor, *Software Agents*. MIT Press, Cambridge, 1997.

[9] M. Ghallab et. al. PDDL-The Planning Domain Definition Language V. 2. Technical Report, report CVC TR-98-003/DCS TR-1165, Yale Center for Computational Vision and Control, 1998.

[10] J. Hendler and D. L. McGuinness. DARPA Agent Markup Language. *IEEE Intelligent Systems*, 15(6):72–73, 2001.

[11] H. Levesque, R. Reiter, Y. Lesperance, F. Lin, and R. Scherl. GOLOG: A Logic programming language for dynamic domains. *Journal of Logic Programming*, 31(1-3):59–84, April-June 1997.

[12] D. Martin, A. Cheyer, and D. Moran. The Open Agent Architecture: A Framework for Building Distributed Software Systems. *Applied Artificial Intelligence*, 13(1-2):92–128, 1999.

[13] S. McIlraith, T. C. Son, and H. Zeng. Mobilizing the Web with DAML-Enabled Web Service. In *Proc. Second Int'l Workshop Semantic Web (SemWeb'2001)*, 2001.

[14] S. McIlraith, T. C. Son, and H. Zeng. Semantic Web Service. *IEEE Intelligent Systems*, 16(2):46–53, 2001.

[15] J. Meseguer. Conditional Rewriting Logic as a Unified Model of Concurrency. *Theoretical Computer Science*, 96(1):73–155, 1992.

[16] R. Milner. Communicating with Mobile Agents: The pi-Calculus. Cambridge University Press, Cambridge, 1999.

[17] S. Narayanan. Reasoning About Actions in Narrative Understanding. In *Proc. International Joint Conference on Artifical Intelligence (IJCAI'1999)*, pages 350–357. Morgan Kaufman Press, San Francisco, 1999.

[18] U. Ogbuji. Using WSDL in SOAP applications: An introduction to WSDL for SOAP programmers. http://www-106.ibm.com/developerworks/library/ws-soap/?dwzone=ws, 2001.

[19] C. Schlenoff, M. Gruninger, F. Tissot, J. Valois, J. Lubell, and J. Lee. The Process Specification Language (PSL): Overview and version 1.0 specification. NISTIR 6459, National Institute of Standards and Technology, Gaithersburg, MD., 2000.

[20] K. Sycara and M. Klusch. Brokering and Matchmaking for Coordination of Agent Societies: A Survey. In Omicini, A, et. al., editor, *Coordination of Internet Agents*. Springer, 2001.

[21] K. Sycara, M. Klusch, S. Widoff, and J. Lu. Dynamic Service Matchmaking Among Agents in Open Information Environments. *ACM SIGMOD Record (Special Issue on Semantic Interoperability in Global Information Systems)*, 28(1):47–53, 1999.

[22] UDDI. The UDDI Technical White Paper. http://www.uddi.org/, 2000.

[23] D. Webber and A. Dutton. Understanding ebXML, UDDI and XML/edi. http://www.xml.org/feature_articles/2000_1107_miller.shtml, 2000.

[24] H.-C. Wong and K. Sycara. A Taxonomy of Middle-agents for the Internet. In *ICMAS'2000*, 2000.

The Emerging Semantic Web
I.F. Cruz et al. (Eds.)
IOS Press, 2002

Searching for Services on the Semantic Web Using Process Ontologies

Mark KLEIN
Center for Coordination Science
Massachusetts Institute of Technology

Abraham BERNSTEIN
Stern School of Business
New York University

Abstract. The ability to rapidly locate useful on-line services (e.g. software applications, software components, process models, or service organizations), as opposed to simply useful documents, is becoming increasingly critical in many domains. As the sheer number of such services increases it will become increasingly more important to provide tools that allow people (and software) to quickly find the services they need, while minimizing the burden for those who wish to list their services with these search engines. This can be viewed as a critical enabler of the 'friction-free' markets of the 'new economy'. Current service retrieval technology is, however, seriously deficient in this regard. The *information retrieval* community has focused on the retrieval of documents, not services per se, and has as a result emphasized keyword-based approaches. Those approaches achieve fairly high recall but low precision. The *software agents* and *distributed computing communities* have developed simple 'frame-based' approaches for 'matchmaking' between tasks and on-line services increasing precision at the substantial cost of requiring all services to be modeled as frames and only supporting perfect matches. This paper proposes a novel, ontology-based approach that employs the characteristics of a process-taxonomy to increase recall without sacrificing precision and computational complexity of the service retrieval process

1. The Challenge

Increasingly, the Semantic Web will be called upon to provide access not just to static *documents* that collect useful *information*, but also to *services* that provide useful *behavior*. Potential examples of such services abound:

- *Software applications* (e.g. for engineering, finance, meeting planning, or word processing) that can invoked remotely by people or software
- *Software components* that can be downloaded for use when creating new applications
- *Process models* that describe how to achieve some goal (e.g. eCommerce business models, material transformation processes, etc)
- *Individuals* or *organizations* who can perform particular functions, e.g. as currently brokered using such web sites as guru.com, elance.com and freeagent.com.

As the sheer number of such services increase it will become increasingly important to provide tools that allow people (and software) to quickly find the services they need, while minimizing the burden for those who wish to list their services with these search engines [1]. This paper describes a set of ideas, based on the sophisticated use of process ontologies, for creating improved service retrieval technologies.

2. Contributions and Limitations of Current Technology

Current service retrieval approaches have serious limitations with respect to meeting these challenges. They either perform relatively poorly or make unrealistic demands of those who wish to index or retrieve services. We review this work below.

Service retrieval technology has emerged from several communities. The information retrieval community has focused on the retrieval of documents, not services per se, and has as a result emphasized keyword-based approaches. The software agents and distributed computing communities have developed simple 'frame-based' approaches for 'matchmaking' between tasks and on-line services. The software engineering community has developed by far the richest set of techniques for service retrieval [2]. We can get a good idea of the relative merits of these approaches by placing them in a *precision/recall* space (Figure 1):

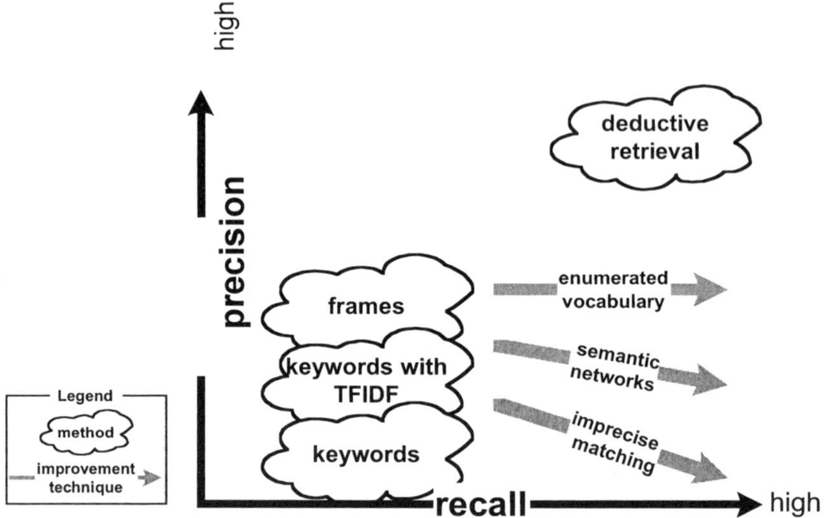

Figure 1: The state of the art in service retrieval.

Recall is the extent to which a search engine retrieves *all* of the items that one is interested in (i.e. avoiding false negatives) while *precision* is the extent to which the tool retrieves *only* the items that one is interested in (i.e. avoiding false positives).

Most search engines look for items (e.g. web pages) that contain the keywords in the query. More sophisticated variants (based on the technique known as TFIDF) look for items in which the searched-for keywords are more common than usual, thereby increasing precision [3]. Typically, no manual effort is needed to list items with such search engines, and queries can be specified without needing to know a specialized query language. Keyword-based approaches are, however, notoriously prone to both low precision and imperfect recall. Many completely irrelevant items may include the keywords in the query, leading to low precision. It is also possible that the query keywords are semantically equivalent but syntactically different from the words in the searched items, leading to reduced recall. Imagine , for example, that we are searching for a service that can offer a loan to cover a $100,000 house addition. Entering the keywords "loan house 100000" into google.com (a keyword-based search service), for example, returns 2,390 documents. While the first two results are promising (a loan calculator and a mortgage calculator somewhat connected to a loan granting organization), the third hit points to a report of a campaign against arms trade, and the fourth shows a junior high-school math-project on how to calculate mortgages. If we enter the same query in altavista.com (which uses TFIDF) we get 24,168,519 'hits'. While the first few hits talk about loans, they do not all provide a loan service. Most of them point to classes that discuss loan calculation techniques and provide some sort of a mortgage calculator.

It is of course somewhat misleading to use web-search engines to assess the likely performance of a keyword-based service retrieval engine. The web contains much more then services. Many documents (like the loan calculation classes mentioned above) have nothing to do with the provision of services. Nevertheless we can take the poor precision of those queries as an indicator of what would happen in a system that relies solely on these techniques for retrieving services. A mortgage calculator is a useful instrument in itself. It does not, however, provide the service of creditworthiness analysis or loan provision. We can, therefore, assume that systems using these techniques would still show low precision.

Several techniques have been developed to address these problems. One is to require that items and queries be described using the same, pre-enumerated, vocabulary [4]. This increases the probability that the same terms will be used in the query and desired items, thereby increasing recall. Another approach is to use semantic nets (e.g. WordNet [5]) that capture the semantic relationships between words (e.g. synonym, antonym, hypernym and hyponym) to increase the breadth of the query and thereby increase recall [6] but this potentially can reduce precision and can result in suboptimal recall because these networks focus on purely linguistic relationships. Search engines like google.com [7] prioritize retrieved documents according to whether they are linked to documents that also contain the searched-for keywords, as a way of increasing precision. Finally, most text-based search engines allow for imprecise matching (e.g. retrieving items that contain some but not all of the query keywords), potentially increasing recall but again at the cost of reduced precision.

We can see then that keyword-based approaches can achieve fairly high recall but at the cost of low precision. The key underlying problem is that keywords are a poor way to capture the semantics of a query or item. If this semantics could be captured more accurately then precision would increase. *Frame*-based approaches [8] [9] [10] [11] [12] have emerged as a way of doing this. A frame consists of attribute value pairs describing the properties of an item. Figure 2 for example shows a frame for an integer averaging service:

Description	a service to find the average of a list of integers
Input	integers
Output	real
Execution Time	number of inputs * 0.1 msec

Figure 2: A frame-based description of an integer sorting service.

Both items and queries are described using frames: matches represent items whose (textual) property values match those in the query. All the commercial service search technologies we are aware of (e.g. Jini, eSpeak, Salutation, UDDI [13]) use the frame-based approach, typically with an at least partially pre-enumerated vocabulary of service types and properties. The more sophisticated search tools emerging from the research community (e.g. LARKS [14]) also make limited use of semantic nets, e.g. returning a match if the input type of a service is equal to *or* a generalization of the input type specified in the query. Frame-based approaches thus do increase precision at the (fairly modest) cost of requiring that all services be modeled as frames.

The frame-based approach is taken one step further in the *deductive retrieval* approach [15] [16] [17] wherein service properties (e.g. inputs, outputs, function, and performance) are expressed *formally* using logic (Figure 3):

```
Name:            set-insert
Syntax:          set-insert(Elem, Old, New)
Input-types:     (Elem:Any), (Old:SET)
Output-types:    (New: SET)
Semantics:
    Precond:
    Postcond:
```

$$\downarrow member(Elem, Old)$$
$$member(Elem, New)$$
$$| \ \forall x(member(x, Old) \ \blacklozenge \ member(x, New)$$
$$| \ \forall y(member(y, New) \ \blacklozenge \ (member(y, old) \int \ y = Elem)$$

Figure 3: A service description for deductive retrieval [15]

Retrieval then consists of finding the items that can be *proved* to achieve the functionality described in the query. If we assume a non-redundant pre-enumerated vocabulary of logical predicates and a complete formalization of all relevant service and query properties, then deductive retrieval can in theory achieve both perfect precision and perfect recall. This approach, however, faces two very serious practical difficulties. First of all, it can be prohibitively difficult to model the semantics of non-trivial queries and services using formal logic. Even the simple set-insert function shown above in Figure 3 is non-trivial to formalize correctly: imagine trying to formally model the behavior of Microsoft Word or an accounting package! The second difficulty is that the proof process implicit in this kind of search can have a high computational complexity, making it extremely slow [15]. Our belief is that these limitations, especially the first one, make deductive retrieval unrealistic as a scalable general purpose service search approach.

Other approaches do exist, but they apply only to specialized applications. One is execution-based retrieval, wherein software components are selected by comparing their actual I/O behavior with the desired I/O behavior. This is approach is suitable only for contexts where observing a few selected samples of I/O behavior are sufficient to prune the service set [18] [19] [20].

3. Our Approach: Exploiting Process Ontologies

Our challenge, as we have seen, can be framed as being able to capture enough service and query semantics to substantively increase precision without reducing recall or making it unrealistically difficult for people to express these semantics. *Our central claim is that these goals can be achieved through the sophisticated use of process ontologies.* We begin by capturing the function(s) of a service as a process model. The service model is then indexed (to facilitate its subsequent retrieval) by placing it and all its components (subtasks and so on) into the appropriate sections of the ontology. Queries are also expressed as (partial) process models. The matching algorithm then finds all the services whose process models match that of the query, using the semantic relationships encoded in the process ontology. Our approach can thus be viewed as having the following functional architecture:

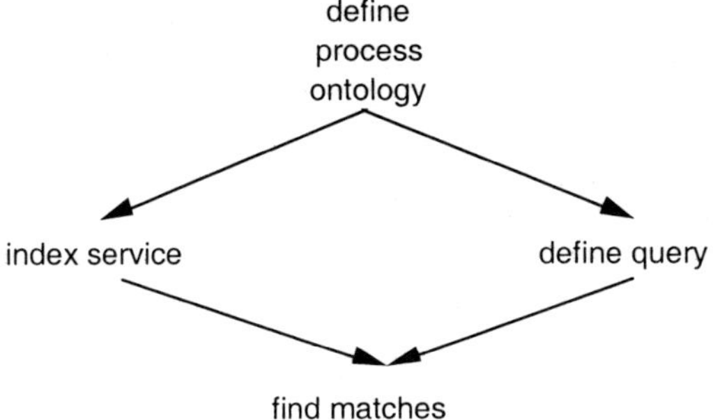

Figure 4: Functional architecture of our proposed service retrieval technology.

We will consider each element of the functional architecture in the sections below.

3.1 Define Process Ontology

Our approach differs from previous efforts in that it is based on highly expressive process models arranged into a fully-typed process ontology. The key concepts underlying this ontology are an extension of those developed by the MIT Process Handbook project. The Handbook is a process knowledge repository which has been under development at the Center for Coordination Science (CCS) for the past eight years [21] [22]. The Handbook is under active use and development by a highly distributed group of more than 40 scientists, teachers, students and sponsors for such diverse purposes as adding new process descriptions, teaching classes, and business process re-design. We believe the current Handbook process ontology represents an excellent starting point for indexing on-line services because it is focused on business processes which is what a high proportion of on-line services are likely to address.

The Handbook takes advantage of several simple but powerful concepts to capture and organize process knowledge: *attributes, ports, decomposition, dependencies, exceptions* and *specialization.*

> *Process Attributes:* Like most process modeling techniques, the Handbook allows processes to be annotated with attributes that capture such information as a textual description, typical performance values (e.g. how long a process takes to execute), as well as pre-, post- and during- conditions.

> *Decomposition:* Also like most process modeling techniques, the Handbook uses the notion of *decomposition*: a process is modeled as a collection of activities that can in turn be broken down ("decomposed") into subactivities.

> *Ports:* Ports describe the I/O-behavior of an activity. They describe the types of resources the activity uses and produces, and are as a result important for assessing the match between a service specification and a query.

> *Dependencies:* Another key concept we use is that coordination can be viewed as the management of *dependencies* between activities [21]. Every dependency can include an associated *coordination mechanism*, which is simply the process that manages the *resource* flow and thereby coordinates the activities connected by the dependency. Task inputs and outputs are represented as *ports* on those tasks. A key advantage of representing processes using these concepts is that they allow us to

highlight the 'core' activities of a process and abstract away details about how they coordinate with each other, allowing more compact service descriptions without sacrificing significant content.

Exceptions: Processes typically have characteristic ways they can fail and, in at least some cases, associated schemes for anticipating and avoiding or detecting and resolving them. This is captured in our approach by annotating processes with their characteristic 'exceptions', and mapping these exceptions to processes describing how these exceptions can be handled [23].

Specialization: The final key concept is that processes and all their key elements (ports, resources, attributes, and exceptions) appear in type taxonomies, with very generic classes at one extreme and increasingly *specialized* ones at the other, so process models are fully typed. The taxonomies place items with similar semantics (e.g. processes with similar purposes) close to each other, the way books with similar subjects appear close to each other in a library: Processes that vary along some identifiable dimension can be grouped into *bundles*; where processes can appear in more than one bundle. Bundles subsume the notion of 'faceted' classification [4], well-known in the software component retrieval community, because bundles, unlike facets, can include a whole ontology branch as opposed to simply a flat set of keywords, allowing varying abstraction levels and the use of synonyms.

As shown in Figure 5, an activity is thus defined by specifying its decomposition (i.e., the activities it contains), its interface (as defined by the ports it contains), the dependencies between its sub-activities, and the attributes defined for each of those entities (not shown). Each activity can be linked to the kinds of exceptions it can face, and these exceptions can be linked in turn to the processes if any used to handle (anticipate and avoid, or detect and resolve) them.

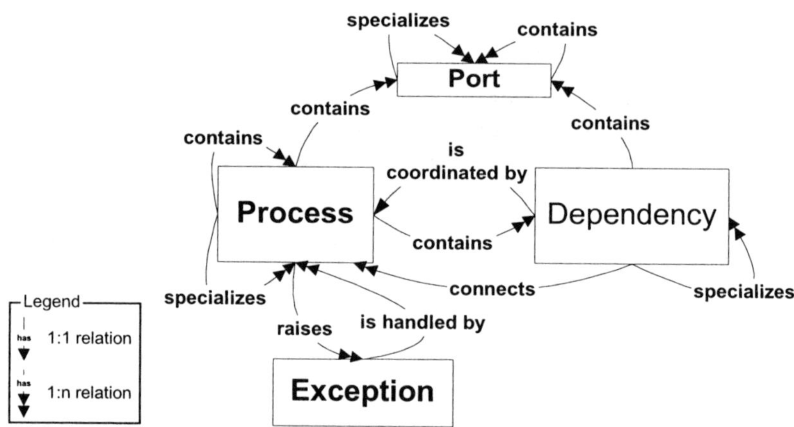

Figure 5: Partial meta-model for our process ontology (attributes not shown).

Every type of entity has its own specialization hierarchy into which it can be placed, making this a fully-typed process description approach. There is thus a specialization hierarchy for processes, resources, exceptions and so on. The "Sell loan" process, for example, is a specialization of the more general "Sell financial service" process. It, furthermore, specializes into more specific processes such as "Sell reserve credit," "Sell Credit Card," and "Sell mortgage" (Figure 6):

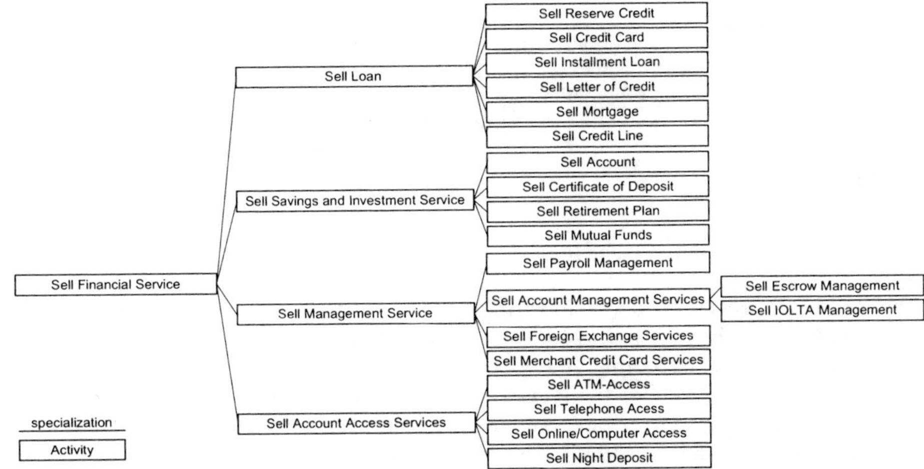

Figure 6: Specialization hierarchy for grant loan

Each of the elements of the "Sell loan" process is also a member of the overall specialization hierarchy. "Analyze credit-worthiness," for example, is a specialization of the more general "Perform financial analysis" and specializes to more specific processes such as "Analyze creditworthiness using scoring" and "Analyze creditworthiness using PE-ratio," etc.

This process representation has equal or greater formal expressiveness than other full-fledged process modeling languages (e.g. IDEF [24], PIF [25], PSL [26] or CIMOSA [27]) as well as greater expressiveness than the frame-based languages used in previous service retrieval efforts, by virtue of adding such important concepts as full typing, resource dependencies, ports, task decompositions, and exceptions.

The growing Handbook database currently includes over 5000 process descriptions ranging from specific (e.g. for a university purchasing department) to generic (e.g. for resource allocation and multi-criteria decision making). A subset of this database (containing a representative selection of process models but no exception-related information) is accessible over the Web at http://ccs.mit.edu/eph/

3.2 Index Services

Services are indexed into the process ontology so that they may be retrieved readily later on. Indexing a service in our approach comes down to placing the associated process model, and all of its components (attributes, ports, dependencies, subtasks and exceptions) in the appropriate place in the ontology. The fact that a substantial process ontology exists in the Process Handbook means that parties wishing to index a service can construct their service specification from already existing elements in the ontology, and then customizing them as necessary.

Imagine for example that we want to index a service that sells mortgages. The Handbook ontology already includes a general 'sell loan' process (Figure 7):

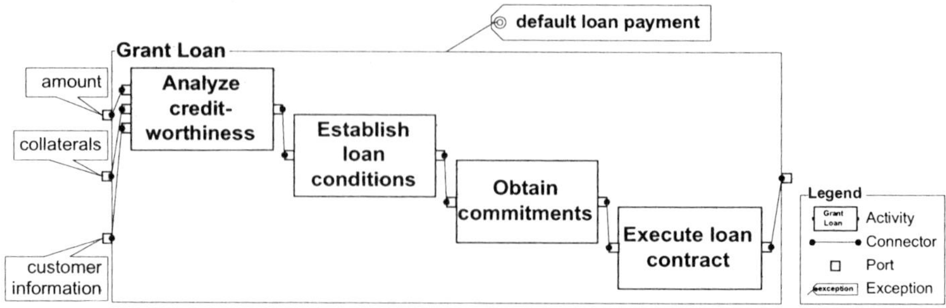

Figure 7: The loan selling service process model.

The 'sell loan' process model includes most of the requisite elements, including key sub-activities such as analyzing creditworthiness, establishing the loan's conditions, obtaining the commitments, and "executing" the loan contract. It also includes ports describing the process inputs (e.g. the size of the loan ("amount"), the collateral provided for the loan, information about the customer) and outputs (the loan itself). To simplify this example we omitted dependencies and exceptions. The mortgage provider, therefore, need only create a specialization of the 'sell loan' process and make the few changes specific to mortgage loans, e.g. further specifying the types of customer information it wishes and type of creditworthiness analysis performed, elements that can also be defined by specializing existing elements in the process ontology. (Figure 8):

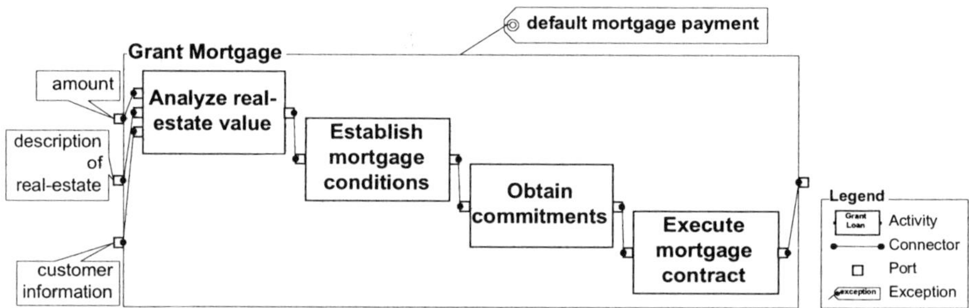

Figure 8: The mortgage selling service process model.

The Handbook project has developed sophisticated Windows-based tools for process indexing, based on this define-by-specialization principle, that have been refined over nearly eight years of daily use. Using these tools, most process models can indexed in a matter of minutes.

Note that when modeling a service, one needs in theory to account for all the possible uses the service may be put to. What to some users may be a side effect of a service may be a key attribute for others. To pick a homely example, a dog-walking service may be desired as a way to provide the dog exercise, or simply as a way to make sure the dog is cared for while the owner is out on an errand. This would suggest that a process model needs to be indexed under specializations representing all of its possible uses, which is difficult at best. As we shall see below, however, we can define query algorithms that, using query mutation operators, can potentially retrieve processes not explicitly indexed as serving a given purpose, thereby reducing the service-indexing burden.

We can, however, take the manual indexing approach described above one important step further. A key criterion for a successful service retrieval approach is minimizing the manual effort involved in listing new services with the search engine. Ideally services can be classified automatically. Automatic classification is predicated on having a similarity metric so one can place a process under the class it is most similar to. Previous efforts for automatic service classification have used similarity metrics based on either:

♦ Automatically calculated word frequency statistics for the natural language documentation of the service [28] [29] [30]
♦ Manually developed frame-based models of the service [9]

The first approach is more scalable because no manual effort is needed, but the latter approach results in higher retrieval precision because frame-based models, as we have seen, better capture service semantics. We can use a ontology-based approach to improve on these approaches by developing tools for [semi-] automated classification of process models. Process models, in the form of flowcharts for example, are typically created as part of standard programming practice, so in many if not most cases the services we want to index will already have process models defined for them. These models may even in some cases already be classified into some kind of process ontology. The greater expressiveness of process models as compared to standard frame-based service models (process models often include task decomposition information, for example, but frame-based models do not) means that we can define similarity metrics that are more accurate than those that have been used previously. These metrics can use word frequency statistics augmented with semantic networks to compute similarity of natural language elements, combined with taxonomic reasoning and graph-theoretic similarity measures to assess structural and type similarities. At the least, we believe that this technique should greatly speed manual service indexing by providing the human user with a short list of possible locations for a service. Ideally, it will allow a human user to be taken out of the loop entirely. If fully automated indexing turns out to be feasible, then we can imagine on-line services being indexed using Internet "worms" analogous to those currently used by keyword-based search tools.

3.3 Define Queries

It is of course possible that we can do without query definition entirely once services have been indexed into a process ontology. In theory one can simply browse the ontology to find the services that one is interested in, as in [31]. Our own experience with the Process Handbook suggests however that browsing can be slow and difficult for all except the most experienced human users, because of the size of the process ontology. This problem is likely to be exacerbated when, as with online services, the space of services is large and dynamic.

To address this challenge we have begun to define a query language called PQL (the Process Query Language) designed specifically for retrieving full-fledged process models from a process ontology [32]. Process models can be straightforwardly viewed as entity-relationship diagrams made up of entities like tasks connected by relationships like 'has-subtask'. PQL queries are built up as combinations of two types of clauses that check for given entities and relationships:

       Entity <entity> isa <entity type> :test <predicate>
       Relationship <source entity> <relationship type> <target entity> :test <predicate>

The first clause type matches any entity of a given type. The second primitive matches any relationship of a given type between two entities. Any bracketed item <> can be replaced by a variable (with the format ?<string>) that is bound to the matching entity and passed to subsequent query clauses. The predicates do further pruning of what constitutes a match.

Let us consider some simple examples. Imagine we are searching for a loan service that accepts real estate as collateral (which includes mortgages), as follows:

```
Entity ?proc isa sell-loan                          // finds a specialization of
"Sell loan"

Relationship ?proc has-port ?port1                  // looks for a port that accepts
real-
Entity ?port1 isa input-port                        // estate as a collateral
Relationship ?port1 propagates-resource ?res1
Entity ?res1 isa real-estate
Entity ?port1 has-attribute ?attr1
Entity ?attr1 isa name
Relationship ?attr1 has-value ?val :test (= ?val "collateral")

Relationship ?proc has-port ?port2                  // looks for a port that
"produces"
Entity ?port2 isa output-port                       // money
Relationship ?port2 propagates-resource ?res2
Entity ?res2 isa money
```

Query 1: A query for mortgage services.

This type of query is imaginably within the capabilities of frame-based query languages, especially if enhanced with a semantic network such as WordNet [5], since it references only the type and I/O for a service. Existing linguistically-oriented semantic networks do not, however, include a service-oriented process taxonomy like that incorporated in the Handbook, so we can expect that recall will be less than optimal using this approach.

We can go substantially further, however, using an ontology-based approach. Query 2 below, for example, retrieves a financing solution that has at least one internet-based step:

```
Entity ?proc isa sell-loan                          // finds a specialization of
"Sell loan"

Relationship ?proc has-subtask ?sub                 // has sub-process that is
internet
Entity ?sub isa internet-process                    // based

Relationship ?proc has-port ?port1                  // looks for a port that accepts
real-
Entity ?port1 isa input-port                        // estate as a collateral
Relationship ?port1 propagates-resource ?res1
Entity ?res1 isa real-estate
Entity ?port1 has-attribute ?attr1
Entity ?attr1 isa name
Relationship ?attr1 has-value ?val :test(= ?val "collateral")

Relationship ?proc has-port ?port2                  // looks for a port that
"produces"
```

    Entity ?port2 isa output-port   // money
    Relationship ?port2 propagates-resource ?res2
    Entity ?res2 isa money

Query 2: A query for internet-based financing services.

This useful capability – searching for services based on *how* they achieve their purpose – can *not* be achieved using frame-based languages since they do not capture process decompositions.

Another novel and powerful feature of the ontology-based approach is the ability to search based on how the service handles *exceptions*. Query 2 could be refined, for example, by adding a clause that searches for loan processes that provide insurance for handling payment defaults:

    Entity ?proc isa sell-loan

    ...

    Relationship ?proc has-exception ?exc
    Entity ?exc isa payment-default
    Relationship ?exc is-handled-by ?proc2
    Entity ?proc2 isa insurance-process

Query 3: A query refinement that searches for payment default insurance.

Searching based on a services' exception handling processes is also not well-supported by frame-based techniques. We can see, in short, that an ontology-based approach offers substantively greater query expressiveness than keyword or frame-based approaches, by virtue of having a substantive process taxonomy, and by being able to represent process decompositions and exception handling.

PQL, like any query language, is fairly verbose and requires that users be familiar with its syntax. More intuitive interfaces suitable for human users are possible. One approach exploits the process ontology. It is straightforward to translate any process model into a PQL query that looks for a service with that function. Users can thus use the Handbook process modeling tools to express a query as a combination and refinement of existing elements in the process ontology, in much the same way new services are indexed. An advantage of specifying a query in this way is that the elements in the process ontology can give the user additional ideas concerning what to look for. Someone looking for a mortgage service, for example, might not initially think to check for whether or not that service provides mortgage insurance. If they define the query as a specialization of the generic 'sell loan' process, however, they may note that that process has a possible 'payment default' exception, and they mya as a result be inspired to search for mortgage services that handle that exception in a way the user prefers.

Other possibilities exist. One can reduce the query definition burden by allowing users to enter queries using a restricted subset of English (an approach that has been applied successfully to traditional database access). Substantial progress has also been made in defining graphical metaphors for query definition (e.g. see [33]). These approaches can of course be combined, so that for example a simple natural language query returns some candidates classes that are selected from and refined to define the final, more complete, query.

3.4 Find Matches

The algorithm for retrieving matches given a PQL query is straightforward. The clauses in the PQL query are tried in order, each clause executed in the variable binding environment accumulated from the previous clauses. The sets of bindings that survive to the end represent the matching services. There is one key problem, however, that has to be accounted for; what we can call *modeling differences*. It is likely that in at least some cases a service may be modeled in a way that is semantically equivalent to but nevertheless does not syntactically match a given PQL query. The service model may, for example, include a given subtask several levels down the process decomposition, while in the query that subtask may be just one level down. The service model may express using several resource flows what is captured in the query as a single more abstract resource flow. The service model may simply be missing some type or resource flow information tested for in the query. This problem is exacerbated by the possibility of multiple service ontologies. As has been pointed out in [34], while we can expect the increasing prevalence of on-line ontologies to structure all kinds of knowledge including service descriptions, there will almost certainly be many partially-mapped ontologies as opposed to a single universally adopted one. This will likely increase the potential for modeling differences, e.g. if queries and services are defined using different ontologies. In order to avoid false negatives we must therefore provide a retrieval scheme that is tolerant of such modeling differences.

We can explore for this purpose the use of semantics-preserving query mutation operators. Imagine we have a library of operators that can syntactically mutate a given PQL query in a way that (largely) preserves its semantics. Some examples of such operators include:

♦ allow a type specification to be more general
♦ allow a subtask to be any number of levels down the task decomposition hierarchy
♦ allow 'siblings' or 'cousins' of a task to constitute a match
♦ relax the constraints on a parameter value
♦ remove a subtask

One can use mutation operators to broaden a search to allow for the discovery of novel alternatives. One could for example apply mutation operator (a) to Query 4 above so that it searches for "Sell" processes, not just "Sell loan" processes. This would result in additional hits like "Sell real-estate," a service which would sell the property to raise money, or "Sell real-estate lease," which would lease the property to generate funds. Assuming a homeowner would want to raise money for an extension, the first of those two additional options would not be desirable, as the property would be sold off. The second option, though, is often used. The key point to be made here is that the mutation operation broadened the search in a way that was *semantically motivated*, thereby avoiding the precipitous decline in precision typical of other imprecise matching techniques.

A second important potential use of mutation operators is to address the incomplete indexing issue described in section 3.2. It will often be the case that a user may be searching for all processes that serve a purpose not represented by any single element in the process ontology. For example, one may be searching for all the ways to raise money, but the different options may not all share a single generalization. One can address this issue by using mutation operators to define a query that searches for processes with *similar substeps,* regardless of what part of the process ontology they are indexed in. So we can, for example, search for all processes that offer money given some kind of collateral. This would return such options as services for getting a mortgage, raising money on the stock market, and so on.

4. Contributions of this Work

This paper has described a set of ideas that exploit the use of process model representations of service semantics, plus process ontologies, to improve service retrieval. These ideas offer the potential for the following important benefits:

Increased Precision: Our approach differs from previous efforts in that it models service semantics more fully than keyword or frame-based approaches, without imposing the unrealistic modeling burden implied by deductive retrieval approaches. This translates into greater retrieval precision.

Increased Recall: Modeling differences between queries and service descriptions can reduce recall, but this can be addressed in a novel way through the use of semantics-preserving query mutation operators.

While query definition and service indexing using process models is potentially more burdensome than simply entering a few keywords, we believe that existing "define-by-specialization" process modeling techniques developed in the Handbook project, coupled with our proposed advances in search algorithms and automated process model classification, should result in an acceptable increase in the query definition and service indexing burden when traded off against the increase in retrieval precision and recall.

To date we have developed an initial version of a PQL interpreter as well as a small set of semantics-preserving query mutation operators [32], which has demonstrated the viability of the query-by-process-model concept. While we have not yet evaluated PQL's performance in detail yet, it is clear that its primitive query elements have low computational complexity. Query performance can in addition be increased by using such well-known techniques as query clause re-ordering. Our future efforts will involve comparing the precision and recall of our approach with other search engines, refining the query definition and mutation schemes, and implementing and evaluating automated process classification techniques.

5. References

[1] Bakos, J.Y., *Reducing Buyer Search Costs: Implications for Electronic Marketplaces*. Management Science, 1997. **43**.

[2] Mili, H., F. Mili, and A. Mili, *Reusing software: issues and research directions*. IEEE Transactions on Software Engineering, 1995. **21**(6): p. 528-62.

[3] Salton, G. and M.J. McGill, *Introduction to modern information retrieval*. McGraw-Hill computer science series. 1983, New York: McGraw-Hill. xv, 448.

[4] Prieto-Diaz, R., *Implementing faceted classification for software reuse*. 12th International Conference on Software Engineering, 1990. **9**: p. 300-4.

[5] Fellbaum, C., ed. *WordNet: An Electronic Lexical Database*. 1998, MIT Press: Cambridge MA USA.

[6] Magnini, B., *Use of a lexical knowledge base for information access systems*. International Journal of Theoretical & Applied Issues in Specialized Communication, 1999. **5**(2): p. 203-228.

[7] Brin, S. and L. Page. *The anatomy of a large-scale hypertextual Web search engine*. in *Computer Networks & ISDN Systems*. 1998. Netherlands: Elsevier.

[8] Henninger, S., *Information access tools for software reuse*. Journal of Systems & Software, 1995. **30**(3): p. 231-47.

[9] Fernandez-Chamizo, C., et al., *Case-based retrieval of software components*. Expert Systems with Applications, 1995. **9**(3): p. 397-421.

[10] Fugini, M.G. and S. Faustle. *Retrieval of reusable components in a development information system*. in *Second International Workshop on Software Reusability*. 1993: IEEE Press.

[11] Devanbu, P., et al., *LaSSIE: a knowledge-based software information system*. Communications of the ACM, 1991. **34**(5): p. 34-49.

[12] ESPEAK, *Hewlett Packard's Service Framework Specification*. 2000, HP Inc.

[13] Richard, G.G., *Service advertisement and discovery: enabling universal device cooperation*. IEEE Internet Computing, 2000. **4**(5): p. 18-26.

[14] Sycara, K., et al. *Matchmaking Among Heterogeneous Agents on the Internet*. in *AAAI Symposium on Intelligent Agents in Cyberspace*. 1999: AAAI Press.

[15] Meggendorfer, S. and P. Manhart. *A Knowledge And Deduction Based Software Retrieval Tool*. in *6th Annual Knowledge-Based Software Engineering Conference*. 1991: IEEE Press.

[16] Chen, P., R. Hennicker, and M. Jarke. *On the retrieval of reusable software components*. in *Proceedings Advances in Software Reuse. Selected Papers from the Second International Workshop on Software Reusability*. 1993.

[17] Kuokka, D.R. and L.T. Harada, *Issues and extensions for information matchmaking protocols*. International Journal of Cooperative Information Systems, 1996. **5**: p. 2-3.

[18] Podgurski, A. and L. Pierce, *Retrieving reusable software by sampling behavior*. ACM Transactions on Software Engineering & Methodology, 1993. **2**(3): p. 286-303.

[19] Hall, R.j. *Generalized behavior-based retrieval (from a software reuse library)*. in *15th International Conference on Software Engineering*. 1993.

[20] Park, Y., *Software retrieval by samples using concept analysis*. Journal of Systems & Software, 2000. **54**(3): p. 179-83.

[21] Malone, T.W. and K.G. Crowston, *The interdisciplinary study of Coordination. ACM Computing Surveys*, 1994. **26**(1): p. 87-119.

[22] Malone, T.W., et al., *Tools for inventing organizations: Toward a handbook of organizational processes*. Management Science, 1999. **45**(3): p. 425-443.

[23] Klein, M. and C. Dellarocas, *A Knowledge-Based Approach to Handling Exceptions in Workflow Systems*. Journal of Computer-Supported Collaborative Work. Special Issue on Adaptive Workflow Systems., 2000. **9**(3/4).

[24] NIST, *Integrated Definition for Function Modeling (IDEF0)*. 1993, National Institute of Standards and Technology.

[25] Lee, J., et al. *The PIF Process Interchange Format and Framework Version 1.1*. in *European Conference on AI (ECAI) Workshop on Ontological Engineering*. 1996. Budapest, Hungary.

[26] Schlenoff, C., et al., *The essence of the process specification language*. Transactions of the Society for Computer Simulation, 1999. **16**(4): p. 204-16.

[27] Kosanke, K., *CIMOSA: Open System Architecture for CIM*. 1993: Springer Verlag.

[28] Frakes, W.b. and B.a. Nejmeh, *Software reuse through information retrieval*. Proceedings of the Twentieth Hawaii International Conference on System Sciences, 1987. **2**: p. 6-9.

[29] Maarek, Y.s., D.M. Berry, and G.e. Kaiser, *An information retrieval approach for automatically constructing software libraries*. IEEE Transactions on Software Engineering, 1991. **17**(8): p. 800-13.

[30] Girardi, M.R. and B. Ibrahim, *Using English to retrieve software*. Journal of Systems & Software, 1995. **30**(3): p. 249-70.

[31] Latour, L. and E. Johnson. *Seer: a graphical retrieval system for reusable Ada software modules*. in *Third International IEEE Conference on Ada Applications and Environments*. 1988: IEEE Comput. Soc. Press.

[32] Klein, M. *An Exception Handling Approach to Enhancing Consistency, Completeness and Correctness in Collaborative Requirements Capture*. in *Third ISPE International Conference on Concurrent Engineering*. 1996. Toronto, Ontario, Canada: Technomic Publishing Company.

[33] Spoerri, A. *InfoCrystal: a visual tool for information retrieval management*. in *Second International Conference on Information and Knowledge Management*. 1993. Washington, D.C.: ACM Press.

[34]   Hendler, J., *Agents on the Semantic Web*. IEEE Intelligent Systems, 2001. **16**(2): p. 30-37.

The Emerging Semantic Web
I.F. Cruz et al. (Eds.)
IOS Press, 2002

CREAting relational Metadata (CREAM) — a framework for semantic annotation

[1]Siegfried Handschuh, [1,2]Steffen Staab, [1,3]Alexander Maedche

[1]Institute AIFB, University of Karlsruhe, D-76128 Karlsruhe, Germany
`http://www.aifb.uni-karlsruhe.de/WBS`
`{sha,sst,ama}@aifb.uni-karlsruhe.de`

[2]Ontoprise GmbH, Haid-und-Neu Straße 7, 76131 Karlsruhe, Germany
`http://www.ontoprise.de`

[3]FZI Research Center for Information Technologies,
Haid-und-Neu Straße 10-14, 76131 Karlsruhe, Germany
`http://www.fzi.de/wim`

> *"The Web is about links;*
> *the Semantic Web is about the relationships implicit in those links."*
> Dan Brickley

Abstract. Richly interlinked, machine-understandable data constitutes the basis for the Semantic Web. Annotating web documents is one of the major techniques for creating metadata on the Web. However, annotation tools so far are restricted in their capabilities of providing richly interlinked and truely machine-understandable data. They basically allow the user to annotate with plain text according to a template structure, such as Dublin Core. We here present CREAM (Creating RElational, Annotation-based Metadata), a framework for an annotation environment that allows to construct *relational metadata*, i.e. metadata that comprises class instances and relationship instances. These instances are not based on a fix structure, but on a domain ontology. We discuss some of the requirements one has to meet when developing such a framework, e.g. the integration of a metadata crawler, inference services, document management and information extraction, and describe its implementation, *viz.* Ont-O-Mat a component-based, ontology-driven annotation tool.

1 Introduction

Research about the WWW currently strives to augment syntactic information already present in the Web by semantic metadata in order to achieve a Semantic Web that human and software agents alike can understand. RDF(S) or DAML+OIL are languages that have recently advanced the basis for extending purely syntactic information, *e.g.* HTML documents, with semantics. Based on these recent advancements one of the the most urgent challenges now is a knowledge capturing problem, *viz.* how one may turn existing syntactic resources into interlinked knowledge structures that represent relevant underlying information. This paper is about a framework for facing this challenge, called CREAM[1], and about its implementation, Ont-O-Mat.

The origin of our work facing this challenge dates back to the start of the seminal KA2 intiative [1], *i.e.* the initiative for providing semantic markup on HTML pages for the knowledge acquisition community. The basic idea then was that manual knowledge markup on web pages was too error-prone and should therefore be replaced by a *simple* tool that should help to avoid syntactic mistakes.

Developing our CREAM framework, however, we had to recognize that this knowledge capturing task exhibited some intrinsic difficulties that could not be solved by a *simple* tool. We here mention only some challenges that immediately came up in the KA2 setting:

- **Consistency**: Semantic structures should adhere to a given ontology in order to allow for better sharing of knowledge. For example, it should be avoided that people confuse complex instances with attribute types.

- **Proper Reference**: Identifiers of instances, *e.g.* of persons, institutes or companies, should be unique. For instance, in KA2 metadata there existed three different identifiers of our colleague Dieter Fensel. Thus, knowledge about him could not be grasped with a straightforward query.[2]

- **Avoid Redundancy**: Decentralized knowledge provisioning should be possible. However, when annotators collaborate, it should be possible for them to identify (parts of) sources that have already been annotated and to reuse previously captured knowledge in order to avoid laborious redundant annotations.

- **Relational Metadata**: Like HTML information, which is spread on the Web, but related by HTML links, knowledge markup may be distributed, but it should be semantically related. Current annotation tools tend to generate template-like metadata, which is hardly connected, if at all. For example, annotation environments often support Dublin Core [14], providing means to state, e.g., the name of authors, but not their IDs[3].

- **Maintenance**: Knowledge markup needs to be maintained. An annotation tool should support the maintenance task.

- **Ease of use**: It is obvious for an annotation environments to be useful. However, it is not trivial, because it involves intricate navigation of semantic structures.

- **Efficiency**: The effort for the production of metadata is a large restraining threshold. The more efficiently a tool support the annotation, the more metadata will produce a user. These requirement stand in relationship with the ease of use. It depends also on the automation of the annotation process, e.g. on the pre-processing of the document.

---

[1]CREAM: Creating RElational, Annotation-based Metadata.

[2]The reader may see similar effects in bibliography databases. E.g., query for James (Jim) Hendler at the otherwise excellent DBLP: http://www.informatik.uni-trier.de/~ley/db/.

[3]In the web context one typically uses the term 'URI' (uniform resource identifier) to speak of 'unique identifier'.

CREAM faces these principal problems by combining advanced mechanisms for inferencing, fact crawling, document management and — in the future — information extraction. Ont-O-Mat, the implementation of CREAM, is a component-based plug-in architecture that tackles this broad set of requirements.[4]

In the following we first sketch usage scenarios (Section 2). Then, we explain our terminology in more detail, derive requirements from our principal considerations above and explain the architecture of CREAM (Section 3). We describe our actual tool, Ont-O-Mat, in Section 4. Before we conclude, we contrast CREAM with related work, namely knowledge acquisition tools and annotation frameworks.

2 Scenarios for CREAM

We here summarize three scenarios, the first two have been elaborated in[25]:

The first scenario extends the objectives of the seminal KA2 initiative. The KA2 portal provides a view onto knowledge of the knowledge acquisition community. Besides of semantic retrieval as provided by the original KA2 initiative, it allows comprehensive means for navigating and querying the knowledge base and also includes guidelines for building such a knowledge portal. The potential users provide knowledge, e.g. by annotating their web pages in a decentralized manner. The knowledge is collected at the portal by crawling and presented in a variety of ways.

The second scenario is a knowledge portal for business analysts that is currently constructed at Ontoprise GmbH. The principal idea is that business analyst review news tickers, business plans and business reports. A considerable part of their work requires the comparison and aggregation of similar or related data, which may be done by semantic queries like"Which companies provide B2B solutions?", when the knowledge is semantically available. At the Time2Research portal they will handle different types of documents, annotate them and, thus, feed back into the portal to which they may ask questions.

The third scenario [21] is the application of semantic web technologies for tourism information systems. Here the WWW accessible information about touristic packages, travel or lodging arrangement is annotated in order to enable a finding, integrating, or connecting information based on these relational metadata.

3 Design of CREAM

In this section we explain basic design decisions of CREAM, which are founded on the general problems sketched in the introduction above. In order to provide a clear design rationale, we first provide definitions of important terms we use subsequently:

- **Ontology**: An ontology is a formal, explicit specification of a shared conceptualization of a domain of interest [9]. In our case it is constituted by statements expressing definitions of DAML+OIL classes and properties [8].

- **Annotations**: An annotation in our context is a set of instantiations attached to an HTML document. We distinguish *(i)* instantiations of DAML+OIL classes, *(ii)* instantiated properties from one class instance to a datatype instance — henceforth called attribute instance

---

[4]The core Ont-O-Mat can be downloaded from: http://annotation.semanticweb.org.

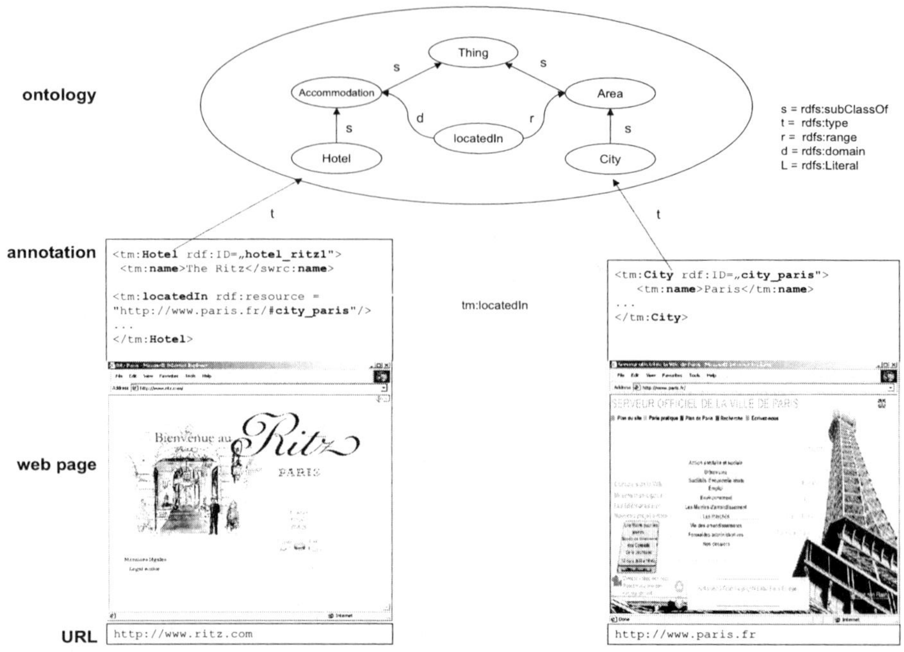

Figure 1: Annotation example

(of the class instance), and *(iii)* instantiated properties from one class instance to another class instance — henceforth called relationship instance.

Class instances have unique URIs. Instantiations may be attached to particular markups in the HTML documents, *viz.* URIs and attribute values may appear as strings in the HTML text.

- **Metadata**: Metadata are data about data. In our context the annotations are metadata about the HTML documents.

- **Relational Metadata**: We use the term relational metadata to denote the annotations that contain relationship instances.

  Often, the term "annotation" is used to mean something like "private or shared note", "comment" or "Dublin Core metadata". This alternative meaning of annotation may be emulated in our approach by modeling these notes with attribute instances. For instance, a comment note "I like this paper" would be related to the URL of the paper via an attribute instance 'hasComment'.

  In contrast, relational metadata contain statements like 'the hotel Ritz is located in the city Paris', *i.e.* relational metadata contain relationships between class instances rather than only textual notes.

Table 1: Design Rationale — Linking Challenges with Required Modules

Requirement General Problem	Document Viewer	Ontology Guidance	Crawler	Storage		
				Replication Annotation Inference Server	Document Management	Information Extraction
Consistency		X		X		
Proper Reference			X	X		
Avoid Redundancy			X	X	X	
Relational Metadata		X	X	X		
Maintenance					X	X
Ease of use	X	X				X
Efficiency	X	X	X	X	X	X

Figure 1 illustrates our use of the terms "ontology", "annotation" and "relational metadata". It depicts some part a tourism ontology[5]. Furthermore it shows two homepages, viz. pages about the Ritz and Paris (`http://www.ritz.com` and `http://www.paris.fr`, respectively) with annotations given in an XML serialization of RDF facts. For the hotel and the city there are instances denoted by corresponding URIs (`hotel_ritz1` and `city_paris`). The `tm:name` of `hotel_ritz1` is "The Ritz". In Addition, there is a relationship instance between them: "locatedIn". This information 'spans' the two pages.

3.1 Requirements for CREAM

The difficulties sketched in the introduction directly feed into the design rationale of CREAM. The design rationale links the challenges with the requirements. This results in a N:M mapping (neither functional nor injective). An overview of the matrix is given in Table 1. It shows which modules (requirements) are mainly used to answer challenges set forth in the introduction, *viz.*:

- **Document Viewer**: The document viewer visualizes the web page contents. The annotator may easily provide annotations by highlighting text that serves as input for attribute instances or the definition of URIs. The document viewer must support various formats (HTML, PDF, XML, etc.).

- **Ontology Guidance**: The annotation framework needs guidance from the ontology. In order to allow for sharing of knowledge, newly created annotations must be consistent with a community's ontology. If annotators instantiate arbitrary classes and properties the semantics of these properties remains void. Of course the framework must be able to adapt to varying ontologies in order to reflect different foci of the annotators.

  Furthermore, the ontology is important in order to guide annotators towards creating relational metadata. We have done some preliminary experiments and found that subjects

---

[5]currently only available in German at http://ontobroker.semanticweb.org/ontos/compontos/tourism_l1.daml.

have more problems with creating relationship instances than with creating attribute instances (cf. [24]). Without the ontology they would miss even more cues for assigning relationships between class instances.

Both ontology guidance and document viewer should be easy to use: Drag'n'drop helps to avoid syntax errors and typos and a good visualization of the ontology can help to correctly choose the most appropriate class for instances.

- **Crawler:** The creation of relational metadata must take place *within* the Semantic Web. During annotation annotaters must be aware of which entities exist in the part of the Semantic Web they annotate. This is only possible if a crawler makes relevant entities immediately available. So, annotators may look for proper reference, i.e. decide whether an entity already has a URI (e.g. whether the entity named "Dieter Fensel" or "D. Fensel" has already been identified by some other annotators) and thus only annotators may recognize whether properties have already been instantiated (e.g. whether "Dieter Fensel" has already be linked to his publications). As a consequence of annotators' awareness relational metadata may be created, because class instances become related rather than only flat templates are filled.

- **Annotation Inference Server**: Relational metadata, proper reference and avoidance of redundant annotation require querying for instances, i.e. querying whether and which instances exist. For this purpose as well as for checking of consistency, we provide an annotation inference server in our framework. The annotation inference server reasons on crawled and newly annotated instances and on the ontology. It also serves the ontological guidance, because it allows to query for existing classes and properties.

- **Document Management**: In order to avoid redundancy of annotation efforts, it is not sufficient to ask whether instances exist at the annotation inference server. When an annotator decides to capture knowledge from a web page, he does not want to query for all single instances that he considers relevant on this page, but he wants information, whether and how this web page has been annotated before. Considering the dynamics of HTML pages on the web, it is desirable to store annotated web pages together with their annotations. When the web page changes, the old annotations may still be valid or they may become invalid. The annotator must decide based on the old annotations and based on the changes of the web page.

  A future goal of the document management in our framework will be the semi-automatic maintenance of annotations. When only few parts of a document change, pattern matching may propose revision of old annotations.

- **Information Extraction**: Even with sophisticated tools it is laborious to provide semantic annotations. A major goal thus is semi-automatic annotation taking advantage of information extraction techniques to propose annotations to annotators and, thus, to facilitate the annotation task. Concerning our environment we envisage two major techniques: First, "wrappers" may be learned from given markup in order to automatically annotate similarly structured pages (cf., e.g., [17]). Second, message extraction like systems may be used to recognize named entities, propose co-reference, and extract some relationship from texts (cf., e.g., [23]).

Besides of the requirements that constitute single modules, one may identify functions that cross module boundaries:

- Storage: CREAM supports two different ways of storage. The annotations will be stored inside the document that is in the document management component, but it is also stored in the annotation inference server.

- Replication: We provide a simple replication mechanism by crawling annotations into our annotation inference server.

3.2　Architecture of CREAM

The architecture of CREAM is depicted in Figure 2. The complete design of CREAM comprises a plug-in structure, which is flexible with regard to adding or replacing modules. Document viewer and ontology guidance module together constitute the major part of the graphical user interface. Via plug-ins the core annotation tool, Ont-O-Mat, is extended to include the capabilities outlined above. For instance, a plug-in for a connection to a document management system provides document management and retrieval capabilities that show the user annotations of a document he loads into his browser. This feature even becomes active when the user does not actively search for already existing annotations. Similarly, Ont-O-Mat provides extremely simple means for navigating the taxonomy, which means that the user can work without an inference server. However, he only gets the full-fledged semantics when the corresponding plug-in connection to the annotation inference server is installed.

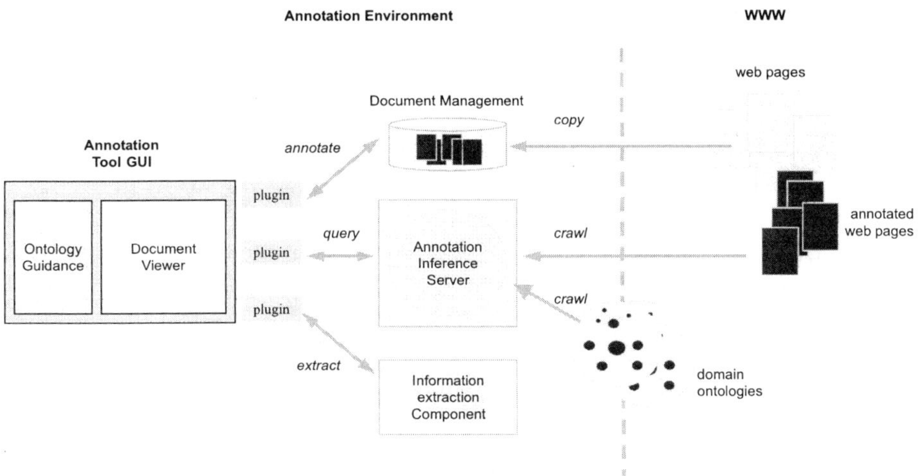

Figure 2: Architecture of CREAM.

4 Implementation: Ont-O-Mat

This section describes Ont-O-Mat, the implementation of our CREAM framework. Ont-O-Mat is a component-based, ontology-driven markup tool. The architectural idea behind CREAM is a component-based framework, thus, being open, flexible and easily extensible.

In the following subsection we refer to the concrete realization and the particular technical requirements of the components. In subsection 4.2 we describe the functionality of Ont-O-Mat based on an example ontology for annotation that is freely available on the web.

4.1 Ont-O-Mat services and components

The architecture of Ont-O-Mat provides a plug-in and service mechanism. The components are dynamically plug-able to the core Ont-O-Mat. The plug-in mechanism notifies each installed component, when a new component is registered. Through the service mechanism each component can discover and utilize the services offered by another component [11]. A service represented by a component is typically a reference to an interface. This provides among other things a de-coupling of the service from the implementation and allows therefore alternative implementations.

The Ont-O-Mat services have been realized by components according to the requirements listed in subsection 3.1. So far we have realized the following components: a comprehensive user-interface, component for document-management, an annotation inference-server and a crawler:

- **Document Viewer and Ontology Guidance**: There are various ways how the gained knowledge database can be visualized and thus experienced. On the one hand, the system can be used as a browser. In the annotated web pages, the extracted text fragments are then highlighted and an icon after each fragment is visible. By clicking on the icon, the name of the assigned class or attribute will be shown. On the other hand, the user can browse the ontology and retrieve for one class all instances or for one instance all attributes.

  The underlying data model used for Ont-O-Mat has been taken from the comprehensive ontology engineering and learning system ONTOEDIT / TEXT-TO-ONTO (see [20]).

  Ont-O-Mat works currently in "read-only–mode" with respect to the ontology and only operates on the relational metadata defined on top of the given ontology.

- **Document Management**: A component for document management is required in order to avoid duplicate annotations and existing semantic annotations of documents should be recognized. In our current implementation we use a straight forward file-system based document management approach.

  Ont-O-Mat uses the URI to detect the re-encounter of previously annotated documents and highlights annotations in the old document for the user. Then the user may decide to ignore or even delete the old annotations and create new metadata, he may augment existing data, or he may just be satisfied with what has been previously annotated. In order to recognize that a document has been annotated before, but now appears under a different URI, Ont-O-Mat computes similarity with existing documents by simple information retrieval methods, e.g. comparison of the word vector of a page. If thereby a similarity is discovered, this is indicated to the user, so that he can check for congruency.

- **Annotation Inference Server**: The annotation inference server reasons on crawled and newly annotated instances and on the ontology. It also serves the ontological guidance, because it allows to query for existing classes and properties. We use Ontobroker's [4] underlying F-Logic [16] based inference engine SiLRI [3] as annotation inference server. The F-Logic inference engine combines ordering-independent reasoning in a high-level logical language with a well-founded semantics.

- **RDF Crawler**: As already mentioned above, the annotation must take place right within the Semantic Web and not isolated. Therefore, we have built a RDF Crawler[6], a basic tool that gathers interconnected fragments of RDF from the Web and builds a local knowledge base from this data.

  In general, RDF data may appear in Web documents in several ways. We distinguish between *(i)* pure RDF (files that have an extension like "*.rdf"), *(ii)* RDF embedded in HTML and *(iii)* RDF embedded in XML. Our RDF Crawler relys on Melnik's RDF-API[7] that can deal with the different embeddings of RDF described above. One general problem of crawling is the applied filtering mechanism: Baseline document crawlers are typically restricted by a predefined depth value. Assuming that there is an unlimited amount of interrelated information on the Web (hopefully this will soon hold about RDF data as well), at some point RDF fact gathering by the RDF Crawler should stop. We have implemented a baseline approach for filtering: At the very start of the crawling process and at every subsequent step we maintain a queue of all the URIs we want to analyze. We process them in the breadth-first-search fashion, keeping track of those we have already visited. When the search goes too deep, or we have received sufficient quantity of data (measured as number of links visited or the total web traffic or the amount of RDF data obtained) we may quit.

- **Information Extraction**: We currently integrate this component in our Ont-O-Mat tool. Actually, we are near finishing an integration of Amilcare [2], a learnable information extraction component. Amilcare is a system that learns information extraction rules from manually marked-up input. Ont-O-Mat will therefore be able to suggests relevant part of the texts for annotation.

4.2 Using Ont-O-Mat — An Example

Our example is based on the tourism ontology. It models the area of the tourism industry, accommodations, landmarks, areas, places of interest etc. and properties between them. It is available in the form of DAML+OIL classes and properties, in pure RDF-Schema and in F-Logic. In the following we shortly explain how Ont-O-Mat may be used for creating relational metadata based on this ontology.

The annotation process is started either with an annotation inference server or the server process is fed with metadata crawled from the web and the document server. Figure 3 shows the screen for navigating the ontology and creating annotations in Ont-O-Mat. The right pane displays the document and the left panes show the ontological structures contained in the

---

[6] RDF Crawler is freely available for download at:http://ontobroker.semanticweb.org/rdfcrawler
[7] http://www-db.stanford.edu/~melnik/rdf/api.html

ontology, namely classes, attributes and relations. In addition, the left pane shows the current semantic annotation knowledge base, i.e. existing class instances, attribute instances and relationship instances created during the semantic annotation.

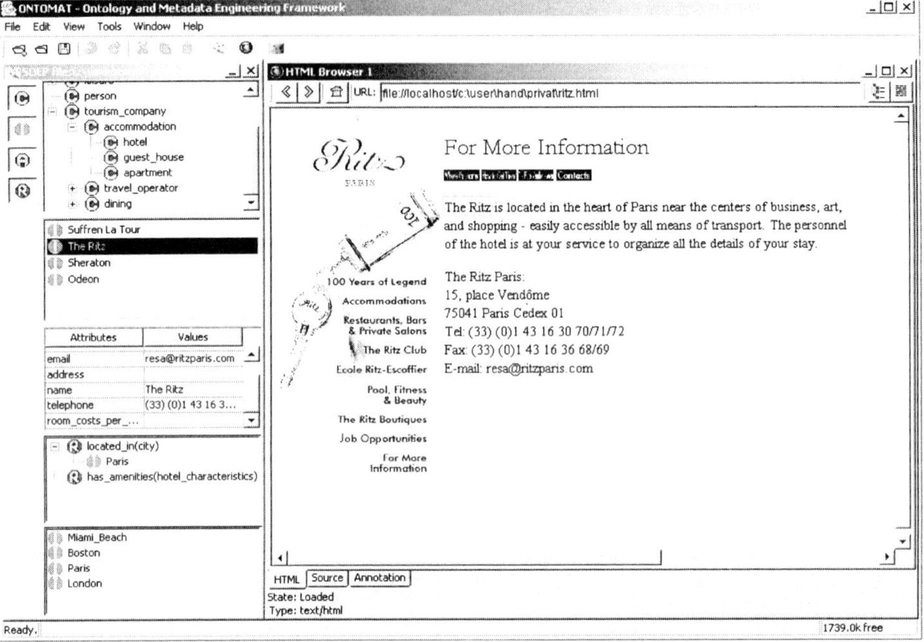

Figure 3: Ont-O-Mat Screenshot.

1. First of all, the user browses a document by entering the URL of the web document that he would like to annotate. This step is quite familiar from existing browsers.

2. Then the user selects a text fragment by highlighting it and takes a look on the ontology which fits in the topic and is therefore loaded and visible in ontology browser.

3. There are two possibilities for the text fragment to be annotated: as an instance or as a property. In the case of an instance, the user selects in the ontology the class where the text fragment fits in, e.g. if he has the text fragment "The Ritz", he would select the class "Hotel". By clicking on the class, the annotation gets created and thus the text fragment will be shown as an instance of the selected class in the ontology at the ontology browser.

4. To each created instance, literal attributes can be assigned. The choice of the predefined attributes depends on the class the instance belongs to, e.g. the class "Hotel" has the attributes name, address, email, and telephone number. The attributes can be assigned to the instance by highlighting the appropriate text fragment of the web document and dragging it to the related property field.

5. Furthermore, the relationships between the created instances can be set, e.g. *The Ritz* "is located in" *Paris* and "offers the event" *Rendez-Vous with the Vintners*. Ont-O-Mat preselects class instances according to the range restrictions of the chosen relation, e.g. the "located in" of a Hotel must be an Area. Therefore only Areas are offered as potential fillers to the "located in" relation of the Ritz.

5   Comparison with Related Work

CREAM can be compared along three dimensions: First, it is a framework for mark-up in the Semantic Web. Second, it can be considered as a particular knowledge acquisition framework vaguely similar to Protégé-2000[7]. Third, it is certainly an annotation framework, though with a different focus than ones like Annotea [15].

5.1   Knowledge Markup in the Semantic Web

We know of three major systems that intensively use knowledge markup in the Semantic Web, viz. SHOE [13], Ontobroker [4] and WebKB [22]. All three of them rely on knowledge in HTML pages.

They all started with providing manual mark-up by editors. However, our experiences (cf. [6]) have shown that text-editing knowledge mark-up yields extremely poor results, viz. syntactic mistakes, improper references, and all the problems sketched in the introduction.

The approaches from this line of research that are closest to *CREAM* is the *SHOE Knowledge Annotator*[8].

The SHOE Knowledge Annotator is a Java program that allows users to mark-up web-pages with the SHOE ontology. The SHOE system [18] defines additional tags that can be embedded in the body of HTML pages. The Knowledge Annotater is less user friendly compared with our implementation Ont-O-Mat. It shows the ontology in some textual lists, whereas Ont-O-Mat gives a graphical visualization of the ontologies. Furthermore, in SHOE there is no direct relationship between the new tags and the original text of the page, i.e. SHOE tags are not annotations in a strict sense.

5.2   Comparison with Knowledge Acquisition Frameworks

The CREAM framework is specialized for creating class and property instances and for populating HTML pages with them. Thus, it does not function as an ontology editor, but rather like the instance acquisition phase in the Protégé-2000 framework [7]. The obvious difference of CREAM to the latter is that Protege does not (and does not intend to) support the particular web setting, *viz.* managing and displaying web pages.

5.3   Comparison with Annotation Frameworks

There are a lot of — even commercial — annotation tools like ThirdVoice[9], Yawas [5], CritLink [26] and Annotea (Amaya) [15].

---

[8]http://www.cs.umd.edu/projects/plus/SHOE/KnowledgeAnnotator.html
[9]http://www.thirdvoice.com

These tools all share the idea of creating a kind of user comment on the web pages. The term "annotation" in these frameworks is understood as a remark to an existing document. As mentioned before, we would model such remarks as attribute instances only in our framework. For instance, a user of these tools might attach a note like "A really nice hotel!" to the name "The Ritz" on a web page.

Annotea actually goes one step further. It allows to rely on an RDF schema as a kind of template that is filled by the annotator. For instance, Annotea users may use a schema for Dublin Core and fill the author-slot of a particular document with a name. This annotation, however, is again restricted to attribute instances. The user may also decide to use complex RDF descriptions instead of simple strings for filling such a template. However, he then has no further support from Amaya that helps him providing syntactically correct statements with proper references.

To summarize, CREAM is used to generate really machine-understandable data and addresses all the problems that come from this objective: relational metadata, proper reference and consistency.

6 Conclusion and Future Plans

CREAM is a comprehensive framework for creating annotations, relational metadata in particular — the foundation of the future Semantic Web. The framework comprises inference services, crawler, document management system, ontology guidance, and document viewers.

Ont-O-Mat is the reference implementation of CREAM framework. The implementation supports so far the user with the task of creating and maintaining ontology-based DAML+OIL markups, i.e. creating of class, attribute and relationship instances. Ont-O-Mat include an ontology browser for the exploration of the ontology and instances and a HTML browser that will display the annotated parts of the text. Ont-O-Mat is Java-based and provides a plugin interface for extensions for further advancement.

There is some ongoing work regarding the CREAM framework. In this paper we described the a-posteriori annotation step as it is useful and necessary when the content of a web document already exist. But future web documents should ideally be build already containing markup. We propose that an author needs the possibility to easily combine authoring of a web page and the creation of relational metadata describing its content. In fact, it is preferable to hide the border between authoring and annotation as far as possible. We have extended the CREAM framework and the tool Ont-O-Mat in order to reflect this [10].

Annotation not only creates metadata it also reuse metadata. To know and use existing metadata is important. Some sources for this metadata are either relational databases or annotated webpages and even P2P-Networks. We developed a REVERSE[10] component, which allows to connect to an relational database and to define mappings from the database tables to the ontology, and finally to extract the data as instances. Further we are working on a specialized Crawler. A focused Crawler[19] which finds Web documents, that correspond to the interests of the user. The search can be focused by indication of relevant example documents. Preferences of the user can be indicated in the reference to a Ontology. The CREAM framework will become really powerful when we exploit existing resources for metadata and combine it with the creation of new relational metadata.

---

[10] http://kaon.aifb.uni-karlsruhe.de/REVERSE

Nevertheless our analysis of the semantic annotation task is far from being complete. Some further important issues we want to mention here are:

- **Information Extraction**: We have done some first steps to incorporate information extraction. However, our future experiences will have to show how and how well information extraction integrates with semantic annotation.

- **Multimedia Annotation**: This requires considerations about time, space and synchronization.

- **Changing Ontologies**: Ontologies on the web have characteristics that influence the annotation process. Heflin & Hendler [12] have elaborated on changes that affect annotation. Future annotation tools will have to incorporate solutions for the difficulties they consider.

- **Active Ontology Evolvement**: Annotation should feed back into the actual ontologies, because annotators may find that they should consider new knowledge, but need revised ontologies for this purpose. Thus, annotation affects ontology engineering and ontology learning.

Our general conclusion is that providing semantic annotation, relational metadata in particular, is an important complex task that needs comprehensive support. Our framework CREAM and our tool Ont-O-Mat have already proved very successful in leveraging the annotation process. They still need further refinement, but they are unique in their design and implementation.

7   Acknowledgements

The research presented in this paper would not have been possible without our colleagues and students at the Institute AIFB, University of Karlsruhe, and Ontoprise GmbH. We thank Kalvis Apsitis (now: RITI Riga Information Technology Institute), Stefan Decker (now: Stanford University), Michael Erdmann, Mika Maier-Collin, Leo Meyer and Tanja Sollazzo. Research for this paper was partially financed by US Air Force in the DARPA DAML project "OntoAgents" (01IN901C0).

References

[1] R. Benjamins, D. Fensel, and S. Decker. KA2: Building Ontologies for the Internet: A Midterm Report. *International Journal of Human Computer Studies*, 51(3):687, 1999.

[2] Fabio Ciravegna. Adaptive Information Extraction from Text by Rule Induction and Generalisation. In *Proceedings of the 17th International Joint Conference on Artificial Intelligence (IJCAI)e*, Seattle, Usa, August 2001.

[3] S. Decker, D. Brickley, J. Saarela, and J. Angele. A Query and Inference Service for RDF. In *Proceedings of the W3C Query Language Workshop (QL-98), http://www.w3.org/TandS/QL/QL98/, Boston, MA, December 3-4*, 1998.

[4] S. Decker, M. Erdmann, D. Fensel, and R. Studer. Ontobroker: Ontology Based Access to Distributed and Semi-Structured Information. In R. Meersman et al., editors, *Database Semantics: Semantic Issues in Multimedia Systems*, pages 351–369. Kluwer Academic Publisher, 1999.

[5] L. Denoue and L. Vignollet.   An annotation tool for Web browsers and its applications to information retrieval.   In *In Proceedings of RIAO2000*, Paris, April 2000.   http://www.univ-savoie.fr/labos/syscom/Laurent.Denoue/riao2000.doc.

[6] M. Erdmann, A. Maedche, H.-P. Schnurr, and Steffen Staab. From Manual to Semi-automatic Semantic Annotation: About Ontology-based Text Annotation Tools. In *P. Buitelaar & K. Hasida (eds). Proceedings of the COLING 2000 Workshop on Semantic Annotation and Intelligent Content*, Luxembourg, August 2000.

[7] H. Eriksson, R. Fergerson, Y. Shahar, and M. Musen. Automatic Generation of Ontology Editors. In *Proceedings of the 12th Banff Knowledge Acquisition Workshop, Banff, Alberta, Canada*, 1999.

[8] Reference description of the DAML+OIL (March 2001) ontology markup language. http://www.daml.org/2001/03/reference.html, March 2001.

[9] T. R. Gruber. A Translation Approach to Portable Ontology Specifications. *Knowledge Acquisition*, 6(2):199–221, 1993.

[10] Siegfried Handschuh and Steffen Staab. Authoring and annotation of web pages in cream. In *Proceeding of the WWW2002 - Eleventh International World Wide Web Conferenceb (to appear)*, Hawaii, USA, May 2002.

[11] Siegfried Handschuh. OntoPlugins – a flexible component framework. Technical report, University of Karlsruhe, May 2001.

[12] J. Heflin, J. Hendler, and S. Luke. Applying Ontology to the Web: A Case Study. In *Proceedings of the International Work-Conference on Artificial and Natural Neural Networks, IWANN'99*, 1999.

[13] J. Heflin and J. Hendler. Searching the Web with SHOE. In *Artificial Intelligence for Web Search. Papers from the AAAI Workshop. WS-00-01*, pages 35–40. AAAI Press, 2000.

[14] Dublin Core Metadata Initiative. http://purl.oclc.org/dc/, April 2001.

[15] J. Kahan, M. Koivunen, E. Prud'Hommeaux, and R. Swick. Annotea: An Open RDF Infrastructure for Shared Web Annotations. In *Proc. of the WWW10 International Conference. Hong Kong*, 2001.

[16] M. Kifer, G. Lausen, and J. Wu. Logical Foundations of Object-Oriented and Frame-Based Languages. *Journal of the ACM*, 42, 1995.

[17] N. Kushmerick. Wrapper Induction: Efficiency and Expressiveness. *Artificial Intelligence*, 118(1), 2000.

[18] S. Luke, L. Spector, D. Rager, and J. Hendler. Ontology-based Web Agents. In *Proceedings of First International Conference on Autonomous Agents*, 1997.

[19] A. Maedche, M. Ehrig, S. Handschuh, L. Stojanovic, and R. Volz. Ontology-Focused Crawling of Web Documents and RDF-based Metadata. In *Subbmited to the 1st International Semantic Web Conference (ISWC2002)*, 2002.

[20] A. Maedche and S. Staab. Ontology Learning for the Semantic Web. *IEEE Intelligent Systems*, 16(2), 2001.

[21] A. Maedche and S. Staab. Applying Semantic Web Technologies to Tourism Information Systems. In *Proceedings of the International Conference on Information and Communication Technologies in Tourism, ENTER 2002*, Innsbruck, Austria, January 23 2002.

[22] P. Martin and P. Eklund. Embedding Knowledge in Web Documents. In *Proceedings of the 8th Int. World Wide Web Conf. (WWW'8), Toronto, May 1999*, pages 1403–1419. Elsevier Science B.V., 1999.

[23] *MUC-7 — Proceedings of the 7th Message Understanding Conference*. http://www.muc.saic.com/, 1998.

[24] S. Staab, A. Maedche, and S. Handschuh. Creating Metadata for the Semantic Web: An Annotation Framework and the Human Factor. Technical Report 412, Institute AIFB, University of Karlsruhe, 2001.

[25] S. Staab and A. Maedche. Knowledge Portals — Ontologies at work. *AI Magazine*, 21(2), Summer 2001.

[26] Ka-Ping Yee. CritLink: Better Hyperlinks for the WWW, 1998. http://crit.org/ ping/ht98.html.

The Emerging Semantic Web
I.F. Cruz et al. (Eds.)
IOS Press, 2002

181

Indexing a Web Site with a Terminology Oriented Ontology

E. Desmontils & C. Jacquin
IRIN, Université de Nantes
2, Rue de la Houssinière, BP 92208
F-44322 Nantes Cedex 3, France
{desmontils,jacquin}@irin.univ-nantes.fr
http://www.sciences.univ-nantes.fr/irin/indexGB.html

Abstract. This article presents a new approach in order to index a Web site. It uses ontologies and natural language techniques for information retrieval on the Internet. The main goal is to build a structured index of the Web site. This structure is given by a terminology oriented ontology of a domain which is chosen a priori according to the content of the Web site. First, the indexing process uses improved natural language techniques to extract well-formed terms taking into account HTML markers. Second, the use of a thesaurus allows us to associate candidate concepts with each term. It makes it possible to reason at a conceptual level. Next, for each candidate concept, its capacity to represent the page is evaluated by determining its level of representativeness of the page. Then, the structured index itself is built. To each concept of the ontology are attached the pages of the Web site in which they are found. Finally, a number of indicators make it possible to evaluate the indexing process of the Web site by the suggested ontology.

keywords : Information Retrieval on the Internet, Web Pages Indexing, Ontologies, Semantic Indexing.

1 Introduction

Searching for information on the Internet means accessing multiple, heterogeneous, distributed and highly evolving information sources. Moreover, provided data are highly changeable: documents of already existing sources may be updated, added or deleted; new information sources may appear or some others may disappear (definitively or not). In addition, the network capacity and quality is a parameter that cannot be entirely neglected. In this context, the question is: how to search for relevant information on the Web more efficiently? Many search engines help us in this difficult task. A lot of them use centralized databases and simple keywords to index and to seek the information. Within such systems, the recall[1] is often relatively high. Conversely, the precision[2] is weak. An intelligent agent supported by the Web site may greatly improve the retrieval process ([4], [1]). In this context, this agent knows its

---

[1]Recall is defined as the number of relevant documents retrieved divided by the total number of relevant documents in the collection

[2]Precision is defined as the number of relevant documents retrieved divided by the total number of documents retrieved

pages content, is able to perform a knowledge-based indexing process on Web pages and is able to provide more relevant answers to queries. In information retrieval processes, the major problem is to determine the specific content of documents. To highlight a Web site content according to a knowledge, we propose a semi-automatic process, which provides a content based index of a Web site using natural language techniques. In contrast with classical indexing tools, our process is not based on keywords but rather on the concepts they represent.

In this paper, we firstly present the general indexing process (section 2). After having exposed the characteristics of used ontologies (section 3), we will indicate how the representativeness of a concept in a page is evaluated (section 4) and, finally, how this process is evaluated itself (section 5).

2   Overview of the indexing process

The main goal is to build a structured index of Web pages according to an ontology. This ontology provides the index structure. Our indexing process can be divided into four steps (figure 1):

1. For each page, a flat index is built. Each term of this index is associated with its weighted frequency. This coefficient depends on each HTML marker that describes each term occurrence.

2. A thesaurus makes it possible to generate all candidate concepts which can be labeled by a term of the previous index. In our implementation, we use the Wordnet thesaurus ([23]).

3. Each candidate concept of a page is studied to determine its representativeness of this page content. This evaluation is based on its weighted frequency and on the relations with the other concepts. It makes it possible to choose the best sense (concept) of a term in relation to the context. Therefore, the more a concept has strong relationships with other concepts of its page, the more this concept is significant into its page. This contextual relation minimizes the role of the weighted frequency by growing the weight of the strongly linked concepts and by weakening the isolated concepts (even with a strong weighted frequency).

4. Among these candidate concepts, a filter is produced via the ontology and the representativeness of the concepts. Namely, a selected concept is a candidate concept that belongs to the ontology and has an high representativeness of the page content (the representativeness exceeds a threshold of sensitivity). Next, the pages which contain such a selected concept are assigned to this concept into the ontology.

Some measures are evaluated to characterize the indexing process. They determine the adequacy between the Web site and the ontology. These measures take into account the number of pages selected by the ontology, the number of concepts included in the pages... The index is built as a XML file ([28]) and is independent of Web pages.

Our process is semi-automatic. It enables the user to have a global view of the Web site. It also makes it possible to index a Web site without being the owner of these pages. We do not regard it as a completely automatic process. Adjustments should be carried out by the user. The counterpart of this automatisation is, obviously, a worse precision of the process. Lastly, compared to the annotation approach, our indexing process improves information retrieval: it

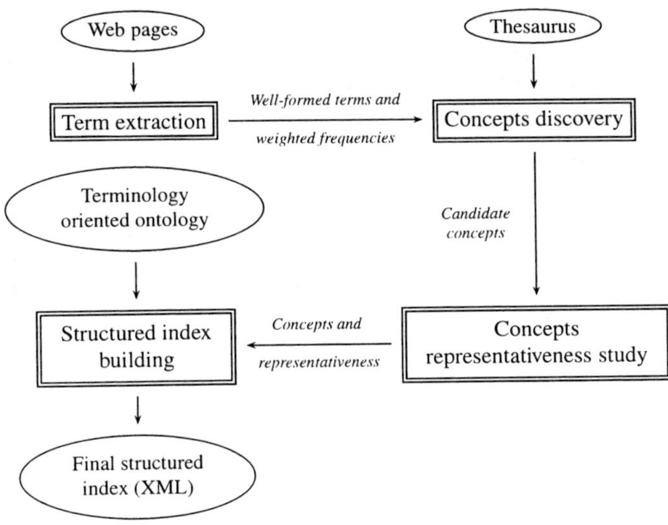

Figure 1: The indexing process

makes it possible to reach directly the pages concerning a concept. By contrast, the annotation approach requires to browse all the pages of the Web site to find this same information. Now, we will study two significant elements: the ontology and the method to evaluate the concepts.

3 Terminology oriented ontologies

3.1 Ontology definition

The term ontology comes from philosophy. In this context, its definition is: «*systematic explanations of the existence*». Furthermore, researchers in Knowledge Engineering give other more suitable definitions with their concerns. In this context, their definitions are strongly dependent on the author's point of view and on his use of ontologies [12, 13]. Some have a formal point of view and work on abstract models of ontologies while others have a more pragmatic approach.

We have chosen this definition of ontology: "*an ontology provides the common vocabulary of a specific domain and defines, more or less formally, terms meaning and some of their relationships*" ([11]). In our context, we thus call ontology a hierarchy of concepts defines in a more or less formal way. For instance, figure 2 shows an extract of the SHOE ontology concerning the American universities.

3.2 Terminology oriented ontology

The concepts of ontologies are usually represented only by a single linguistic term (a label). However, in our context, this term can be at the same time ambiguous (it represents several candidate concepts) and not always unique (existence of synonyms). As a result, within the

```
    <?xml version="1.0" encoding="ISO-8859-1"
        standalone="no"?>
<!DOCTYPE ontology SYSTEM "http://.../onto.dtd">
<ontology id="university-ont" version="2.1"
            description="...">
  <def-category name="Department"
                isa="EducationOrganization"
                short="university department"/>
  <def-category name="Program"
                isa="EducationOrganization"
                short="program"/>
  <def-category name="ResearchGroup"
                isa="EducationOrganization"
                short="research group"/>
  <def-category name="University"
                isa="EducationOrganization"
                short="university"/>
  <def-category name="Activity"
                isa="SHOEEntity"
                short="activity"/>
  <def-category name="Work"
                isa="Activity"
                short="work"/>
  <def-category name="Course"
                isa="Work"
                short="teaching course"/>
  ...
</ontology>
```

Figure 2: Extract of the SHOE ontology concerning the American universities

framework of texts written in natural language, it is necessary to determine the whole set of the synonyms (candidate labels) to define in a single way a concept. Such process can be found in a manual way in OntoSeek ([14]) or in a semi-automatic way in Mikrokosmos ([25]).

In our context, an ontology is a set of concepts each one represented by a term (a label) and a set of synonyms of this term, and a set of relationships connecting these concepts by the specific/generic relationship, the composition relationship,... Currently, the only relationship we take into account is the "isa" relationship. We call this type of ontology a terminology oriented ontology. Note that our ontologies do not reflect all the inherent aspects to formal ontologies ([11]). Our ontologies are close by their structure to those used in the SHOE project ([21]). Moreover, we choose XML format ([28]) to store our ontologies and our indexing results. The used DTD is rather similar to the SHOE DTD but we made modifications and extensions to this last.

We thus propose a process which makes it possible to determine all the candidate labels of a concept. This process is based on a thesaurus and uses a number of heuristics similar with those proposed by the Mikrokosmos project. The general principle of these heuristics is to try to make a correspondance between the paths according to the "isa" relationship in the ontology and the paths of hypernyms in the thesaurus. According to the "matching degree", a more or less large confidence is given to such or such set of synonyms (concept). Let us note that experiments using the relationship of composition have not improved the results.

The user can manually finish the disambiguation process of the labels. Indeed, the process can not always select in an unquestionable way the good set of synonyms. The definitions of the sets of candidate synonyms are presented in order to help to this final choice.

However, the process gives results rather satisfactory since it chooses the good sense for nearly 75% of the labels associated with the concepts of the Universities ontology (SHOE project [21]) and for 95% of the label after several modifications (contradictions with the used thesaurus were deleted).

These evaluations were determined with ontologies for which the whole set of the labels associated with the concepts was manually disambiguated. Of course, this disambiguation process depends on the thesaurus used (in our case Wordnet).

4   Index building

The other important part of our process is the indexing process and the evaluation of the importance of a concept in a HTML page. There are two essential steps: (1) terms extraction from Web pages and calculus of the weighted frequency and (2) determination of candidate concepts and the calculus of the representativeness of a concept.

4.1   Terms extraction

The well-formed terms extraction process starts by (1) removing HTML markers from Web pages, (2) dividing the text into independent sentences, and (3) lemmatising words included in the page. Next, Web pages are annotated with part of speech tags using the Brill tagger ([3]). As a result, each word in a page is annotated with its corresponding grammatical category (noun, adjective...). Finally, the surface structure of sentences is analyzed using term patterns (Noun, Noun+Noun, Adjective+Noun...)[7] to provide well-formed terms . For each selected term, we calculate its weighted frequency. The weighted frequency takes into account the frequency of the term and especially the HTML markers which are linked with each of its occurrences. We can notice that the frequency is not a main criterion. Indeed, we work with pages which are of rather restricted size compared to large corpora used in NLP (Natural Language Processing). The influence of the marker depends on its role in the page. For example, the marker "TITLE" will give a considerable importance to the term (*10) whereas the marker "B" (for bold font) has a quite less influence (* 2). The table 1 gives the weight of the most significant markers (the markers weights were determined in an experimental way [10]). In a Web page containing n different terms, for a given term T_i (with i in $1..n$), the weighted frequency $F(T_i)$ is determined as the sum of the p weights of HTML markers associated with the p term occurrences. The result is then normalized. This calculus is shown in formula (1) and (2) where $M_{i,j}$ corresponds to the HTML marker weight associated with the jth occurrence of the term T_i.

$$F(T_i) = \frac{P(T_i)}{max_{k=1..n}(P(T_k))} \tag{1}$$

```xml
<?xml version="1.0" encoding="ISO-8859-1"
      standalone="no"?>
<!DOCTYPE ontology SYSTEM "http://.../onto.dtd">
<ontology id="university-ont" version="3.0">
  <def-category name="Course" short="teaching course"
               isa="Work">
    <sense name="Course" no="1" origin="WN"
          definition="..." convenience="1.0">
      <synset>class#4,course of instruction#1,
             course of study#2,course#1</synset>
    </sense>
  </def-category>
  <def-category name="Department"
               short="university department"
               isa="EducationOrganization">...
  </def-category>
  <def-category name="University" short="university"
               isa="EducationOrganization">
    <sense name="University" no="3" origin="WN"
          definition="..." convenience="1.0">
      <synset>university#3</synset></sense>
  </def-category>
  <def-category name="Program" short="program"
               isa="Information">
    <sense name="Program" no="4" origin="WN"
          definition="..." convenience="1.0">
      <synset>course of study#1,curriculum#1,program#4,
             syllabus#1</synset></sense>
  </def-category>
  <def-category name="ResearchGroup"
               short="research group"
               isa="EducationOrganization">
    <sense name="ResearchGroup" no="0" origin="TECH"
          definition="" convenience="1.0">
      <synset>research group#0</synset></sense>
  </def-category>
  <def-category name="Activity" short="activity"
               isa="HumanActivity">...
  </def-category>
  <def-category name="Work" short="work"
               isa="Activity">...
  </def-category>...
</ontology>
```

Figure 3: Extract of the terminology oriented ontology concerning the American university

$$P(T_i) = \sum_{i=1}^{p} (M_{i,j}) \qquad (2)$$

HTML marker description	HTML marker	Weight
Document title	<TITLE></TITLE>	10
Keyword	<meta name="keywords" ... content=...>	9
Hyper-link	<A HREF=...></A>	8
Font size 7	<FONT SIZE=7></FONT>	5
Font size +4	<FONT SIZE="+4"></FONT>	5
Font size 6	<FONT SIZE=6></FONT>	4
Font size +3	<FONT SIZE="+3"></FONT>	4
Font size +2	<FONT SIZE="+2"></FONT>	3
Font size 5	<FONT SIZE=5></FONT>	3
Heading level 1	<H1></H1>	3
Heading level 2	<H2></H2>	3
Image title	<IMG ... ALT="...">	2
Big marker	<BIG></BIG>	2
Underlined font	<U></U>	2
Italic font	<I></I>	2
Bold font	<B></B>	2
...	...	...

Table 1: Higher coefficients associated with HTML markers

Table 2 shows some results extracted from an experiment on a Web page. Terms are sorted according to the weighted frequency coefficient.

4.2   Page concepts determination

During the term extraction process, well-formed terms and their weighted frequency coefficient were respectively extracted and calculated. The well-formed terms are different forms representing a particular concept (for example "chair", "professorship"...). In order to determine not only the set of terms included in a page but also the set of concepts in a page, a thesaurus is used. Our experiments use the WordNet thesaurus ([23]). The process to generate candidate concepts is quite simple: from extracted terms, all candidate concepts (all senses) are generated using a thesaurus. A sense is represented by a list of synonym (this list is unique for a given concept). Then for each candidate concept, the representativeness is calculated according to the weighted frequency and the cumulative similarity of the concept with the other concepts in the page. This last one is based on the similarity between two concepts.

We first define the similarity measure between two concepts which makes it possible to evaluate the semantic distance between these two concepts. This measure is defined relatively to a thesaurus and to the hypernyms relationship. In our context, we use the similarity measure defined by [29]. They propose a similarity measure related to the edge distance in the way it takes into account the most specific subsumer of the two concepts, characterizing their commonalities, while normalizing in a way that accounts for their differences. Their measure is shown in formula 3 where c is the most specific subsumer of c_1 and c_2, $depth(c)$ is the number of edges from c to the taxonomy root, and $depth_c(c_i)$ with i in $\{1, 2\}$ is the number of edges from c_i to the taxonomy root through c.

Terms	Weighted frequency
uw	1.00
cse	0.59
uw cse	0.45
computer	0.41
university	0.37
seattle	0.30
article	0.30
science	0.26
research	0.24
professor	0.24
...	...
computer science	0.18
...	...
university of washington	0.16
...	...
program	0.15
...	...
news	0.12
...	...
information	0.09
...	...
message	0.01
...	...

Table 2: Extracted terms and their weighted frequency (sorted according to the weighted frequency). Results coming from http://www.cs.washington.edu/news/

$$sim(c_1, c_2) = \frac{2 * depth(c)}{depth_c(c_1) + depth_c(c_2)} \qquad (3)$$

This measure performs a little worse than the Resnik's measure ([26]) but better than the traditional edge-counting measure (see related works for more details).

For evaluating the relative importance of a concept in a page, we define its cumulative similarity. The cumulative similarity measure associated with a concept in a page, noted $\widehat{sim}$, is the sum of all the similarity measures calculated between this concept and all the other concepts included in the studied page. In this formula, a specific concept is unified with the corresponding synset (set of synonyms) in WordNet. The measure is shown in formula 4[3], where l_k synsets are associated with a term T_k, and there are m terms in the studied Web pages.

$$\widehat{sim}(synset_i(T_k)) = \sum_{j \in [1,k-1] \cup [k+1,m]} \sum_{l=1}^{l_j} sim(synset_i(T_k), synset_l(T_j)) \qquad (4)$$

In this calculus, all similarities are not been taken into account in order to discriminate the results: a threshold is applied. Finally, we determine a representativeness coefficient which

---

[3] $\widehat{sim}(synset_i(T_k))$ is normalized

determines the representativeness of a concept in a document. The coefficient is a linear combination of the weighted frequency and of the cumulative similarity of a concept (formula 5)[4]. This coefficient is the major one to qualify answer to a request. The empirical values for α and β are respectively 2 et 1.

$$representativeness(synset_i(T_k)) = \frac{\alpha * F(synset_i(T_k)) + \beta * \widehat{sim}(synset_i(T_k))}{\alpha + \beta} \quad (5)$$

The table 3 shows the effect of the representativeness on the concepts order (terms found in the page are in bold font). Some concepts are higher in the table 3 than in the table 2. For instance, news#1 (weighted frequency 0.12, representativeness 0.51) or information#1 (weighted frequency 0.1, representativeness 0.59). This is a good result for a page related to a news page. If we analyse the result more in details, the concepts: news#4 and news#2 have a representativeness equal to 0.49. This is not very different from the degree of news#1 which is equal to 0.51. The explanation is that Wordnet includes too much fine-grained sense distinctions. In fact, in the thesaurus, the three previous concepts have all the same subsumer. Then, an automatic process cannot distinguish these three concepts. Wordnet was built by linguist and is not always effective in NLP [25].

5 Associating concepts and synsets

At this point, we have on the one hand a terminology oriented ontology and on the other hand candidate concepts with their representativeness coming from HTML pages. In the next step, candidate concepts are matched with concepts of the ontology. If a concept is in the ontology and in a Web page, the URL of this page and its representativeness are added to the ontology.

To evaluate the appropriateness of an ontology according to a set of HTML pages, five typical coefficients are calculated. These coefficients are normalized. The first four coefficients define:

- the rate of concepts directly involved in HTML pages, called *the Direct Indexing Degree or DID*;

- the rate of concepts indirectly involved in HTML pages (calculated by the way of the generic/specific relationship), called *the Indirect Indexing Degree or IID*;

- the rate of pages concerned with the ontology concepts, called *the Ontology Cover Degree or OCD*, which gives the number of Web pages that involve at least one concept of the ontology;

- the Mean of the Representativeness of the candidate Concepts (MRC).

These coefficients (DID, IID, OCD, MRC) are evaluated for different thresholds applied on the representativeness (0 to 1 with a step equals to 0.02). For each coefficient its weighted mean (WM) is calculated. For instance, formula 6 presents the calculus of the weighted mean for the direct indexing degree (DID).

---

[4]The representativeness is normalized. $F(synset_i(T_k))$ is the normalized sum of all the weighted frequency related to $synset_i(T_k)$.

Concepts	Weighted frequency	Representativeness
uw#0	1.0	1.0
award#2, accolade#1, honor#1, honour#2, laurels#1	0.20	0.7
computer#1, data processor#1, electronic computer#1, information processing system#1	0.41	0.68
information#1, info#1	0.1	0.59
cse#0	0.59	0.59
university#2	0.37	0.58
course of study#1, **program#4**, curriculum#1, syllabus#1	0.15	0.53
calculator#1, reckoner#1, figurer#1, estimator#1, **computer#2**	0.41	0.51
news#1, **intelligence#4**, tidings#1, word#3	0.12	0.51
news#2	0.09	0.49
news#4	0.09	0.49
voice#6	0.01	0.51
voice#2, vocalization#1	0.01	0.51
message#2, **content#2**, subject matter#1, substance#6	0.01	0.51
language#1, linguistic communication#1	0.01	0.51
article#3, clause#2	0.30	0.5
submission#1, **entry#4**	0.01	0.5
subject#1, topic#1, theme#1	0.01	0.5
university#3	0.37	0.42
...	...	...

Table 3: Extracted concepts after the calculus of the representativeness degree (sorted according to the representativeness). Results coming from http://www.cs.washington.edu/news/

$$\overline{DID_{s,o}} = \sum_{i=0}^{1} (i * DID_{i,s,o}) \tag{6}$$

This calculus privileges the concepts which are more representative of the pages. A representative ontology of a site has the weighted mean nearly equal to 1. This evaluation depends on the thesaurus used because it depends on the used relationships. Finally, the global evaluation of the indexing process (OSAD: Ontology-Site Adequacy Degree) is a linear combination of these weighted means. Currently, the coefficients are evaluated in an experimental way. The equation 7 gives the present evaluation where s is a Web site and o an ontology. The experiment shows that a value of 0.3 for the representativeness gives good results. Below this threshold, too many concepts with a low representativeness are kept. For this threshold, the discrimination of concepts is relatively effective (the larger the Web pages are, the more effective the process is).

$$OSAD_{s,o} = \frac{\overline{IID_{s,o}}}{2} + \overline{DID_{s,o}} + 2 * \overline{OCD_{s,o}} + 2 * \overline{MRC_{s,o}} \tag{7}$$

The figure 4 presents indexing results related to the Web site: "http://www.cs.washington.edu/" (1315 HTML pages). This is the site of the department of computer science of the Washington university. It was chosen because of its a priori adequacy with our ontology. However, the

Ontology-Site Adequacy Degree (OSAD) is not very high (56%). The explanation is that the used ontology (the SHOE ontology with some extensions and modifications) does not cover all the studied domain. For instance, the studied site has numerous personal Web pages which are rarely indexed by the ontology. Figure 5 presents an extract of the structured index.

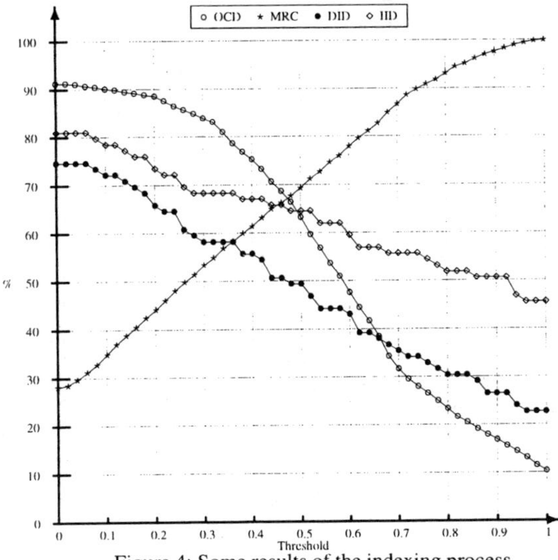

Figure 4: Some results of the indexing process

The indexing process can highlight concepts, which do not match with concepts of ontologies. In this case, we may search for ontologies related to this index. In the future, we will be able to start again the indexing process when the content of the site evolves or when ontologies are updated. This process can only be executed on modified pages.

The evaluation process enables us to evaluate the adequacy between the pages of the site and the ontology and thus to adopt various strategies depending on the coefficients value:

1. the coefficients are correct: the structured index is kept and exploited;

2. the coefficients are not correct:

   (a) the pages which are not suitable are deleted (the OCD and/or the MRC coefficient are low);

   (b) the ontology is updated (the DID coefficient is low);

   (c) a new ontology is chosen and the index is built again (the whole set of coefficients is low);

6   Exploitation of our approach for query answering

Most of search engines use simple keywords to index web pages. Queries are often made up of a list of keywords connected by logical operator ("and", "or"...). In our context, we

```xml
<?xml version="1.0" encoding="ISO-8859-1" standalone="no"?>
<!DOCTYPE ontology SYSTEM "http://.../onto.dtd">
<ontology id="university-ont" version="3.0" description="">
 <def-category name="University" short="university"
               isa="EducationOrganization">
   <sense name="University" no="3" origin="wn" convenience="1.0">
     <synset>university#3</synset>
     <page name="http://www.cs.washington.edu/info/contact/"
           frequence="0.5" representativeness="0.4"/>
     <page name="http://www.cs.washington.edu/info/aboutus/"
           frequence="0.54" representativeness="0.49"/>
     <page name="http://www.cs.washington.edu/education/courses/590m/"
           frequence="0.4" representativeness="0.4"/>
     <page name="http://www.cs.washington.edu/outreach/"
           frequence="0.28" representativeness="0.34"/>
     <page name="http://www.cs.washington.edu/mssi/"
           frequence="0.5" representativeness="0.43"/>
     <page name="http://www.cs.washington.edu/general/overview.html"
           frequence="0.87" representativeness="0.81"/>
     <page name="http://www.cs.washington.edu/education/courses/599/"
           frequence="0.4" representativeness="0.35"/>
     <page name="http://www.cs.washington.edu/workforce/tnt/"
           frequence="0.25" representativeness="0.35"/>...
   </sense>
 </def-category>
 <def-category name="Department" short="university department"
               isa="EducationOrganization">
   <sense name="Department" no="1" origin="wn" convenience="1.0">
     <synset>department#1,section#11</synset>
     <page name="http://www.cs.washington.edu/education/courses/444/"
           frequence="0.29" representativeness="0.31"/>
     <page name="http://www.cs.washington.edu/lab/facilities/la2.html"
           frequence="0.5" representativeness="0.41"/>
     <page name="http://www.cs.washington.edu/ARL/"
           frequence="0.21" representativeness="0.32"/>
     <page name="http://www.cs.washington.edu/"
           frequence="0.33" representativeness="0.37"/>
     <page name="http://www.cs.washington.edu/desktop_refs.html"
           frequence="0.5" representativeness="0.43"/>
     <page name="http://www.cs.washington.edu/news/jobs.html"
           frequence="0.44" representativeness="0.46"/>
     <page name="http://www.cs.washington.edu/admin/newhires/faq.html"
           frequence="0.29" representativeness="0.32"/>
     <page name="http://www.cs.washington.edu/info/videos/index.html"
           frequence="0.39" representativeness="0.38"/>
     <page name="http://www.cs.washington.edu/affiliates/corporate/"
           frequence="0.5" representativeness="0.51"/>...
   </sense>
 </def-category>...
</ontology>
```

Figure 5: Extract of the structured index based on the terminology oriented ontology concerning the American universities

use the terminology oriented ontology and the structured index in order to improve the query answering process. Queries are not only processed at the terminological level but also at the conceptual level. This approach provides several improvements:

1. a user's query is expanded: terms are transformed into concepts;

2. logical operators have a richer semantics than in the simple keywords world;

3. the answers are more suitable to a user's query.

The query expansion is thus improved by the use of ontologies. Often, when a user proposes a query which contains terms connected by logical operators, these terms are often ambiguous. In our approach, terms are replaced by their associated concepts. The candidate concepts are first selected in the ontology. Then, the other concepts of the query and the logical operators are studied. Finally, if a term is still associated with several candidate concepts, the user's assistance is required. If set of query terms are not associated with any concepts at the end of this process, they are regarded as not relevant for the site. According to the logical operator, either they are suppressed from the query or the query has no response.

The conceptually expanded query can be exploited to seek pages corresponding precisely to its content. The ontology makes it possible to improve the interpretation of the used logical operators. Currently, in one hand, the "and" and "or" operators have the same interpretation as in the traditional keywords approach. In the other hand, the "no" and "near" operators have a different semantics. For a query containing a "no" operator, we add to the concerned concept, all the concepts which are more specific than this concept according to the "isa" relationship. So, all pages containing these concepts will be rejected. The "near" operator is not related to the distance between words (number of words between two words) as in the classical approach. But, it is related to a semantic distance between concepts according to the similarity measure [29] used to calculate the representativeness coefficient. In our context, the "near" operator becomes an unary operator and makes it possible to add to the query all the concepts semantically connected to the targeted concept and in its neighborhood.

7　Related works

Our choices differ from related works especially from work on annotation of Web page like KA2 ([9], [2]), SHOE ([21]) or WebKB([22]). These two projects annotate manually Web pages using semantic tags. SHOE proposes a set of *Simple HTML Ontology Extension* to annotate Web pages with ontology-based knowledge concerning page contents. In this context, an agent can use this knowledge to manage effectively information requests.

In all the cases, the goal is to use semantic information to improve the information retrieval. However, in these approaches, annotations are strongly linked to document. The author of pages progressively indicates handled knowledge where it appears. The problem is that any modification or new generation of the pages requires to remake entirely or partly the annotations. Nevertheless, the precision of this process is extremely fine. Moreover, the methods based on annotation are manual or semi-manual (an user interface helps the user to annotate the document [16]). Therefore, they are very time expensive and can be carried out only by specialists ([15]).

However, this manual process is time expensive, complex, and information and knowledge are mixed. The information management difficulty is thus increased ([15]). In addition, semantically annotated documents are not today and perhaps may be never available on the Web. These two projects work on restricted domain and scaling up to the entire Web is a titanic task ([15]). Moreover, in this context, all Web page builders have to accept to annotate their own pages. The consensus needed by this protocol is far to be widely admitted and is at the opposite of the Web philosophy. Another project is the "WebKB" project ([22]). It proposes another manual process to annotate Web pages using an ontology represented with a conceptual graph ([27]), which is built using a linguistic thesaurus. Even if the used language is different from the two previous projects, annotations are also included in the HTML pages. Moreover, the thesaurus is only used to extend the ontology. It is not used to automatically index natural language documents.

Like in OntoSeek project ([14]), our approach adds linguistic attributes to ontologies using the WordNet thesaurus to improve our semi-automatic Web site knowledge discovery. Guarino calls this process a *disambiguation process*. However, the manual process OntoSeek uses ontologies not to define the knowledge of a Web site but to find user's data in a large classical database of Web pages. Another project proposes a similar process: the Mikrokosmos project ([25]) to provide a knowledge base for machine translation process. This process is another semi-automatic process (the user can improve manually the disambiguation results). It studies several heuristics. The most important are an hierarchical heuristics and a similarity heuristics. The hierarchical heuristics uses the generic/specific relationship in the ontology and the hypernyms relationship in the thesaurus. For [25], the hierarchical heuristics seems to be the more effective to select senses. Therefore, we choose to use this heuristics and to improve it.

Some projects of the KDD (Knowledge Discovery in Databases) community are interested by extracting knowledge from Web sites. [8] apply techniques of KDD to keywords which are attached to the documents and which are then regarded as attributes. These mining techniques use statistical analysis to discover association rules and interesting patterns over keywords distributions and associations. Other researchers [18] use terms automatically extracted from documents to characterize the document and to find associations which connect the terms to the documents. Another approach is to apply KDD techniques after the use of information extraction techniques, which transform information located in texts into a structured database [6]. Other approaches [20] mix NLP techniques and KDD techniques to extract automatically information from documents. They do not use keywords as attribute but use concepts which are acquired by the way of a thesaurus. The approach of the last authors seems the most interesting because they do not work any more with simple keywords but with the concepts included in documents. Compared to KDD techniques like [20], we also work on conceptual level instead on the simple keywords level. But we take the option to have linguistic processing much finer and especially we privilege an a priori knowledge on the studied domain (one or several ontologies). [20] use a priori knowledge on the studied domain (a thesaurus) exclusively to extract the concepts of the pages. In our approach, the concepts are also extracted from the pages using a thesaurus, but the indexing process itself is also based on an ontology of the domain. [24] asserts besides that for an effective extraction of knowledge, a priori knowledge on the studied domain (for example ontologies) is essential.

Many measures of similarity are defined in related works. For [19], the information shared by two concepts is indicated in an "isa" taxonomy by the most specific concept that subsumes them. The semantic similarity of two concepts in a taxonomy is the distance between the nodes corresponding to the items which are compared (edge-counting). The shorter the path from one node to another is, the more similar they are. Given multiple paths, one takes the length of the shortest one.

A widely acknowledged problem ([26]) with this approach is that it relies on the notion that links in the taxonomy represent uniform distances (but it is most of the time false). [26] describes an alternative way to evaluate semantic similarity in a taxonomy based on the notion of information content. All links in a taxonomy are weighted with an estimated probability (concept occurrences in corpora), which measures the information content of a concept. The main idea is: the more concepts share information, more similar they are. The information shared by two concepts is indicated by the information content of the concepts that subsumes them in the taxonomy. The probability P of a concept c is based on the probability associated with the concept plus the probability associated with all its descendant concepts. $P(c)$ is then used to calculate the information content of a concept c which is equal to $-log(P(c))$.

8   Conclusions

In this paper, we have presented a semi-automatic process to index a Web site by its content. This process builds a structured index coming from an ontology and pages of a Web site. After the construction of a flat index where all terms have a weighted frequency, we determine candidate concepts associated with these terms. For each concept, a representativeness coefficient is calculated. Finally, the most representative concepts in a Web page are selected, and those which belong to the ontology are kept. The final structured index is organized according to the ontology. With each ontology concepts a set of Web pages is associated from where the potential concepts were extracted.

This process comprises a number of advantages on the traditional indexing methods (only based on keyword retrieval) and even on the methods of Web site annotation:

1. selected pages contain not only the keywords but also the required concepts ;

2. these concepts are representative of the topics treated in selected pages ;

3. terms which are responsible of the page selection are not always those of the request but can be synonyms ;

4. pages can comprise not only the required concepts but also more specific ones ;

5. the importance of a concept depends not only on its term frequency but also on the HTML markers which describe it and on its relations with the other concepts of the page...

The indexing process can be used not only for retrieving information but also for valuing the appropriateness of a Web site with regard to a domain or a knowledge. This latter case enables us to classify a Web site in a hierarchical index of a classical search engine (Yahoo !, Excite...). Note that such hierarchies can be themselves considered as general ontologies ([17]).

Currently, other Web sites on American universities are indexed in order to compare their results to those of the Washington university. In order to improve the indexing results, we may also improve the coverage degree of the ontology on our studied domain. We study also other relationships than the generic/specific relationship in order to improve the process of concepts extraction. We have developed a measure according to the composition relationship, but we must also evaluate it in an experimental way.

The results presented in this paper can be used in various applications. They are currently being incorporated within the Bonom Multi-agent system ([5], [4]) to search for relevant information on the Internet. The system involves different types of agents among which "site agents" which encapsulate information sources. The methods we propose are implemented within the site agents. They greatly improve the site analysis process and the query answering process.

References

[1] N. Ashish and C. A. Knowblock, "Semi-Automatic Generation Internet Information Sources", In 2nd IFCIS Conference on Cooperative Information Systems (CoopIS), Charleston, SC, 1997.

[2] V. R. Benjamins, D. Fensel, A. Gomez-Perez, S. Decker, M. Erdmann, E. Motta, and M. Musen. "Knowledge Annotation Initiative of the Knowledge Acquisition Community KA2". In Proceedings of the 11th Banff knowledge acquisition for knowledge-based system workshop, Banff, Canada, 1998, pp. 18-23.

[3] E. Brill, "Transformation-based error-driven learning and natural language processing: a case study in Part-of-speech Tagging". Computational Linguistics, vol. 21, 1995, pp. 543-565.

[4] S Cazalens, E Desmontils, C Jacquin, and P Lamarre, "A Web Site Indexing Process for an Internet Information Retrieval Agent System", International Conference on Web Information Systems Engineering (WISE'2000), IEEE Computer Society Press, Hong-Kong, 19-20 June, 2000, pp. 245-249.

[5] S. Cazalens and P. Lamarre, "An organization of Internet agents based on a hierarchy of information domains", In Proceedings MAAMAW, Yves Demazeau and Francisco J. Garijo editors, may 2001

[6] J. Cowie and W. Lehnert. "Information extraction". In Communications of the ACM, number 1, volume 39, january 1996.

[7] B. Daille, "Approche mixte pour l'extraction de terminologie : statistique lexicale et filtres linguistiques", PHD Thesis, Paris 7, 1994.

[8] R. Feldman and I. Dagan. "Knowledge discovery in textual databases (KDT)". In First international conference on knowledge discovery (KDD'95), Montreal, august 1995.

[9] D. Fensel, S. Decker, M. Erdmann, and R. Studer. "Ontobroker: Or How to Enable Intelligent Access to the WWW". In Proceedings of the 11th Banff Knowledge Acquisition for Knowledge-Based System Workshop (KAW'98), Banff, Canada, 1998.

[10] J. Gamet. "indexation de pages web". Rapport de DEA informatique, université de Nantes, 1998.

[11] A. Gomez-Perez. "Développements récents en matière de conception, de maintenance et d'utilisation des ontologies". In Proceedings of colloque Terminologie et intelligence artificielle de Nantes, 10-11 mai 1999, revue terminologies nouvelles, pp. 9-20.

[12] T. Gruber, "A Translation Approach to Portable Ontology Specification". In Knowledge Acquisition journal, vol 5, pp 199-220, 1993.

[13] N. Guarino. "Some Organizing Principles for a Unified Top-Level Ontology". In Spring Symposium series on ontological engineering, pp 57-63, 1997

[14] N. Guarino, C. Masolo, and G. Vetere, "OntoSeek: Content-Based Access to the Web", IEEE Intelligent Systems and Their Applications, Elsevier Science, 14(3), 1999, pp. 70-80.

[15] J. Heflin, J. Hendler, and S. Luke, "Applying Ontology to the Web: A Case Study", In International Work-Conference on Artificial and Natural Neural Networks (IWANN), 1999.

[16] J. Kahan, M. Koivunen, E. Prud'Hommeaux and R.R. Swick "Annotea: An Open RDF Infrastructure for Shared Web Annotations", In proceedings of the WWW'10 conferences, Hong Kong 2001

[17] Y. Labrou and T. Finin, "Yahoo! as an Ontology - Using Yahoo! Categories to Describe Documents", In Proceedings of CIKM'99, Kansas City, MO, Oct. 1999, pp. 180-187.

[18] S. Lin and al. "Extracting classification knowledge of internet documents with mining term associations: a semantic approach". In International ACM-SIGIR conference on research and development in information retrieval (SIGIR-98).

[19] J. H. Lee, M. H. Kim, and Y. J. Lee, "information retrieval based on conceptual distance in IS-A hierarchies", journal of documentation, 49(2) , 1993, pp 188-207.

[20] S. Loh, L.k. Wives and J Palazzo M de Oliveira. "Concept-based knowledge discovery in texts extracted from the web". In journal SIGKDD explorations, number 1, volume 2, pp 29-39, 2000.

[21] S. Luke, L. Spector, and D. Rager. "Ontology-Based Knowledge Discovery on the World-Wide-Web". In Proceedings of the workshop on Internet-based information system, AAAI'96, Portland, Oregon, 1996.

[22] P. Martin and P. Eklund, "Embedding Knowledge in Web Documents", In Proceedings of the 8th International World Wide Web Conference, Toronto, Canada, May 11-14, 1999 (http://www8.org).

[23] G. A. Miller, "WordNet: an Online Lexical Database", International Journal of Lexicography, 3(4), 1990, pp. 235-312.

[24] D. Mattox, L. Seligman and K. Smith, "Rapper: a wrapper generator with linguistic knowledge", In ACM workshop on information and data management, 2000.

[25] T. O'Hara, K. Mahesh, and S. Niremburg, "Lexical Acquisition with WordNet and Microkosmos Ontology", workshop on "usage of WordNet in natural language processing systems", 8 pages, Coling-ACL'98

[26] P. Resnik, "Semantic similarity in a taxonomy : an information-based measure and its application to problems of ambiguity in natural language", journal of artificial intelligence research, 11, July 1999, pp. 95-130.

[27] J. F. Sowa, "Conceptual Structures, Information Processing in Mind and Machine", Addison Wesley Publishing Company, 1984

[28] W3C. "Extensible Markup Language (XML) 1.0". W3C Recommendation, Reference: REC-xml-19980210, 10 February 1998, http://www.w3.org/TR/REC-XML

[29] Z. Wu and M. Palmer, "verb semantics and lexical selection", In Proceedings of the 32nd annual meeting of the association for computational linguistics, Las Cruses, New Mexico, 1994

[30] B. Yuwono and D. L. Lee. "WISE: A World Wide Web Resource Database System". IEEE Transactions on Knowledge and Data Engineering, 8(4), 1996, pp. 548-554.

Part 3:
Interoperability, Integration, and Composition

A Framework for Ontology Integration

Diego Calvanese, Giuseppe De Giacomo, Maurizio Lenzerini
Dipartimento di Informatica e Sistemistica
Università di Roma "La Sapienza"
Via Salaria 113, 00198 Roma, Italy
`{calvanese,degiacomo,lenzerini}@dis.uniroma1.it`

Abstract. One of the basic problems in the development of techniques for the semantic web is the integration of ontologies. Indeed, the web is constituted by a variety of information sources, each expressed over a certain ontology, and in order to extract information from such sources, their semantic integration and reconciliation in terms of a global ontology is required. In this paper, we address the fundamental problem of how to specify the mapping between the global ontology and the local ontologies. We argue that for capturing such mapping in an appropriate way, the notion of *query* is a crucial one, since it is very likely that a concept in one ontology corresponds to a *view* (i.e., a query) over the other ontologies. As a result query processing in ontology integration systems is strongly related to view-based query answering in data integration.

1   Introduction

One of the basic problems in the development of techniques for the semantic web is the integration of ontologies. Indeed, the web is constituted by a variety of information sources, and in order to extract information from such sources, their semantic integration and reconciliation is required. In this paper we deal with a situation where we have various local ontologies, developed independently from each other, and we are required to build an integrated, global ontology as a mean for extracting information from the local ones. Thus, the main purpose of the global ontology is to provide a unified view through which we can query the various local ontologies.

Most of the work carried out on ontologies for the semantic web is on which language or which method to use to build the global ontology on the basis of the local ones [13, 2]. For example, the Ontology Inference Layer (OIL) [13, 2] proposes to use a restricted form of the expressive and decidable DL studied in [4] to express ontologies for the semantic web.

In this paper, we address what we believe is a crucial problem for the semantic web: how do we specify the mapping between the global ontology and the local ontologies. This aspect is the central one if we want to use the global ontology for answering queries in the context of the semantic web. Indeed, we are not simply using the local ontologies as an intermediate step towards the global one. Instead, we are using the global ontology for accessing information in the local ones. It is our opinion that, although the problem of specifying the mapping between the global and the local ontologies is at the heart of integration in the web, it is not deeply investigated yet.

We argue that even the most expressive ontology specification languages are not sufficient for information integration in the semantic web. In a real world setting, different ontologies are build by different organizations for different purposes. Hence one should expect the same information to be represented in different forms and with different levels of abstraction in the various ontologies. When mapping concepts in the various ontologies to each other, it is very likely that a concept in one ontology corresponds to a *view* (i.e., a *query*) over the other ontologies. Observe that here the notion of "query" is a crucial one. Indeed, to express mappings among concepts in different ontologies, suitable query languages should be added to the ontology specification language, and considered in the various reasoning tasks, in the spirit of [4, 5]. As a result query processing in this setting is strongly related to view-based query answering in data integration systems [20, 16]. What distinguishes ontology integration from data integration as studied in databases, is that, while in data integration one assumes that each source is basically a databases, i.e., a logical theory with a single model, such an assumption is not made in ontology integration, where a local ontology is an arbitrary logical theory, and hence can have multiple models.

Our main contribution in this paper is to present a general framework for an ontology of integration where the mapping between ontologies is expressed through suitable mechanisms based on queries, and to illustrate the framework proposed with two significant case studies.

The paper is organized as follows. In the next section we set up a formal framework for ontology integration. In Sections 3 and 4, we illustrate the so called global-centric approach and local-centric approach to integration, and we discuss for each of the two approaches a specific case study showing the subtleties involved. In Section 5 we briefly present an approach to integration that goes beyond the distinction between global-centric and local-centric. Finally, Section 6 concludes the paper.

2 Ontology integration framework

In this section we set up a formal framework for *ontology integration systems* (OISs). We argue that this framework provides the basis of an *ontology of integration*. For the sake of simplicity, we will refer to a simplified framework, where the components of an OIS are the global ontology, the local ontologies, and the mapping between the two. We call such systems "one-layered". More complex situations can be modeled by extending the framework in order to represent, for example, mappings between local ontologies (in the spirit of [12, 6]), or global ontologies that act as local ones with respect to another layer.

In what follows, one of the main aspects is the definition of the semantics of both the OIS, and of queries posed to the global ontology. For keeping things simple, we will use in the following a unique semantic domain Δ, constituted by a fixed, infinite set of symbols.

Formally, an OIS $\mathcal{O}$ is a triple $\langle \mathcal{G}, \mathcal{S}, \mathcal{M}_{\mathcal{G},\mathcal{S}} \rangle$, where $\mathcal{G}$ is the global ontology, $\mathcal{S}$ is the set of local ontologies, and $\mathcal{M}_{\mathcal{G},\mathcal{S}}$ is the mapping between $\mathcal{G}$ and the local ontologies in $\mathcal{S}$.

Global ontology. We denote with $\mathcal{A}_{\mathcal{G}}$ the alphabet of terms of the global ontology, and we assume that the global ontology $\mathcal{G}$ of an OIS is expressed as a theory (named simply $\mathcal{G}$) in some logic $\mathcal{L}_G$.

Local ontologies. We assume to have a set $\mathcal{S}$ of n local ontologies $\mathcal{S}_1, \ldots, \mathcal{S}_n$. We denote with $\mathcal{A}_{\mathcal{S}_i}$ the alphabet of terms of the local ontology $\mathcal{S}_i$. We also denote with $\mathcal{A}_{\mathcal{S}}$ the union of all the $\mathcal{A}_{\mathcal{S}_i}$'s. We assume that the various $\mathcal{A}_{\mathcal{S}_i}$'s are mutually disjoint, and each one is disjoint from the alphabet $\mathcal{A}_{\mathcal{G}}$. We assume that each local ontology is expressed as a theory (named simply $\mathcal{S}_i$) in some logic $\mathcal{L}_{\mathcal{S}_i}$, and we use $\mathcal{S}$ to denote the collection of theories $\mathcal{S}_1, \ldots, \mathcal{S}_n$.

Mapping. The mapping $\mathcal{M}_{\mathcal{G},\mathcal{S}}$ is the heart of the OIS, in that it specifies how the concepts[1] in the global ontology $\mathcal{G}$ and in the local ontologies $\mathcal{S}$ map to each other.

Semantics. Intuitively, in specifying the semantics of an OIS, we have to start with a model of the local ontologies, and the crucial point is to specify which are the models of the global ontology. Thus, for assigning semantics to an OIS $\mathcal{O} = \langle \mathcal{G}, \mathcal{S}, \mathcal{M}_{\mathcal{G},\mathcal{S}} \rangle$, we start by considering a *local model* $\mathcal{D}$ for $\mathcal{O}$, i.e., an interpretation that is a model for all the theories of $\mathcal{S}$. We call *global interpretation* for $\mathcal{O}$ any interpretation for $\mathcal{G}$. A global interpretation $\mathcal{I}$ for $\mathcal{O}$ is said to be a *global model for $\mathcal{O}$ wrt $\mathcal{D}$* if:

- $\mathcal{I}$ is a model of $\mathcal{G}$, and

- $\mathcal{I}$ satisfies the mapping $\mathcal{M}_{\mathcal{G},\mathcal{S}}$ wrt $\mathcal{D}$.

In the next sections, we will come back to the notion of satisfying a mapping wrt a local model. The semantics of $\mathcal{O}$, denoted $sem(\mathcal{O})$, is defined as follows:

$$sem(\mathcal{O}) = \{\ \mathcal{I}\ |\ \text{there exists a local model } \mathcal{D} \text{ for } \mathcal{O}$$
$$\text{s.t. } \mathcal{I} \text{ is a global model for } \mathcal{O} \text{ wrt } \mathcal{D}\ \}$$

Queries. Queries posed to an OIS $\mathcal{O}$ are expressed in terms of a query language $\mathcal{Q}_{\mathcal{G}}$ over the alphabet $\mathcal{A}_{\mathcal{G}}$ and are intended to extract a set of tuples of elements of Δ. Thus, every query has an associated arity, and the semantics of a query q of arity n is defined as follows. The answer $q^{\mathcal{O}}$ of q to $\mathcal{O}$ is the set of tuples

$$q^{\mathcal{O}} = \{\langle c_1, \ldots, c_n \rangle\ |\ \text{for all } \mathcal{I} \in sem(\mathcal{O}),\ \langle c_1, \ldots, c_n \rangle \in q^{\mathcal{I}}\ \}$$

where $q^{\mathcal{I}}$ denotes the result of evaluating q in the interpretation $\mathcal{I}$.

As we said before, the mapping $\mathcal{M}_{\mathcal{G},\mathcal{S}}$ represents the heart of an OIS $\mathcal{O} = \langle \mathcal{G}, \mathcal{S}, \mathcal{M}_{\mathcal{G},\mathcal{S}} \rangle$. In the usual approaches to ontology integration, the mechanisms for specifying the mapping between concepts in different ontologies are limited to expressing direct correspondences between terms. We argue that, in a real-world setting, one needs a much more powerful mechanism. In particular, such a mechanism should allow for mapping a concept in one ontology into a *view*, i.e., a query over the other ontologies, which acquires the relevant information by navigating and aggregating several concepts.

Following the research done in data integration [17, 16], we can distinguish two basic approaches for defining this mapping:

- the *global-centric approach*, where concepts of the global ontology $\mathcal{G}$ are mapped into queries over the local ontologies in $\mathcal{S}$;

- the *local-centric approach*, where concepts of the local ontologies in $\mathcal{S}$ are mapped to queries over the global ontology $\mathcal{G}$.

We discuss these two approaches in the following sections.

---

[1] Here and below we use the term "concept" for denoting a concept of the ontology.

3   Global-centric approach

In the global-centric approach (aka global-as-view approach), we assume we have a query language $\mathcal{V}_S$ over the alphabet $\mathcal{A}_S$, and the mapping between the global and the local ontologies is given by associating to each term in the global ontology a *view*, i.e., a query, over the local ontologies. The intended meaning of associating to a term C in $\mathcal{G}$ a query V_s over $\mathcal{S}$, is that such a query represents the best way to characterize the instances of C using the concepts in $\mathcal{S}$. A further mechanism is used to specify if the correspondence between C and the associated view is *sound, complete,* or *exact*. Let $\mathcal{D}$ be a local model for $\mathcal{O}$, and $\mathcal{I}$ a global interpretation for $\mathcal{O}$:

- $\mathcal{I}$ satisfies the correspondence $\langle C, V_s, sound \rangle$ in $\mathcal{M}_{\mathcal{G},\mathcal{S}}$ wrt $\mathcal{D}$, if all the tuples satisfying V_s in $\mathcal{D}$ satisfy C in $\mathcal{I}$,

- $\mathcal{I}$ satisfies the correspondence $\langle C, V_s, complete \rangle$ in $\mathcal{M}_{\mathcal{G},\mathcal{S}}$ wrt $\mathcal{D}$, if no tuple other than those satisfying V_s in $\mathcal{D}$ satisfies C in $\mathcal{I}$.

- $\mathcal{I}$ satisfies the correspondence $\langle C, V_s, exact \rangle$ in $\mathcal{M}_{\mathcal{G},\mathcal{S}}$ wrt $\mathcal{D}$, if the set of tuples that satisfy C in $\mathcal{I}$ is exactly the set of tuples satisfying V_s in $\mathcal{D}$.

We say that $\mathcal{I}$ *satisfies* the mapping $\mathcal{M}_{\mathcal{G},\mathcal{S}}$ wrt $\mathcal{D}$, if $\mathcal{I}$ satisfies every correspondence in $\mathcal{M}_{\mathcal{G},\mathcal{S}}$ wrt $\mathcal{D}$.

The global-centric approach is the one adopted in most data integration systems. In such systems, sources are databases (in general relational ones), the global ontology is actually a database schema (again, represented in relational form), and the mapping is specified by associating to each relation in the global schema one relational query over the source relations. It is a common opinion that this mechanism allow for a simple query processing strategy, which basically reduces to unfolding the query using the definition specified in the mapping, so as to translate the query in terms of accesses to the sources [20]. Actually, when we add constraints (even of a very simple form) to the global schema, query processing becomes even harder, as shown in the following case study.

3.1   A case study

We now set up a global-centric framework for ontology integration, which is based on ideas developed for data integration over global schemas expressed in the Entity-Relationship model [3]. In particular, we describe the main components of the ontology integration system, and we provide the semantics both of the system, and of query answering.

The OIS $O = \langle \mathcal{G}, \mathcal{S}, \mathcal{M}_{\mathcal{G},\mathcal{S}} \rangle$ is defined as follows:

- The *global ontology* $\mathcal{G}$ is expressed in the *Entity-Relationship model* (or equivalently as *UML class diagrams*). In particular, $\mathcal{G}$ may include:

    - typing constraints on relationships, assigning an entity to each component of the relationship;

    - mandatory participation to relationships, saying that each instance of an entity must participate as i-th component to a relationship;

    - ISA relations between both entities and relationships;

- typing constraints, functional restrictions, and mandatory existence, for attributes both of entities and of relationships.

- The *local ontologies* S are constituted simply by a relational alphabet $\mathcal{A}_S$, and by the extensions of the relations in $\mathcal{A}_S$. For example, such extensions may be expressed as relational databases. Observe that we are assuming that no intensional relation between terms in $\mathcal{A}_S$ is present in the local ontologies.

- The *mapping* $\mathcal{M}_{G,S}$ between G and S is given by a set of correspondences of the form $\langle C, V_s, sound \rangle$, where C is a concept (i.e., either an entity, a relationship, or an attribute) in the global ontology and V_s is a query over S. More precisely,

  - The mapping associates a query of arity 1 to each entity of G.

  - The mapping associates a query of arity 2 to each entity attribute A of G. Intuitively, if the query retrieves the pair $\langle x, y \rangle$ from the extension of the local ontologies, this means that y is a value of the attribute A of the entity instance x. Thus, the first argument of the query corresponds to the instances of the entity for which A is defined, and the second argument corresponds to the values of the attribute A.

  - The mapping associates a query of arity n to each relationship R of arity n in G. Intuitively, if the query retrieves the tuple $\langle x_1, \ldots, x_n \rangle$ from the extension of the local ontologies, this means that $\langle x_1, \ldots, x_n \rangle$ is an instance of R.

  - The mapping associates a query of arity $n + 1$ to each attribute A of a relationship R of arity n in G. The first n arguments of the query correspond to the tuples of R, and the last argument corresponds to the values of A.

As specified above, the intended meaning of the query V_s associated to the concept C is that it specifies how to retrieve the data corresponding to C in the global schema starting from the data at the sources. This confirms that we are following the global-as-views approach: each concept in the global ontology is defined as a view over the concepts in the local ontologies. We do not pose any constraint on the language used to express the queries in the mapping. Since the extensions of local ontologies are relational databases, we simply assume that the language is able to express computations over relational databases.

To specify the semantics of a data integration system, we have to characterize, given the set of tuples in the extension of the various relations of the local ontologies, which are the data satisfying the global ontology. In principle, one would like to have a single extension as model of the global ontology. Indeed, this is the case for most of the data integration systems described in the literature. However, we will show in the following the surprising result that, due to the presence of the semantic conditions that are implicit in the conceptual schema G, in general, we will have to account for a set of possible extensions.

Example 1. Figure 1 shows the global schema G_1 of a data integration system $\mathcal{O}_1 = \langle G_1, S_1, \mathcal{M}_1 \rangle$, where Age is a functional attribute, Student has a mandatory participation in the relationship Enrolled, Enrolled isa Member, and University isa Organization. The schema models persons who can be members of one or more organizations, and students who are

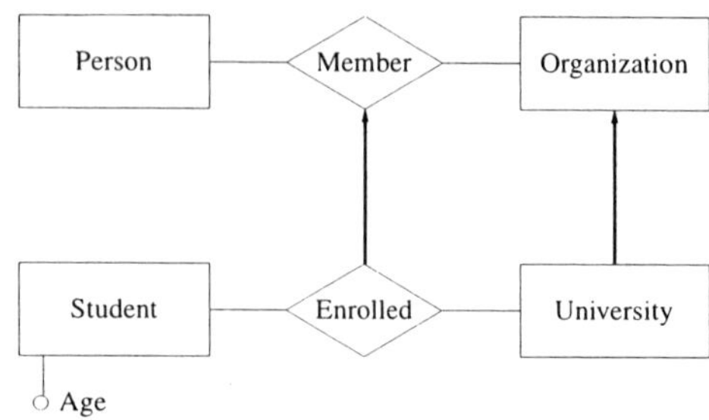

Figure 1: Global ontology of Example 1

enrolled in universities. Suppose that $\mathcal{S}$ is constituted by $S_1, S_2, S_3, S_4, S_5, S_6, S_7, S_8$, and that the mapping $\mathcal{M}_1$ is as follows:

$$
\begin{aligned}
\mathsf{Person}(x) &\leftarrow S_1(x) \\
\mathsf{Organization}(x) &\leftarrow S_2(x) \\
\mathsf{Member}(x, y) &\leftarrow S_7(x, z) \wedge S_8(z, y) \\
\mathsf{Student}(x) &\leftarrow S_3(x, y) \vee S_4(x) \\
\mathsf{Age}(x, y) &\leftarrow S_3(x, y) \vee S_6(x, y, z) \\
\mathsf{University}(x) &\leftarrow S_5(x) \\
\mathsf{Enrolled}(x, y) &\leftarrow S_4(x, y)
\end{aligned}
$$

∎

From the semantics of the OIS $\mathcal{O}$ it is easy to see that, given a local model $\mathcal{D}$, several situations are possible:

1. No global model exists. This happens, in particular, when the data in the extension of the local ontologies retrieved by the queries associated to the elements of the global ontology do not satisfy the functional attribute constraints.

2. Several global models exist. This happens, for example, when the data in the extension of the local ontologies retrieved by the queries associated to the global concepts do not satisfy the ISA relationships of the global ontology. In this case, it may happen that several ways exist to add suitable objects to the elements of $\mathcal{G}$ in order to satisfy the constraints. Each such ways yields a global model.

Example 2. Referring to Example 1, consider a local model $\mathcal{D}_1$, where S_3 contains the tuple $\langle t_1, a_1 \rangle$, and S_6 contains the tuple $\langle t_1, a_2, v_1 \rangle$. The query associated to Age by the mapping $\mathcal{M}_1$ specifies that, in every model of $\mathcal{O}_1$ both tuples should belong to the extension of Age. However, since Age is a functional attribute in $\mathcal{G}_1$, it follows that no model exists for the OIS $\mathcal{O}_1$. ∎

Example 3. Referring again to Example 1, consider a local model $\mathcal{D}_2$, where S_1 contains p_1 and p_2, S_2 contains o_1, S_5 contains u_1, S_4 contains t_1, and the pairs $\langle p_1, o_1 \rangle$ and $\langle p_2, u_1 \rangle$ are in the join between S_7 and S_8. By the mapping $\mathcal{M}_1$, it follows that in every model of $\mathcal{O}_1$, we have that $p_1, p_2 \in$ Person, $\langle p_1, o_1 \rangle, \langle p_2, u_1 \rangle \in$ Member, $o_1 \in$ Organization, $t_1 \in$ Student, and $u_1 \in$ University. Moreover, since $\mathcal{G}_1$ specifies that Student has a mandatory participation in the relationship Enrolled, in every model for $\mathcal{O}_1$, t_1 *must* be enrolled in a certain university. The key point is that nothing is said in $\mathcal{D}_2$ about *which* university, and therefore we have to accept as models all interpretations for $\mathcal{O}_1$ that differ in the university t_1 is enrolled in. ∎

In the framework proposed, it is assumed that the first problem is solved by the queries extracting data from the extension of the local ontologies. In other words, it is assumed that, for any functional attribute A, the corresponding query implements a suitable data cleaning strategy (see, e.g., [15]) that ensures that, for every local model $\mathcal{D}$ and every x, there is at most one tuple (x, y) in the extension of A (a similar condition holds for functional attributes of relationships).

The second problem shows that the issue of query answering with incomplete information arises even in the global-as-view approach to data integration. Indeed, the existence of multiple global models for the OIS implies that query processing cannot simply reduce to evaluating the query over a single relational database. Rather, we should in principle take *all* possible global models into account when answering a query.

It is interesting to observe that there are at least two different strategies to simplify the setting, and overcome this problem that are frequently adopted in data integration systems [17, 20, 16]:

- Data integration systems usually adopt a simpler data model (often, a plain relational data model) for expressing the global schema (i.e., the global ontology). In this case, the data retrieved from the sources (i.e., the local ontologies) trivially fits into the schema, and can be directly considered as the unique database to be processed during query answering.

- The queries associated to the concepts of the global schema are often considered as exact. In this case, analogously to the previous one, it is easy to see that the only global extension to be considered is the one formed by the data retrieved by the extension of the local ontologies. However, observe that, when data in this extension do not obey all semantic conditions that are implicit in the global ontology, this single extension is not coherent with the global ontology, and the OIS is inconsistent. This implies that query answering in meaningless. We argue that, in the usual case of autonomous, heterogeneous local ontologies, it is very unlikely that data fit in the global ontology, and therefore, this approach is too restrictive, in the sense that the OIS would be often inconsistent.

The fact that the problem of incomplete information is overlooked in current approaches can be explained by observing that traditional data integration systems follow one of the above mentioned simplifying strategies: they either express the global schema as a set of plain relations, or consider the sources as exact (see, for instance, [11, 19, 1]).

In [3] we present an algorithm for computing the set of certain answers to queries posed to a data integration system. The key feature of the algorithm is to reason about both the query and the global ontology in order to infer which tuples satisfy the query in all models of the OIS. Thus, the algorithm does not simply unfold the query on the basis of the mapping, as usually done in data integration systems based on the global-as-view approach. Indeed, the algorithm is able to add more answers to those directly extracted from the local ontologies, by exploiting the semantic conditions expressed in the conceptual global schema.

Let $\mathcal{O} = \langle \mathcal{G}, \mathcal{S}, \mathcal{M}_{\mathcal{G},\mathcal{S}} \rangle$ be an OIS, let $\mathcal{D}$ be a local model, and let Q be a query over the global ontology $\mathcal{G}$. The algorithm is constituted by three major steps.

1. From the query Q, obtain a new query $expand_G(Q)$ over the elements of the global ontology G in which the knowledge in G that is relevant for Q has been compiled in.

2. From $expand_G(Q)$, compute the query $unfold_{\mathcal{M}_{G,S}}(expand_G(Q))$, by unfolding $expand_G(Q)$ on the basis of the mapping $\mathcal{M}_{G,S}$. The unfolding simply substitutes each atom of $expand_G(Q)$ with the query associated by $\mathcal{M}_{G,S}$ to the element in the atom. The resulting $unfold_{\mathcal{M}_{G,S}}(expand_G(Q))$ is a query over the relations in the local ontologies.

3. Evaluate the query $unfold_{\mathcal{M}_{G,S}}(expand_G(Q))$ over the local model $\mathcal{D}$.

The last two steps are quite obvious. Instead, the first one requires to find a way to compile into the query the semantic relations holding among the concepts of the global schema $\mathcal{G}$. A way to do so is shown in [3]. The query $expand_G(Q)$ returned by the algorithm is exponential wrt to Q. However, $expand_G(Q)$ is a union of conjunctive queries, which, if the queries in the mapping are polynomial, makes the entire algorithm polynomial in data complexity.

Example 4. Referring to Example 3, consider the query Q_1 to $\mathcal{O}_1$:

$$\mathsf{Q}_1(x) \leftarrow \mathsf{Member}(x, y) \wedge \mathsf{University}(y)$$

It is easy to see that $\{\mathsf{p}_2, \mathsf{t}_1\}$ is the set of certain answers to Q_1 with respect to $\mathcal{O}_1$ and $\mathcal{D}_2$. Thus, although $\mathcal{D}_2$ does not indicate in which university t_1 is enrolled, the semantics of $\mathcal{O}_1$ specifies that t_1 is enrolled in a university in all legal database for $\mathcal{O}_1$. Since Member is a generalization of Enrolled, this implies that t_1 is in $\mathsf{Q}_1^{\mathcal{O}}$, and hence is in $unf_{\mathcal{M}_1}(exp_{\mathcal{G}_1}(\mathsf{Q}_1))$ evaluated over $\mathcal{D}_2$. ∎

4 Local-centric approach

In the local-centric approach (aka local-as-view approach), we assume we have a query language $\mathcal{V}_G$ over the alphabet $\mathcal{A}_G$, and the mapping between the global and the local ontologies is given by associating to each term in the local ontologies a *view*, i.e., a query over the global ontology. Again, the intended meaning of associating to a term C in S a query V_g over $\mathcal{G}$, is that such a query represents the best way to characterize the instances of C using the concepts in $\mathcal{G}$. As in the global-centric approach, the correspondence between C and the associated view can be either sound, complete, or exact. Let $\mathcal{D}$ be a local model for $\mathcal{O}$, and $\mathcal{I}$ a global interpretation for $\mathcal{O}$:

- $\mathcal{I}$ satisfies the correspondence $\langle V_g, C, sound \rangle$ in $\mathcal{M}_{G,S}$ wrt $\mathcal{D}$, if all the tuples satisfying C in $\mathcal{D}$ satisfy V_g in $\mathcal{I}$,

- $\mathcal{I}$ satisfies the correspondence $\langle V_g, C, complete \rangle$ in $\mathcal{M}_{G,S}$ wrt $\mathcal{D}$, if no tuple other than those satisfying C in $\mathcal{D}$ satisfies V_g in $\mathcal{I}$,

- $\mathcal{I}$ satisfies the correspondence $\langle V_g, C, exact \rangle$ in $\mathcal{M}_{G,S}$ wrt $\mathcal{D}$, if the set of tuples that satisfy C in $\mathcal{D}$ is exactly the set of tuples satisfying V_g in $\mathcal{I}$.

As in the global-centric approach, we say that $\mathcal{I}$ *satisfies* the mapping $\mathcal{M}_{G,S}$ wrt $\mathcal{D}$, if $\mathcal{I}$ satisfies every correspondence in $\mathcal{M}_{G,S}$ wrt $\mathcal{D}$.

Recent research work on data integration follows the local-centric approach [20, 16, 18, 6, 8]. The major challenge of this approach is that, in order to answer a query expressed over the global schema, one must be able to reformulate the query in terms of queries to the sources. While in the global-centric approach such a reformulation is guided by the correspondences in the mapping, here the problem requires a reasoning step, so as to infer how to use the sources for answering the query. Many authors point out that, despite its difficulty, the local-centric approach better supports a dynamic environment, where local ontologies can be added to the systems without the need for restructuring the global ontology.

4.1 A case study

We present here an OIS architecture based on the use of Description Logics to represent ontologies [6, 7]. Specifically, we adopt the Description Logic $\mathcal{DLR}$, in which both classes and n-ary relations can be represented [4]. We first introduce $\mathcal{DLR}$, and then we illustrate how we use the logic to define an OIS.

4.1.1 The Description Logic $\mathcal{DLR}$

Description Logics[2] (DLs) are knowledge representation formalisms that are able to capture virtually all class-based representation formalisms used in Artificial Intelligence, Software Engineering, and Databases [9, 10].

One of the distinguishing features of these logics is that they have optimal reasoning algorithms, and practical systems implementing such algorithms are now used in several projects.

In DLs, the domain of interest is modeled by means of *concepts* and *relations*, which denote classes of objects and relationships, respectively. Here, we focus our attention on the DL $\mathcal{DLR}$ [4, 6], whose basic elements are *concepts* (unary relations), and *n-ary relations*. We assume to deal with an alphabet $\mathcal{A}$ constituted by a finite set of atomic relations, atomic concepts, and *constants*, denoted by P, A, and a, respectively. We use R to denote arbitrary relations (of given arity between 2 and n_{max}), and C to denote arbitrary concepts, respectively built according to the following syntax:

$$C \;::=\; \top_1 \mid A \mid \neg C \mid C_1 \sqcap C_2 \mid \exists[i]R \mid (\leq k\,[i]R)$$
$$R \;::=\; \top_n \mid P \mid i/n\!:\!C \mid \neg R \mid R_1 \sqcap R_2$$

where i denotes a component of a relation, i.e., an integer between 1 and n_{max}, n denotes the *arity* of a relation, i.e., an integer between 2 and n_{max}, and k denotes a nonnegative integer. We consider only concepts and relations that are *well-typed*, which means that only relations of the same arity n are combined to form expressions of type $R_1 \sqcap R_2$ (which inherit the arity n), and $i \leq n$ whenever i denotes a component of a relation of arity n.

The semantics of $\mathcal{DLR}$ is specified as follows. An *interpretation* $\mathcal{I}$ is constituted by an *interpretation domain* $\Delta^{\mathcal{I}}$, and an *interpretation function* $\cdot^{\mathcal{I}}$ that assigns to each constant an element of $\Delta^{\mathcal{I}}$ under the unique name assumption, to each concept C a subset $C^{\mathcal{I}}$ of $\Delta^{\mathcal{I}}$, and to each relation R of arity n a subset $R^{\mathcal{I}}$ of $(\Delta^{\mathcal{I}})^n$, such that the conditions in Figure 2 are satisfied. Observe that, the "$\neg$" constructor on relations is used to express difference of relations, and not the complement [4].

A $\mathcal{DLR}$ knowledge base is a set of inclusion assertions of the form

$$C_1 \sqsubseteq C_2 \qquad\qquad R_1 \sqsubseteq R_2$$

---

[2]See `http://dl.kr.org` for the home page of Description Logics.

$$
\begin{aligned}
\top_1^{\mathcal{I}} &= \Delta^{\mathcal{I}} \\
A^{\mathcal{I}} &\subseteq \Delta^{\mathcal{I}} \\
(\neg C)^{\mathcal{I}} &= \Delta^{\mathcal{I}} \setminus C^{\mathcal{I}} \\
(C_1 \sqcap C_2)^{\mathcal{I}} &= C_1^{\mathcal{I}} \cap C_2^{\mathcal{I}} \\
(\exists [i] R)^{\mathcal{I}} &= \{ d \in \Delta^{\mathcal{I}} \mid \exists \langle d_1, \ldots, d_n \rangle \in R^{\mathcal{I}}.\, d_i = d \} \\
(\leq k\,[i] R)^{\mathcal{I}} &= \{ d \in \Delta^{\mathcal{I}} \mid \sharp\{ \langle d_1, \ldots, d_n \rangle \in R_1^{\mathcal{I}} \mid d_i = d \} \leq k \} \\[4pt]
\top_n^{\mathcal{I}} &\subseteq (\Delta^{\mathcal{I}})^n \\
P^{\mathcal{I}} &\subseteq \top_n^{\mathcal{I}} \\
i/n : C^{\mathcal{I}} &= \{ \langle d_1, \ldots, d_n \rangle \in \top_n^{\mathcal{I}} \mid d_i \in C^{\mathcal{I}} \} \\
(\neg R)^{\mathcal{I}} &= \top_n^{\mathcal{I}} \setminus R^{\mathcal{I}} \\
(R_1 \sqcap R_2)^{\mathcal{I}} &= R_1^{\mathcal{I}} \cap R_2^{\mathcal{I}}
\end{aligned}
$$

Figure 2: Semantic rules for $\mathcal{DLR}$ (P, R, R_1, and R_2 have arity n)

where C_1 and C_2 are concepts, and R_1 and R_2 are relations of the same arity. An inclusion assertion $C_1 \sqsubseteq C_2$ (resp., $R_1 \sqsubseteq R_2$) is satisfied in an interpretation $\mathcal{I}$ if $C_1^{\mathcal{I}} \subseteq C_2^{\mathcal{I}}$ (resp., $R_1^{\mathcal{I}} \subseteq R_2^{\mathcal{I}}$). An interpretation is a *model* of a knowledge base $\mathcal{K}$, if it satisfies all assertions in $\mathcal{K}$. $\mathcal{K}$ *logically implies* an inclusion assertion ρ if ρ is satisfied in all models of $\mathcal{K}$.

Finally, we introduce the notion of query expression in $\mathcal{DLR}$. We assume that the alphabet $\mathcal{A}$ is enriched with a finite set of variable symbols, simply called *variables*. A *query expression* Q over a $\mathcal{DLR}$ knowledge base $\mathcal{K}$ is a non-recursive datalog query of the form

$$
Q(\vec{x}) \;\leftarrow\; conj_1(\vec{x}, \vec{y}_1) \vee \cdots \vee conj_m(\vec{x}, \vec{y}_m)
$$

where each $conj_i(\vec{x}, \vec{y}_i)$ is a conjunction of *atoms*, and $\vec{x}$, $\vec{y}_i$ are all the variables appearing in the conjunct. Each atom has one of the forms $R(\vec{t})$ or $C(t)$, where $\vec{t}$ and t are variables in $\vec{x}$ and $\vec{y}_i$ or constants in $\mathcal{A}$, R is a relation of $\mathcal{K}$, and C is a concept of $\mathcal{K}$. The number of variables of $\vec{x}$ is called the *arity* of Q, and is the arity of the relation denoted by the query Q. We observe that the atoms in query expressions are arbitrary $\mathcal{DLR}$ concepts and relations, freely used in the assertions of the KB.

Given an interpretation $\mathcal{I}$, a query expression Q of arity n is interpreted as the set $Q^{\mathcal{I}}$ of n-tuples of constants $\langle c_1, \ldots, c_n \rangle$, such that, when substituting each c_i for x_i, the formula

$$
\exists \vec{y}_1.conj_1(\vec{x}, \vec{y}_1) \vee \cdots \vee \exists \vec{y}_m.conj_m(\vec{x}, \vec{y}_m)
$$

evaluates to true in $\mathcal{I}$.

$\mathcal{DLR}$ is equipped with effective reasoning techniques that are sound and complete with respect to the semantics. In particular, checking whether a given assertion logically follows from a set of assertions is EXPTIME-complete in (assuming that numbers are encoded in unary), and query containment, i.e., checking whether one query is contained in another one in every model of a set of assertions, is EXPTIME-hard and solvable in 2EXPTIME [4].

4.1.2 $\mathcal{DLR}$ local-centric OIS

We now set up a local-centric framework for ontology integration, which is based on ideas developed for data integration over $\mathcal{DLR}$ knowledge bases [6, 5]. In particular, we describe the main components of the ontology integration system, and we provide the semantics both of the system, and of query answering.

In this setting, an OIS $O = \langle \mathcal{G}, \mathcal{S}, \mathcal{M}_{\mathcal{G},\mathcal{S}} \rangle$ is defined as follows:

- The *global ontology* $\mathcal{G}$ is a $\mathcal{DLR}$ knowledge base.

- The *local ontologies* $\mathcal{S}$ are again seen as a set of relations each giving the extension of an ontology-concept in the ontology. We observe that again we have only extensional knowledge on such relations in $\mathcal{S}$.

- The *mapping* $\mathcal{M}_{\mathcal{G},\mathcal{S}}$ between $\mathcal{G}$ and $\mathcal{S}$ is given by a set of correspondences of the form $\langle V_g, T, as \rangle$, where T is a relation of a local ontology, V_g is a query expression over $\mathcal{G}$, and as is either *sound*, *complete*, or *exact*.

Observe that we could partition the global ontology in several parts, one for each local ontology, modeling the intensional knowledge on the local ontology wrt the OIS, plus one for the reconciled global view of such ontologies. By making use of the so called interschema assertions [12] the different parts can be related to each at the intesional level. For simplicity we do not deal with interschema assertion in this case study, however it is immediate to extend the framework presented here to include them as well [6, 7].

Query answering in this setting requires quite sophisticated techniques that take into account the knowledge both in the global ontology and in the mapping in answering a query posed over the global ontology with the data contained in the local ontologies. Such query answering techniques are studied in [5].

Example 5. Consider for example the OIS $\mathcal{O}_d = \langle \mathcal{G}_d, \mathcal{S}_d, \mathcal{M}_d \rangle$ defined as follows:

- The global ontology $\mathcal{G}_d$ is the $\mathcal{DLR}$ knowledge base

$$
\begin{aligned}
\mathsf{American} \sqcap \exists[1](\mathsf{RELATIVE} \sqcap 2{:}\mathsf{Doctor}) &\sqsubseteq \mathsf{Wealthy} \\
\mathsf{Surgeon} &\sqsubseteq \mathsf{Doctor}
\end{aligned}
$$

expressing that Americans who have a doctor as relative are wealthy, and that each surgeon is also a doctor.

- The set $\mathcal{S}_d$ of local ontologies consists of two ontologies, containing respectively the relations T_1 and T_2, with extensions $\{\mathsf{ann}, \mathsf{bill}\}$ and $\{\mathsf{ann}, \mathsf{dan}\}$.

- The mapping $\mathcal{M}_{\mathcal{G},\mathcal{S}}$ is $\{\langle V_1, T_1, sound \rangle, \langle V_2, T_2, sound \rangle\}$, with

$$
\begin{aligned}
V_1(x) &\leftarrow \mathsf{RELATIVE}(x, y) \wedge \mathsf{Surgeon}(y) \\
V_2(x) &\leftarrow \mathsf{American}(x)
\end{aligned}
$$

Given the query expression $Q_w(x) \leftarrow \mathsf{Wealthy}(x)$ over $\mathcal{G}_d$, asking for those who are wealthy, we have that the only answer in $Q_w^{\mathcal{O}_d}$ is ann. Consider an additional local ontology, consisting of a relation T_3 with an extension not containing bill, and mapped to $\mathcal{G}$ by the correspondence $\langle V_3, T_3, exact \rangle$, with $V_3(x) \leftarrow \mathsf{Wealthy}(x)$. Then, from the constraints in $\mathcal{G}_d$ and the information we have on the correspondences, we can conclude that bill is not an answer to the query asking for the Americans. ∎

5　Combining the global-centric and local-centric approaches

The global-centric and the local-centric approach can be combined together into an approach using unrestricted mappings, in which the restrictions on the direction of the correspondence between global and local ontologies are overcome [14]. In the unrestricted approach, we have both a query language $\mathcal{V}_S$ over the alphabet $\mathcal{A}_S$, and a query language $\mathcal{V}_G$ over the alphabet $\mathcal{A}_G$, and the mapping between the global and the local ontologies is given by relating views over the global ontology to views over the local ontologies. Again, the intended meaning of relating the view V_g over the global ontology to the view V_s over the local ontology is that V_s represents the best way to characterize the objects satisfying V_g in terms of the concepts in $\mathcal{S}$. Analogously to the other cases, the correspondences between V_g and V_s can be characterized as sound, complete, or exact. Let $\mathcal{D}$ be a local model for $\mathcal{O}$, and $\mathcal{I}$ a global interpretation for $\mathcal{O}$:

- $\mathcal{I}$ satisfies the correspondence $\langle V_g, V_s, sound \rangle$ in $\mathcal{M}_{G,S}$ wrt $\mathcal{D}$, if all the tuples satisfying satisfying V_s in $\mathcal{D}$ satisfy V_g in $\mathcal{I}$,

- $\mathcal{I}$ satisfies the correspondence $\langle V_g, V_s, complete \rangle$ in $\mathcal{M}_{G,S}$ wrt $\mathcal{D}$, if no tuple other than those satisfying V_s in $\mathcal{D}$ satisfy V_g in $\mathcal{I}$,

- $\mathcal{I}$ satisfies the correspondence $\langle V_g, V_s, exact \rangle$ in $\mathcal{M}_{G,S}$ wrt $\mathcal{D}$, if the set of tuples that satisfy V_g in $\mathcal{I}$ is exactly the set of tuples satisfying V_s in $\mathcal{D}$.

Again, we say that $\mathcal{I}$ *satisfies* the mapping $\mathcal{M}_{G,S}$ wrt $\mathcal{D}$, if $\mathcal{I}$ satisfies every correspondence in $\mathcal{M}_{G,S}$ wrt $\mathcal{D}$.

Example 6. Consider the OIS $\mathcal{O}_u = \langle \mathcal{G}_u, \mathcal{S}_u, \mathcal{M}_u \rangle$, where both $\mathcal{G}_u$ and the two ontologies S_1 and S_2 forming $\mathcal{S}_u$ are simply sets of relations with their extensions.

- The global ontology $\mathcal{G}_u$ contains two binary relations, WorksFor, denoting researchers and projects they work for, and Area, denoting projects and research areas they belong to.

- The local ontology S_1 contains a binary relation InterestedIn denoting persons and fields they are interested in, and the local ontology S_2 contains a binary relation GetGrant, denoting researchers and grants assigned to them, and a binary relation GrantFor denoting grants and projects they refer to.

- The mapping $\mathcal{M}_u$ is formed by the following correspondences

    - $\langle V_1, \text{InterestedIn}, complete \rangle$, with $V_1(r, f) \leftarrow \text{WorksFor}(r, p) \wedge \text{Area}(p, f)$
    - $\langle \text{WorkFor}, V_2, sound \rangle$, with $V_2(r, p) \leftarrow \text{GetGrant}(r, g) \wedge \text{GrantFor}(g, p)$

This situation can be represented neither in the global-centric nor in the local-centric approach. ∎

Query answering in this approach is largely unexplored, mainly because it combines the difficulties of the other ones. However, in a real world setting, this may be the only approach that provides the appropriate expressive power.

6   Conclusions

We have presented a general framework for ontology integration, where a global ontology is used to provide a unified view for querying local ontologies, as in the semantic web. The framework represents a sort of design space for the problem of integrating ontologies within semantic web applications. We have argued that the mapping between the global and the local ontologies is the main aspect of the framework, and we have discussed various approaches for specifying such a mapping. Independently of the approach, we have stressed that the notion of query is crucial for the task of ontology integration.

The two case studies we have presented have shown the need of sophisticated techniques for query answering in an ontology integration system. The two case studies illustrated simplified settings, drawn from data integration. One should expect things to become even more complex when ontology integration is considered in its full generality. Recently several proposals have been made, based on the idea of expressing ontologies as knowledge bases, e.g., in Description Logics [13, 2], and applying automated reasoning techniques for several services in the design of and the interaction with the semantic web. We believe however that such an idea needs to be extended by considering queries as first order citizens and having the ability to reason on them.

References

[1]   M. Bouzeghoub and M. Lenzerini.   Introduction to the special issue on data extraction, cleaning, and reconciliation. *Information Systems*, 26(8):535–536, 2001.

[2]   J. Broekstra, M. Klein, D. Fensel, and I. Horrocks. Adding formal semantics to the Web: building on top of RDF Schema. In *Proc. of the ECDL 2000 Workshop on the Semantic Web*, 2000.

[3]   A. Calì, D. Calvanese, G. De Giacomo, and M. Lenzerini. Accessing data integration systems through conceptual schemas. In *Proc. of the 20th Int. Conf. on Conceptual Modeling (ER 2001)*, 2001.

[4]   D. Calvanese, G. De Giacomo, and M. Lenzerini. On the decidability of query containment under constraints. In *Proc. of the 17th ACM SIGACT SIGMOD SIGART Symp. on Principles of Database Systems (PODS'98)*, pages 149–158, 1998.

[5]   D. Calvanese, G. De Giacomo, and M. Lenzerini. Answering queries using views over description logics knowledge bases. In *Proc. of the 17th Nat. Conf. on Artificial Intelligence (AAAI 2000)*, pages 386–391, 2000.

[6]   D. Calvanese, G. De Giacomo, M. Lenzerini, D. Nardi, and R. Rosati. Description logic framework for information integration. In *Proc. of the 6th Int. Conf. on Principles of Knowledge Representation and Reasoning (KR'98)*, pages 2–13, 1998.

[7]   D. Calvanese, G. De Giacomo, M. Lenzerini, D. Nardi, and R. Rosati. Information integration: Conceptual modeling and reasoning support. In *Proc. of the 6th Int. Conf. on Cooperative Information Systems (CoopIS'98)*, pages 280–291, 1998.

[8]   D. Calvanese, G. De Giacomo, M. Lenzerini, and M. Y. Vardi. View-based query processing and constraint satisfaction. In *Proc. of the 15th IEEE Symp. on Logic in Computer Science (LICS 2000)*, pages 361–371, 2000.

[9]   D. Calvanese, M. Lenzerini, and D. Nardi. Description logics for conceptual data modeling. In J. Chomicki and G. Saake, editors, *Logics for Databases and Information Systems*, pages 229–264. Kluwer Academic Publisher, 1998.

[10]   D. Calvanese, M. Lenzerini, and D. Nardi. Unifying class-based representation formalisms. *J. of Artificial Intelligence Research*, 11:199–240, 1999.

[11] M. J. Carey, L. M. Haas, P. M. Schwarz, M. Arya, W. F. Cody, R. Fagin, M. Flickner, A. Luniewski, W. Niblack, D. Petkovic, J. Thomas, J. H. Williams, and E. L. Wimmers. Towards heterogeneous multimedia information systems: The Garlic approach. In *Proc. of the 5th Int. Workshop on Research Issues in Data Engineering – Distributed Object Management (RIDE-DOM'95)*, pages 124–131. IEEE Computer Society Press, 1995.

[12] T. Catarci and M. Lenzerini. Representing and using interschema knowledge in cooperative information systems. *J. of Intelligent and Cooperative Information Systems*, 2(4):375–398, 1993.

[13] S. Decker, D. Fensel, F. van Harmelen, I. Horrocks, S. Melnik, M. Klein, and J. Broekstra. Knowledge representation on the web. In *Proc. of the 2000 Description Logic Workshop (DL 2000)*, pages 89–97. CEUR Electronic Workshop Proceedings, http://ceur-ws.org/Vol-33/, 2000.

[14] M. Friedman, A. Levy, and T. Millstein. Navigational plans for data integration. In *Proc. of the 16th Nat. Conf. on Artificial Intelligence (AAAI'99)*, pages 67–73. AAAI Press/The MIT Press, 1999.

[15] H. Galhardas, D. Florescu, D. Shasha, and E. Simon. An extensible framework for data cleaning. Technical Report 3742, INRIA, Rocquencourt, 1999.

[16] A. Y. Halevy. Answering queries using views: A survey. *Very Large Database J.*, 10(4):270–294, 2001.

[17] R. Hull. Managing semantic heterogeneity in databases: A theoretical perspective. In *Proc. of the 16th ACM SIGACT SIGMOD SIGART Symp. on Principles of Database Systems (PODS'97)*, 1997.

[18] A. Y. Levy, D. Srivastava, and T. Kirk. Data model and query evaluation in global information systems. *J. of Intelligent Information Systems*, 5:121–143, 1995.

[19] C. Li, R. Yerneni, V. Vassalos, H. Garcia-Molina, Y. Papakonstantinou, J. D. Ullman, and M. Valiveti. Capability based mediation in TSIMMIS. In *Proc. of the ACM SIGMOD Int. Conf. on Management of Data*, pages 564–566, 1998.

[20] J. D. Ullman. Information integration using logical views. In *Proc. of the 6th Int. Conf. on Database Theory (ICDT'97)*, volume 1186 of *Lecture Notes in Computer Science*, pages 19–40. Springer, 1997.

The Emerging Semantic Web
I.F. Cruz et al. (Eds.)
IOS Press, 2002

A Scalable Framework for the Interoperation of Information Sources

Prasenjit Mitra, Gio Wiederhold, and Stefan Decker *
Infolab, Stanford University
Stanford, CA, USA 94305
{mitra, gio, stefan}@db.stanford.edu

Abstract. Resolving heterogeneity among information systems is a crucial necessity if we wish to gain value from the many distributed resources available to us. Problems of heterogeneity in hardware, operating systems, and data structures have been widely addressed, but issues of diverse semantics have been handled mainly in an ad-hoc fashion. In this paper, we present ONION, a system based on a scalable approach to interoperation of information systems that articulates their associated ontologies. An articulation focuses on the semantically relevant intersection of information resources with respect to a type of application. However, ontologies obtained from diverse sources are represented using different formats. We have designed a simple intermediate format - the ONION ontology format - that we transform ontologies to before we generate semantic correspondences or articulations between them.

In ONION, application-dependent articulation rules that capture the correspondence between concepts in different ontologies are established between source ontologies semi-automatically. Finally we present an ontology algebra, based on the articulation rules, for the composition of ontologies.

1 Introduction

Today a large number of diverse information sources - databases, knowledge bases, collections of documents - are available on the Internet. Often, we cannot answer a query by using a single source, and need to compose knowledge from multiple sources. Intelligent searching and querying on the World Wide Web - the largest collection of distributed information and knowledge sources - often requires composing information from heterogeneous information sources. Today, the bulk of this composition is done by the end-user. Not only is this process extremely tedious and time-consuming, but also, often, the end-user does not have any idea about the semantics used by the builder of the information source. In this paper, we present a brief overview of the ONION (ONtology compositION) system, which takes a systematic approach to enable semi-automatic interoperation among heterogeneous information sources.

1.1 Heterogeneity

Most information sources have been independently constructed and are autonomously maintained. Attempts have been made to integrate information from these various information

---

* This work was partially supported by a grant from the Air Force Office of Scientific Research (AFOSR).

sources into a monolithic information source [1], [2]. Such an approach, however, creates maintenance and scalability problems. When an information source is to be added, the large information source must be restructured, and often, this kind of maintenance leads to substantial delays [3].

Some researchers have tried to first build a standard ontology or global schema and then build information sources that conform to that ontology or schema [4], [5]. Even though this approach has worked for small communities, coming up with an agreed-to-standard for knowledge in larger domains is almost impossible, especially among groups that have different applications in mind.

Besides, it is prohibitively expensive to restructure existing knowledge so that it conforms to the standard ontology even if one were able to.

1.2   Maintenance

Everyday new discoveries expand our knowledge and change our views of the universe that we live in. Therefore, even if information sources start off with a common ontology, this ontology has to be updated periodically. The maintainers of the information sources that use the standard ontology will have to agree on the updates being proposed and on the restructuring of the ontology. They may have entirely different applications in mind or may not subscribe to a newly discovered theory. Furthermore, some participants might see the changes required to support the proposed updates as an unnecessary imposition since restructuring the information source will require substantial effort on their part. Thus generating new consensus on updates to the standard ontology is a time-consuming and tenuous process. For quickly changing fields, arriving at a consensus within a short period of time is not even feasible. Therefore, we need a system where the information sources are autonomous.

1.3   A Realistic Setting

We believe that the information sources should be autonomous and that they should not be required to conform to a standard ontology in order for a user to get a composition of knowledge from them. Instead of integrating information sources, we intend to enable interoperation among them.

Unfortunately, the composition of knowledge from multiple independently maintained information sources is a hard problem. Independently constructed information sources are heterogeneous and often use different vocabularies and data formats. The organization of class-subclass hierarchies are substantially different. Often, they use different terms to represent the same concept and the same term to represent entirely different concepts. In order to interoperate among such information sources we need to resolve their semantic heterogeneity.

Karp [6] proposes a strategy for database interoperation. We extend Karp's approach to apply to not only databases, but also to knowledge bases and information sources.

As in [7], [8], and [6], we assume that information sources are independently created and maintained. In Karp's system, each database comes with a schem a which is saved in a Knowledge Base of Databases. Correspondingly, we assume that associated with each information source is an ontology. However, we do not require all ontologies to be saved in a central repository.

The ontologies associated with information sources are based on some existing, known vocabularies and data formats. Native drivers and wrappers provide access to the ontol ogies and help us restructure the information if needed. We establish application-specific *articulation rules*, i.e., rules that establish correspondence between concepts in different ontologies, semi-automatically.

Queries are rewritten using the articulation rules. Before a query is dispatched to a source, the terms in the query are rewritten using the articulation rules that indicate the semantic correspondence between the terms in the query and those in the source. This rewriting ensures that a source gets a query that conforms to the vocabulary and the semantics of the source. During query planning, optimization is enabled based on the algebraic properties of the operations.

In this paper, we describe the ONION system and highlight our approach to interoperation. In Section 2, we describe the common conceptual model that ONION uses for its internal representation of ontologies. In Section 3 we discuss the semi-automatic articulation of ontologies. In Section 4 we outline an Ontology Composition Algebra that we use to compose ontologies. Section 5 concludes the paper.

2　The ONION Ontology Format

ONION's articulation generator needs all source ontologies to conform to a common ontology format. Heterogeneity among information sources needs to be resolved to enable meaningful information exchange or interoperation among them. The two major sources of heterogeneity among the sources are as follows: First, different sources use different data formats and modeling languages to represent their data and meta-data. In the rest of the paper, we will refer to the data format and the modeling language together as the ontology format. Second, sources using the same data format differ in their semantics. The ONION system uses a common ontology format, which we describe below. It first converts all external ontologies to this common format and then resolves the semantic heterogeneity among the objects in the ontologies that it is articulating.

Melnik, et al., [9] have shown how to convert documents from one modeling format to another, e.g., from RDFS [10] to DAML+OIL [11]. We can use wrappers to convert the ontologies represented using the formats that we want to support to the ONION format.

Instead of writing a wrapper to convert all ontologies from their native formats to the ONION format, we could do so declaratively. That is, we could first write rules that transform parts of one ontology from one format to another. However, such an approach is not feasible. Often, the transformations are quite complex and can be more naturally expressed procedurally. Expressing them declaratively requires a very expressive rule language. Deductions in more expressive rule languages are often not tractable. Also, we would have to create and manipulate articulation rules that not only have semantic information but also have information about transforming ontology formats. Besides, by converting to the ONION format, we eliminate the necessity of n^2 pariwise conversions among n ontologies and instead reduce it to n conversions (of all the ontologies to the common format).

We solve the problem of establishing correspondences among ontology formats and the problem of establishing articulations among the concepts in the ontologies differently because we believe that the small number of ontology formats that we intend to support (currently XML, RDF, DAML+OIL) can be converted to use one common format, whereas the number of concepts and thus objects used in ontologies are rather large and creating a huge, integrated, common, global ontology is untenable and if such an ontology could be created it would be unmaintainable.

Information sources were, are and will be modeled using different formats. We do not foresee the creation of a *de facto* standard data format that will be used by all information sources. On the other hand, we need a common ontology format for our internal representation. We use the ONION format to which the source ontologies are converted. ONION then matches the converted ontologies to create the articulation ontology. The common ontology format could be arbitrarily complex so that we could transform all features from various ontology formats minimally. However, to make the articulation generation simple, we take a different approach and strive to keep our model simple.

2.1   A Graph-Oriented Conceptual Model

Our common ontology format is based on the work done by Gyssens, et al.,[12]. At its core, we represent an ontology as a graph. Formally, an ontology $O = (G, R)$ is represented as a directed labeled graph G and a set of rules R. The graph $G = (V, E)$ comprises a finite set of nodes V and a finite set of edges E. R is expressed as Horn clauses.

An edge e is written as (n_1, α, n_2), where n_1 and n_2 are two nodes belonging to the set of nodes V and α is the label of the edge between them. The label of a node n is given by a function $\lambda(n)$ that maps the node to a non-null string. In the context of ontologies, the label is often a noun-phrase that represents a concept. The label α of an edge $e = (n_1, \alpha, n_2)$ is a string given by $\alpha = \delta(e)$. The label of an edge is the name of a semantic relationship among the concepts and it can be null if the relationship is not known. The domain of the functions λ and δ is the universal set of all nodes and edges, respectively (from all graphs), and their range is the set of strings (from all lexicons). For the rest of the paper, we assume that the function λ maps a node to a unique label (i.e., the name of the node in the ontology is concatenated with the name of the ontology). Thus, we will use the label of a node as a unique identifier of the node. To represent an edge, we can substitute the label of a node for a node and write edge $e = (\lambda(n_1), \alpha, \lambda(n_2))$.

The graph in the ONION data format can be expressed using RDF [13]. Each edge in our graph is coded as an RDF sentence, with the two nodes in the edge being the subject and the predicate and the relationship being the property. However, in order to keep our model simple, we have not included the containers that provide collection semantics in RDF. If the children of a node need to be ordered we use a special relationship, as explained below. By choosing RDF, we can use the various tools that are available for RDF and do not have to write parsers and other tools for our model.

Rules in an ontology are expressed in a logic-based language. Although, theoretically, it might make sense to use first-order logic as the rule language due to its greater expressive power, in order to limit the computational complexity we will use a simpler language like Horn Clauses. A typical rule $r \in R$ is of the form :

$$CompoundStatement \implies Statement$$

A *Statement* is of the form $(Concept\ Relationship\ Concept)$. A *Concept* is either a label of a node or a variable that can be bound to one or more nodes in the ontology graph. A *Retationship* expresses a realtion between two *Concepts*.

2.2   *Semantic Relationships in* ONION

The ONION *articulation generator* can improve the semantic matches it derives among concepts in a pair of ontologies if it has some semantic information about the relationships used in the ONION ontology model.

Certain data formats allow only strictly-typed relationships with pre-defined semantics. For instance, relationships like $SubClassOf$, $AttributeOf$, etc., have very clearly defined semantics in most object-relational databases. A system that knows the exact semantics of the relationships in a conceptual model can use the information, for instance, to find better matches between concepts in two ontologies or to perform type-checking and flag errors.

Other models allow any user-defined relationships, without any restriction. For instance, relationships like $OwnerOf$ tend to be interpreted according to the semantics associated with them by the local application. Such relationships need not be strictly typed, and a general system that imports a model allowing them does not know of the application-specific semantic interpretation of the relationships. This approach provides enormous flexibility and can accommodate a large number of relationships. However, since the semantics of these relationships are not exactly known by the system, it cannot use them for matching related concepts or for type-checking.

The ONION data formating encourages the use of a set of strictly-typed relationships with precisely defined semantics. The set of relationships that our articulation generator knows the semantics of is $\{SubClassOf, PartOf, AttributeOf, InstanceOf, ValueOf\}$.

In ONION, we assign the conventional semantics to each of these relationships. Some of these relationships impose type-restrictions on the two nodes they relate. Some of the relationships (like $SubClassOf$, $InstanceOf$) are somewhat similar to those in RDF-Schema but we have chosen a different and much smaller set of relationships to define semantics in ONION so as to maintain its simplicity.

In the following description, we use the term *Literal* to denote a string and the terms $Class$ and $Object$ to denote classes and objects in the sense it is used in object-oriented databases. The semantics of the set of pre-defined relationships available in our common ontology format are as follows:

$SubClassOf$: relates two concepts each of type $Class$. The relationship indicates that one concept is a subclass of another. For example, the statement $(Car\ SubClassOf\ Vehicle)$ denotes that the concept Car is a subclass of concept $Vehicle$. Any instance of the class Car is also an instance of the class $Vehicle$ and all the attributes of the class $Vehicle$ are also attributes of the class Car. The relationship $SubClassOf$ is transitive, and in the absence of an explicit rule in an ontology that states that the $SubClassOf$ relationship is transitive, we will add one to the ontology before reasoning or rewriting the queries using the rules.

$AttributeOf$: This relationship indicates that a concept is an attribute of another concept, e.g., an edge $(ConceptA\ AttributeOf\ ConceptB)$ indicates that $ConceptA$ is an attribute of $ConceptB$. $ConceptB$ is of type $Class$ or of type Object and $ConceptA$ is of type $Class$. This relationship, also referred to as $PropertyOf$ in some information models, has typically the same semantics as attributes in (object-)relational databases . The following rule holds:

$$((A\ AttributeOf\ B)\ \wedge\ (B\ SubClassOf\ C))\ \Longrightarrow\ (A\ AttributeOf\ C)$$

$PartOf$: This relationship indicates that a concept is a part of another concept, e.g., an edge $(Chassis\ PartOf\ Car)$ indicates that $Chassis$ is part of a Car. The first concept is of type *Class* while the second concept can be of type *Class* or *Object*. In relational databases, such relationships are often coded as attributes, but we believe that this relationship is sufficiently different semantically from the relationship *AttributeOf* to warrant separate consideration.

InstanceOf: This relationship indicates that an object is an instance of a class. Therefore, the first concept in the relationship is of type *Object* and the second of type *Class*. For example, an edge (*MyCar InstanceOf Car*) indicates that *MyCar* is an instance of the Class *Car*. The following rule holds:

$$((A \; InstanceOf \; B) \; \wedge \; (B \; SubClassOfC)) \implies (A \; InstanceOf \; C))$$

ValueOf: This relationship is used to indicate the value of an attribute of an object, e.g., ("29" *ValueOf Age*). Thus, the first concept is of type *Literal* and the second of type *Class*. Typically, the second concept (in our example, the class *Age*), in turn, has an edge (in our example (*Age AttributeOf PersonA*)) from the object it describes.

2.3 Sequences

XML is becoming a popular format for expressing data and meta-data on the web. Like SGML and other markup languages primarily designed to express documents, XML imposes order among its elements. By itself, the graphical ONION model, described above, does not impose order among the children of a node. To express order, we introduce a special relationship, namely *Sequence*, which is very similar to the container *Sequence* in RDF. For example, a list ranking cars can be described using the edges

(*MoneyLineRanking Sequence CarRankingList*),
(*CarRankingList* : 1 *HondaAccord*), and
(*CarRankingList* : 2 *FordTaurus*).

The intermediate node *CarRankingList* represents the list object and its elements form an ordered sequence. In an edge of the form (*ConceptA Sequence ConceptB*) the first concept can be a *Class* or an *Object* and the second concept is an *Object* representing the list. The individual elements of the list can be objects or classes and are related to the list-object via the relationships : 1, : 2, . . . , : N, where the list has N elements.

In the ONION format, we do not require that every relationship must belong to the small set of relationships whose semantics are predefined. The model is flexible enough to allow any other user-defined relationship. The articulation generator will not be able to use the relationships, whose semantics it is not aware of, unless the semantics are captured using rules in the source ontology. For example, if the source ontology uses a relationship $Is - A$ and has a rule that says that "Is-A" is transitive, the articulation generator can use that information to generate matches. The articulation rules that the articulation generator generates uses only the relationships whose semantics are predefined to establish correspondences among nodes in the source ontologies.

The articulation generator generates matches among nodes in the two source ontologies that is supplied to it and does not attempt to match relationships among ontologies. The articulation generator uses only relationships whose semantics are clearly defined to it to derive meaningful matches among the nodes and ignores the relationships that it does not know the semantics of. Therefore, if two RDF models have the relationships "Buyer" and

"Owner" and for the purposes of the application we want to generate a match between the two, we need to represent these relationships as nodes in the ONION model and then run the articulation generator to match them.

2.4   Reference and Subsumption

In data formats, especially those used to model documents, like XML, SGML, OEM etc. [14], where there are nested objects and entities, an object is modeled as a subtree in a graph. The entire subtree rooted at a node comprises the object that the node represents. When a query asks for the object, the entire subtree is returned. Such models assume that an object subsumes all objects that are in its subtree. If any relationship needs to be expressed between two objects a reference to the second object is used. The reference is denoted by having a node with the the identifier of the second object and having an edge to this node. The use of this additional node that refers to a different object helps preserve the tree structure of the models, which is required for documents, since they are in essence serialized entities.

In our model, however, even though many of the relationships, with pre-defined semantics, are essentially subsumptive in nature, we intend to keep the concept of an object as simple as possible. Faced with the question of defining the scope of an object in our common data format, we take the minimal approach. In our world, a single node represents a concept: a class, an object, or a value. All edges are referential in nature. Thus, when a query asks to select an object, only the node representing the object is returned and not the entire subtree rooted at the node. This minimal definition of an object helps us keep the articulation rules and the resulting ontology intersections as small as possible. As we will see later, the larger the intersection, the greater the cost when using the articulation to answer queries. Thus we make the choice to keep the definition of an object as simple as possible.

Apart from the graph model, our data format allows us to declaratively supply rules. Some features in other models can be converted using the rules to capture their semantics. If this is not possible, relationships which are not interpreted by ONION can be used. Some features still cannot be expressed using the ONION model.

The common data format is used to bring ontologies to a common format - so that the articulation generator needs to understand only one format. So if a feature cannot be translated into our common data format, it will not be matched with similar features carrying similar semantic messages in other ontologies. However, such information will still be accessible from the individual ontology and the engine associated with the individual sources.

We resolve the heterogeneity with respect to ontology models and modeling languages by building wrappers that convert ontologies using various conceptual models to an ontology in our common data format. However, the second problem of semantic heterogeneity among the concepts used in the source models still remains. In the next section, we will summarize various methods that we use to automatically suggest ontology articulations.

3   Resolving Semantic Heterogeneity

An important requirement for the application scenarios that our system will be used for is high precision. In distinction to research tasks, casual browsing, and web-surfing, the cost of eliminating false hits is very high in business environments. At this point we believe that resolving semantic heterogeneity entirely automatically is not feasible. We, therefore, advocate a semi-automatic approach wherein an automatic *articulation generator* suggests matches between concepts in the two ontologies it is articulating. A human expert, knowledgeable about the semantics of concepts in both ontologies, validates the generated suggested matches using a GUI tool. An expert can delete a suggested match or say that the match is irrelevant for the application at hand. The expert can also indicate new matches that the articulation generator might have missed. The process of constructing an articulation is an iterative process and after the expert is satisfied with the rules generated, they are stored and used when information needs to be composed from the two ontologies.

In order to keep the cost of computation and especially maintenance (which often dominates other costs in established business environments) low, we strive to make the articulations minimal. Currently, the onus is on the expert to keep the articulation minimal. In future, we hope to make the automated heuristics aware of the needs of the application and minimize the articulations.

The matching algorithms that we use can be classified into two types - iterative and non-iterative.

Non-iterative Algorithms

Non-iterative algorithms are ones that generate the concepts that match in the two ontologies in one pass. These algorithms do not generate any new matches based on existing matches. The non-iterative algorithms that we employ involve matching the nodes based on their content.

The articulation generator looks at the words that appear in the label of the two nodes (or associated with the two nodes, e.g., if the nodes are documents or if more elaborate descriptions of the concepts that are represented using the nodes are available) that it seeks to match and generates a measure of the similarity of the nodes depending upon the similarity of the words used in their descriptions or labels.

The non-iterative methods that we currently use primarily refer to dictionaries and the Nexus [15] and also use several semantic indexing techniques based on the context of occurrence of words in a corpus. Since the articulation generator is modular in nature, it should be easy to add any other sophisticated heuristic (like consulting WordNet [16]) that allows us to generate semantic similarity measures between phrases.

Iterative Algorithms

Iterative algorithms require multiple iterations over the two source ontologies in order to generate semantic matches between them. These algorithms look for structural isomorphism between subgraphs of the ontologies, or use the rules available with the ontologies and any seed rules provided by an expert to generate matches between the ontologies. Iterative algorithms are typically used after the non-iterative algorithms have already generated some semantic matches between the ontologies and use these generated matches as its base.

For example, one heuristic we use is to look at the attributes of each node and see if the attributes of the two nodes have matched. If a reasonably large number of attributes are the same, the two nodes are related. If all the attributes of one node are also attributes of another node, the articulation generator indicates that the second node is a subclass of the first node. Another heuristic matches nodes based on the matches between their parent (or child) nodes. The expert has the final decision whether to bless this educated guess generated by the articulation generator.

Due to space limitations, we will not describe in detail all the heuristic algorithms that we use to match ontologies, but refer the interested reader to [17].

In the next section, we will briefly define an Ontology Algebra, which allows us to systematically compose information from diverse information sources. Since we focus on small, well-maintained ontologies in order to achieve high-precision, but we still want to serve substantial applications, we will often have to combine results of prior articulations. The ontology algebra provides the compositional capability, and thus enhances the scalability of our approach.

4 Ontology Composition Algebra

In this section, we present an algebra for Ontology Composition that allows us to compose information systematically. Depending upon the properties of the algebraic operators, we optimize the composition of ontologies.

By retaining a log of the articulation and subsequent composition process, we can also, with minimal adaptations, replay the composition whenever any of the sources change[15]. Without such a capability, integrated ontologies soon became stale and useless. Redoing a substantial integration manually is rare, because of the cost, and the realization that the work will be obsolete again in a short time.

The algebra has one unary operator: Select, and three binary operations:Intersection, Union, and Difference.

4.1 Select

Select: allows us to highlight and select portions of an ontology that are relevant to the task at hand. Given an ontology and a node, t select operator selects the subtree rooted at the node. Given an ontology and a nodes, the select operator selects only those edges in the ontology that connect nodes in the given set.

4.2 Intersection

Each binary operator takes as operands two ontologies that we want to articulate, and generates an ontology as a result, using the articulation rules. The articulation rules are generated by an articulation generation function briefly discussed above.

Intersection is the most important and interesting binary operation. The intersection of two ontologies $O1 = (N1, E1, R1)$, and $O2 = (N2, E2, R2)$ with respect to the set of articulation rule generating f unction AR is:

$OI_{1,2} = O1 \cap_{AR} O2$, where $OI_{1,2} = (NI, EI, RI)$,

$NI = Nodes(AR(O1, O2))$,

$EI = Edges(E1, NI \cap N1) + Edges(E2, NI \cap N2) + Edges(Arules(O1, O2))$,

and $RI = Rules(O1, NI \cap N1) + Rules(O2, NI \cap N2) + AR(O1, O2) - Edges(AR(O1, O2))$.

The nodes in the intersection ontology are those nodes that appear in the articulation rules. The edges in the intersection ontology are the edges among the nodes in the intersection

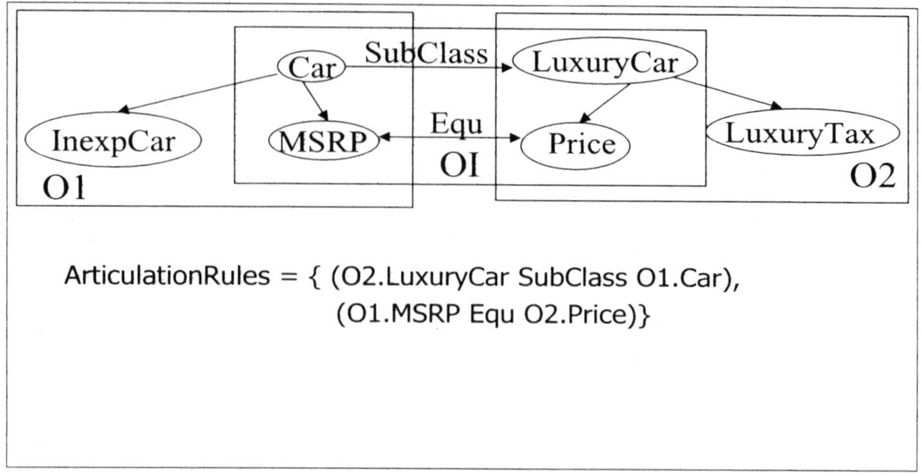

Figure 1: The Intersection Ontology OI of Source Ontologies $O1$ and $O2$

ontology that were either present in the source ontologies or have been established as an articulation rule. The rules in the intersection ontology are the articulation rules that have not already been modeled as edges and those rules present in the source ontology that use only concepts that occur in the intersection ontology.

The articulation rules are of two types - ones that are simple statements expressing binary relationships and the more complex rules expressed in Horn Clauses that are mostly supplied by the expert. An example of rules of the former type is: $(O1.Car SubclassOf O2.Vehicle)$ and one of the more complex logic-based ones is a conjunctive rule of the form: e.g. conjunctive rules of the form $(O1.X InstanceOf O1.Car), (Y PriceOf X), (Y > 30000) \Rightarrow (O1.X SubClassOf O2.LuxuryCar)$. The former set of rules are modeled as edges in the articulation ontology and the second set of rules which require some form of reasoning to derive statements from are left as rules belonging to the articulation ontology. These rules will be processed during the query evaluation process only when necessary.

For all articulation generator functions, we require that $O1 \cap_{AR} O1 = O1$, that is the articulation generator function should generate such articulation rules that upholds the above-mentioned property as a sanity-check. Articulation generator functions that do not satisfy the above equality are *unsound* and for the purposes of our compositions, we do not use any unsound articualtion generator function.

In Figure 1, we show two ontologies $O1$, $O2$, the articulation rules between them and the intersection ontology OI. Equ is a short-hand that we use when to indicate classes that are equivalent in the two ontologies.

Note that since we consider each node as an object instead of the subtree rooted at the node, we will get only the node in the intersection by virtue of its appearing in an articulation rule and not automatically include its attributes or subclasses. Again, a minimal linkage serves our needs better than inclusion of possibly irrelevant concepts. Inclusion of attributes will be required to define subclass relationships among nodes in the source ontologies precisely.

Each node in the intersection has a label which contains the URI of the source in which it appears. If the attributes of the object that it represents are required, the application's query processor has to get that information from the original source. Defining the intersection with a minimal outlook reduces the complexity of the composition task, and the maintenance costs, which all depend upon the size of the articulation.

4.3   Union

The union OU between two ontologies $O1 = (V1, E1, R1)$ and $O2 = (V2, E2, R2)$ is expressed as $OU = O1 \cup_{AR} O2 = (VU, EU, RU)$ where
$VU = V1 \cup V2 \cup VI_{1,2}$,
$EU = E1 \cup E2 \cup EI_{1,2}$,
and $RU = R1 \cup R2 \cup RU_{1,2}$,
and where $OI_{1,2} = O1 \cap_{AR} O2 = (VI_{1,2}, EI_{1,2}, RI_{1,2})$ is the intersection of the two ontologies.
The union operation combines two source ontologies retaining only one copy of the concepts in the intersection. Though queries are often posed over the union of several information sources, we expect this operation to be rarely applied to entire source ontologies. The union of two source ontologies is seldom materialized, since our objective is not to integrate source ontologies but to create minimal articulations and interoperate based on them. However, we do expect that larger applications will often have to combine multiple articulations and here is where the union operation is handy.

4.4   Difference

The difference between two ontologies $O1$ and $O2$, written as $O1 - O2$, between two ontologies $O1 = (V1, E1, R1)$ and $O2 = (V2, E2, R2)$ is expressed as $OD = (VD, ED, RD)$, where $VD = V1 - VI_{1,2}$, $ED = E1 - EI_{1,2}$, and $RD = RI - RI_{1,2}$, and where $OI_{1,2} = O1 \cap_{ARules} O2 = (VI_{1,2}, EI_{1,2}, RI_{1,2})$ is the intersection of the two ontologies. That is, the difference ontology includes portions of the first ontology that are not common to the second ontology. The nodes, edges and rules that are not in the intersection ontology but are present in the first ontology comprise the difference.

4.5   Properties of the Operators

We defined the operators in the algebra on the basis of the articulation rules produced by the articulation generating function. Not surprisingly, most of the properties of the binary operations are based on the properties of the articulation generating function.

For example, the intersection and union operators are commutative if and only if the articulation generation function, on which they are based, is commutative. The commutativity of intersection and union gives the query optimizer the freedom to swap the order of the operands for these operations if required to optimize performance of the query. However, strict commutativity of the articulation generation function might not be achievable or necessary in order to allow the operands to be swapped.

Consider the example where an articulation generator generates articulation rules

$$AR(O1, O2) = (O1.Car\ NM : SubClassOf\ O2.Vehicle)$$

and

$$AR(O2, O1) = (O2.VehicleNM : SuperClassOf"O1.Car")$$

Although the articulation generation function is not commutative, the semantic information contained in the articulation rules are equivalent as long as the relations $SubClassOf$ and $SuperClassOf$ defined in the namespace "NM" are semantically similar after we invert their parameters. Thus, if the rules obtained by swapping the operands are semantically equivalent, we can swap the operands without compromising on the correctness of the result.

To capture this, we define the concept of *semantic commutativity*.

Definition 1. *An articulation generation function, AR, is* semantically commutative *iff $AR(O1, O2) \Leftrightarrow AR(O2, O1) \forall O1, O2$, where $O1$, and $O2$ are ontologies.*

and the necessary and sufficient condition for intersection to be semantically commutative is:

Theorem 1. *An intersection operator is semantically commutative iff the articulation generation function that it uses to derive the articulation rules is semantically commutative.*

To determine the semantic commutativity of articulation generation functions, we need to prove that for any pairs of ontologies, the articulation rules produced by the articulation generation function are in fact semantically equivalent. Automatically proving an articulation generator commutative or semantically commutative might be easy for the $SubClassOf$ and $SuperClassOf$ examples, but is not always feasible. In such cases, ONION requires the programmer of the articulation generation function and/or the expert to indicate whether the function is semantically commutative. In the absence of such information, ONION conservatively assumes that the operation is not semantically commutative if it cannot prove otherwise.

For detailed discussions and proofs of the theorems regarding the necessary and sufficient conditions for the operators to have properties (like commutativity, and associativity), please refer to [18]. We have identified the desired properties that a "well-behaved" articulation generation function should have so that query optimization can be enabled.

Using a formal process minimizes the maintenance costs in two ways: first of all we can recognize when a change in a source does not require a change in the articulation rules, and if a change is required we can rapidly regenerate the affected articulations, and adapt them to the new situation.

5 Conclusion

In this paper we present a brief overview of the ONION system used for the interoperation of information sources. ONION uses a simple data format to which different ontology models are mapped using wrappers. The articulation generator is then applied to ontologies expressed using the sc ONION data format to generate semantic correspondences leading to articulation rules among concepts in the source ontologies. A domain expert validates the generated rules or supplies new rules. These rules form the basis of interoperation among the autonomously maintained information sources. Finally, we briefly highlighted an ontology algebra that provides the formal basis for composition of information and the maintenance of the articulations. The ONION approach supports precise composition of information from multiple diverse sources by not relying on simple lexical matches, but requiring human-validated articulation rules among such sources. This approach allows the reliable exploitation of information sources that are autonomously maintained without any imposition on the sources themselves. The algebra based on the articulation rules allows systematic, composition, which unlike integration is much more scalable. When sources change maintenance is rapid since the effect of the changes can be determined using the algebra and the composition can be regenerated where needed.

References

[1] Cia factbook: http://www.cia.gov/cia/publications/factbook/. 2000.

[2] O. Ritter, P. Kocab, M. Senger, D. Wolf, and S. Suhai. Prototype implementation of the integrated genomic database. *Computers and Biomedical Research*, 27:97–115, 1994.

[3] Diane E. Oliver. *Change Management and Synchronization of Local and Shared Versions of a Controlled Vocabulary*. PhD thesis, Stanford University, 2000.

[4] Information integration using infomaster, http://infomaster.stanford.edu/infomaster-info.html.

[5] Thomas Kirk, Alon Y. Levy, Yehoshua Sagiv, and Divesh Srivastava. The information manifold. In C. Knoblock and A. Levy, editors, *Information Gathering from Heterogeneous, Distributed Environments*, Stanford University, Stanford, California, 1995.

[6] P. D. Karp. A strategy for database interoperation. *Journal of Computational Biology*, 2(4):573–583, 1996.

[7] M. D. Siegel C. H. Goh, S. E. Madnick. Semantic interoperability through context interchange: Representing and reasoning about data conflicts in heterogeneous and autonomous systems http://citeseer.nj.nec.com/191060.html.

[8] C. H. Goh, S. Bressan, S. Madnick, and M. Siegel. Context interchange: new features and formalisms for the intelligent integration of information. *ACM Transactions on Information Systems*, 17(3):270–270, 1999.

[9] S. Melnik. Declarative mediation in distributed systems. In *Proceedings of the International Conference on Conceptual Modeling (ER'00)*, 2000.

[10] Resource description framework(rdf) schema specification 1.0, w3c recommendation http://www.w3.org/tr/rdf-schema. Technical report, 2000.

[11] Daml+oil http://www.daml.org/2001/03/daml+oil-index. 2001.

[12] M. Gyssens, J. Paredaens, and D. Van Gucht. A graph-oriented object database model. In *Proc. PODS*, pages 417–424, 1990.

[13] Resource description framework(rdf) model and syntax specification, w3c recommendation http://www.w3.org/tr/rec-rdf-syntax. 1999.

[14] Serge Abiteboul, Sophie Cluet, and Tova Milo. Correspondence and translation for heterogeneous data. *To appear in Theoretical Computer Science http://osage.inria.fr/verso/PUBLI/all-bykey.php?mytexte=abiteboul*, 2001.

[15] J. Jannink. *A Word Nexus for Systematic Interoperation of Semantically Heterogeneous Data Sources*. PhD thesis, Stanford University, 2000.

[16] Wordnet - a lexical database for english. http://www.cogsci.princeton.edu/wn/. Technical report, Princeton University.

[17] P. Mitra, G. Wiederhold, and J. Jannink. Semi-automatic integration of knowledge sources. In *Proc. of the 2nd Int. Conf. On Information FUSION'99*, 1999.

[18] P. Mitra. An algebra for semantic interoperation of information sources, http://www-db.stanford.edu/ prasen9/alg.txt. Technical report, Infolab, Stanford University, July 2001.

The Emerging Semantic Web
I.F. Cruz et al. (Eds.)
IOS Press, 2002

Overcoming Ontology Mismatches in Transactions with Self-Describing Service Agents

Drew McDermott
Yale University
drew.mcdermott@yale.edu

Mark Burstein
BBN Technologies
burstein@bbn.com

Douglas Smith
Kestrel Institute
smith@kestrel.edu

Abstract. One vision of the "Semantic Web" of the future is that software agents will interact with each other using formal metadata that reveal their interfaces. We examine one plausible paradigm, where agents provide *service descriptions* that tell how they can be used to accomplish other agents' *goals*. From the point of view of these other agents, the problem of deciphering a service description is quite similar to the standard AI planning problem, with some interesting twists. Two such twists are the possibility of having to reconcile contradictory *ontologies* — or conceptual frameworks — used by the agent, and having to rearrange the data structures of a message-sending agent so they match the expectations of the recipient. We argue that the former problem requires human intervention and maintenance, but that the latter can be fully automated.

1   Introduction

Suppose an agent is given the task of buying the paperback edition of "Robo Sapiens" for less than $25.

The agent must carry out several tasks:

1. Find other agents that might be able to help carry out the given action. (A *broker agent* would perform this part.)

2. For each such agent, get a description of what service it provides. This description must be expressed in a formal language, such as DAML (DARPA Agent Markup Language).

3. If the goal description and the service description do not use the same ontology, find a common framework to translate them to. An *ontology* is a "conceptual scheme," a way of talking about the world.[1]

4. Find and execute a *plan* for satisfying its goal, that is, a series of interactions with a given bookseller that result in the agent acquiring a copy of the book. The primitive actions of the plan will be actions that send and receive messages. Building and decoding these messages may require further translation, between what one agent wants to receive and what the other knows.

---

[1] Original meaning: the philosophical study of being. As used in AI, the word "ontology" has come to mean "what is represented as existing."

One of the key questions we address in this paper is how agents' goals and servers' service description can be represented, and what is necessary to make the two mesh. Many treatments of such problems assume that representations can be as simple as lists of keywords and values

```
(``Task: buy; Thing-to-buy: book; Price: (< $25); ....'')
```

Such notations work fine as long as all tasks fit within a preimagined framework, but are unable to express anything novel.

We prefer to use notations that respect the degrees of freedom we're likely to require in the future. It seems inescapable that such notations will have the power of formal logic:

```
(do-for-some (λ (m - Merchant b - Book)
               (and (= (title b) "Robo Sapiens")
                    (sells m b)
                    (< (price m b) (* 25 $))))
             (λ (m - Merchant b - Book)
               (buy-from m 1 b)))
```

$(\text{do-for-some}\ p\ a)$ means, "For some object(s) x satisfying predicate p, do $(a\ x)$." We use Lisp-style notation for logical constructs. Function application is written (*function* $arg_1 \ldots arg_n$), even if the *function* is traditionally written using infix notation. So (* (+ 3 4) 5) is the Lisp way to write (3+4)*5.[2]

The notation (λ (*params*) e) denotes a function whose parameters are *params* and whose value is e. We use the term *body of* the λ-expression to refer to e. Although it's not our emphasis in this paper, all expressions must be *typable,* meaning that it must be possible to assign consistent types to all their subexpressions. When necessary for typability or perspicuity, parameters can have declared types, indicated using the notation (λ (...*param - type*...) ...). λ-expressions have many purposes. The first λ-expression in our example is a predicate, because its body is of type `Proposition`. The second denotes a function from merchants and books to actions, so that applying it to a particular merchant and book yields a particular action, namely, buying one copy of that book from that merchant. The combination of `do-for-some` and λ work together to define a "quantifier" for actions, analogous to the usual existential quantifier $\exists(x \in S)P(x)$ in mathematical logic. The action $(\text{do-for-some}\ p\ a)$ is carried out whenever the agent does $(a\ x)$ for some x satisfying p. There is no presupposition that it achieves this by, say, finding an x that satisfies p, then doing $(a\ x)$. In the present case, it might search for a plan for (buy-from m96 1 b97), where m96 and b97 are placeholder constants labeled with the constraints that b97 be *Robo Sapiens*, and that m96 be a merchant that sells b97 for less than $25. Or it might pursue it in some other way entirely; the logic doesn't care.

In this paper, we focus on the question how these logic-based representations can be used, and in particular what happens after brokers have done their work, so that two or more agents know of each other's existence and possible usefulness. At that point the task becomes getting the agents to talk to each other in order to solve a common problem. For clarity, we will adopt the following terminology: the *planning agent* is the one whose point of view we are taking, i.e., the buyer in our example; the *target agent(s)* are those the planning agent is trying to

---

[2] We depart from Lisp notation in two contexts. We represent finite sets using braces and tuples using angle brackets. Lisp purists may prefer to read {a, b, c} as (set a b c), and <a b c> as (tuple a b c).

interact with. We assume the target agents are not under our control. They share some of the
notational assumptions we make, but we must take their notations as we find them.

2   Using Self-Describing Agents

One of our notational assumptions is that each target agent will have a *service description* embedded in the interface it presents to the world, which one may visualize as a web page. This
description will have an internal and an external form. The external form is "web-friendly,"
in the sense that it looks like XML, and, when appropriate, can be displayed and browsed
through. Such a language is under development under the label "DARPA Agent Markup Language," or DAML (`http://www.daml.org`), which is an extension of RDF, the Resource
Description Framework.

(See `http://www.w3.org/TR/1999/REC-rdf-syntax-19990222`.)

So what we have been writing as

```
(book-isbn book21 "0-262-13383-0")
```

might be encoded on the web more like this:

```
<rdf:Description about=''#book21''>
        <pub:book_isbn>0-262-13383-0</pub:book_isbn>
</rdf:Description>
```

However, these are simply two alternative syntaxes for the same thing, which is represented
internally as an abstract syntactic object.

The first hurdle to overcome is that the two agents must "speak the same language." Two
different booksellers (e.g., Amazon.com and Barnes & Noble) must use the same industry-
specific vocabulary in their service descriptions. If they don't, then we have an *ontology
translation problem,* an issue we'll address in section 3.2, making only two remarks here:
(1) Within an industry there will be strong motivation to adopt a standard vocabulary, as is
indeed already happening with XML; (2) the main place the translation problem will arise is
when satisfying a request requires interaction of agents from multiple communities.

Assuming for now that the service description is in the same language as our service
request, what we have to do is verify that there is a way of carrying out the request by talking
to the target agent. (In general, we may have a collection of target agents to talk to, but we'll
ignore that.)

This kind of verification is close to what AI researchers call a *planning problem*: Given a
description of a system, an initial state of the system, and a goal, find a sequence of actions
that achieve the goal in that system. Here the service description plays the role of system
description and initial state. Once the action sequence has been found, during the *planning
phase*, it must be executed. During this *plan execution* phase, the actions are executed in
order. It is reasonable (we hope) to assume that the planning agent will succeed if it executes
the plan; but there may well be situations where the plan exits prematurely with some sort of
failure indication. In that case the agent may give up, or *replan*, starting from the situation it
finds itself in halfway through the original plan.

Let's look at an example of planning and execution, involving a fictional bookseller we'll call "Nile.com." One thing you can do at Nile.com's web page is find out if they have a book in stock. Nowadays this is done by using the search facility, and visually inspecting the output, looking for phrases such as "In stock, usually ships within 24 hours." In an agent-oriented world, actions such as filling in a form and pushing a button will have dual descriptions in terms of agents sending messages. Similarly, outputs will be defined in terms of formal languages, as well as being displayable for human consumption.

We will formalize this by having `send` and `receive` actions:

- (`send` *agent message*): Send the given message to the given agent; creates a message id that the sending agent can use to identify replies.

- (`receive` *agent message-id*): Receive a message, sent in reply to the original sender's message.

The message to the bookseller is of the form (`search` {<key_1, val_1>, . . . , <key_k, val_k>}).[3] The response is a list of "book descriptions," giving important information about each book that matches the search keys. These descriptions will also be in an XML dialect, but as usual we will use a more compact notation.

So the plan we are looking for might begin:

```
(series (tag s1
           (send Nile.com
                 (test-in-stock
                    <<author "Philip K. Dick">
                     <title "Ubik">>)))
        (tag r2 (receive Nile.com (value s1))))
           (test (= (value r2) empty-set)
                 (fail (not-in-stock ...))
                 ...))
```

In this plan, the `tags` allow us to give names to steps in the plan. The `value` of a step is the result it returns. The value of `s1` is a message id that later `receives` can refer to. The value of `r2` is the set of tuples received in answer to the `in-stock` query.

To formalize this in terms a planner can understand, we create *action definitions* such as

```
(:action (send ?a - agent ?msg - Message)
    :vars (?id - Message-id)
    :value ?id
    :effect (reply-pending ?a ?id ?msg))

(:action (receive ?a - agent ?id - Message-id)
    :vars (?msg - Message)
    :precondition (reply-pending ?a ?id ?msg)
    :effect (forall (?d - (Lst (Tup Attribute String))
                     ?sv - Message)
```

---

[3] As before, what's actually sent is a piece of XML. This is an ongoing area of research; W3C's effort is described at `http://www.w3.org/MarkUp/Forms/`.

```
(when (and (= ?msg (test-in-stock ?d))
           (this-step-val ?sv))
      (know-val (has-in-stock ?a ?d)
                ?sv))))
```

This is an extension of PDDL (Planning Domain Definition Language) notation, which is in standard use in the AI planning world[8, 9]. The details of the notation are not important here, but the gist is that sending a message creates a message id, so that a later reception can know what it's a response to. In addition, in the case where the message sent was an "in-stock" inquiry, one result of the action is that the planning agent knows whether the target agent has the book in stock. In other words, by executing this action the planning agent will have acquired new information.

This way of representing the effects of `receive` is too clumsy for practical use, because to be realistics the effect specification would have to list the effects of all the possible `send`s that the `receive` could be in answer to. A better idea is to have assertions of the form

```
(message-exchange  message-id
                   sent-message
                   received-message
                   effect)
```

and have the `:effect` field of `:receive` consult these assertions:

```
:effect (when (and (this-step-val ?sv)
                   (message-exchange ?id ?smsg ?sv ?e))
              ?e)
```

Obviously, an AI planner can solve problems involving actions that acquire information only if it can reason about situations in which it doesn't already know everything. As it happens, many planning algorithms, including some of the most efficient, cannot. They require it to be the case that the initial state of the world, the set of possible actions, and the effects of every action are all known. The only uncertainty is which action sequence will bring about a desired result. There has been much research on relaxing these assumptions, but no approach that is obviously correct.

Fortunately, the version of the problem we are confronted with is not as bad as the general case, because our agent knows at planning time exactly what it will and will not know at plan-execution time. In addition, we can avoid tackling extremely general formalizations of what it means for an agent to know something. For automated agents, we can appeal to the difference between computable and noncomputable terms. A term is *computable*[4] if it can be "evaluated," yielding a canonical term for an object of its type. For instance, the term `(+ 5 4)` is computable, because we can hand it to a programming-language processor and get back 9. We will use the term *computational* for a term like 9 that is canonical in the sense alluded to, meaning that it can take part in further computations using standard algorithms. We write `(val (+ 5 4) 9)`, where `val` is a variant of equality that applies only to computable terms and their computational values. By contrast, `(number-of-planets sun)`, while it may also happen to denote nine, is not a computational representation of nine in the way the

---

[4]We adopt this term with some hesitation, because its usual meaning has somewhat different connotations. However, we can't think of a better one.

term 9 is. It is not even computable, because we cannot simply ask a Lisp system to evaluate
(number-of-planets sun) and expect to get back 9.[5]
A plausible principle for agents is

> *To know something is to have a computable term whose value*
> *is (a computational representation of) that something.*

We formalize this principle by introducing predicates expressing what the planning agent
knows. (We currently do not provide for reasoning about what the target agents know; we
believe that there is little symmetry between the two cases, because even if the planning
agent believes that a target agent has a computable term denoting something, the planning
agent won't know what that term is or how to evaluate it.)

One such predicate is (know-val e r), which means that the agent knows the value
of expression e, and that the value is the value of computable term r. For example, the agent
might record

```
(know-val (book-isbn book21) (value step14))
```

meaning that (val (value step14) s) if and only if s is a string giving a legal ISBN
(International Standard Book Number) for book21. Here we make use of the fact that after
a plan step p has been executed, (value p) is a computable term.

We will also require a predicate (know-val-is e r v), which is roughly equivalent
to

```
(and (know-val e r) (val r v)))
```

except that the planner will avoid trying to make such a goal true by changing the value of r.

A computational term representing a finite set is the familiar $\{r_1, \ldots, r_k\}$, where r_i is
a computational term representing the i'th element of the set. Sometimes it is sufficient for
an agent to have a partial listing of a set. To represent that situation, we have two further
predicates

- (known-elements S r): Meaning that r is a computable term whose value is a
  computational representation of the set of all objects the planning agents knows to be
  elements of S.

- (known-elements-are S r $\{r_1, \ldots, r_k\}$): In which the elements are spelled out.

2.1 Proposed Planning Algorithm

Most previous work in the area of planning with incomplete knowledge—so-called *contin-gent planning*—has been done in the context of partial-order planning [4, 11, 12]. This fact is
mainly a historical accident, because work on planning with incomplete knowledge happened
to coincide with a period when partial-order planning was popular.

We are adding a contingent-planning ability to our Unpop planner [7], which is in the
family of *estimated-regression search* planners [1]. These systems build a plan by starting
with a null series of actions and adding actions to its trailing end. At each stage, it attempts

---

[5]Of course, there may be programs, say, a front end to a database of astronomical facts, in which one can do
exactly this; in that context the term (number-of-planets sun) *would* be computable.

to add the action that will maximally reduce the estimated effort required to finish the plan. The effort is estimated by constructing a tree of subgoals that relates the original goal to the current situation. The branches of the tree are simplified versions of the actual sequence of actions that will be required to solve the problem. The tree, called the *regression graph*, can be computed efficiently, but is only a heuristic estimate of the actual actions required, because many interactions between actions are ignored.

To handle contingent planning, Unpop must be modified thus:

1. The output of the planner can't be a simple sequence of actions; it must include `if-then-else` tests that send execution in different directions based on information gathered.

2. As a consequence, the space searched by the planner cannot be a simple space of action sequences. One alternative would be to let the space be the set of "action trees," each branch of which corresponds to a sequence. However, this idea has a couple of bugs that we will discuss below.

3. Given a goal of the form `(know-val` e `...)`, the planner must either verify that the planning agent already knows e, or find an action whose `value` can be be used to construct e. For a goal of the form `(send` a m `)`, the planner must verify that it knows, or can come to know, sufficient information to build m

To deal with this last issue, the planner must index actions by the values they compute, in much the way that planners traditionally index them by the effects they can bring about. However, there are some differences. There will seldom be an exact alignment between what the planning agent knows and what it needs to know. For instance, if the value of an action `(ask-name ?c)` is `<(last-name ?c) (first-name ?c)>`, and the planning agent wants to know the last-name of D, it will have a goal `(know-val (last-name D) ?r)`. The term `(last-name D)` can be extracted from the action value by using the function `(elt` t i `)`, which gets the i'th element of a tuple t. So all the planner has to do is propose the action `(ask-name D)`, which will have, among other things, the effect `(know-val (last-name D) (elt (value` S `) 1))`, assuming S is the step with action `(ask-name D)`. A bit of care must be taken here to ensure that S is a placeholder for the correct step, which of course doesn't exist yet. We discuss this issue at greater length in section 3.1.

Let's look more closely at the search-space issue. As we said above, the most straightforward idea is to think of a partially constructed plan as a tree of actions, with the branch points occurring after information-gathering steps. A plan is completed successfully when every branch leads to a successful conclusion. One bug with this idea is that it may be asking too much to require every branch of a plan to succeed. Often there is a "normal" result of an information-gathering step, such that it is reasonable to expect the normal result to occur. If it might not occur, the best thing for the planner to do is tack on a short branch saying "Give up!" The resulting branching plan has one branch that succeeds and one that fails, which is perfectly all right. If Nile.com might not have your book, that is no reason to give up on the attempt to deal with them. Hence rather than require all branches to succeed, we require just one to succeed, hopefully the most likely one.

Another problem has to do with efficiency. Suppose a plan has a branch point fairly early, leading to subplans P_1 and P_2. In general, the planner has to do a search through different partial versions of P_1 and P_2. Suppose it eventually finds versions P_{11}, P_{12}, ..., P_{1m} of P_1, and versions P_{21}, ... P_{2n} of P_2. Using the tree representation, we must represent these as mn distinct trees. The numbers m and n might be around 50 in a realistic case, so we have 2500 different plans to think about. Worse, the computation the planner does for, say, $P_{1,23}$ is the same regardless of whether it is paired with $P_{2,13}$ or $P_{2,32}$, so the planner will have to do the same work over and over.

The best search space therefore turns out to be the one we started with: a set of sequences of steps, each representing a partial plan. The only difference is that each sequence may be annotated with zero or more *knowledge notes* recording what the planner will have learned at various points in the sequence. There is also a difference in what the planner must do when a complete sequence is found. It now may discard all the competing plans that reflect the same knowledge notes, and keep working on plans that represent other knowledge states. For instance, the planner may find a plan for buying a book assuming that there is a paperback edition. Having found it, it may continue to look for a plan to handle the case where it discovers that there is no paperback edition.

When the planner runs out of patience, it returns however many branches it can cobble together. If during execution it diverges from the branches it predicted would succeed, it must replan. In some such cases, the new information it has will allow it to find a good plan; but many times the problem will just not have a solution.

2.2 Scripts and Hierarchical Planning

So far, we seem to be assuming that service descriptions contain specifications of the effects of individual atomic transactions with the server. These are indeed important, but in practice many servers will also provide "scripts," that is, standard sequences of transactions that can be used to accomplish common goals.

For instance, a bookseller might provide a script for the action `(buy-from m n d)`, meaning "Buy n copies of something answering to the description d." (To keep things simple, we suppress the price argument we used earlier.) That script might look like:

```
(:method buy-from
    :params (?m - Merchant
             ?quant - Integer
             ?d - Item-description)
    :vars (?r - (Set ISBN) ?isbn - ISBN)
    :precondition
        (and (forall (x) (if (?d x) (is Book x)))
             (know-val-is (image book-isbn
                               (set-of-all ?d))
                          ?r {?isbn}))
    :expansion
        (series (send ?m
                   (verify-in-stock ?isbn))
            ...))
```

The notation `(set-of-all ?d)` is the set of all objects matching description `?d`. In traditional notation that would be written $\{x \mid (\text{?d } \text{?x})\}$. The function

```
(image f l)
```

creates a list with elements $(f\ l_0)$, $(f\ l_1)$, ..., $(f\ l_{n-1})$, so

```
(image book-isbn ...)
```

changes a list of books into a list of their ISBNs, a computational object.

The idea behind scripts is that if the planning agent just wants to carry out the action `(buy-from ...)`, or any action that fits one of the scripts, it can save searching for a plan by just finding and tuning the appropriate script. (Tuning might include filling in actions to achieve goals for which the script supplies no action.)

This style of planning is usually called *hierarchical*, because the problem is to instantiate hierarchies of actions using large building blocks rather than assembling sequences of individual actions. Hierarchical planning is fairly well understood, and tends to be efficient when it is applicable at all (because the script writer has done most of the work already). There is an interesting research question here about how to get a planner to do both hierarchical and sequential planning. Our approach will be to augment the notion of partial plan to include partially expanded scripts as well as open goals, but the focus of this paper is on agent-communication issues, so we won't go into this any further. However, we do point out that the goal we started with, `(do-for-some ...(λ(...) (buy-from m 1 b)))`, is actually an *action* rather than a *propositional goal*, so we've been assuming that actions are part of problem specifications all along.

3   Ontology and Data Structure Translation

It's time we turned to our principal topic, which is how to cope with ontology and data-structure mismatch. We begin with the latter.

3.1   Glue Code

Assuming that the planning agent and target agent use the same ontology, there is still a potential mismatch problem. Suppose that the planning agent is dealing with a book seller that offers a discount if you order 10 or more books, not counting bulk orders. Somewhat artificially, let's suppose that the planning agent is responsible for sending the total at some point. That is, the planner contemplates executing the action:

```
(send G (non-bulk-total
            (size (set-of-all
                    (λ (b)
                       (intention (buy-from G 1 b)))))))
```

This looks complex, so let's break it down into parts.

```
(set-of-all (λ (b) (intention (buy-from G 1 b))))
```

is the set of all books b such that the planning agent intends to buy exactly 1 copy of b from G. The function `non-bulk-total` is a constructor that builds a message to send to the target agent — a computational object.

Obviously, the planning agent should know what it plans to buy. Using the principle of section 2, that means it must have a computable term for it. Suppose the following is true in the initial situation:

```
(know-val (image (λ(b k)
                    <(name (author b)) (title b) k>)
                  (set-of-all
                     (λ (b k)
                        (intention
                           (buy-from G k b)))))
           pending-orders)
```

This formula states that the computable variable `pending-orders` contains (by stipulation) a set of triples *<author title quantity>* for every book the planning agent intends to buy some quantity of. Let's explain that more gradually. The `set-of-all` expression here is similar to the one we need to send, except that it denotes a set of tuples *<b k>* for every book *b* that the agent plans to buy *k* copies of. These tuples are not computational, but we can convert it to something that is by using `image`. While a book or an author is an abstract object in a universe of discourse, the name of the book or author is just a string, and the number of copies the agent intends to buy is represented as a sequence of binary digits. Furthermore, the use of `know-val` announces that the variable stored in `pending-orders` is computable, and its value will be a purely computational object, namely an ordinary tuple holding two strings and an integer.

The message the agent needs to send, and the data it has in its possession, are tantalizingly closely related, but not identical. We need a procedure that translates from what the agent knows to what it needs to send. We call such a procedure *glue code,* because it connects two things together. In [2] we discussed how to generate glue code automatically; the same approach will work in this context, with some minor modifications to the assumptions we make about the source side. In the original paper we assumed that the things the agent "knows" are strung together in a tuple; now we posit that these entities are the values of an unordered collection of computable terms, of which only a subset may be relevant to building a particular data structure.

Space does not permit us to explain in detail how the algorithm works. We treat the glue-code-generation problem as finding a computable function f such that

$$(f \text{ "things agent knows"}) \; = \; \text{"things agent needs"}$$

The right-hand side is called the *target*, the arguments to f are called the *source*. The algorithm operates by transforming the target until it contains only terms that appear in the source, in which case f can be produced by λ-abstraction (replacing terms with variables).

The output of the algorithm in our example should be

```
(non-bulk-total
    (size (filter (λ (b k) (= k 1))
                  pending-orders)))
```

The value of

```
(filter p l)
```

is a copy of list l containing just the elements satisfying predicate p. In this context, it means that we discard from `pending-orders` all the tuples corresponding to bulk orders.

The planning context adds another dimension to the problem of glue-code generation. In addition to the computable terms that the planner knows about, it must also entertain the possibility of generating new computable terms of the form (`value` *step*), where *step* is a new step added to the plan. The open research question is how to fit this into the computation of the regression graph.

3.2   Ontology Translation

We now turn to the most difficult problem that web-based agents must cope with, the problem of reconciling disparate ontologies, or representational frameworks. The reason it is so difficult is that it often requires subtle judgments about the relationships between the meanings of formulas in one notation and the meanings of formulas in another. Furthermore, there is no obvious "oracle" that will make these judgments. For instance, we cannot assume that there is an overarching (possibly "global") ontology that serves as a court of appeals for semantic judgments. There are times when such a strategy will work, but only after someone has provided a translation from each of the disparate ontologies to the overarching framework, and there is no reason to expect either of these translation tasks to be any easier than the one we started with. Indeed, the more the overarching framework encompasses, the harder it will be to relate local ontologies to it. Hence the work of ontology reconciliation inevitably involves a human being to do the heavy lifting. The most we can hope for is to provide a formal definition of the problem, and software tools[6] to aid in solving it.

The goal of these tools is to develop and maintain *ontology transformations*. An ontology transformation is a mechanism for translating a set of facts expressed in one ontology (O_1) into a set of expressions in another ontology (O_2), such that the new set "says the same thing" as the original set.

Ontology translation is partly a matter of syntax and partly a matter of logic. The logical issues include:

- *Vocabulary:* What symbols does the ontology use and what do they refer to?

- *Expressiveness:* What logical constructs are allowed?

The expressiveness issue may not sound ontological, but it can be. For instance, if the ontology allows us to talk about possible truth, it may commit us to assuming the existence of possible but nonactual worlds in which propositions false in this world are true.

In addition to such purely logical issues, computational questions about how facts are structured and accessed are often mixed into the ontology question. Examples:

- *Implicit content:* What facts are represented implicitly in a given formalism? For instance, if the formalism allows a list of objects at a certain point, does it imply that the list comprises all the objects with a certain property?

- *Indexing:* How are facts associated with "keys" so that they can be retrieved when necessary? Specifically, is every fact associated with a class of object it is true of?

- *Efficiency:* Is the language restricted in such a way as to make some class of inferences more efficient?

---

[6]Such as those described by [10].

Past work in the area of ontology transformation [6, 3] has addressed both logical and computational issues. We think it is more enlightening to separate them out. From the point of view of logic, computational issues affect mainly the *concrete syntax* of an ontology. Therefore it ought to be possible to find an abstract version O_a of any ontology O, such that any set of facts expressed in O can be translated into a set of facts in O_a. Furthermore, all abstract ontologies use the *same* syntax, so that there is no longer any need to mix syntactic and computational issues into logical ones. In other words, we assume that an ontology transformation $O_1 \rightarrow O_2$ can always be factored into three transformations $O_1 \rightarrow O_{1a} \rightarrow O_{2a} \rightarrow O_2$. This may not seem like an improvement at first, but it has some advantages. First, it allows us to focus on abstract→abstract transformations, and put syntax on the back burner. Second, the translation $O \rightarrow O_a$ should not be very difficult, because it is essentially a matter of "parsing" a set of facts; going in the other direction, $O_a \rightarrow O$ is a matter of "generating" the concrete representation of a set of facts. Third, the transformation $O \leftrightarrow O_a$ has to be done just once for each ontology.

One might object that not all the content of a set of facts can be pulled out and made into explicit formulas, and therefore that our decomposition, however tidy, will not work in practice. We take this objection seriously, but for now our principal reply is that for ontologies in which it is valid the transformation problem is not very well defined no matter what approach you take to it.

Hence we will continue to employ our tactic of focusing on abstract rather than concrete data structures. We will assume that all facts are expressed in terms of *formal theories*, each of which we take to contain the following elements:

1. A set of *types*.

2. A set of *symbols*, each with a type.

3. A set of *axioms* involving the symbols.

In addition we introduce the concept of a *dataset,* that is, a set of facts expressed using a particular ontology. This concept abstracts away from the actual representations of, say, Nile.com's current inventory, and treats it as a set of identifiers and facts about them, which uses symbols from that ontology.

Once we have cleared away the syntactic underbrush, the ontology-transformation problem becomes much clearer. One is likely, in fact, to see it as trivial. Suppose one bookseller has a theory O_1 with a predicate (in-stock x - Book t - Duration), meaning that x is in stock and may be shipped in time t. Another bookseller expresses the same information in its theory O_2, with two predicates, (in-stock y - Book) and (deliverable d - Duration y - Book). We are presented with a dataset D_1 that is in terms of O_1, which contains fragments such as

```
(:constants ubik blade-runner - Book)
(:axioms (in-stock ubik (* 24 hr))
         (in-stock blade-runner (* 4 day))
         ...)
```

To translate this into an equivalent dataset that uses O_2, we must at least find a translation for the axioms. The types and constants need to be handled as well, but we'll set that aside for a moment. We will use the notation $D_1 \rightarrow D_2$ as a mnemonic for this sort of transformation problem.

With this narrow focus, it becomes almost obvious how to proceed: Treat the problem as a deduction from the terms of one theory to the terms of the other. That is, combine the two theories by "brute force," tagging every symbol with a subscript indicating which theory it comes from. Then all we need to do is supply a "bridging axiom" such as

```
(forall (b t) (iff (in-stock₁ b t)
                   (and (in-stock₂ b)
                        (deliverable₂ t b)))))
```

which we can use to translate every axiom in D_1. More precisely, we can use it to augment the contents of D_2. Any time we need an instance of `(in-stock₂ x)` and `(deliverable₂ y x)`, the bridging axiom will tell us that `(in-stock₂ ubik)` and `(deliverable₂ (* 24 hr) ubik)` are true (and maybe other propositions as well). We then discard the subscripts, and we're done. Furthermore, elementary type analysis tells us that `ubik` is of type $Book_2$.

This idea is similar to the *lifting axioms* of [5]. The main difference is that they focused on axioms of the form (`if` *(axiom in one domain) axiom in another)*, whereas we use `iff`. The reason for the difference is that we are interested in inferring facts of the form `(not (in-stock₂ x))`; we could avoid this sort of inference if we could rely on a closed-world assumption for the predicate `in-stock`.

Of course, the deductive approach does not solve all problems. Here is a list of some of the remaining issues:

1. It is potentially reckless to reduce ontology transformation to theorem proving. In the example, the required deduction was easy, but in general it could be undecidable, after finding zero, one, or two axioms, whether there are any more. However, we are inclined to think that most of the theorem-proving problems that arise during ontology translation are straightforward.

2. We attached subscripts to predicates and types, but not to other identifiers. That implies that we can just take a symbol like `ubik` over to the target theory. But suppose the target dataset must be compatible with some existing O_2 dataset, and the symbol `ubik` is already in use. In principle the deductive framework can accommodate this situation, by including a test for whether `ubik₁` and `ubik₂` refer to the same object, i.e., whether we can prove `(= ubik₁ ubik₂)`. It is often easy to show that they are not equal, by showing that they are of different types. But suppose we can't prove either that the two identifiers are equal or that they are unequal. What do we do then? Also, do we have to test all pairs of symbols for equality? (Two symbols could easily be provably equal even though they are spelled differently.)

We glossed over similar problems with variables and types, when we wrote `(forall (x y) ...)`, implying that `x` and `y` could live in both ontologies. We may want to allow that as a special case, but in the general case it is necessary to provide transformations for the values of variables. To modify our example somewhat, suppose that the types of the arguments of `deliverable` are actually `Integer` and `Book`, so that `(deliverable 24 b)` means that b ships within 24 hours. But let's also suppose that the symbol `Book` happens to denote exactly the same sort of thing in both domains. Then our bridging axiom might become:

```
(forall (b - Book
         t₁ - Duration₁ t₂ - Integer)
    (if (= t₁ (* t₂ hr)))
        (iff (in-stock₁ b₁ t₁)
             (and (in-stock₂ b₂)
                  (deliverable₂ t₂ b₂)))))))
```

Note that equality and Integer are not domain-specific. (Put another way, there is a standard ontology where such general-purpose things live, and all other ontologies inherit from it.)

3. As has been observed before, two ontologies often carve the world up differently. They may have different "granularity," meaning that one makes finer distinctions than the other; of course, O_1 might make finer distinctions than O_2 in one respect, coarser distinctions in another.

The last issue is likely to be the most troublesome. Here's an example: Suppose O_1 is the ontology we have been drawing examples from, a standard for the mainstream book industry. Now suppose O_2 is an ontology used by the *rare* book industry. The main difference is that the rare-book people deal in individual books, each with its own provenance and special features (e.g., an autograph by the author). Hence the word "book" means different things to these two groups. For the mainstream group, a book is an abstract object, of which there are assumed to be many copies. If a customer buys a book, it is assumed that he or she doesn't care which copy is sent, provided it's in good condition. For the rare-book industry, a book is a particular object. It may be an "instance" of an abstract book, but this is not a defining fact about it.

For example, if you buy Walt Whitman's *Leaves of Grass* from Amazon.com, you can probably choose from different publishers, different durabilities (hardcover vs. paperback, page weight), different prices, and various other features (scholarly annotations, large print, spiral binding, etc.). However, you certainly can't choose exactly which copy you will receive of the book you ordered; and you probably can't choose which poems are included, even though Whitman revised the book throughout his life. The versions in print today include the last version of each poem included in any edition.

If you buy the book from RareBooks.com, then there is no such thing as an abstract book of which you wish to purchase a copy. Instead, every concrete instance of *Leaves of Grass* must be judged on its own merits. Indeed, making this purchase is hardly a job for an automated agent, although it could be useful to set up an agent to tell you when a possibly interesting copy comes into the shop.

Let's look at all this more formally. Suppose that the planning agent uses the industry-standard ontology (O_2), and the broker puts it in touch with RareBooks.com, with a note that although it bills itself as selling books, its service description uses a different ontology (O_1). If after trying more accessible sources the planning agent's goal can't be achieved, then the broker may search for an existing ontology transformation that can be used to translate RareBooks's service description from O_1 to O_2.[7]

Let us sketch what some of the bridging axioms between O_1 and O_2 might look like. In particular, we need to infer instances of (is Book₂ x) given various objects of type

---

[7] If it can't find one, all it can do is notify the maintainers of the ontologies of the problem; there is no way for the broker, the planning agent, or the end user to find a transformation on the fly.

$Book_1$ with various properties. Objects of type $Book_2$ we will call *commodity books*; an example is the Pocket Books edition of *Mein Kampf*. Objects of type $Book_1$ we will call *collectable books*; an example is a copy of *Mein Kampf* once owned by Josef Stalin. It is roughly true that many, but not all, rare books can be thought of as instances of particular commodity books. Two rare books are instances of the same commodity book if they have the same publisher, the same title, the "same" contents, and the same characteristics (e.g., hardcover, large print, and such).[8] We can produce the following bridge axioms:

```
(:functions (book-type x - Book₁) - Book₂)
(:axioms (forall (b1₁ b2₁ - Book₁)
            (iff (and (= (publisher₁ b1₁)
                         (publisher₁ b2₁))
                      (= (title₁ b1₁) (title₁ b2₁))
                      (= (phys-charac₁ b1₁)
                         (phys-charac₁ b2₁))
                      (< (revision-dif₁ b1₁ b2₁) 1.5))
                 (= (book-type b1₁) (book-type b2₁)))))
         (forall (b₁ - Book₁)
            (= (buy₁ b₁)
               (buy₂ (book-type b₁)))))))
```

This should all be self-explanatory, except for the predicate `revision-dif`, which we suppose is in use in the rare book business to express how many revisions are found between an earlier and later copy of an author's work. We have introduced a new function `book-type`, which maps individual collectable books to their types, which are commodity books.

For axioms such as these to do the planning agent any good, it must be possible for the planning agent to use them to translate a rare-book dealer's service description. Suppose the agent is trying to buy a copy of *Lady Chatterly's Other Lover*, a little-known[9] sequel to D.H. Lawrence's famous work. Having exhausted the usual sources, it attempts to deal with RareBooks.com. The planning agent first translates the service description, so that all actions are in terms of (book-type *b*) instead of *b*. Assuming it can find a way to carry out its plan, at the last stage it must translate its messages back into talking about collectable books. This requires producing glue-code in the combined axiom set. Similarly, the first step in deciphering a message from the target agent is to apply glue code to rearrange the data structures into something the planning agent can decode.

4 Conclusions

Here are the main points we have tried to make:

1. Interagent communication requires a sophisticated level of representation of knowledge states, action definitions, and plans.

2. This representation can only be logic-based; no other notation has the expressive power. Embedding this logic in some form of **XML/RDF/DAML** notation is a good idea for

---

[8] An easy way to tell if they are the same would be to check if they have the same ISBN, but the ISBN system has been in effect for only thirty years, so it won't apply to many rare books.

[9] in fact, fictitious

web-based agents, but puts nontrivial demands on the representational power of those notations.

3. In spite of the expressivity, there are algorithms for manipulating logic-based expressions that might overcome computational-complexity problems.

4. In particular, planning algorithms are a natural fit to the idea of a *service description*. The service description specifies the possible interactions with an agent; a plan is a sequence of interactions to achieve a specific goal. Finding such plans is more or less what planning algorithms do.

5. Planning algorithms will, however, have to be extended in various ways, in order to cope with disparities between what it knows and what the target agent wants to receive.

6. There are two key disparities that must be dealt with: ontology mismatches and data-structure mismatches. The former requires human management of a formal inter-theory inference process. The latter requires automatic generation of "glue code" to translate data structures.

This is obviously work in progress. We are in the process of adapting our Unpop planner to handle hierarchical and contingency planning, and connecting it to the glue-code generator. We are building the architecture for managing ontology transformations.

Acknowledgements: This work was supported by DARPA, the Defense Advanced Research Projects Agency. Thanks to Dejing Dou for input.

References

[1] B. Bonet, G. Loerincs, and H. Geffner. A fast and robust action selection mechanism for planning. In *Proc. AAAI-97*, 1997.

[2] M. Burstein, D. McDermott, D. Smith, and S. Westfold. Derivation of glue code for agent interoperation. In *Proc. 4th Int'l. Conf. on Autonomous Agents*, pages 277–284, 2000.

[3] H. Chalupsky. Ontomorph: A translation system for symbolic logic. In *Proc. Int'l. Con. on Principles of Knowledge Representation and Reasoning*, pages 471–482, 2000. San Francisco: Morgan Kaufmann.

[4] O. Etzioni, S. Hanks, D. Weld, D. Draper, N. Lesh, and M. Williamson. An approach to planning with incomplete information. In *Proc. Third International Conf. on Knowledge Representation and Reasoning*, pages 115–125, 1992. Morgan Kaufmann.

[5] G. Frank, A. Farquhar, and R. Fikes. Building a large knowledge base from a structured source. *IEEE Intelligent Systems*, 14(1), 1999.

[6] T. Gruber. Ontolingua: A Translation Approach to Providing Portable Ontology Specifications. *Knowledge Acquisition*, 5(2):199–200, 1993.

[7] D. McDermott. A Heuristic Estimator for Means-ends Analysis in Planning. In *Proc. International Conference on AI Planning Systems*, pages 142–149, 1996.

[8] D. McDermott. The Planning Domain Definition Language Manual. Technical Report 1165, Yale Computer Science, 1998. (CVC Report 98-003).

[9] D. McDermott. The 1998 Ai Planning Systems Competition. *AI Magazine*, 21(2):35–55, 2000.

[10] P. Mitra, G. Wiederhold, and M. Kersten. A graph-oriented model for articulation of ontology interdependencies. In *Proc. of Conf. on Extending Database Technology (EDBT 2000)*, 2000.

[11] M. Peot and D. Smith. Conditional nonlinear planning. In J. Hendler, editor, *Proceedings of the First International Conf. on AI Planning Systems*, pages 189–197. 1992.

[12] L. Pryor and G. Collins. Planning for contingencies: A decision-based approach. *J. of Artificial Intelligence Research* , 4:287–339, 1996.

An Infrastructure for Formally Ensuring Interoperability in a Heterogeneous Semantic Web

Jérôme Euzenat
INRIA Rhône-Alpes
655 avenue de l'Europe, 38330 Montbonnot Saint-Martin (France)
Jerome.Euzenat@inrialpes.fr

Abstract. Because different applications and different communities require different features, the semantic web might have to face the heterogeneity of languages for expressing knowledge. Yet, it will be necessary for many applications to use knowledge coming from different sources. In such a context, ensuring the correct understanding of imported knowledge on a semantic ground is very important. We present here an infrastructure based on the notions of transformations from one language to another and of properties satisfied by transformations. We show, in the particular context of semantic properties and description logics markup language, how it is possible (1) to define transformation properties, (2) to express, in a form easily processed by machine, the proof of a property and (3) to construct by composition a proof of properties satisfied by compound transformations. All these functions are based on extensions of current web standard languages.

1. Introduction

The idea of a "semantic web" [1] supplies the (informal) web as we know it with interlinked annotations expressed in a machine-processable form. Taking advantage of this semantic web will require the manipulation of knowledge representation formalisms.

There are several reasons why the semantic web could suffer from diversity and heterogeneity. One main reason is that it depends on content providers who have diverse goals and focal points that will not lead them to invest on the same area of the semantic web. Yet these areas of interest will overlap meaningfully and putting part of their content together will be required for taking advantage of them in unexpected applications [16]. Another reason arises from the observation that the web sites and web pages are increasingly generated on demand depending on (1) the device on which they will be displayed and (2) the preferences of the users. There is no reason why the semantic web resources would not require the same kind of operations. There are several other reasons for expecting heterogeneity including legacy knowledge bases and systems, learning curves, etc.

Because we think that nothing better can happen to the semantic web than having well suited languages for each task while preserving interoperability, we aim at providing a path towards this goal. This paper is a short description of the technicalities involved in a solution to interoperability despite diversity.

Imagine a second-hand hardware provider company willing to build a semantic web support for its business involving repair and printers. Because the company core competence is neither technical support, nor printers, it will prefer to reuse knowledge models (or ontologies, which can be briefly described as conceptual schemes of knowledge bases) from authoritative sources. Additionally, the company has decided to use a particular representation and deduction formalism for processing knowledge (similar to the SHIQ language for which the FaCT reasoner can perform subsumption test). This company has been able to locate, on the emerging semantic web, a technical support ontology written in DAML-ONT and a printer ontology written in OIL that fulfill its requirements.

The problem then consists of importing these two ontologies in the SHIQ language. The solution will resort to transforming each ontology into a common format and transforming this format into a form compatible with SHIQ. This can be achieved by a homemade transformation or by assembling transformations available through the web (see Figure 1). Of course, the transformation system engineer will choose transformations that satisfy the desired properties (here it is consistency preservation). To that extent, the properties are advertised for each transformation. But, how to be sure that the assertions are correct (they can be erroneous, or valid within a specific context...)? There are two basic alternatives to this problem: trusting or checking.

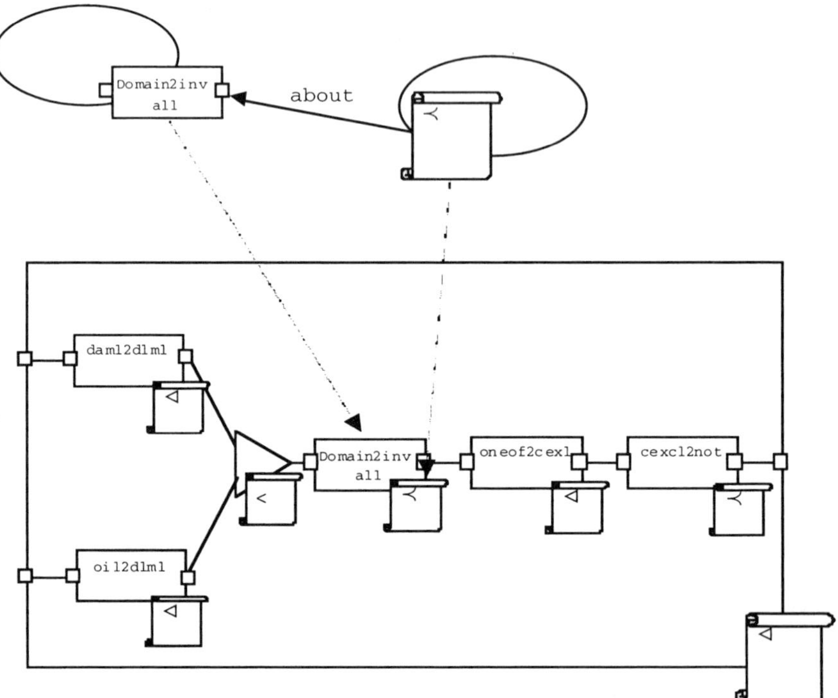

Figure 1 : The complete construction of a transformation, by composing more elementary transformations gathered from the web, and the proof of consequence preservation by composing lemmas.

Checking is possible if the proofs of the asserted properties are available somewhere. It will then be possible to check the properties satisfied by the transformations and to deduce those satisfied by the compound transformations. Then, the transformation system engineer will be able to publish the new compound transformation and the proofs of its properties. This shall contribute to the global web of transformations,

The framework presented here is distributed, modular, incremental (i.e., anyone can add a new transformation, a new assertion or a new proof at any time without compromising already obtained results) and ensures a high level of safety. In these matters, it is fully adequate for the semantic web.

The remainder presents the building blocks of such an infrastructure. The presentation is based on the simple example above (the complete example has been implemented in DLML and XSLT). First, we describe DLML, an XML encoding of knowledge representation languages and the kind of transformations that can be performed on these languages (§2). Then several consequence-preserving properties are introduced (§3). The proofs of these properties are expressed in such a way that machines can manipulate them (§4). Last, we introduce an environment for building, checking, proving and publishing transformations and proofs by composition (§5).

2. A family of representation languages : DLML

In order to simplify the presentation and to facilitate the transformations, we will restrict ourselves to a set of languages that act as pivot languages between the actual representation languages used in the semantic web.

In this presentation, a language L will be a set of expressions. A representation (r) is a subset of L. In this framework, a model of a set of assertions $r \subseteq L$, is an interpretation I satisfying all the assertions in r (the set of all models of r is noted $M_L(r)$). An expression δ is said to be a consequence of a set of expression r if it is satisfied by all models of r (this is noted $r|=_L\delta$). A family of languages is a set L of languages that share constructors having the same interpretation in all the languages. The "family of languages" approach is interesting, because it enables a fast implementation of meaning-preserving transformations. Using a family of languages makes the representations easier to understand because the elements have the same meaning across languages. It will enable the fragmentation of these transformations into unit transformations and the precise characterization of the transformation properties.

The description logics, for which an extensive language hierarchy has been defined [9], are a good example of a family of languages. This presentation will focus on our "Description Logic Markup Language" (DLML) on which we have carried out experiments. DLML [11] is a modular system of document type description (DTD) encoding the syntax of many descriptions logics (§2.1). The actual system contains the description of more than 40 constructors and 25 logics. To DLML is associated a set of transformations (written in XSLT) enabling the conversion of a representation from one logic to another (§2.2).

We do not put forth DLML as the standard language of the semantic web but rather as one of the many languages that can be used for transformation purposes. DLML is used here as a proof of concept. The general framework, however, will work with other languages including RDF and other XML based languages, like those presented in introduction.

2.1 Modular Encoding

Description logics allow the manipulation of two kinds of terms: concepts and roles. Below are one role description stating that the `InkPrinter` concept can be applied the role `inktype` and one concept description stating that a `ColorInkPrinter` is an `InkPrinter` whose `inktype`(s) are all instances of the `ColorInkType` concept.

```
inktype ≤ (domain InkPrinter)
ColorInkPrinter ≤ (and InkPrinter (all inktype ColorInkType))
```

Term descriptions are built from sets of atomic concept (resp. role) names and term constructors. They are constrained by equations of the kind above where two terms are related by a formula constructor (here ≤). A terminology is a set of such equations.

Concept terms are interpreted as sets of individuals of the domain of interpretation and roles are sets of pairs of individuals. The interpretation I of the constructors above is:

$$
\begin{aligned}
I((\text{and } c_1,\dots c_n)) &= & I(c_1) \cap \dots I(c_n) \\
I((\text{all } r\ c)) &= & \{\, x \in D \mid \forall y\ ;\ \langle x,y \rangle \in I(r) \Rightarrow y \in I(c) \} \\
I((\text{inv } r)) &= & \{ \langle x,y \rangle \mid \langle y,x \rangle \in I(r) \} \\
I((\text{domain } c)) &= & \{ \langle x,y \rangle \mid x \in I(c) \}
\end{aligned}
$$

As usual, a model of a terminology is an interpretation I which satisfies all the assertions of the terminology.

DLML takes advantage of the modular design of description logics by describing individual constructors separately. The modular encoding of the description logics is made of three kind of DTD: atoms (introducing the atomic terms), term constructors (e.g., `all`, `and`, `not`) and formula constructors (e.g., =, ≤). An arbitrary number of these XML files are put together in order to form a particular logic.

Below is the content of the DTD of the INV (converse of a role) constructor that can be applied to any role description:

```
<!ELEMENT INV (%RDESC;)>
```

We have also defined the notion of Document Semantic Description (DSD) which enables the description of the formal semantics of an XML language (just like the DTD or schemas express the syntax). To the DTD above is associated a DSD describing the semantics of the operator (i.e., $I((\text{inv } r))=(I(r))^{-1}$):

```
<dsd:denotation match="INV">
  <mml:eq/>
  <mml:apply>
    <mml:inverse/> <!-- converse for binary relations -->
    <dsd:apply-interpretation select="*[1]"/>
  </mml:apply>
</dsd:denotation>
```

In the experimental DSD language, the XML elements are identified by XPATH [7] expressions (INV or `*[1]` standing for any term of constructor INV and any first argument of the term). The syntax is very similar to that of XSLT [6] (with `denotation`, `interpretation` and `apply-interpretation` corresponding to `template` and `apply-template`). The remaining expressions are mathematical symbols expressed in MathML [4].

The DLML family of languages provides the DTD and DSD of all the covered operators and can build automatically those of a particular logic from its DLML description. The DLML logic descriptions are like the following:

```
<?xml version="1.0" encoding="UTF-8" standalone="no" ?>
<!DOCTYPE dlml:logic SYSTEM "dlml.dtd">

<dlml:logic name="shiq" version="1.0">
        <dlml:atoms/>

        <dlml:cop name="anything"/>
        <dlml:cop name="nothing"/>
        <dlml:cop name="and"/>
        <dlml:cop name="or"/>
        <dlml:cop name="not"/>
        <dlml:cop name="all"/>
        <dlml:cop name="some"/>
        <dlml:cop name="csome"/>
```

```
        <dlml:cop name="catleast"/>
        <dlml:cop name="catmost"/>
        <dlml:rop name="inv"/>
        <dlml:rop name="trans"/>

        <dlml:cint name="cprim"/>
</dlml:logic>
```

From this description, two XSLT transformations can generate the DTD and DSD corresponding to the language. They can be used for expressing SHIQ terminologies in XML.

2.2   Transformations

What can such a DTD for description logics be good for? Once a language is encoded in XML, it is very easy to transform syntactically a representation into another one. A transformation is an algorithmic manner to generate one representation from another (not necessarily in the same language). A transformation $\tau:L{\to}L'$, from a representation r of L generates a representation $\tau(r)$ in L'.

More precisely, we take advantage of the XSLT transformation language ("XML Style Language Transformations" [6]) recommended by W3C, to which we have added a compound transformation description language (see §5.1).

The first application is the import and export of terminologies from a description logic. In our example, the representations in OIL and DAML-ONT are imported in DLML through transformations. Then, the result is exported to SHIQ (the FaCT system [2] has an XML entry point). These transformations are simple XSLT stylesheets.

More elaborate transformations can be developed. The imported representations are then merged and three successive steps (inspired from those of OIL [13]) are applied to the result: the three steps concern the suppression of the DOMAIN constructor with the help of the ALL and INV constructors (`domain2allinv`), the suppression of the ONE-OF constructor with the introduction of new exclusive concepts (`oneof2orcexcl`) and the elimination of the exclusion introducers with the help of the NOT constructor (`cexcl2not`).

The piece of stylesheet presented below converts a terminology containing the DOMAIN restrictions on roles (attributes) in a terminology which replaces them by a ALL constraint on the inverse (INV) of the role applied on the whole universe (ANYTHING). For instance, it will convert:

$$\text{inktype} \leq (\text{domain InkPrinter})$$

into:

$$\text{AnyThing} \leq (\text{all (inv inktype) InkPrinter})$$

Both formulas equally say that only `InkPrinters` can have the `inktype` attribute.

```
<xsl:template match="TERMINOLOGY">
  <TERMINOLOGY>
    <xsl:comment>Introduction of the DOMAIN</xsl:comment>
    <CPRIM>
      <ANYTHING />
      <AND>
        <xsl:apply-templates select="RPRIM " mode="gatherdomain" />
      </AND>
    </CPRIM>
    <xsl:comment>The terminology</xsl:comment>
    <xsl:apply-templates />
  </TERMINOLOGY>
</xsl:template>

<!-- gather domains in role introduction and add this for root -->
```

```
<xsl:template match="RPRIM " mode="gatherdomain">
  <ALL>
    <INV>
        <RATOM><xsl:value-of select="RATOM[1]/text()"/></RATOM>
    </INV>
    <xsl:apply-templates select="DOMAIN/*" />
  </ALL>
</xsl:template>

<!-- usual processing -->

<xsl:template match="*|@*|text()">
  <xsl:copy><xsl:apply-templates select="*|@*|text()"/></xsl:copy>
</xsl:template>

<xsl:template match="RPRIM">
  <RPRIM>
     <RATOM><xsl:value-of select="RATOM[1]/text()"/></RATOM>
     <xsl:choose>
       <xsl:when test="DOMAIN">
         <ANYRELATION/>
       </xsl:when>
       <xsl:otherwise><xsl:copy-of select="."/></xsl:otherwise>
     </xsl:choose>
  </RPRIM>
</xsl:template>
```

This stylesheet gathers all the DOMAIN constraints of relations in a range (ALL) constraint of the inverse (INV) of the relation and applies it to ANYTHING. Then, it reproduces the whole terminology with domain constraints suppressed (i.e., replaced by ANYRELATION) [1].

Such transformations are assembled for transforming terminologies in one logic into another, equivalent, one. This is what is achieved in the example of figure 1.

3. Semantic properties

Operationally, the content of the previous section is sufficient for importing a representation from one language to another. However, it does not provide any idea of what properties are satisfied by each transformation step, nor by the transformation process as a whole. In order for the semantic web to be safely used by machines, it is necessary to define what properties have to be satisfied by the transformations (§3.1). We focus here on semantic properties. In the context of families of languages we have described a set of more precisely characterized semantic properties which are presented in the following subsections (§3.2-3.4).

3.1   Transformation properties

A property is a Boolean predicate about the transformation (e.g., "preserving information" is such a predicate — it is true or false of a transformation — and is satisfied if there exists an algorithmic way to recover r from $\tau(r)$). We consider more closely preservation properties which preserve (or counter-preserve) an order relation between the source representation (r) and the target representation ($\tau(r)$). There can be many such

---

[1] This transformation is not sufficient to eliminate all occurrences of domain. For instance, `(all (domain C) C')` has to be transformed into `(or (not C) (all anyrelation C'))`. But this is sufficient for our purpose.

properties (content or structure preservation, trackability, and confidentiality...) affecting different aspects of the representation. They can be roughly classified as:

— Syntactic properties : like the completion ($\tau(r)\propto r$, in which $\propto$ denotes structural subsumption between representations) ;

— Semantic properties : like consequence preservation (i.e., equation 2 below) ;

— Semiotic properties : like interpretation preservation (let σ be the interpretation rules and $|\!\equiv_i$ be the interpretation of individual i, $\forall\delta\in L$, $\forall i,j$, $r,\sigma|\!\equiv_i\delta\Rightarrow\tau(r),\tau(\sigma)|\!\equiv_j\tau(\delta)$).

In the context of the communication of formal representations, we would like to warrant semantic properties related to the interpretation of representations. This can be based on model theory. In the context of the "family of languages" approach, we identified several such properties.

3.2 Language inclusion

The simplest transformation is the transformation from one logic to a syntactically more expressive one (i.e., which adds new constructors). The transformation is then trivial, yet useful, because the initial representation is valid in the new language; it is thus identity:

$$\forall\delta\in L, r|=_L\delta \Rightarrow r|=_{L'}\delta$$

This trivial interpretation of semantic interoperability is one strength of the "family of languages" approach because, in the present situation, nothing has to be done for gathering knowledge. For this case, one can define the relation between two languages L and L' as $L<L'$ which has to comply with $L\subseteq L'$.

This simple property is satisfied by the merge operation that puts together the two representations issued from the DAML-ONT translation and the OIL translation.

3.3 Interpretation preservation

The previous proposal is restricted in the sense that only expressions of the source language are allowed in the target language, though there exist equivalent non-syntactically comparable languages. This is the case of the description logic languages ALC and ALUE which are known to be equivalent while none has all the constructors of the other[2]. For that purpose, one can define $L \prec L'$ if and only if the interpretations are preserved, i.e.,

$$\exists\tau_\prec; \forall\delta\in L, \forall\langle I, D\rangle; I(\tau_\prec(\delta)) = I(\delta)$$

This property is satisfied by the `domain2allinv` and `cexcl2not` transformations.

The $\tau_\prec$ transformation is not easy to produce (and can generally be computationally expensive) but we show, in §4.1, how this can be practically achieved.

3.4 Consequence preservation

Consequence preservation is here what comes closest to preserving the meaning of representation. It specifies that the consequences (what is true in all models) of the source are also consequence of the target representation (modulo transformation). This can be defined by:

$$\forall r\subseteq L, \forall\delta\in L, r|=_L\delta \Rightarrow \tau(r)|=_{L'}\tau(\delta)$$

---

[2] This is true if we consider that the languages here are those described by their names: AL+negation vs. AL+disjunction+qualified existentials. Of course, because they have the same expressivity all the constructors of each language can be defined in the other. But this equivalence must be proved first.

3.5   Consistency preservation

Preserving consistency is a very weak property (it is true of any transformation that only forgets knowledge). However, transformations that preserve consistency can be used for checking the consistency of a knowledge base: if the target knowledge base is inconsistent, then the source is too. A transformation τ preserve consistency if and only if:

$$\forall r \subseteq L, \ M_L(r) \neq \emptyset \Rightarrow M_{L'}(\tau(r)) \neq \emptyset$$

If for a couple of languages L and L' there is a consistency preserving transformation, then this is noted $L \triangleleft L'$. The transformation `oneof2orcexcl` that converts the `one-of` into disjunction (`or`) is consistency preserving.

4. Proofs, annotations and proof-checking

The approach to semantic interoperability defended here is based on transformations and their properties. Hence, in order to ensure formally the properties of transformations, one must exhibit a proof of the property. In fact, the proof and the transformation can be strongly tied together to the extent that they are built together (§4.1). In such a case, the publication of the proof is as important as the publication of the transformation (§4.2). The proof can be checked thus providing confidence with the corresponding transformation (§5.2).

4.1   From proofs to transformations

When providing transformations from one language to another, it is useful to prove the properties that are satisfied by the transformations (e.g., that the transformation terminates or that it preserves interpretations). For instance, the proof that the `domain2allinv` transformation preserves interpretations is as follows (inference rules are in brackets):

$$
\begin{array}{lll}
 & r \leq (\texttt{domain}\ C) & [\text{hypothesis}](0) \\
\Rightarrow & I(r) \subseteq I((\texttt{domain}\ C)) & [\text{dsd/syn-to-sem}](1) \\
\Rightarrow & I(r) \subseteq \{\langle x,y\rangle \in D^2;\ y \in I(C)\} & [\text{dsd/expand-interp}](2) \\
\Rightarrow & \forall \langle x,y\rangle \in I(r),\ y \in I(C) & [\text{sets/incl-in}](3) \\
\Rightarrow & \forall x \in D,\ \forall y,\ \langle x,y\rangle \in I(r) \Rightarrow y \in I(C) & [\text{pc/quant-intro}](4) \\
\Rightarrow & \forall x \in D,\ \forall y\ \langle x,y\rangle \in \{\langle w,z\rangle;\ \langle z,w\rangle \in I(r)\} \Rightarrow y \in I(C) & [\text{set/in-incl}](5) \\
\Rightarrow & D \subseteq \{x \in D,\ \forall y;\ \langle x,y\rangle \in \{\langle w,z\rangle;\ \langle z,w\rangle \in I(r)\} \Rightarrow y \in I(C)\} & [\text{dsd/retract-interp}](6) \\
\Rightarrow & D \subseteq \{x \in D;\ \forall y;\ \langle x,y\rangle \in I((\texttt{inv}\ r)) \Rightarrow y \in I(C)\} & [\text{dsd/retract-interp}](7) \\
\Rightarrow & I(\texttt{AnyThing}) \subseteq \{x \in D;\ \forall y;\ \langle x,y\rangle \in I((\texttt{inv}\ r)) \Rightarrow y \in I(C)\} & [\text{dsd/retract-interp}](8) \\
\Rightarrow & I(\texttt{AnyThing}) \subseteq I((\texttt{all}\ (\texttt{inv}\ r)\ C)) & [\text{dsd/retract-interp}](9) \\
\Rightarrow & \texttt{AnyThing} \leq (\texttt{all}\ (\texttt{inv}\ r)\ C) & [\text{dsd/sem-to-syn}](10)
\end{array}
$$

This proof, like many language equivalence proofs in description logics, shows that whatever term built from some term constructor (here DOMAIN) is expressible with other term constructors (here ALL, INV and ANYTHING), though preserving the interpretation of the terms. One characteristic of such proofs in compositional languages is that they are constructive: they exhibit a transformation from one language to the other. They can thus be translated into a transformation (and this results in the XSLT example presented in §2.2).

Another example is the transformation from ALUE to ALC, which is based on the argument that any NOT constructor can be pushed down the term structure:

$$(\text{not } c) \Leftrightarrow (\text{anot } c) \qquad \text{for } c \text{ atomic}$$

$$(\text{not } (\text{anot } c)) \Leftrightarrow c$$

$$(\text{not } (\text{not } c)) \Leftrightarrow c$$

$$(\text{not } (\text{all } r\, c)) \Leftrightarrow (\text{csome } r\, (\text{not } c))$$

$$(\text{not } (\text{and } c_1,\ldots c_n)) \Leftrightarrow (\text{or } (\text{not } c_1)\ldots (\text{not } c_n))$$

$$(\text{not } (\text{some } r)) \Leftrightarrow (\text{all } r\, \text{Nothing})$$

Each line here corresponds to a proof like above. This proof can be turned into a transformation, which applies the rules (from left to right) recursively on the structure of the terms. In DLML, many of the transformations across languages have been designed together with their proofs. We did this for the above transformations. This principle, which is the instantiation of the Curry-Howard correspondence to transformations, can be applied to many transformations.

4.2 Proof annotations

If the designers build proofs of some properties, it is desirable, especially in a worldwide-distributed environment, to publish these proofs. It is thus useful to be able to represent them. The representation of the proof itself can be provided in MathML [4], a language for representing mathematical formulas, and OMDoc [14], a language extending MathML towards the expression of mathematical macrostructures (e.g., theories, theorems, axioms, and proofs). In this formalism, the two first steps of the proof above would look like:

```
<omd:proof id='domain2allinvpr' for='domainelim' theory='dlml'>
  <omd:hypothesis id='domain2allinv_0'/>
  <omd:derive id='domain2allinv_1'>
    <omd:FMP>
      <omd:assumption id='domain2allinv_0'>
        <OMOBJ>
          <dl:rprim>
            <dl:ratom>r</dl:ratom>
            <dl:domain>
              <dl:catom>C</dl:catom>
            </dl:domain>
          </dl:rprim>
        </OMOBJ>
      </omd:assumption>
      <omd:conclusion id='domain2allinv_1cl'>
        <OMOBJ>
          <mml:apply><mml:subset/>
            <dsd:apply-interpretation>
              <dl:ratom>r</dl:ratom>
            </dsd:apply-interpretation>
            <dsd:apply-interpretation>
              <dl:domain><dl:catom>C</dl:catom></dl:domain>
            </dsd:apply-interpretation>
          </mml:apply>
        </OMOBJ>
      </omd:conclusion>
    </omd:FMP>
    <omd:method><omd:ref theory='dsd' name='syn-to-sem'/></omd:method>
    <omd:premise xref='domain2allinv_0'/>
```

```
    </omd:derive>
    <omd:derive id='domain2allinv_2'>
      <omd:FMP>
        <omd:assumption id='domain2allinv_1cl'/>
        <omd:conclusion id='domain2allinv_2cl'>
          <OMOBJ>
            <mml:apply><mml:subset/>
              <dsd:apply-interpretation>
                <dl:ratom>r</dl:ratom>
              </dsd:apply-interpretation>
              <dsd:apply-interpretation>
                <dl:domain><dl:catom>C</dl:catom></dl:domain>
              </dsd:apply-interpretation>
            </mml:apply>
          </OMOBJ>
        </omd:conclusion>
      </omd:FMP>
      <omd:method><omd:ref theory='dsd' name='expand-interp'/>
      </omd:method>
      <omd:premise xref='domain2allinv_1cl'/>
      <omd:conclusion>
    </omd:derive>
    ...
    <omd:derive id='domain2allinv_10'>
      <omd:FMP>
        <omd:assumption id='domain2allinv_9cl'/>
        <omd:conclusion id='domain2allinv_10cl'>
          <OMOBJ>
            <dl:cprim>
              <dl:anything/>
              <dl:all>
                <dl:inv><dl:ratom>r</dl:ratom></dl:inv>
                <dl:catom>C</dl:catom>
              </dl:all>
            </dl:cprim>
          </OMOBJ>
      </omd:conclusion>
      </omd:FMP>
      <!-- this is substitution of interpretation by its definition -->
      <omd:method><omd:ref theory='dlml' name='completeness'/>
      </omd:method>
      <omd:premise xref='domain2allinv_9cl >
    </omd:derive>
    <omd:conclude id='domain2allinv_10'>
      <omd:FMP>
        <omd:assumption id='domain2allinv_9cl'/>
        <omd:conclusion id='domain2allinv_10cl'>
          <OMOBJ>
            <dl:cprim>
              <dl:anything/>
              <dl:all>
                <dl:inv><dl:ratom>r</dl:ratom></dl:inv>
                <dl:catom>C</dl:catom>
              </dl:all>
            </dl:cprim>
          </OMOBJ>
      </omd:conclusion>
      </omd:FMP>
      <!-- this is substitution of interpretation by its definition -->
      <omd:method><omd:ref theory='dlml' name='completeness'/>
      </omd:method>
    </omd:conclude>
</omd:proof>
```

The namespace prefix are omd for OMDoc, mml for MathML, dsd for DSD and dl for DLML. We took some liberty with OMDoc (e.g., instead of OpenMath objects — OMOBJ — we put MathML expressions, because DSD is based on MathML instead of OpenMath). However, the relevant part is the ability of OMDoc for representing proofs.

It is also useful to attach the property and the proof to the transformations. One solution consists of adding it to the transformation structure. There are two problems with this solution: the XSLT language does not enable this, though Transmorpher does, and this would prevent people who are not owner of the transformation to claim properties and publish proofs. Hence the best solution seems to use RDF for annotating the transformations from the outside.

5. Composing transformations, composing proofs

In a family of languages, composing transformations can be a very convenient way to transform from one language to another. This is what has been proposed in the introductory example. Each elementary transformation can be used in various compound transformations. We have developed a system, Transmorpher, for dealing with such composition of more elementary transformations (called transformation flows, §5.1). Transmorpher is an environment for defining transformations and assembling them, on one hand, annotating them by properties they satisfy or those they must satisfy and proving the properties of compound transformations on the other hand. The proof of properties of components can be gathered from the web and checked (§5.2) and the proof of the compound transformation can be obtained by composing the properties of the components (§5.3). Once the proofs are produced, both the transformation and the proof can be exported to the web (§5.4).

5.1   Transmorpher

In order to prove or check the properties of transformations, it is necessary to have a representation of these transformations. The XSLT language enables the expression of a transformation in XML but is relatively difficult to analyze. In order to overcome that problem, we have designed and developed in collaboration with the FluxMedia Company, the Transmorpher environment [12]. It is a layer on top of XSLT allowing the expression of complex transformation flows such as the one of Figure 2 (which is that of the example). A transformation flow is the composition of elementary transformation instances whose input/output are connected by channels. A transformation flow is itself a transformation.

One of the goals of Transmorpher is the encapsulation of XSLT, used for performing the transformations, such that transformations are easier to analyze through special purpose syntax and hierarchical decomposition. This should facilitate the description of proofs through "Lemmas" attached to component transformations.

Transmorpher enables the definition and processing of generic transformations of XML documents. It provides XSLT extensions for:
— Describing straightforwardly simple transformations (removing elements, replacing attribute names, merging documents...) and applying regular expression substitution;
— Composing transformations by connecting their (multiple) input and output;
— Applying transformations until closure;
— Calling external transformation engines (such as XSLT).

Transmorpher describes the transformation flows in XML. Input/output channels carry the information, mainly XML, from one transformation to another. Transformations can be other transformation flows or elementary transformations. Transmorpher provides a set of abstract elementary transformations (including their execution model) and one default instantiation. Among elementary transformations are external calls (e.g., XSLT), dispatchers, serializers, query engines, iterators, mergers, generators and rule sets. Figure 2 presents the representation of the above transformation flow in Transmorpher graphic format.

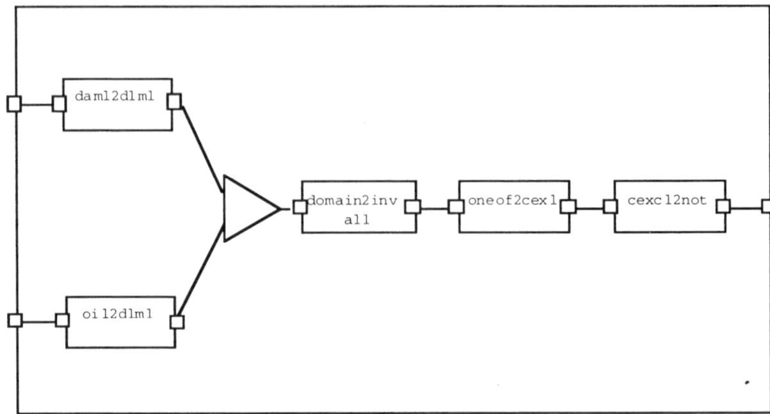

Figure 2 : Transmorpher description of the importation of DAML-ONT and OIL fragments into the DLML representation of SHIQ.

Transmorpher is made of a set of documented Java classes (which can be refined or integrated into other software) and a transformation flow processing engine. A transformation flow can be expressed by programming in Java or providing an XML description. Figure 2 is the description of the following transformation flow:

```xml
<process name="assemble-onto"  in="i1 i2"  out="o">
  <apply-external type="xslt"  name="daml2dlml" in="i1" out="o1"/>
    <with-param name="file">daml21daml.xsl</with-param>
  </apply-external>
  <apply-external type="xslt"  name="oil2dlml"  in="i2"  out="o2">
    <with-param name="file">oil2loil.xsl</with-param>
  </apply-external>
  <merge type="concat"  name="1daml+1daml" in="o1 o2"  out="o3">
  <apply-external type="xslt"  name="domain2allinv"
     file="domain2allinv.xsl"  in="o3"  out="o4"/>
    <with-param name="file">oil2loil.xsl</with-param>
  </apply-external>
  <apply-external type="xslt"  name="oneof2cexclor"  in="o4"  out="o5">
    <with-param name="file">oneof2or.xsl</with-param>
  </apply-external>
  <apply-external type="xslt"  name="cexcl2not"  in="o5"  out="o">
    <with-param name="file">cexcl2not.xsl</with-param>
  </apply-external>
</process>
```

An extension of Transmorpher consists of attaching assertions to the transformations in a transformation flow in order to tell if a property is assumed, proved or to be checked. This will allow real experimentation of proving properties of compound transformations.

## 5.2	Towards proof checking

Proof-carrying code [17] is an infrastructure in which a program is provided with the proof of the properties that it satisfies. A client system that wants to run the former program will check the proof against this program in order to ensure that it can do it safely.

These principles can be applied to the verification of the transformations and their properties.

In order to be able to check proofs of semantic properties such as consequence preservation, it is necessary to have (a) the representation of the transformation which is provided by XSLT or by Transmorpher, (b) the semantics of the transformation language, (c) the representation of the semantics of the logics provided by their DSD and (d) the representation of the proof like the one described above. Of these elements, the only missing one is the representation of the semantics of XSLT. There are several attempts, however, to provide a semantics for XSLT fragments that can be used [18, 3]. Another path consists of defining a transformation language simpler than XSLT but with a clean semantics. This is partly the case of Transmorpher.

Checking is the opposite of trusting. Both approaches have different advantages: trusting does not require to spend time checking the arguments while checking does not require to maintain a heavy model of trust and is independent of who provides the arguments. Proof-carrying code can be applied to non trusted items. So if someone needs particular transformations satisfying particular properties, (s)he can try to find such transformations and proof of properties on the web and check them.

Unlike watermarking, proof-carrying code does not require any alteration of the transformation because it checks the proof against the program. The program can have been modified, if the checker finds that the proof is still valid, then this is all that is required. It is not even required that the proofs are provided with the program. In fact, someone can publish an automatic proof of the termination of the above transformation web site not connected to the DLML one and the proof-checker must be able to decide if the proof is valid or not.

5.3   Proof by composition

Once the properties of elementary transformations are available, either by checking, trusting or proving, an interesting point is the elaboration of the proof of properties for transformation flows.

If each of these more elementary transformations is annotated by the assertion of the properties it satisfies, the property concerning the compound transformation remains to be computed. A very simple example is the termination property on finite input that is preserved through composition, but not by iteration until saturation. Interpretation preservation for its part is preserved through both composition and iteration.

This can be exemplified with the properties that have been considered in §3. It is possible to establish the composition table of transformation properties. In the example of Figure 1, since language inclusion and interpretation preservation entail consistency preservation, the whole transformation is consistency preserving. It is thus possible to use the FaCT prover to check the consistency of the result of the transformation.

5.4   Safe transformation development cycle

The techniques presented here provide a framework in which transformations from one representation language to another are available from the network and proofs of various properties of these transformations are attached to them. It is noteworthy that transformations and proofs do not have to come from the same origin. They can be produced by any mean (including manual design).

The transformation system engineers can gather these transformations and their proofs, check the proofs before importing them in the transformation development environment. They will then be able to create a new transformation flow and generate the proofs of the required properties. Finally, the transformation and its proof can be published on the network.

Given two languages with their semantics, in order to transform representations in one language into representations in the other that satisfy some properties, the following transformation edition process (see Figure 1) can be attempted:

1. Fetching transformations that can help performing part of the task ;
2. Fetching assertions and proofs about these transformations ;
3. Checking the proof or trusting the assertions of properties about the transformations ;
4. Composing transformations into a global transformation that is supposed to do the transformation;
5. Proving that this composition preserves the properties that are required by the global transformation;
6. Publishing transformation, assertions and proofs for others to use it.

Then, the problem proposed in introduction will be reduced to: gather available ontologies, create a safe transformation flow for importing them in the current knowledge processing environment and apply the transformation flow. The transformation flow can be applied at any time for updating the compound ontology and its properties will remain valid as long as the languages remain the same.

6. Conclusion

We have presented a framework for formally ensuring semantic interoperability in the semantic web. Interoperability is assured by transformations that have to satisfy some client-defined properties. The proofs of properties are encoded in a machine-readable way so that the client can check them. Transmorpher enables the composition of these transformations into a more elaborate one whose proofs of properties can be facilitated by simple composition of the properties of its components (either proof-checked or trusted).

If enough actors are interested in sharing transformations safely instead of developing again and again the same transformation, the architecture presented in this paper enables the formal and modular realization of safe transformations. We believe that there will be a strong need of such a framework in the context of the growing use of XML and XML transformations inside and across companies. In fact, if semantic properties are more related to the semantic web, many other properties of general interest can be taken into account by this framework.

The main strength of the framework is not its sophistication, but rather its relative simplicity. Its distributed, modular and incremental characteristics make it adapted to the web. No doubt that it will not be practical in all cases, but it works for cases like the one presented.

This framework is very close to that of proof-carrying code [17] of which it is an instantiation on particular programs and properties. Moreover it is fully based on widely available XML technologies (XML, XPATH, XSLT, MATHML, OMDOC, RDF) or local extensions (DLML, DSD, Transmorpher). For a description of complementary work on the topic of semantic interoperability (e.g., [15, 5, 8]), see [10].

This infrastructure is a prospective framework for which many pieces are already available and several of them linked together. The main part of it, with the notable exception of proof-checking, has already been implemented as a proof of concept. The DLML framework is operational and several experiments have been made with XSLT transformations. Transmorpher, though still evolving, is available and used by several projects. The OMDoc and DSD languages are available as first drafts.

We have some examples of proof (mainly of interpretation preservation) in description logics that should constitute a first test for the application of these concepts. We also have examples of transformations between heterogeneous representations (e.g., description logics and syllogistic).

The proof-checker is the difficult point because we will need one that can interface easily with the kind of proofs required by the framework. There are two issues to be solved next: generalization and scalability.

Generalization requires a lot of fundamental work about topics such as generalizing from DLML to other representation languages (we have superficially investigated syllogisms and considered DAML-ONT as a description logic language), generalizing semantics properties, generalizing to other (e.g., structural, semiotic) properties, generalizing the kind of proofs required. We are currently committed to investigate the semantic properties more thoroughly.

Robustification and scalability will be required in order to consider the workability of the whole system. Positive elements are the intrinsic distribution of our framework and the fact that any element can be replaced by another with similar interface.

Acknowledgements

The author is indebted to Heiner Stuckenschmidt who proposed the introductory example for presentation of the "family of languages" approach. Anonymous reviewers are thanked for suggesting several improvements of the paper.

References

[1] Tim Berners-Lee, James Hendler, Ora Lassila, The semantic web, *Scientific american* 284(5):35-43, 2001, `http://www.scientificamerican.com/2001/0501issue/0501berners-lee.html`

[2] Sean Bechhofer, Ian Horrocks, Peter Patel-Schneider, Sergio Tessaris, A proposal for a description logic interface, Proc. int. workshop on description logics, Linköping (SE), CEUR-WS-22, 1999 `http://www.ceur-ws.org/Vol-22/bechhofer.ps`

[3] Geert Jan Bex, Sebastian Maneth, Frank Neveu, A formal model for an expressive fragment of XSLT, *Lecture notes in computer science* 1861:1137-1151, 2000

[4] David Carlisle, Patrick Ion, Robert Miner, Nico Poppelier (eds.), Mathematical markup language (MATHML) version 2.0, Recommendation, W3C, 2001 `http://www.w3.org/TR/MathML2`

[5] Hans Chalupsky, OntoMorph: a translation system for symbolic knowledge, Proceedings of 7th international conference on knowledge representation and reasoning (KR), Breckenridge, (CO US), pp471-482, 2000

[6] James Clark (ed.), XSL transformations (XSLT) version 1.0, Recommendation, W3C, 1999 `http://www.w3.org/TR/xslt`

[7] James Clark, Stephen DeRose (eds.), XML path language (XPATH) version 1.0, Recommendation, W3C, 1999. `http://www.w3.org/TR/xpath`

[8] Mihai Ciocoiu and Dana Nau, Ontology-based semantics, Proceedings of 7th international conference on knowledge representation and reasoning (KR), Breckenridge, (CO US), pp539-546, 2000 `http://www.cs.umd.edu/~nau/papers/KR-2000.pdf`

[9] Francesco Donini, Maurizio Lenzerini, Daniele Nardi, Andrea Schaerf, Deduction in concept languages: from subsumption to instance checking, *Journal of logic and computation* 4(4):423-452, 1994

[10] Jérôme Euzenat, Towards a principled approach to semantic interoperability, Proc. IJCAI workshop on Ontologies and information sharing, Seattle (WA US) , pp19-25, 2001 http://www.ceur-ws.org/Vol-47/euzenat.pdf

[11] Jérôme Euzenat, Preserving modularity in XML encoding of description logics, Proc. 13th description logic workshop, pp20-29, Stanford (CA US), 2001 ftp://ftp.inrialpes.fr/pub/exmo/publications/euzenat2001e.ps.gz

[12] Jérôme Euzenat, Laurent Tardif, XML transformation flow processing, *Markup languages: theory and practice* 3(3):285-311, 2002 to appear

[13] Ian Horrocks, A denotational semantics for Standard OIL and Instance OIL, 2000, http://www.ontoknowledge.org/oil/downl/semantics.pdf

[14] Michael Kohlhase, OMDoc : an open markup format for mathematical documents, SEKI report SR-00-02, Universität des Saarlandes, Saarebrucken (DE), 2000 http://www.mathweb.org/src/mathweb/omdoc/doc/omdoc/omdoc.ps

[15] Claudio Masolo, Criteri di confronto e costruzione di teorie assiomatiche per la rappresentazione della conoscenza: ontologie dello spazio e del tempo, Tesi di dottorato, Università di Padova, Padova (IT), 2000

[16] Prasenjit Mitra, Gio Wiederhold and Stefan Decker, A Scalable Framework for the Interoperation of Information Sources, this book, 2002

[17] George Necula, Compiling with proofs, PhD thesis, Carnegie Mellon university, Pittsburgh (PA US), 1998

[18] Philip Wadler, A formal semantics of patterns in XSLT, *Markup technologies*, 1999 http://www.cs.bell-labs.com/who/wadler/papers/xsl-semantics/xsl-semantics.pdf

The Emerging Semantic Web
I.F. Cruz et al. (Eds.)
IOS Press, 2002

Toward Semantic Interoperability in Agent-based Coalition Command Systems

David N. Allsopp, Patrick Beautement, John Carson and Michael Kirton
{d.allsopp, p.beautement, j.carson, m.kirton}@signal.QinetiQ.com

QinetiQ Ltd,
Malvern Technology Centre,
St Andrews Road, Malvern,
Worcestershire, WR14 3PS
United Kingdom

Abstract. The Coalition Agents Experiment (CoAX) is an international collaboration carried out under the auspices of DARPA's Control of Agent-Based Systems (CoABS) programme. The overall aim of CoAX is to demonstrate how an agent-enabled infrastructure, based upon the CoABS Grid, can enhance interoperability between heterogeneous components, including actual military systems, in a realistic scenario. The scenario is based on a peace-enforcement operation in the year 2012 in 'Binni' (a mythical state in Africa) which requires a mix of Coalition forces to work together.

The agent infrastructure allows the construction of a coalition command support system, with agents grouped into domains to reflect real-world organisational and national boundaries. Each domain is a community of agents that has its own secure communications, capabilities and information spaces, and is governed by policies at the domain, host, virtual machine and agent levels.

Communications between agents, whilst given some minimal semantic grounding via the use of conversation policies, should in future utilise emerging semantic web technology. In particular, the Resource Description Framework (RDF) and the DARPA Agent Mark-up Language (DAML) promise to deliver a greater degree of semantic interoperability. This paper describes practical experiences taking initial steps towards this goal, implementing agents that use a query language to exchange data between RDF models and implementing a prototype RDF browser. We discuss the specific requirements for querying, merging and attributing of RDF data by agents in a coalition environment, and the particular restrictions affecting agents on controlled networks, rather than on the web. Finally, some challenges and requirements for the future are outlined.

1. Introduction

In order to demonstrate how planning, visualisation and execution activities in coalition operations can be augmented by agent technology, a collaborative programme of work has been put together under DARPA's Control of Agent-Based Systems programme (CoABS). This work involves 16 partner organisations, and is entitled the Coalition Agents Experiment (CoAX) [1,2].

This paper begins with an introduction to the challenges of coalition operations and our technical approach to solving them, and gives an overview of the CoAX demonstrations. It then outlines the infrastructure and systems in the current demonstration and the techniques used to integrate them. In evaluating this demonstration, areas that would benefit from semantic web technology are noted.

Our initial work on implementing agents that use RDF, including a basic query language and a RDF browser, is then described. This is followed by discussion of the benefits gained from this approach and the limitations of the current technology, in particular the querying and merging of RDF models and the attribution of data via the reification mechanism. The importance of software tools for rapid integration is emphasised. Finally, we note the potential advantages of the emerging DAML language [3] over RDF, and discuss future work.

2. Background

The year is 2012, and climate change in the Sudanese plain of East Africa has enabled the production and export of wheat in large quantities. The only way to transport this increasing volume of food to the European market is by sea. Competition over sea port access has led the government of Gao to launch a pre-emptive strike to open a corridor to the sea, declaring the annexed area to be the independent country of Binni. This action has incensed the government of neighbouring Agadez, who have launched repeated guerrilla activities to dislodge the Gao forces. Because of this dangerously unstable situation in Binni, the UN has passed a Resolution to create and deploy a UN War Avoidance Force for Binni (UNWAFB).

"Binni - Gateway to the Golden Bowl of Africa" [4] is a hypothetical scenario based on the Sudanese Plain. The countries of Gao, Agadez and Binni are fictitious, as are the events, organisations and personalities that lead to the crisis requiring UN intervention.

The vignette used for the CoAX experiment concerns a specific operation in which the UN forces are attempting to keep mutually hostile forces apart long enough to enable peace negotiations (figure 1). Incomplete, changing information, as well as deliberate misinformation from some parties hampers the UN efforts.

2.1 Coalition operations

Coalition military operations will become an increasingly important feature in future years. In any military operation, enabling commanders to have access to timely and relevant information is crucially important to a successful outcome. The difficulties are compounded in the virtual organisation of the coalition since there will be a mixture of equipment, operational procedures, languages, etc. Moreover, there is a pressing need to set up such organisations rapidly in order to respond decisively to emerging crises.

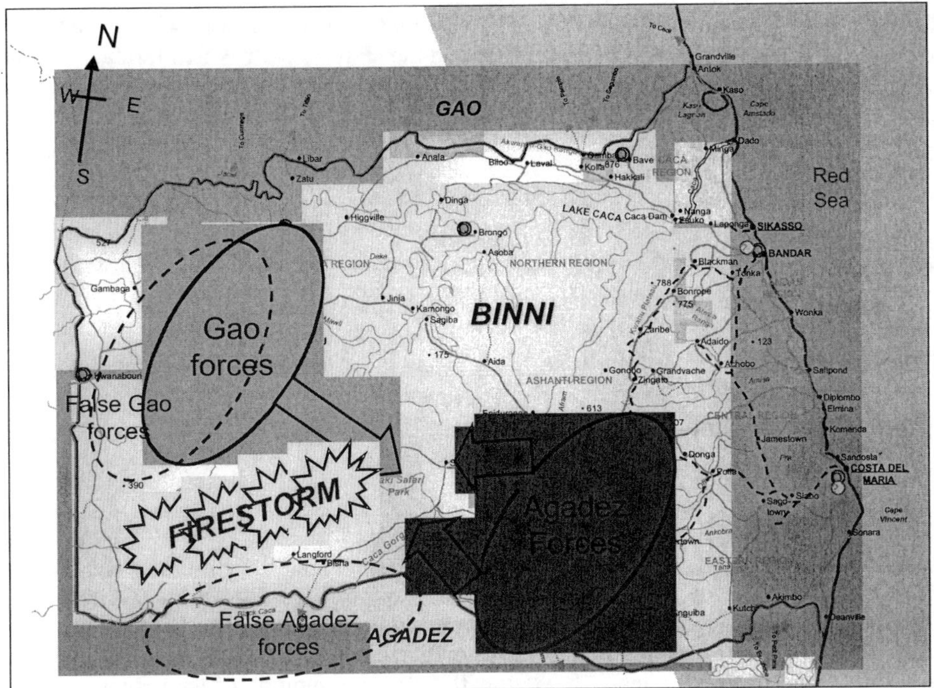

Figure 1. The fictional nation of Binni. The UN forces are considering a controversial firestorm to separate the warring forces of Gao and Agadez. Misinformation from Gao agents initially leads the UN to believe that the forces are further to the west than is in fact the case.

2.2 Technical approach

From a technical perspective, coping with the inherent heterogeneity and tight time-scales are major challenges. Traditional approaches to software integration are too inflexible to share information between such disparate command systems at short notice. Agent-oriented approaches are believed to offer advantages in such environments [5].

The principal motivation of the CoAX experiment is to investigate the conjecture that software agent technology can provide an advanced infrastructure able to support the demanding information, command and control requirements of a coalition force [2].

For the purposes of this research, an agent is defined as a software entity acting on behalf of, or mediating the actions of, a human user and having the ability to autonomously carry out tasks to achieve goals or support the activities of the user. Here, agents are supporting a community of human experts; they must not 'take over' or become obtrusive or obstructive. Their purpose is to help people cope with the complexities of working collaboratively in a distributed information environment. Agents operate mostly behind the scenes, integrated into familiar tools and methods of working, linking and fusing disparate sources of information as available — tasks well-matched with semantic web technologies. The CoAX project is producing a series of staged demonstrations of increasing complexity, showing agents and agent-wrapped legacy systems communicating over the CoABS Grid [6], developed at Global InfoTek, Inc (GITI). The Grid is a framework for federating heterogeneous systems. Although the Grid is being developed with a military application in mind, it is a general-purpose agent framework with potential use by a variety of applications.

In recent demonstrations, agents are grouped into domains, using the Knowledgeable Agent-oriented System (KAoS) from Boeing and the University of West Florida's Institute for Human and Machine Cognition (IHMC) [7]. This system enables domain policies to be changed at runtime; for example, to cut off communications with a domain containing hostile agents or to drastically reduce CPU and network resources to agents launching a denial-of-service attack.

The current demonstration at the time of writing has grown to 25 agents grouped into 6 domains; elements of this demonstration are outlined below. The full demonstrations (documents, images and video) may be seen in detail on the CoAX web-site [1]. The demonstration is genuinely heterogeneous, comprising systems and agents from at least 6 different organisations (including two real military systems) with more to be added in future demonstrations for 2001 and beyond.

3. Current demonstration

3.1 CoABS Grid Infrastructure

At the most basic level, the agents and systems to be integrated require infrastructure for discovery of other agents, and messaging between agents. This is provided by the CoABS Grid. Based on Sun's Jini services [8], the Grid allows registration and advertisement of agent capabilities, and communication by message passing. Agents can be added or removed, or their advertisements updated, without reconfiguration of the network. Agents are automatically purged from the registry after a short time if they fail. Multiple lookup services may be used, located by multicast or unicast protocols.

In addition, the Grid provides functionality such as logging, visualisation, encryption and authentication.

3.2 Knowledgeable Agent-oriented System (KAoS)

At a higher level, the KAoS framework is used to group agents into domains, to facilitate policy administration. Agents in a domain are subject to the policies of that domain. A given domain can extend across host boundaries and, conversely, multiple domains can exist concurrently on the same host. Policies can be scoped variously to individual agent instances, agents of a given class, agents running on a given host or instance of a platform (e.g., a single Java VM), or agents in a given domain or sub-domain [7]. The KAoS Policy Administration Tool (KPAT), a graphical user interface to domain management functionality, has been developed to make policy specification, revision, and application easier for administrators without specialised training.

The concept of policy-based management necessarily extends beyond typical security concerns. For example, KAoS policies will ultimately be used to represent not only *authorisation, encryption, access* and *resource control* policies, but also *conversation policies, mobility policies, domain registration policies,* and various forms of *obligation policies.*

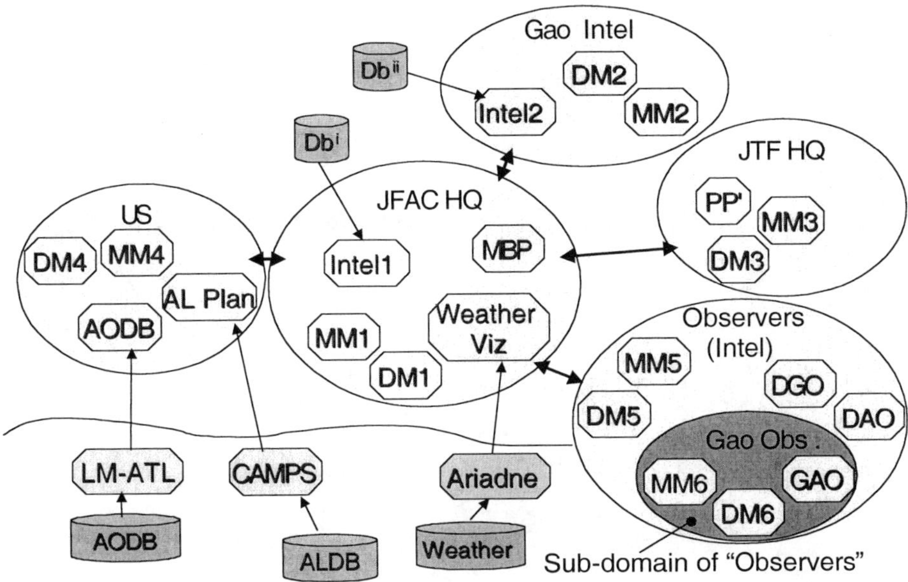

Figure 2. Agents are shown grouped into domains. Each domain contains two specialised agents: the Domain Manager (DM) and Matchmaker (MM). There are domains for countries (the US, and the fictional country of Gao), for coalition structures (such as the Joint Forces Air Component HQ), and for functional groups (Observers). Some agents (shown below the line) are not domain-aware, such as CAMPS; these have domain-aware proxies within the domains. Various agents are associated with databases (DB).

The KAoS policy representation is currently very simple but an implementation of a more sophisticated DAML-based policy representation will be available later this year (2001). The domain structure of the current demonstration is shown in figure 2. Each domain contains two specialised agents, the Domain Manager, which enforces (directly or indirectly) the domain policies, and the Matchmaker, which provides functionality similar to the Grid registry.

KAoS also provides support for defining and using *conversation policies*: the structuring of messages for particular purposes or speech acts, such as Inform, Query, Request and others. Each basic policy forms a finite state machine, where each message, labelled with a verb identifying its purpose, represents a transition between states [9]. More general constraint-based DAML policy representations and mechanisms incorporating additional communications aspects, such as time limits, and the ability to compose policies from smaller fragments, are under development [10].

3.3 Systems integrated

The demonstration, at the time of writing, includes 25 agents from about six different organisations, grouped into six domains, written using three different programming languages. Some of the main elements are described briefly below.

3.3.1 Master Battle Planner (MBP)

A core agent in the demonstration is MBP – a highly effective visual planning-tool for air operations. MBP assists air planners by providing them with an intuitive visualisation on which they can manipulate the air intelligence information, assets, targets and missions, using a map-based graphical user interface (figure 3).

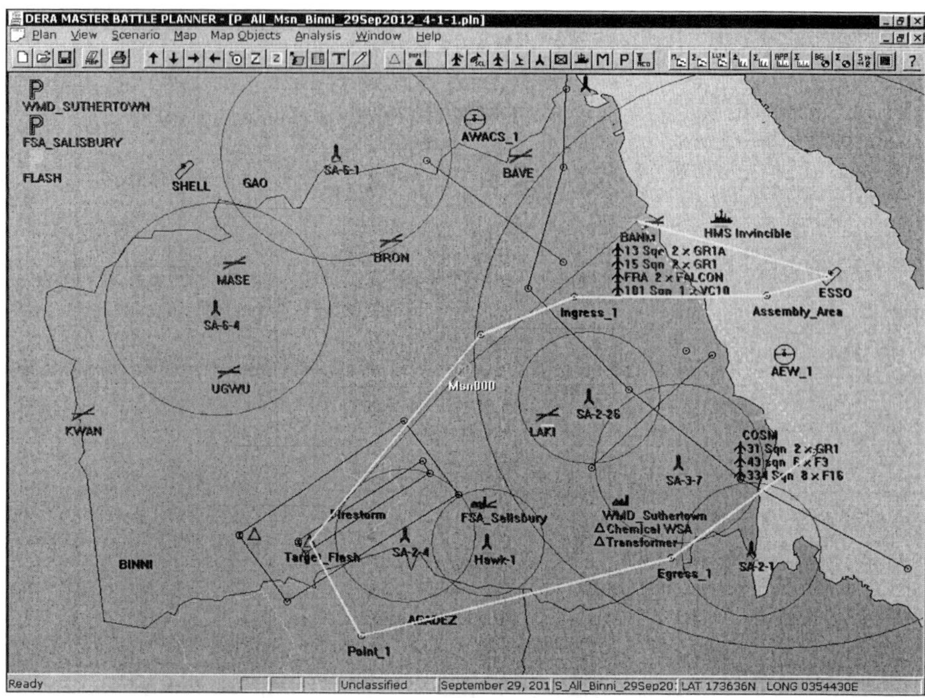

Figure 3. Master Battle Planner map display of the fictional countries of Binni, Gao, and Agadez. A selected mission is highlighted, proceeding from an airbase (BANM), to refuelling tanker (ESSO), to the target via waypoints and airspaces, and back to base by a different route.

The operator can interact with these operational entities and can plan individual air missions (or complex packages of missions) by dragging and dropping offensive units onto targets on the map. Supporting / defensive elements are added in the same way. The system provides the operator with analytical tools to assess the planned air operations.

MBP is a monolithic C++ application, which has been agent-enabled by wrapping it in Java code, using the Java Native Interface, and providing a proxy agent which communicates with the wrapper using the JavaSpaces API [11]. The agent enabling of MBP allows it to receive scenario data (targets, assets, airspaces etc) from other agents, and update this information continuously. Information concerning other air missions can be accepted and merged with missions planned within MBP; export of mission data to other agents is under development.

3.3.2 Consolidated Air Mobility Planning System (CAMPS)

The second real military system integrated into the demonstration is AFRL's CAMPS Mission Planner. CAMPS develops notional schedules for aircraft to pick up and deliver cargo within specified time windows. It takes into account numerous constraints on aircraft capabilities, port capabilities, etc. [12–14].

In the demonstration scenario, CAMPS schedules airlifts of cargo into Binni. These airlift flights could potentially conflict with offensive air missions, so the scheduled flights are requested from the CAMPS agent, translated by another agent, and sent to MBP, forming part of the normal MBP air visualisation.

This is an interesting example, as only partial translation is possible; CAMPS and MBP differ fundamentally in their definition of air missions. A CAMPS mission consists of an arbitrary collection of flights, where a flight is a single journey from A to B by a single aircraft. However, an MBP mission consists of a starting point and a route, *which must return to the starting point* (perhaps by a different path), and may consist of multiple aircraft. CAMPS can therefore produce routes that have no fully valid representation in MBP, although they could be partially represented or indicated graphically. This is a fundamental limit on the achievable degree of interoperability.

3.3.3 Ariadne

In a similar manner, weather information extracted from web-sites by the Ariadne system from USC/ISI is gathered by the WeatherViz agent (figure 2). It is translated and forwarded to MBP, again forming part of the normal picture of the air situation. Ariadne facilitates access to web-based data sources via a wrapper/mediator approach [15,16]. Wrappers that make web sources look like databases can be rapidly constructed; these interpret a request (expressed in SQL or some other structured language) against a web source and return a structured reply. The mediator software answers queries efficiently using these sources as if they formed a single database. Translation of the XML from Ariadne into the XML expected by MBP was initially handled by custom code, but can now be performed more easily using XSL Transformations [17].

3.3.4 Process Panel

The Artificial Intelligence Applications Institute (AIAI) of the University of Edinburgh has provided its IP^2 Process Panel agent (PP, figure 2), which provides user level, configurable task and process management aids for inter-agent co-operation [18]. Each user may have their own panel to reflect their role in a co-operative process. The Process Panel keeps track of the air planning process through inter-agent messages.

3.3.5 NOMADS agents

The NOMADS mobile agent system from IHMC is used in the demonstration to allow untrusted agents (Gao Observer) to run in the Observer domain (figure 2). The Aroma virtual machine provides dynamic resource control mechanisms, protecting the host from a malicious or buggy agent [19]. When a denial-of-service attack is mounted by an agent from Gao, the excessive usage of CPU, disk and network is detected and a change of policy is automatically executed, in concert with the KAoS domain management mechanisms. A human operator can then choose to lower the resource limits even further using KPAT.

3.3.6 Future additions

Future demonstrations for 2001 and beyond have introduced further agent systems and capabilities. These include a multi-level co-ordination agent from the University of Michigan [20]; a field observation system using Dartmouth College's D'Agents technology [21]; and eGents (agents communicating over e-mail) from Object Services and Consulting, Inc [22]. This demonstration extends into the execution phase of coalition operations, showing near real-time visualisation of air operations based upon data from agents.

4. Evaluation of demonstration

4.1 Aims and achievements

The aim of this demonstration was to investigate how software agent technology can provide an advanced coalition infrastructure. We were successful in integrating a variety of real military systems and agents, and were able to demonstrate increased functionality and interoperability between previously stand-alone systems. The systems were written separately by different organisations, in different languages, under different operating systems. Dynamic data sources were an important feature, removing the reliance on static data files. Agents also integrated data from disparate systems seamlessly as far as the user was concerned; weather and airlift missions were merged into the MBP view of air operations, for example.

Agent enabling of real legacy systems via wrappers was found viable, even where the original system made no allowance for integration with other systems.

Using KAoS, the ability to group agents into domains was demonstrated, and to change the domain policies dynamically; for example, to cut off communications with a domain containing hostile agents. Using KAoS domain management tools in conjunction with the Aroma virtual machine also allowed dynamic resource limits to be applied to individual agents to prevent denial-of-service attacks.

4.2 What is missing?

However, the vision of the CoAX project is to achieve rapid, dynamic coalition formation, in which agent domains are created and removed on-the-fly, and agents come and go. Interoperability between agents should be achieved very rapidly, with as little human intervention as possible. Agent interoperability *was* achieved relatively easily, due to the discovery and messaging facilities provided by the CoABS Grid, but message structures, primarily in XML, were pre-agreed, or translators were hand-coded. This process is time-consuming. Tools such as XSLT can accelerate the process (and for rapid integration, graphical tools based on languages such as XSLT may still be valuable) but are still human driven. A fundamental problem for such agents is that there is no mechanism for sharing terms and relations (via shared or partially shared ontologies). Consequently, messages have no unambiguous meaning (even to humans) outside of the agent that generates them. XML provides shared syntax, but not shared meaning.

4.3 How can semantic web technology help?

Berners-Lee *et al* write: [23] "Some low-level service-discovery schemes are currently available, such as Microsoft's Universal Plug and Play, which focuses on connecting different types of devices, and Sun Microsystems's Jini, which aims to connect services. These initiatives, however, attack the problem at a structural or syntactic level and rely heavily on standardisation of a predetermined set of functionality descriptions. Standardisation can only go so far, because we can't anticipate all possible future needs. The Semantic Web, in contrast, is more flexible."

The CoABS Grid infrastructure used in this work is based upon Sun's Jini, but requires only *one* standard interface – the 'AgentRep' which provides inter-agent messaging functionality, with arbitrary message content. It is therefore possible to combine the discovery services of Jini and the messaging, security, logging and other services of the CoABS Grid with machine-understandable semantics by writing messages in emerging Semantic Web languages such as the Resource Description Framework (RDF) and the DARPA Agent Mark-up Language (DAML).

5. Initial work

The aim of this initial work was to implement simple agents using a semantic web language to exchange data about our demonstration scenario. Practical experience with RDF and RDF Schema will assist in understanding the issues involved and assessing the current technology.

5.1 Special features of the Coalition domain

There are some differences between the web and the networks expected in a command information system.

Hendler [24] predicts that on the web we will not see large complex consistent ontologies, carefully constructed by expert AI researchers, and shared by a great number of users. Rather, we will see a great number of small ontological components largely created of pointers to each other and developed by web users in much the same way that web content is currently created. There has been little work so far on developing explicit ontologies for coalition operations; we expect that the situation will improve as benefits from the initial semantic web technology are realised.

A coalition network could perhaps be regarded as being 'on the edge of the web', consisting of multiple fire-walled networks with guarded portals between them, and between them and the web itself. A greater degree of control will be present. Medium size ontologies would be expected, constructed with care by individual coalition members and groups of members, but not all directly interoperable or consistent with each other. The challenge is to map between them at short notice. In a best-case scenario, many of these ontologies would use standard ontology libraries developed over time for common domains. Complete mapping is not always possible, as noted in the description earlier (section 3.3.2) of mapping data between MBP and CAMPS. There is a need for techniques and tools to handle this, perhaps detecting and flagging the problematic elements for human attention. Hendler [24] notes that there are many possible techniques to map between ontologies, and that this is an interesting challenge for the future.

Some of the initial interest in semantic web technology has focussed on the mark-up of conventional web pages with semantic metadata for improved search engines and web-crawling agents. In a coalition system, some data may be utilised in this way, but the main focus is on inter-agent messages expressed directly in RDF or another semantic web language. It is important to note that not all agents in a command system will have direct access to the WWW, for obvious security reasons.

5.2 Resource Description Framework (RDF)

Our initial work was based on RDF and RDF Schema (RDFS), following the initial W3C Recommendation and the release of a number of parsers, APIs and frameworks for RDF. Due to the time scales of this project, it was essential to investigate technologies available now, as well as potential for the future. We regard RDF as an initial test-bed for investigating semantic web issues, and a stepping-stone to future technologies.

DAML promises a far greater level of power but is still at an early stage of development as far as tools are concerned. For rapid coalition integration, effective tools are the essential requirement. A powerful and expressive language is not useful in practice until it can be written, modified and applied rapidly, by those without expertise in logic: "A crucial aspect of creating the Semantic Web is to enable users who are not logic experts to create machine-readable Web content" [24].

There is also an interesting correspondence between RDF and DCADM (Defence Command and Army Data Model), the UK Ministry of Defence's preferred – and indeed in many cases, mandated – solution [25]. DCADM is a combination of two technologies. The first is an innovative immutable datastore. In most datastores when a record is modified the old version is overwritten by the new version. In the DCADM immutable datastore, both versions are preserved. This has considerable potential advantages in the sort of Command and Control systems that are envisaged as the primary applications of DCADM. The datastore can support multiple competing values, reflecting the uncertainty factor present in the 'fog of war', and it maintains a complete audit trail of who changed what values and when.

The second component of DCADM is a metadata model that can be used to describe the data models that form the basis for interoperability. In this respect, DCADM and RDF provide essentially equivalent facilities. Data models developed in DCADM are readily translated into RDF, and vice versa.

We have implemented simple agents, running on the CoABS Grid inside KAoS domains, which can store and query RDF databases. They make use of basic RDF Schema ontologies for defining the class and property hierarchy and the range and domain constraints on properties and their values. The entities in the scenario fall into a number of superclasses, such as mobile or fixed objects, natural features or man-made installations, locations, airspaces, or activities. Basic constraints apply: physical objects possess a location; vehicles can have a speed; airfields have runways. RDF Schema cannot however express many other features of the domain; even the fact that friends are disjoint from enemies.

The agents need to acquire information from other agents, and from their own databases. We have therefore implemented a simple RDF query language and query engine with an SQL-like syntax, similar to other recent query languages [26,27]. Most RDF query language proposals appear to be client-server oriented, assuming fast access by the client to a local database in-memory or on disk. However, with a mainly peer-to-peer model, where access via messages over a network may be slow, special features may be required.

As an alternative to returning individual values of properties matched by a query, the query engine can return the sub-graph of triples matched by the query, as a complete RDF document, using a query of the form:

```
select triples where <constraint list>
```

This allows the returned data to be directly parsed and merged into an agent's database. Returning complete RDF documents in this way supplies the context necessary when using asynchronous messaging; if individual context-free values were returned they would have to be somehow matched up with large numbers of outstanding queries.

Queries may be formed which return the sub-graph accessible from a specified resource, so an agent can ask for everything known about a resource in a single query, using the form:

```
select reachable <resource>
```

Without this feature, a potentially very large number of queries would be required.

Reading or editing raw RDF syntax is difficult, and rapidly becomes impractical as the number of triples increases. In the process of developing the experimental schemas, a prototype RDF browser has been implemented. This allows the user to seamlessly navigate through both the schema and data, searching for resources either by type or via the query language. All resources are clickable hotlinks, and a history is kept, allowing navigation of an RDF graph in the now-familiar style of a web browser. Namespaces are automatically abbreviated to namespace prefixes, e.g. 'rdf:type'. In figure 4, scenario data from the CoAX demonstration is being queried for resources of a specified type; the properties of a selected resource can then be viewed. In figure 5, the classes in the corresponding RDF Schema are being examined; super-classes and properties related to the selected class are shown.

This browser was not intended to replace dedicated ontology editors, but to provide tighter support for the specific features of RDF, to handle data and schema seamlessly, and handle large numbers of instances. Some ontology editors do not support features of RDF such as the sub-property hierarchy, global properties, and multiple domains and ranges for properties; in general they cannot handle arbitrary RDF. The aim is to facilitate the creation and examination of models without having to hand-code RDF in XML; there is a lack of mature tools for this at present.

Desirable enhancements to the browser include:
- support for displaying and checking reified statements and containers;
- filtering data by origin and timestamp;
- enhanced namespaces support including filtering by namespace;
- editing support (selection of sub-graphs and multiple nodes; clean deletion of entire objects, collections, and reified statements);
- graphical display of portions of an RDF graph.

Recent work on the browser has allowed views to be 'pluggable'; right-clicking on any resource displays a dynamically-created menu of possible actions that can be performed upon that resource by the currently available views. For example, one can either view a class in the class browser, or choose to treat it as an instance, and list its properties directly.

6. Discussion

6.1 Advantages of RDF

RDF provides a formal data model for representing entities (resources) and the relations between them, and a syntax for XML serialisation of data models. RDF describes directed labelled graphs, rather than just labelled trees as in XML. The use of RDF is a move away from inflexible XML data structures and DTDs, allowing more natural handling of partial data, which inevitably occur in uncertain military environments, and multiple competing values for properties.

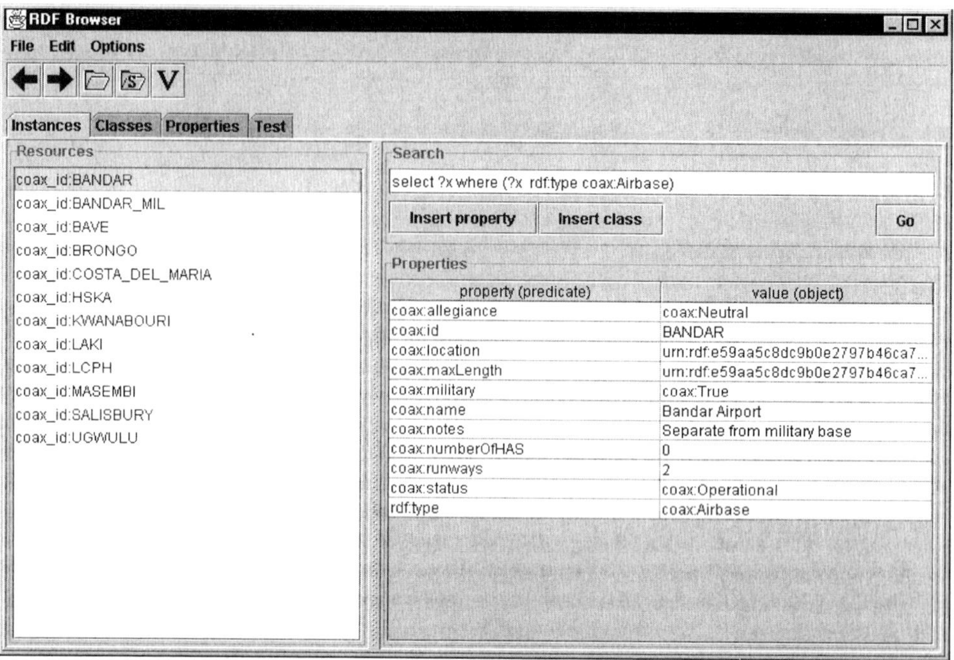

Figure 4. RDF browser. A search for resources of a specified type has been performed; these resources are listed on the left. All the properties of the selected resource (Bandar Airbase) are shown – these form hotlinks that can be explored further by clicking on them. Literals are not hotlinks, and are shown in a different colour.

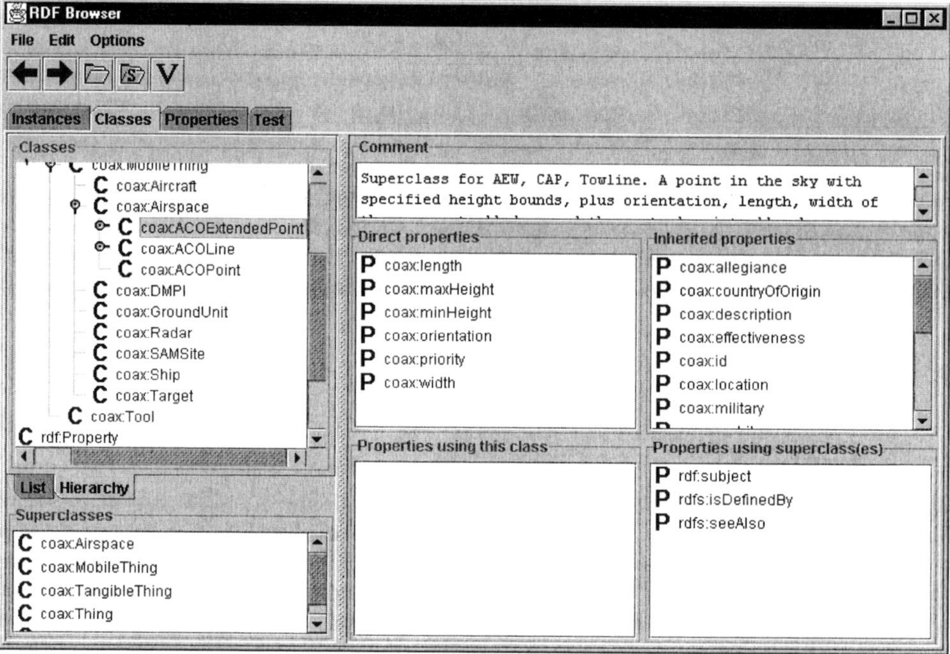

Figure 5. RDF Browser class display, showing superclasses, properties of the class (both direct and inherited) and usage of this class by other properties.

For example, a system that represents an entity such as a radar installation may store many attributes such as location, allegiance, range, type and so on; yet if a radar is detected electronically at a great distance, we know very little about it and cannot 'fill in all the blanks' of a database form or XML DTD. Rather, data arrive gradually from disparate sources and must be merged together. Partial data records or changes in document structure can be problematic when handling XML, although more recent XML technologies such as XPath and XQuery have increased flexibility to some extent. These advances also counter the size and complexity of code previously required to handle XML trees.

RDF Schema adds a very basic ontological framework, although it appears from the many discussions on the RDF mailing lists that the semantics of RDF and RDFS are unclear in the current specifications [28]. This may be hindering the development of systems with formal semantics on the top of RDF, such as DAML. Very basic inference is possible using the RDFS class and property hierarchy definitions, and property restrictions [24]. This is already used to some extent by current query engines.

Although this seems trivial, it offers a substantial improvement over the keyword searches that web users suffer at present, and a qualitatively different capability from semantics-free XML data. In many cases, the level of power needed to achieve significant benefits in interoperability is quite small, and so RDF and RDF Schema are useful in themselves. For example, in this coalition scenario, it is easy to search for data about any damaged friendly ground units, without needing to know their exact type. One could also learn their exact types (subclasses of the class *GroundUnit*) in the same query. Simple constraints on properties would allow queries to also specify particular regions in space or time. A flexible query interface to agents creates possibilities for all kinds of useful (and perhaps unforeseen) interactions between systems, in contrast with rigid one-to-one message links.

6.2 Current limitations

The growing industry support for XML points to an XML-based solution for semantic mark-up, yet RDF is verbose and not easily readable or writeable by humans. 'Notation 3' [29] is an interesting experiment with a more concise syntax (with additional logic elements). Authoring and processing tools would of course make the syntax less of an issue.

For rapid integration of agents, tools are the emphasis, not languages. A more powerful language is of no use in this domain if it cannot be deployed easily. Tools and APIs are needed throughout the lifecycle of the data – creation, checking, storing, querying and inference, mapping and converting.

Judging from the large volume of debate on the RDF mailing lists, the development of such tools appears to be suffering delays due to the substantial number of unresolved issues concerning the RDF and RDF Schema standards, and their interpretation [28].

A practical problem encountered is that there is an assumption in some APIs and parsers that schemas will always be loaded over the web from their home site (rather than being cached) which is not realistic on a coalition network.

6.3 Querying requirements

A query language allows agents to seek and exchange information, especially when enhanced by a schema/ontology, but of course we rely on agents understanding the same query language, and there is no standard query language for RDF.

A standard language is of less importance when querying local databases or web documents; any suitable language could be used. In a community of heterogeneous agents there is a need to talk to other agents in a common tongue, or at least translate down to some 'lowest common denominator'.

A variety of languages have been developed [26, 27, 30–33] with differing capabilities. Many do not yet deal with some of the more controversial aspects of RDF such as reification and collections. Kokkelink [34] has suggested work on standard RDF querying by attempting to re-use previous experience with XML in the development of XPath, XQuery and XSL Transformations.

In the absence of a standard query language, a simple technique for gaining rapid interoperability at the expense of increased messaging load is the use of a remote model interface. The majority of current RDF frameworks allow an RDF graph (model) to be queried using a single triple where each of the subject, predicate and/or object can be a wildcard. This can be regarded as the lowest common denominator for querying. Instead of sending complex queries for a remote agent to process, the work could be done locally, sending multiple messages invoking only the basic query method of the remote agent. As far as the initiating agent is concerned, the process is the same as querying a local (albeit very slow) model database (figure 6). Primitive agents can be made to support complex queries, and agents using differing query languages can be rapidly integrated, although the load on the network will greatly increase.

One could also send a mobile agent implementing complex queries to a remote host, interrogate agents there using low-level messages, and return the results. This could reduce the network load but requires more sophisticated infrastructure, especially for security issues.

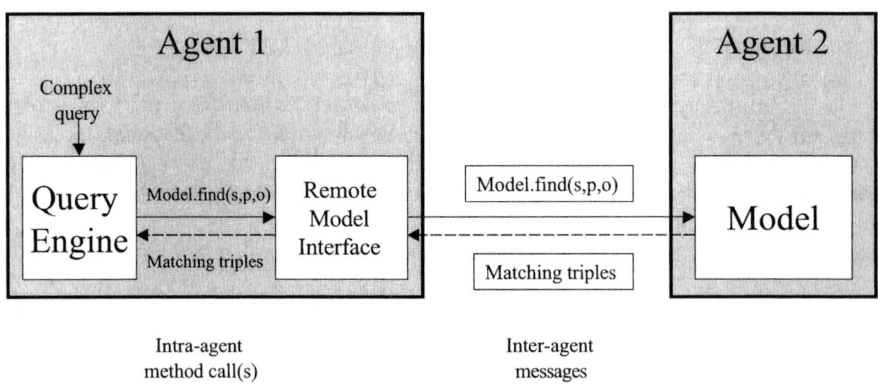

Figure 6. Use of a remote model interface, allowing Agent 1 to perform complex querying of the more primitive Agent 2, which only supports matching of single wild-carded triples.

6.4 Merging models

A fundamental process in a command information system is the collection and fusion of data from many sources. Merging data from multiple RDF sources (agents) into a single model raises several issues. Firstly, the identification of redundant anonymous resources. Anonymous resources are usually assigned locally unique identifiers by the parser; if the data in an RDF model originates from multiple documents, the same (anonymous) resource in different documents will normally receive two different identifiers. For example, figure 7 shows data obtained from three separate sources, which require merging. Unfortunately, it does not seem possible to determine in general whether the duplication is intended, and therefore whether the redundancy can safely be eliminated. Cardinality restrictions, available in DAML, could help to resolve this issue. For example, in RDF, either of the graphs in figure 8 might be chosen. Can John Smith only have one weight? It might initially appear so, but suppose the data track his weight during a diet! Each weight would then be valid for a particular point in time, and could possess equivalent values in various units.

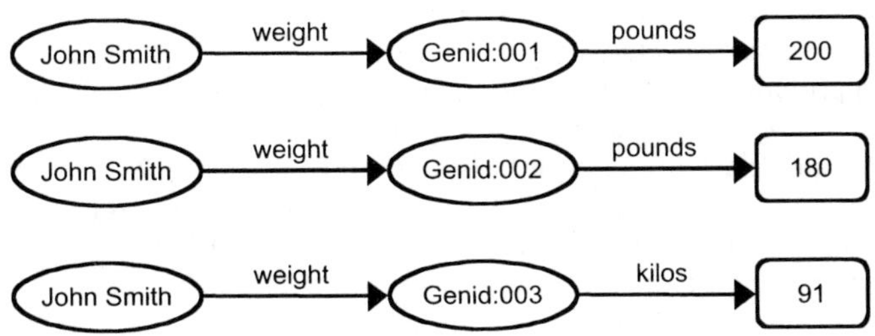

Figure 7. Three RDF data models which we are attempting to merge. The anonymous middle nodes are assigned a locally unique identifier by the parser, but we cannot determine unambiguously whether they are in fact the same resource.

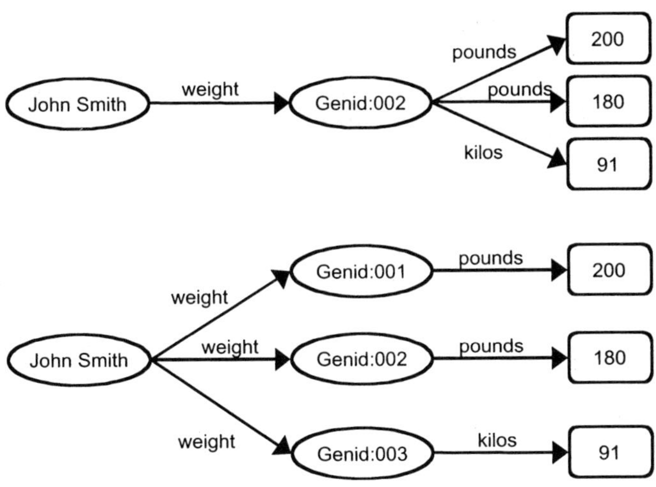

Figure 8. Two possible results of merging the models in figure 7.

Secondly, merging of RDF *Bags* or *Alternatives* cannot be achieved without renumbering all the member attributes (*rdf:_n*) of one of the collections. Merging of *Sequences* does not necessarily make sense in general. Other problems with the RDF containers have been identified [28]; for example, adding an element to an RDF *Bag* requires one to know all the existing elements.

6.5 Attribution

As mentioned earlier, it is valuable for an agent operating in an uncertain environment to store multiple competing values, and maintain an audit trail of changes. As levels of trust and other factors change, the most reliable or up-to-date data can be selected. In a military coalition context this ability is essential.

Reification provides part of the solution; we can reify statements and attach additional data (timestamp, origin, trust values) to them. In the example above, it would then be possible to determine that John Smith weighed 200 pounds (91 Kg) last year but only 180 pounds last week, although the initial value was measured by his doctor and the recent value is his own optimistic claim! However, once the criteria for selecting competing data values have been chosen, we still need to query the data as easily as if it were 'flat'. Most current APIs and query languages do not appear to provide a solution yet. Reification is a contentious issue in RDF with a number of problems identified. The concept of contexts has been introduced as an improvement [28,35].

In practical cases, it may be that no decision can be made automatically; to assist human decisions, there is a need for ways of visualising the changes in data according to time, or source.

6.6 DAML versus RDF(S)

The case for DAML is strongly made in several recent papers [24,36], and centres on DAML's greater expressive power and formal semantics. RDF(S) is not considered to provide sufficient expressive power for many applications.

DAML+OIL, an ontology language based upon description logics and encoded in RDF, provides a rich set of constructs not available in RDF(S). In addition to defining classes and properties, one can express the disjointness or equivalence of classes and a variety of restrictions on the usage of classes and properties, such as cardinality. Additional information can be expressed about properties, for example stating that they are transitive. New classes can be constructed by taking the complement of another class or the intersection of other classes. A Property can be declared as the inverse of other properties. In recent versions, DAML+OIL has also been integrated with the XML Schema datatypes. Rule and query languages (DAML-Rules and DAML-Query) are under development.

Some of the incompatibilities between RDF(S) and DAML have recently been resolved by the RDF Working group. Firstly, the semantics of *domain* and *range* were originally different from those in RDF Schema. Secondly, the RDF Schema specification demanded that the subclass relation between classes must be acyclic. DAML+OIL deliberately has no such restriction. Finally, parsers based on the current RDF specification will not support the daml:collection parse type, although a pre-processing stage can overcome this problem. The DAML collections address the previously mentioned problems with RDF Bags (section 6.4).

6.7 What next ?

Initial proof-of-concept contributions to the CoAX experiment will involve replacing some of the XML communication links with RDF to compare the relative complexity and robustness of the code. The simple agents used for this will provide a test-bed for showing the increased flexibility of RDF(S), for example assembling partial data from several sources to form a complete description, and queries assisted by the class hierarchy defined in the schema. Agents supporting a common query language, or a remote model interface, are far more accessible to other agents, greatly increasing the interaction possibilities.

We also wish to explore the use of RDF Reification or Contexts [35] for tagging data with their origin, reliability, timestamp etc. This is obviously of crucial importance in a command information system where it is essential to be able to roll back or exclude false or inaccurate data. There is much scope here for work on tools to visualise the data, providing different views of the data filtered by time, origin, etc.

A further step would be the interoperation of agents without fully shared terminology, via translator agents. There are interesting practical issues in handling the agent conversation policies with interruptions to request translation of terms.

Further steps, such as more expressive ontologies and the use of inference rules, move into the territory of DAML; we expect that emerging DAML tools and the DAML-Query and DAML-Rules languages will provide us with an opportunity to explore these capabilities. As previously noted, we are collaborating with IHMC on specification and implementation of a DAML-based policy representation (KAoS Policy Language, or KPL), which will used to represent both simple atomic policies (e.g., Java permissions) and complex constructions. Representation of both authorisations (i.e., permitting, permitting with qualification, or forbidding some action) and obligations (i.e., requiring some action to be performed) will be possible. We expect that an initial specification of KPL will be available later this year (2001).

7. Conclusions

Although RDF and RDF Schema have a number of flaws, they are useable for a variety of applications and for agent experimentation. In the context of CoAX, for example, they allow richer interactions between agents, and more useful and complex queries. Thus, RDF and RDF Schema still offer interesting possibilities and can contribute significantly to agent interoperability in a coalition setting. Alongside the development of languages, tools and agents, expertise in constructing ontologies for coalition operations will be needed. Some of the flaws will be addressed by the emerging DAML family of languages; others relate to the RDF data model and syntax; these need to be addressed. There is also a profusion of RDF query languages, although work toward a standard has been proposed.

DAML adds the formal semantics and expressiveness demanded by the logic community, but is incomplete as yet; we look forward to future developments, particularly in the area of tools for creating, parsing, checking, querying and reasoning with the languages.

One of the greatest challenges ahead lies in the development of mechanisms for merging or mapping between ontologies automatically, as far as possible, and fusing data from disparate sources, enabling heterogeneous agent systems to interoperate rapidly and effectively. It is important to acknowledge that any fundamental differences between systems (such as described in section 3.2.2 will always be a barrier to complete interoperability.

Acknowledgements

QinetiQ work was carried out as part of the Technology Group 10 of the UK Ministry of Defence Corporate Research Programme. We acknowledge the contributions of the following CoAX partners:

- Ariadne web wrapper/mediator (University of Southern California, Information Sciences Institute)
- Consolidated Air Mobility Planning System (CAMPS) (Global InfoTek, Inc / BBN Technologies / Air Force Research Laboratories).
- Knowledgeable Agent-oriented System (KAoS) Policy-Based Tools and Framework (University of West Florida, Institute for Human and Machine Cognition / Boeing).
- EMAA / CAST agents (Lockheed Martin Advanced Technology Laboratories).
- NOMADS Mobile Agent System (University of West Florida, Institute for Human and Machine Cognition).
- Process and Task Management tools (University of Edinburgh, Artificial Intelligence Applications Institute).
- The DARPA CoABS Grid (Global InfoTek Inc, ISX Corporation).

We would like to thank our QinetiQ colleagues Chris Walker and Don Brealey for provision of the Master Battle Planner (MBP) tool for Air Battle Planning, and Sergey Melnik of Stanford University for provision of RDF API software.

The views and conclusions contained herein are those of the authors and should not be interpreted as necessarily representing official policies or endorsements, either express or implied, of the UK MoD, DARPA, the Air Force Research Laboratory, the US Government, the University of Edinburgh or the University of West Florida.

References

[1] Coalition Agents eXperiment: http://www.aiai.ed.ac.uk/project/coax/

[2] David Allsopp, Patrick Beautement, Jeffrey M. Bradshaw, John Carson, Michael Kirton, Niranjan Suri and Austin Tate, *Software agents as facilitators of coherent coalition operations*, 6th International Command and Control Research and Technology Symposium, 19-21 June 2001, US Naval Academy, Annapolis, MD, USA.

[3] DARPA Agent Mark-up Language: http://www.daml.org/

[4] R. A. Rathmell, *A Coalition Force Scenario 'Binni – Gateway to the Golden Bowl of Africa'*, Proceedings of the International Workshop on Knowledge-Bases Planning for Coalition Forces, (ed. A. Tate) pp. 115-125, Edinburgh, Scotland, 10-11 May 1999.

[5] Nicholas R. Jennings, *An agent-based approach for building complex software systems*, Communications of the ACM, April 2001/Vol. 44, No. 4, pp 35-41.

[6] CoABS Grid: http://coabs.globalinfotek.com/

[7] Jeffrey M. Bradshaw, Niranjan Suri, Martha Kahn, Phil Sage, Doyle Weishar and Renia Jeffers, *Terraforming Cyberspace: Toward a policy-based grid infrastructure for secure, scalable, and robust execution of Java-based multi-agent systems*, IEEE Computer, 49-56, July 2001.

[8] Jini: http://www.sun.com/jini/

[9] Jeffrey M. Bradshaw, Stewart Dutfield, Pete Benoit and John D. Woolley, *KAoS: Toward an industrial-strength generic agent architecture*, In J. M. Bradshaw (Ed.), *Software Agents*, 1997, pp. 375-418,

Cambridge, MA: AAAI Press/The MIT Press.

[10] Jeffrey M. Bradshaw, Mark Greaves, Heather Holmback, Wayne Jansen, Tom Karygiannis, Barry Silverman, Niranjan Suri, and Alex Wong, *Agents for the masses?* In J. Hendler (Ed.) Special issue on agent technology, IEEE Intelligent Systems, March/April, 53-63.

[11] JavaSpaces: http://www.sun.com/jini/specs/

[12] Mark Burstein, and Douglas Smith, *A Portable, Interactive Transportation Scheduling Tool Using a Search Engine Generated from Formal Specifications*, Proceedings of the Third International Conference on Artificial Intelligence Planning Systems, B. Drabble (ed.), The AAAI Press, Menlo Park, CA, May, 1996 ISBN 0-929280-97-0.

[13] Thomas Emerson and Mark Burstein, *Development of a Constraint-based Airlift Scheduler by Program Synthesis from Formal Specifications*, Proceedings of the 1999 Conference on Automated Software Engineering, Orlando, FL, September, 1999.

[14] Mark Burstein, George Ferguson, and James Allen, *Integrating Agent-Based Mixed-Initiative Control with an Existing Multi-Agent Planning System*, Proceedings of the Fourth International Conference on MultiAgent Systems, Boston, MA, 2000.

[15] Craig A. Knoblock and Steven Minton, *The ariadne approach to web-based information integration*, IEEE Intelligent Systems , 13(5), September/October 1998.

[16] Ariadne: http://www.isi.edu/info-agents/ariadne/

[17] XSL Transformations: http://www.w3.org/Style/XSL/

[18] AIAI's IX Technology: http://www.aiai.ed.ac.uk/project/ix/

[19] N. Suri, J. M. Bradshaw, M. R. Breedy, P. T. Groth, G. A. Hill and R. Jeffers, *Strong mobility and fine-grained resource control in NOMADS*, Proceedings of the 2nd International Symposium on Agents Systems and Applications and the 4th International Symposium on Mobile Agents (ASA/MA 2000), Zurich, Switzerland; Berlin: Springer-Verlag

[20] Michigan MCA: http://ai.eecs.umich.edu/people/durfee/COABS/

[21] Dartmouth College: http://actcomm.dartmouth.edu/

[22] OBJS eGents: http://www.objs.com/agility/

[23] Tim Berners-Lee, James Hendler and Ora Lassila, *The Semantic Web*, Scientific American, May 2001 http://www.scientificamerican.com/2001/0501issue/0501berners-lee.html

[24] James Hendler, *Agents and the Semantic Web*, IEEE Intelligent Systems, vol. 16, no. 2, March/April 2001, pp. 30-37. http://www.cs.umd.edu/~hendler/AgentWeb.html

[25] Robert Andrews, *Data Interoperability with DCADM and XML*, DERA internal report DERA/CIS/CIS3/TR000265/1.0, March 2000

[26] RDFDB: http://web1.guha.com/rdfdb/query.html#query

[27] Squish: http://swordfish.rdfweb.org/rdfquery/

[28] RDF issue tracking: http://www.w3.org/2000/03/rdf-tracking

[29] Notation 3: http://www.w3.org/DesignIssues/Notation3.html

[30] RQL: http://139.91.183.30:9090/RDF/

[31] RDFQL: http://www.intellidimension.com/RDFQLmanual.html

[32] RDFQuery: http://www.w3.org/TandS/QL/QL98/pp/rdfquery.html

[33] XWMF: http://nestroy.wi-inf.uni-essen.de/xwmf/

[34] RDFPath: http://zoe.mathematik.Uni-Osnabrueck.DE/QAT/

[35] RDF Contexts: http://public.research.mimesweeper.com/RDF/RDFContexts.html

[36] Sheila A. McIlraith, Tran Cao Son, and Honglei Zeng, *Semantic Web Services,* IEEE Intelligent Systems, vol. 16, no. 2, March/April 2001, pp. 46-53.

The Emerging Semantic Web
I.F. Cruz et al. (Eds.)
IOS Press, 2002

Object Interoperability for Geospatial Applications: A Case Study

Isabel F. Cruz[1]
University of Illinois at Chicago

Paul W. Calnan
Worcester Polytechnic Institute

Abstract. In this paper, we analyze a geospatial application for visualizing U.S. election results in order to show the problems that need to be solved in the mapping between different XML representations and their conceptual models. We propose a framework that provides a number of core classes that allow applications to treat XML documents as graphs and to evaluate XPath expressions against such document graphs. We also propose a mechanism that allows information to be exchanged between document types. Our goal is to ultimately attain an overall framework for interoperation where maintenance problems are minimized. To achieve this, we anticipate the need for introducing metadata in the semantic layer that will guide the translation process between document types.

Keywords: Geospatial applications, object interoperability, technologies for interoperability.

1 Introduction

In statewide geospatial applications, hundreds of systems need to be integrated. In these applications, challenges in achieving interoperability are at the semantic level (e.g., different classification schemes) and at the data structure level (e.g., different XML DTDs). Current approaches that deal with this problem require the intervention of a human expert to perform the mapping between XML representations or to map between the conceptual models for those representations. Also, changes in the representations will typically entail specific code changes by a human expert. A recently proposed layered model [12] partitions this problem by considering the requirements of different layers: syntax, object, semantic, and application.

This paper discusses our approach to interoperability in the object layer using XML [2], developed as a part of a framework for geospatial data visualization applications. Applications using our framework should be able to seamlessly pull data from multiple XML data sources. Thus, we focus on the backend portions that allow for querying and integrating data from multiple XML sources.

---

[1] Corresponding author. Address: Department of Computer Science, University of Illinois, Chicago, IL 60607-7053, USA. Email address: ifc@cs.uic.edu.

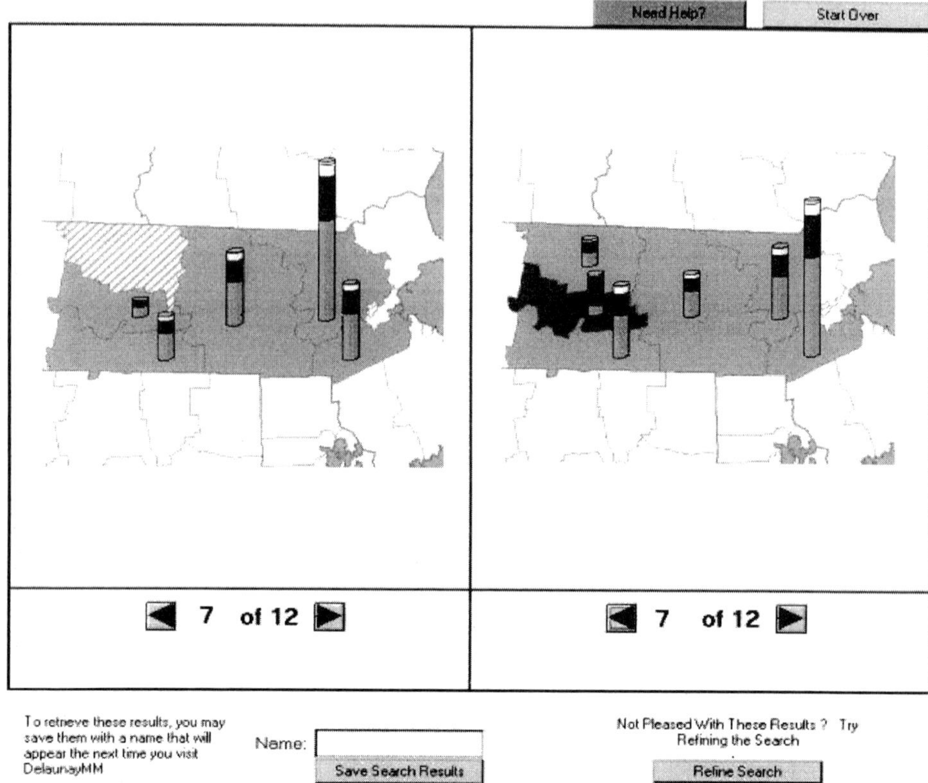

Figure 1: User interface for the election scenario

In developing our framework, we have focused on a number of application scenarios. In this paper, we examine our election results scenario. In this scenario, we create an application that will visualize results from the 2000 U.S. Presidential Election, superimposing vote totals and campaign donations over a given region on a map. Users will be able to search for a geographic area in the United States, choose which data to display (e.g., demographic information, votes cast per candidate, campaign donations, etc.), and then view that data on a map of the region. Data can be displayed at multiple granularities, depending on what the user wants to see (e.g., the user can display a map of Massachusetts with county boundaries showing election results for each county and then zoom in on a map of Worcester County showing election results and campaign donations for each municipality). A screen shot from this scenario is shown in Figure 1.

XML was chosen as our data representation language because it is quickly becoming the new standard for information interchange. The main appeal of XML is that it allows users to define their own document types, and then store and exchange documents conforming to that document type. A document type declaration is used to accomplish this. Document type declarations serve to identify the root element of a document, but can also contain a document type definition (DTD) [1]. This provides users a way of declaring the markup, syntax, and structure of a given document type. This also provides the parser a way of determining whether a document is valid (i.e., conforms to a DTD), rather than just well formed (i.e., uses correct XML syntax).

Allowing everyone to create their own document types makes data exchange easier, but it also makes data interoperability more difficult. Different organizations could model the same information with different document types [1]. It is trivial to load and view documents with different document types, but integrating the data between them is potentially quite difficult.

In this paper, we concentrate on providing a general-purpose application framework that allows data to be interchanged between various XML document types. We utilize XPath to concisely describe a path through the document graph and to select a number of nodes whose values can be aggregated. Finally, we introduce the concept of a *geospatial authority*. Authoritative geospatial information about the region being covered by a given application is collected in an XML document. This document serves as the source for geospatial relationships at the core of the application. For instance, in our election scenario, we maintain a geospatial authority containing the names of all of the states, the counties contained in those states, and the municipalities contained in those counties. This provides us with a means of query refinement by providing context for a given geospatial query (e.g., a search for the string "Worcester" would yield matches in New York, Vermont, Massachusetts, Wisconsin, Missouri, and Pennsylvania—the authority allows us to ask the user for clarification in which "Worcester" is desired). This also provides us with context and a starting point when looking up data in other documents, as seen in the examples given below.

Our framework is implemented in Java 1.3 and uses Apache's Xalan-Java 2 API for XML, XPath, and XSLT processing.

The paper is organized as follows: In Section 2, we examine treating an XML document as a graph, using the Document Object Model (DOM) and XPath as a means of traversing the graph. In Section 3, we present a number of classes that form the core of the backend of our application framework. In Section 4, we introduce our lookup mechanism that allows users to interchange data from one document type to another. Finally, in Section 5, we examine issues that remain open or that need to be addressed to complete our framework.

2 XML As a Graph

XML is actually a collection of W3C recommendations that define the syntax and semantics of XML and its related technologies [1]. The core XML recommendation is the XML Information Set (or Infoset) [5], which models the core abstractions of XML as a set of information items [1]. Information items represent the pieces of an XML document, what is required of them, and how they behave. The items modeled in the Infoset are reflected in the Document Object Model (DOM) [10]. The DOM allows programmers to access XML documents uniformly, regardless of the underlying implementation.

When an XML document is loaded using a DOM compliant parser, a DOM tree is returned. The DOM provides interfaces to the following information items: documents, document fragments, document types, entities, entity references, elements, attributes, processing instructions, comments, text, CDATA sections, and notations.

We note that documents whose elements contain references to other elements (e.g., IDREFs) can be considered to be a graph, rather than a tree. However, in the DOM, references are not considered to be edges, thus maintaining the tree structure. Therefore, an XML document is primarily tree-structured, so we can use terms like child, parent, and sibling.

Also worth noting is the XPath [4] engine in the Xalan-Java API. XPath provides a simple way of expressing a path through a document tree to select a set of nodes. When a path expression is evaluated, the XPath facilities select a set of nodes relative to a context node. Any information item represented in the DOM (and consequently any information item in any document) can be selected by an XPath expression. Using XPath expressions to traverse an XML document is much more concise and easier to understand than using the DOM. Also, after analyzing a DTD, it is possible to generate XPath expressions for the body of the accessor methods necessary to perform the graph operations described above.

3   Framework Core Classes

Our framework provides a number of core classes, shown below in Figure 2, that allow applications to treat XML documents as graphs, to perform XSL transformations on an XML document, to evaluate XPath expressions against a document, and to perform inter-document lookups.

The base class that we use in the framework is the `XMLObject` class. In our Java implementation, the `XMLObject` class contains a reference to a node in the DOM tree. Through this node reference, it is possible to retrieve any data contained in the node, as well as any nodes linked to that node in the DOM tree. This class also provides an interface to the XPath facilities in the Xalan-Java API. The node referenced by an `XMLObject` object is used as the context node when evaluating XPath expressions. When an XPath expression is evaluated, a set of DOM nodes matching that expression are selected and placed in a DOM `NodeList`. The `NodeList` interface is wrapped by the `XPathResult` class, which allows users to cast the ith node in the list to a `Boolean`, `Double`, `Integer`, `Node`, or `String`. Coupled with prior knowledge of attribute types (determined by a domain expert, or in the future by analyzing an XML Schema for a given document type), this allows typed access to data in the document.

The `XPathResult` class also provides aggregate operations for the set of nodes that match a given XPath expression. Once a set of nodes is selected, it is often necessary to traverse the set, accumulating data. Rather than have the application designer write code to perform these aggregate operations, we provide such code in our framework. The aggregate operations that are provided are listed in Figure 3.

There are three subclasses of the `XMLObject` class: `XMLData`, `XMLSource`, and `LookupResult`. The `XMLData` class represents elements in the DOM tree and is the basis for treating a document as a homogeneous graph. It encapsulates many of the DOM methods that relate only to elements (i.e., retrieving attribute names, retrieving attribute values by attribute name, retrieving children, ancestors, and siblings). It also translates the name and namespace of an element into the type of the graph node. `XMLData` objects are instantiated by the `XMLSource` class. `XMLSource` objects represent XML documents and allow users to load and parse documents, to serialize documents out to a stream, and to retrieve the root node of a document as an `XMLData` object. The `XMLSource` class also provides access to the XSLT [3] facilities (discussed below) provided in the Xalan-Java API. The `LookupResult` class encapsulates the resulting data from an inter-document lookup (discussed below).

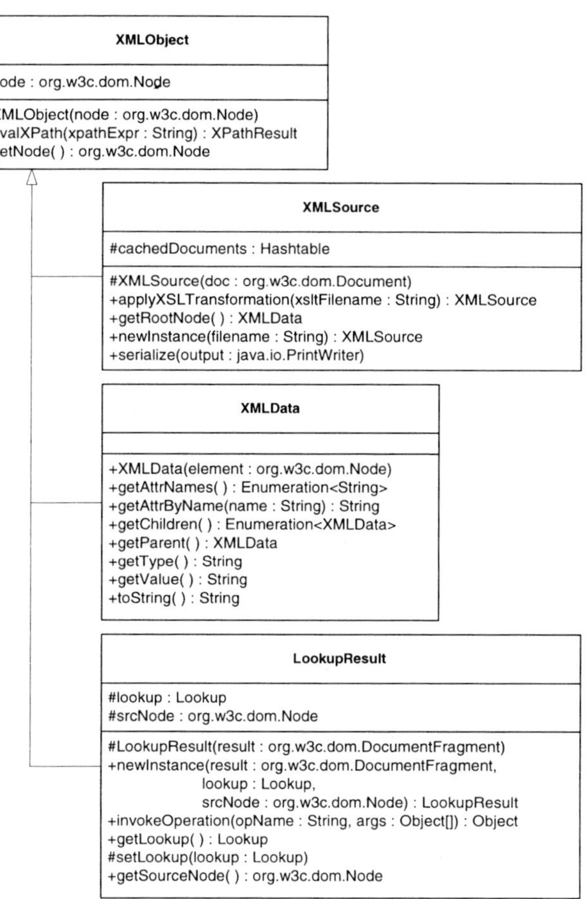

Figure 2: UML class diagram of core framework classes

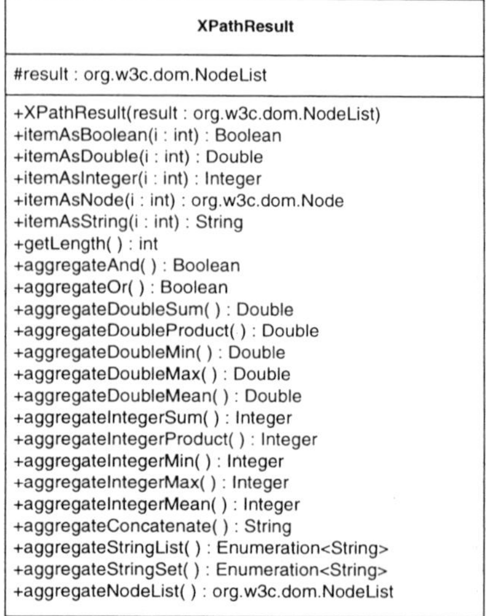

Figure 3: UML class diagram for the XPathResult class

3.1   Example using the Framework Core Classes

In our election scenario, we start with an XML document that we call the *geospatial authority*, which contains geographic information about the area being covered by the application (in this case, the United States). For simplicity, we consider an authority document that contains state elements, which in turn contain county elements, which in turn contain municipality elements. The DTD for the geospatial authority is shown below:

```
<!ELEMENT state        (county+)>
<!ELEMENT county       (municipality+)>
<!ELEMENT municipality EMPTY>


<!ATTLIST state        name CDATA #REQUIRED>
<!ATTLIST county       name CDATA #REQUIRED>
<!ATTLIST municipality name CDATA #REQUIRED>
```

This would suggest that subclasses of XMLData are needed for states, counties, and municipalities. Each of these classes would have an accessor method that would allow the user to retrieve the name, as well as the region(s) contained by that region (e.g., retrieve all counties for a given state, or retrieve the municipality named "Worcester" from Worcester county in Massachusetts). There are also documents for each state containing election results. Potentially, each state can have a different DTD, and consequently, a different structure for its results document. For simplicity, we will examine the DTDs for election results from only two states, Massachusetts and Maine:

MA_results.dtd

```
<!ELEMENT state        (county+)>
<!ELEMENT county       (municipality+)>
<!ELEMENT municipality (candidate+)>
<!ELEMENT candidate    EMPTY>

<!ATTLIST state        name CDATA #REQUIRED>
<!ATTLIST county       name CDATA #REQUIRED>
<!ATTLIST municipality name CDATA #REQUIRED>
<!ATTLIST candidate    name CDATA #REQUIRED
                       votes CDATA #REQUIRED>
```

ME_results.dtd

```
<!ELEMENT state        (county+)>
<!ELEMENT county       (municipality+)>
<!ELEMENT municipality (ward+)>
<!ELEMENT ward         (precinct+)>
<!ELEMENT precinct     (candidate+)>
<!ELEMENT candidate    EMPTY>

<!ATTLIST state        name   CDATA #REQUIRED>
<!ATTLIST county       name   CDATA #REQUIRED>
<!ATTLIST municipality name   CDATA #REQUIRED>
<!ATTLIST ward         id     CDATA #REQUIRED>
<!ATTLIST precinct     id     CDATA #REQUIRED>
<!ATTLIST candidate    name   CDATA #REQUIRED
                       votes  CDATA #REQUIRED>
```

This represents the general structure of the election result data as presented at the Massachusetts and Maine state websites. In order to better understand these DTDs, Figure 4 shows the E-R diagrams of these document types.

Note that in the diagram, the cardinality of all relationships is one-to-many. This is due to the fact that, in the DTD, all subelements have the "+" qualifier, meaning that one or more instances of that subelement can appear. While this is fine for the state-to-county relationship and the county-to-municipality relationship, it does not tell the whole story for candidates. The municipality- or precinct-to-candidate relationship should have a cardinality of many-to-many, since there are many municipalities or precincts and many candidates. However, the DTD does not reflect this—it only states that each municipality or precinct can have more than one candidate. To determine a many-to-many relationship, it would be necessary to examine the actual data.

When we discussed the geospatial authority document we stated that classes for states, counties, and municipalities would be desirable. However, since each state's results document could potentially have a different structure, it would be unfeasible to define a separate state, county, municipality, and candidate class for each state's election results. It would make more sense to have just one state, county, and municipality class for the entire application and

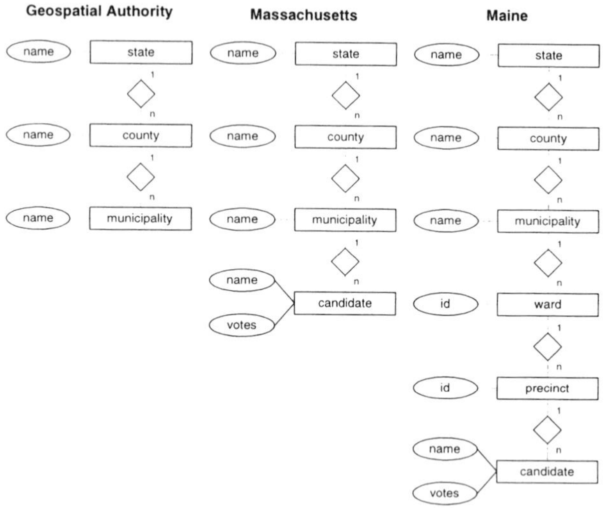

Figure 4: DTD E-R Diagrams

let the framework classes handle the necessary translation between the underlying XML formats of the various election result documents. To accomplish this, we introduce our lookup mechanism.

4 Lookups

Interoperability hinges upon a system that is able to seamlessly interchange data between various document types. Data from one document needs to be selected, possibly restructured, and then linked to data in another document. Our framework provides a way of linking data in this manner using what we call *lookups*. This section discusses the features of our lookup mechanism and some of the design rationale behind those features. We will illustrate this using a running example from our election scenario: defining a lookup for Massachusetts election results for municipalities.

Lookups in our system are specified declaratively in a lookup specification document. This document, stored in XML, allows application designers to specify all lookup types for an application. Each lookup is given a name, a description, and an identifier, as shown below:

```
<?xml version='1.0' standalone='no'?>
<!DOCTYPE lookup-spec SYSTEM 'lookup-spec.dtd'>

<lookup-spec>
<lookup name='MA Municipal Results'
        description='Massachusetts election results per
                    municipality'
        id='1'>
```

4.1   Predicates

Any node in an XML document used by our system can potentially have any number of lookups associated with it. Therefore, we first need a way in which we can define predicates that determine whether a lookup exists from a given source node. These predicates are expressed as XPath expressions. When checking if a node is associated with a lookup, the predicate XPath expressions are evaluated using this source node as the context node. If all of the predicates evaluate to non-null results, we can consider this node associated with this lookup and can proceed to execute the lookup. In our example, we only want to link municipalities in the geospatial authority to municipalities in the Massachusetts election results document. Consequently, we define the following predicates:

```
<predicate>
<!-- ensure that the source node is a municipality -->
self::municipality
</predicate>

<predicate>
<!-- ensure that the source node is in Massachusetts -->
ancestor::state[attribute::name='Massachusetts']
</predicate>
```

4.2   Arguments

Lookups actually link *entities* (that is, entities in the database sense; these entities are expressed in XML as elements) in different documents, not actual instances of the entities. In other words, lookups act as a link between different data types, not their objects. It may only be possible to state a lookup in terms of variables whose values depend on the context of the lookup being performed (i.e., the source node's context). For instance, in our running example linking a municipality in Massachusetts with a municipality in the election results, one lookup can serve all municipalities in the state. Contextual data, such as the county and municipality name, is necessary for the lookup to be performed, but cannot be determined until the lookup is about to be executed. Therefore, we provide a mechanism for defining arguments whose values are computed before executing the lookup and then substituted into the body of the lookup. These arguments are associated with an XPath expression. When the lookup is about to be executed from a given source node, the XPath expression is evaluated using the source node as the context node, and the resulting value is substituted for the argument name in the body of the lookup. For example, we would need to define arguments for county and municipality names in order to properly link a municipality to the election results:

```
<argument>
   <name>$county_name</name>
   <value>parent::county/attribute::name</value>
</argument>

<argument>
   <name>$municipality_name</name>
```

```
<value>attribute::name</value>
</argument>
```

4.3   Lookups: XPath or XSLT

The next step is to define the actual body of the lookup. There are two types of lookups supported by our framework. The first type of lookup involves simply selecting a set of nodes in a document using an XPath expression. To specify an XPath lookup, the actual XPath expression can be stated directly in the lookup specification document. The second type of lookup involves restructuring a subset of the data in a document using XSLT. To specify an XSLT lookup, the name of the XSLT file can be stated in the lookup specification document. When the time comes to execute a given lookup, the XPath expression or XSLT file is loaded, argument values are evaluated and substituted, and the lookup is performed. It is also necessary to state the file name of the target document. In our example, we want to find the municipality element in the target document and to select all children of that municipality. The XPath lookup to accomplish this, written in terms of the variables given above, is shown here:

```
<target-document>
MA_election_results.xml
</target-document>

<!--
  Start at the root, trace through the tree to find the
  municipality, and select all children of the municipality.
  -->
<xpath-expr>
/child::state[attribute::name='Massachusetts'] \
  /child::county[attribute::name='$county_name']   \
  /child::municipality[attribute::name='$municipality_name'] \
  /child::*
</xpath-expr>
```

4.4   Linking the Results

When an XPath expression is evaluated, a `NodeList` or a `NodeIterator` containing the selected nodes is returned. When an XSLT file is evaluated, the resulting DOM tree structure is returned. While DOM trees that result from XSL transformations can have XPath expressions evaluated against them, `NodeLists` and `NodeIterators` that result from XPath expressions cannot. It would be useful to organize these results in such a manner that XPath expressions can be evaluated against them. Similarly, we would like to be able to cache and possibly serialize these results. It would be nice if we could simply add these nodes as children of the lookup's source node, but this is not allowed by the DOM because it could potentially make the containing document invalid. However, the DOM provides the `DocumentFragment` interface for representing lightweight collections of nodes. The `DocumentFragment` interface is intended to support movement of nodes for operations such as "cut" and "paste" [10]. Also, since `DocumentFragments` are nodes, XPath expressions can be evaluated against them.

We can specify that the XSLT part of the Xalan-Java API produce a `DocumentFrag-ment` with the results of the transformation. For XPath lookups, we can simply take each node in the resulting `NodeList` or `NodeIterator` and add that node as a child of a `DocumentFragment`.

Our framework provides the `LookupResult` class, a subclass of `XMLObject`, to store the resulting `DocumentFragment`. The details of this class are discussed later on, but it is worth noting here that in the lookup specification, the application designer can specify which result class to instantiate with the lookup results. Either `LookupResult`, or a subclass of it, can be specified to take the lookup results. In our running example, we simply use the `LookupResult` class:

```
<result-class>LookupResult</result-class>
```

4.5 Operations: Accessing the Results

Once a lookup is performed, code is needed to access the data contained in the nodes that result from the lookup. Potentially, each lookup can select nodes from different documents containing different structures. Therefore, each lookup would require its own class to be instantiated with the appropriate code to access its data. However, this can quickly become cumbersome as the number of lookups increase. Also, if the structure of the various documents change, those classes would need to be rewritten. In our election scenario, each state could potentially require a separate class for lookups for its election results. While these classes could be arranged into an inheritance hierarchy, having 50 election result classes would be a little excessive. It would be more useful if accessor methods could be defined at the lookup level.

Accessor methods can be defined using XPath expressions that will be evaluated using the `DocumentFragment` as the context node. The return values for such accessor methods can be computed using our aggregate operations discussed above. The application designer can therefore define accessor operations in the lookup specification using a name, aggregation type, and an XPath expression for the body of the operation. Parameters can also be defined when extra context is needed for the operation. Default values for those parameters can also be given, where necessary.

In our running example, we would define the following two operations:

```
<!-- select all candidate names, return a set of strings -->
<operation name='getCandidateNames' aggregation='sset'>
  <body>
    child::candidate/attribute::name
  </body>
</operation>


<!-- select vote total for a candidate, return an integer -->
<operation name='getVotesByCandidate' aggregation='isum'>
  <parameter>
    <name>$candidate_name</name>
  </parameter>
```

```
<body>
  child::candidate[attribute::name='$candidate_name'] \
  /attribute::votes
</body>
</operation>
</lookup>
</lookup-spec>
```

If all election result lookups define operations with the same name, multiple classes to represent the election results would no longer be needed. Rather, we can use one subclass of `LookupResult`. Operations defined in the lookup specification can be invoked using the `invokeOperation()` method provided by the `LookupResult` class. In our subclass, we can provide methods (e.g., `getCandidateNames()` and `getVotesByCandidate()`), which simply call `invokeOperation()` with the appropriate parameters.

4.6   The Lookup Specification

As stated above, all lookups are specified in an XML document. These documents must conform to the lookup specification DTD (`lookup-spec.dtd`), shown below:

```
<!ELEMENT lookup-spec       (lookup+)>
<!ELEMENT lookup            (predicate+,
                             argument*,
                             target-document,
                             (xpath-expr | xslt-file),
                             result-class,
                             operation*)>
<!ATTLIST lookup name          CDATA #REQUIRED
                 description CDATA #REQUIRED
                 id          ID     #REQUIRED>
<!ELEMENT predicate         (CDATA)>
<!ELEMENT argument          (name,
                             value)>
<!ELEMENT name              (CDATA)>
<!ELEMENT value             (CDATA)>

<!ELEMENT target-document (CDATA)>
<!ELEMENT xpath-expr        (CDATA)>
<!ELEMENT xslt-file         (CDATA)>
<!ELEMENT result-class      (CDATA)>

<!ELEMENT operation          (parameter*,
                              body)>
<!ATTLIST operation name          CDATA #REQUIRED
                    aggregation (nodelist |
                          and | or |
                          dsum | dprod | dmin | dmax | dmean |
```

```
                                       isum | iprod | imin | imax | imean |
                                       concat | slist | sset) #REQUIRED>
<!ELEMENT parameter           (name, default-value?)>
<!ELEMENT default-value       (CDATA)>
<!ELEMENT body                (CDATA)>
```

5   Conclusion and Open Issues

In this paper, we analyzed a geospatial application for the U.S. elections as a means of illustrating the problems that need to be solved in the mapping between different XML representations and their conceptual models. The framework that we presented allows application designers to treat XML documents as homogeneous graphs and to evaluate XPath expressions and XSL transformations against a document. Our framework also allows application designers to define a set of lookups that integrate data from multiple documents. Data retrieved using a lookup can also have operations defined for it declaratively in a lookup specification.

We anticipate the need for introducing metadata in the semantic layer to guide the translation process between document types. In this section, we discuss metadata issues in the semantic layer and a number of other issues that still need to be investigated.

5.1   Metadata, Semantics, and Ontologies

A certain amount of metadata is necessary for a domain expert or application designer to appropriately identify the entities that can be linked and how the lookups should be performed. In some cases, this metadata is available from the DTD or from another external source that describes that document type. In other cases, this metadata may be implied. For example, one can reasonably expect measurements in documents from Europe to be in metric units, while measurements in documents from the United States to be in feet and inches, even though this information is not explicitly stated anywhere in the document. Some conversions may be handled by XSLT, but some may require more complicated computations and consequently must be performed by another mechanism.

There are also naming issues that need to be taken into consideration. For instance, it is possible for a geographic entity to have multiple accepted spellings (e.g., Foxboro, MA vs. Foxborough, MA; or Mt. Washington vs. Mount Washington). Often times, foreign place names have multiple accepted English spellings, and this too must be taken into consideration. In some cases, this can be handled using a crosswalk table or some other form of dictionary data structure. In other cases, the accepted spellings of a place name may depend on the current context or the location of that place.

Further research is also needed to see how to use ontologies, especially as presented in [8] and [9], in our system.

5.2   Technical Issues

We need an engine capable of executing graph queries. With such an engine, it may be possible to take a graph query language that supports aggregation, such as G+ [7, 6], and compile queries in that language into XPath expressions or another XML based query language.

We can also look at performance issues, especially in a distributed environment. Each XML document that we are interoperating between can potentially be stored on a different server. We need to look at different ways of caching and processing data. We also are examining different security schemes for accessing the various XML data sources.

At this point in the development of our framework, much of the code necessary to perform the tasks described above must be written by hand. This may become too complex to be practical. In the future, we plan to analyze all DTDs that will be supported by and application and generate the necessary code to perform many of the tasks described above. It would still be necessary for the application designer or a domain expert to determine the links between the different document types. It may be possible, however, to automatically or semi-automatically generate the lookup specifications necessary to execute the lookups, but more research is needed in this area. In order to generate any code based on a DTD, it is first necessary to parse the DTD to determine its structure. This can be done by creating a DTD graph, using algorithms described in [11] and [13]. From there, we can begin to examine code generation for XPath-based accessor methods in the lookup specification. It may also be possible to automatically or semi-automatically generate the lookup code (using either XPath or XSLT). Code generation can be supplemented by the input of the application designer or domain expert via a visual tool that displays E-R diagrams based on a given DTD.

5.3   Document Structure

The election scenario example shown throughout this paper is somewhat contrived (the actual data was originally retrieved in HTML format from a website and then converted to XML) as we have created all of the documents and defined their structure. Obviously, in a real-world application, the document structures could potentially be quite different, requiring more restructuring of the data.

We also need to examine the effects that changing a document type would have on code that has already been written or generated. Ideally, our final framework would be sufficiently powerful to handle such changes.

6   Acknowledgements

We would like to thank Nancy Wiegand and Steve Ventura for discussions on the subject of statewide geospatial applications and the referees for their suggestions.

This research was supported in part by the Advanced Research and Development Activity (ARDA) and the National Imagery and Mapping Agency (NIMA) under Award Number NMA201-01-1-2001, and by the National Science Foundation under CAREER Award IRI-9896052 and Award EIA-0091489. The views and conclusions contained in this document are those of the authors and should not be interpreted as necessarily representing the official policies or endorsements, either expressed or implied, of the National Imagery and Mapping Agency or the U.S. Government.

References

[1] D. Box, A. Skonnard, and J. Lam. *Essential XML Beyond Markup*. Addison-Wesley, 2000.

[2] T. Bray, J. Paoli, and C. M. Sperberg-McQueen. Extensible Markup Language (XML) 1.0 (Second Edition). W3C Recommendation, 2000.

[3] J. Clark. XSL Transformations (XSLT) Version 1.0. W3C Recommendation, 1999.

[4] J. Clark and S. DeRose. XML Path Language (XPath) Version 1.0. W3C Recommendation, 1999.

[5] J. Cowan and R. Tobin. XML Information Set. W3C Candidate Recommendation, 2001.

[6] I. Cruz and T. Norvell. Aggregative Closure: An Extension of Transitive Closure. In *IEEE International Conference on Data Engineering*, pages 384–390, 1989.

[7] I. F. Cruz, A. O. Mendelzon, and P. T. Wood. G+: Recursive Queries Without Recursion. In *Expert Database Conference*, pages 355–368, 1988. Also in Larry Kershberg, editor, *Expert Database Systems*, The Benjamin/Cummings Publishing Company, Inc., Redwood City, California, pages 645-666, 1989.

[8] M. Erdmann and R. Studer. How to Structure and Access XML Documents with Ontologies, 2001. DKE 36(3): 317–335.

[9] F. Fonseca. Gis_ontology.com. In *GIScience*, 2000. http://www.giscience.org/GIScience2000/papers/218-Fonseca.pdf.

[10] A. Le Hors, P. Le Hégaret, L. Wood, G. Nicol, J. Robie, M. Champion, and S. Byrne. Document Object Model (DOM) Level 2 Core Specification Version 1.0. W3C Recommendation, 2001.

[11] D. Lee and W. Chu. Constraints-Preserving Transformation from XML Document Type Definition to Relational Schema. In *Proc. 19th Int'l Conf. on Conceptual Modeling*. Springer-Verlag, October 2000.

[12] S. Melnik and S. Decker. A Layered Approach to Information Modeling and Interoperability on the Web. In *ECDL 2000 Workshop on the Semantic Web*, Lisbon, Portugal, September 2000.

[13] J. Shanmugasundaram, K. Tufte, G. He, C. Zhang, D. DeWitt, and J. Naughton. Relational Databases for Querying XML Documents: Limitations and Opportunities. In *Proceedings of the 25 th VLDB Conference*, Edinburgh, Scotland, 1999.

Author Index